Contemporary Innovations in Reporting and Analysis

Fábio Albuquerque
Instituto Politécnico de Lisboa, Portugal

Paula Gomes dos Santos
Lisbon Accounting and Business School, Instituto Politécnico de Lisboa, Portugal & COMEGI, Portugal

Published in the United States of America by
IGI Global Scientific Publishing
701 East Chocolate Avenue
Hershey, PA, 17033, USA
Tel: 717-533-8845
Fax: 717-533-8661
E-mail: cust@igi-global.com
Website: https://www.igi-global.com

Copyright © 2025 by IGI Global Scientific Publishing. All rights reserved. No part of this publication may be reproduced, stored or distributed in any form or by any means, electronic or mechanical, including photocopying, without written permission from the publisher.
Product or company names used in this set are for identification purposes only. Inclusion of the names of the products or companies does not indicate a claim of ownership by IGI Global Scientific Publishing of the trademark or registered trademark.

Library of Congress Cataloging-in-Publication Data

CIP Data Pending
ISBN:979-8-3693-5923-5
eISBN:979-8-3693-5925-9

Vice President of Editorial: Melissa Wagner
Managing Editor of Acquisitions: Mikaela Felty
Managing Editor of Book Development: Jocelynn Hessler
Production Manager: Mike Brehm
Cover Design: Phillip Shickler

British Cataloguing in Publication Data
A Cataloguing in Publication record for this book is available from the British Library.

All work contributed to this book is new, previously-unpublished material.
The views expressed in this book are those of the authors, but not necessarily of the publisher.
This book contains information sourced from authentic and highly regarded references, with reasonable efforts made to ensure the reliability of the data and information presented. The authors, editors, and publisher believe the information in this book to be accurate and true as of the date of publication. Every effort has been made to trace and credit the copyright holders of all materials included. However, the authors, editors, and publisher cannot assume responsibility for the validity of all materials or the consequences of their use. Should any copyright material be found unacknowledged, please inform the publisher so that corrections may be made in future reprints.

Editorial Advisory Board and List of Reviewers

Iryna Alves, *Lisbon Accounting and Business School (ISCAL), Instituto Politécnico de Lisboa, Portugal*

João Borralho, *Lusófona University, Portugal*

Kurt Desender, *Universidad Carlos III de Madrid, Spain*

Ana Isabel Dias, *Lisbon Accounting and Business School (ISCAL), Instituto Politécnico de Lisboa, Portugal & Research Center on Accounting and Taxation (CICF), Instituto Politécnico do Cávado and Ave, Portugal*

Flory Dieck-Assad, *Tecnologico de Monterrey, Mexico*

Alexandra Domingos, *Lisbon Accounting and Business School (ISCAL), Instituto Politécnico de Lisboa, Portugal*

Azzouz Elhamma, *Ibn Tofaîl Universit, Morocco*

João Marcelo Alves Macêdo, *Federal University of Paraíba, Brazil*

María-Pilar Martín-Zamora, *University of Huelva, Spain*

Pedro Pinheiro, *Lisbon Accounting and Business School (ISCAL), Instituto Politécnico de Lisboa, Portugal & Center for Research in Organizations Markets and Industrial Management (COMEGI), Universidade Lusíada, Portugal*

Carlos Pinho, *Universidade Aberta, Portugal*

Mónica López Puertas-Lamy, *Universidad Carlos III de Madrid, Spain*

Maria Albertina Rodrigues, *Lisbon Accounting and Business School (ISCAL), Instituto Politécnico de Lisboa, Portugal & CETRAD-Europeia, Centre for Interdisciplinary Development Studies, Universidade Europeia, Universidade de Trás os Montes e Alto Douro, Portugal*

Daniel Silva, *Federal University of Pernambuco, Brazil*

Muhammad Usman Tariq, *Abu Dhabi University, UAE & University of Glasgow, UK*

Table of Contents

Preface xiv

Acknowledgment xviii

Chapter 1
Navigating New Frontiers: Integrative Approaches in Accounting and
Auditing Education and Practice 1
    Muhammad Usman Tariq, Abu Dhabi University, UAE & University
        College Cork, Ireland

Chapter 2
Success Story on Business Decision Making Using Artificial Intelligence: A
Positive Vision of Disruptive Technologies 27
    Flory Dieck-Assad, Tecnologico de Monterrey, Mexico

Chapter 3
Exploring the Potential Influences of Blockchain Technology in Financial
Reporting 65
    Pedro Pinheiro, ISCAL, Instituto Politécnico de Lisboa, Portugal &
        COMEGI, Portugal
    Andreia Gomes, ISCAL, Instituto Politécnico de Lisboa, Portugal
    Ana Isabel Dias, ISCAL, Instituto Politécnico de Lisboa, Portugal &
        CICF, IPCA, Barcelos, Portugal

Chapter 4
The Use of Robotic Process Automation in Brazilian Accounting Firms: A
Study of the Perception of Accounting Professionals 95
    João Marcelo Alves Macêdo, Federal University do Paraíba, Brazil
    Yanne Yasmim Gouveia Silva, Federal University of Paraíba, Brazil
    Ariane Silva Moura, Federal University of Paraíba, Brazil
    George Rogers Andrade Silva, Federal University of Paraíba, Brazil
    Gelyel Estevan dos Santos, Federal University of Rio Grande do Norte,
        Brazil

Chapter 5
Digitalization of Financial Reporting: Its Role in Improving Corporate
Efficiency and Transparency 123
    María-Pilar Martín-Zamora, University of Huelva, Spain
    João Miguel Capela Borralho, University Lusófona, Portugal

Chapter 6
An Assessment of the Sentiments Behind the IASB's Standards: An
Exploratory Analysis of IAS 37 165
    Fábio Albuquerque, ISCAL, Instituto Politécnico de Lisboa, Lisboa,
        Portugal & CICF, IPCA, Barcelos, Portugal
    Paula Gomes dos Santos, ISCAL, Instituto Politécnico de Lisboa,
        Portugal & COMEGI, Portugal

Chapter 7
Perceived Benefits of IFRS Adoption in Morocco and French Speaking Sub-
Saharan African Countries 183
    Azzouz Elhamma, Ibn Tofaîl University, Morocco

Chapter 8
Exploring the Matters by ESG Dimensions Disclosed Within the European
Entities' Materiality Matrices: Are There Differences Explained by the
Entities' Specific Characteristics? 211
    Miguel Gomes, ISCAL, Instituto Politécnico de Lisboa, Portugal
    Fábio Albuquerque, ISCAL, Instituto Politécnico de Lisboa, Portugal &
        CICF, IPCA, Barcelos, Portugal
    Maria Albertina Rodrigues, ISCAL, Instituto Politécnico de Lisboa,
        Portugal & CETRAD-Europeia, Centre for Interdisciplinary
        Development Studies, Universidade Europeia, Portugal

Chapter 9
Application of Governance, Risk Management, and Compliance Practices
in the Public Service, in Light of the Tam Model: A Study at the Federal
Institute of Bahia 245
    Rômulo Brito Oliveira, Universidade de Pernambuco, Brazil
    Luiz Carlos Miranda, Universidade de Pernambuco, Brazil
    Carlos Pinho, Universidade Aberta, Portugal

Chapter 10
Gender Diversity and Audit Fees Across Diverse Institutional Settings 297
  Kurt Desender, Universidad Carlos III de Madrid, Spain
  Mónica López Puertas-Lamy, Universidad Carlos III de Madrid, Spain

Compilation of References 331

About the Contributors 395

Index 399

Detailed Table of Contents

Preface xiv

Acknowledgment xviii

Chapter 1
Navigating New Frontiers: Integrative Approaches in Accounting and
Auditing Education and Practice 1
    Muhammad Usman Tariq, Abu Dhabi University, UAE & University
      College Cork, Ireland

The chapter delves into the integrative approaches in accounting and auditing education and practice by addressing the revolutionary changes that have taken place in the accounting and auditing fields due to technology, the ever-changing nature of the regulations, and the expectations of the society. It further discusses the technologies, like AI, blockchain, and data analytics, which improve productivity and increase effectiveness and compliance in finance. The chapter also shows how accounting and auditing are no longer limited to only technical frameworks, but include cultural, social, and moral aspects, such as sustainability and social responsibility. By the means of case descriptions and best practices, it demonstrates new trends in educational approaches and effective integration of digital media and information, subject-area practices in curricula. In addition, it considers the issues that are connected with work-life imbalance, diversity, and minority issues in the occupation.

Chapter 2
Success Story on Business Decision Making Using Artificial Intelligence: A Positive Vision of Disruptive Technologies... 27
    Flory Dieck-Assad, Tecnologico de Monterrey, Mexico

This chapter presents the advantages of using technological advancements such as artificial intelligence (AI) tools to enhance the traditional decision-making process of an accountant in the area of reporting and analysis. Throughout the chapter, the reader will discover a wide array of applications that the AI ecosystem (robo-advisors, virtual assistants, chatbots, etc.) offers to simplify data analysis and improve tactical decision-making for targeting new paths of growth for any company. It tells the success story of an accountant who was promoted to chief accounting officer (CAO) by enhancing the vision of the firm's path of growth through the use of AI tools, based on real data. AI will not replace professional accountants; on the contrary, with the help of AI, accountants can give strategic insights to improve the financial welfare of any firm by providing innovative data analysis faster and allowing the accountant more time to digest the analysis and provide better and informed tactical decision-making to target a newer vision of the company in the short and long term.

Chapter 3
Exploring the Potential Influences of Blockchain Technology in Financial Reporting 65
    Pedro Pinheiro, ISCAL, Instituto Politécnico de Lisboa, Portugal & COMEGI, Portugal
    Andreia Gomes, ISCAL, Instituto Politécnico de Lisboa, Portugal
    Ana Isabel Dias, ISCAL, Instituto Politécnico de Lisboa, Portugal & CICF, IPCA, Barcelos, Portugal

This study aims to assess the influences that blockchain technology may have on financial reporting as the first presents unique characteristics that may contribute to transparency, immutability, security, and real-time availability of the latter. Hence, 11 interviews were conducted with professionals related to professors' professionals of accounting, and specialists in blockchain technology, to collect their perceptions on the subject. It was possible to conclude that blockchain technology may influence financial reporting mainly by enhancing its reliability, a qualitative characteristic referred to in the conceptual framework for financial reporting. In turn, reliability, associated with neutrality, ensures authenticity, transparency, and confidence in the information derived from a blockchain system. This study contributes to the literature with new empirical evidence, so that the pros and cons of the adoption of this technology may change the paradigm of obtaining how financial information is analyzed in more detail.

Chapter 4

The Use of Robotic Process Automation in Brazilian Accounting Firms: A Study of the Perception of Accounting Professionals 95

    João Marcelo Alves Macêdo, Federal University do Paraíba, Brazil
    Yanne Yasmim Gouveia Silva, Federal University of Paraíba, Brazil
    Ariane Silva Moura, Federal University of Paraíba, Brazil
    George Rogers Andrade Silva, Federal University of Paraíba, Brazil
    Gelyel Estevan dos Santos, Federal University of Rio Grande do Norte, Brazil

Recently, there have been changes in the work processes of Brazilian accounting firms, with the implementation of systems automation, the integration of accounts payable and receivable systems, and payroll systems with accounting systems. The objective of this study was to analyze the perceptions of Brazilian accounting professionals about the implementation of robotic process automation (RPA) in their work routines. RPA was considered a strategic tool that aims to optimize time and expand business. A quantitative and descriptive approach was adopted, using an online questionnaire on Google Forms, which was answered virtually by 210 professionals. The participants' opinions regarding the use of RPA, their experiences, benefits, and challenges faced were considered. It was concluded that RPA automates repetitive tasks and frees accounting professionals for strategic and more complex activities. This study contributes to the management of accounting firms by optimizing processes and routines, especially their productivity.

Chapter 5

Digitalization of Financial Reporting: Its Role in Improving Corporate Efficiency and Transparency 123

    María-Pilar Martín-Zamora, University of Huelva, Spain
    João Miguel Capela Borralho, University Lusófona, Portugal

Digitalized financial processes are redefining 21st-century business landscapes. One area that has undergone significant transformation is financial reporting, which involves the preparation and presentation of essential reports that enhance strategic decision making and regulatory compliance. Automation and data processing play a crucial role in this context by enhancing the efficiency, accuracy, and transparency of the reports generated. This chapter explores in detail how advances in these two areas of digitalization are revolutionizing financial reporting and then analyzes the relevant technologies and their benefits and challenges, as well as best practices for their implementation. Regulatory guidelines are also examined in terms of their implications and future trends in digital financial reporting.

Chapter 6
An Assessment of the Sentiments Behind the IASB's Standards: An
Exploratory Analysis of IAS 37 165
    Fábio Albuquerque, ISCAL, Instituto Politécnico de Lisboa, Lisboa,
        Portugal & CICF, IPCA, Barcelos, Portugal
    Paula Gomes dos Santos, ISCAL, Instituto Politécnico de Lisboa,
        Portugal & COMEGI, Portugal

This exploratory study aims to assess the aspects related to the message tone, magnitude, subjective-objective distinction, and thematic area behind the text collected from the International Accounting Standards Board (IASB) standard that outlines the accounting for provisions, contingent liabilities and contingent assets, i.e., International Accounting Standard (IAS) 37 - Provisions, Contingent Liabilities and Contingent Assets. The study uses archival research as a method and content analysis as a technique. The analysis is supported by an application programming interface, which uses text analytics based on natural language processing and machine learning. The findings show a most predominant negative approach underlying the message, regardless of the aspects under assessment, which also have a higher level of magnitude on average. Furthermore, messages are mostly subjective or of an unknown nature, particularly for those related to more technical aspects of IAS 37. Finally, those aspects present reduced scores of their classification within the "Business and Finance."

Chapter 7
Perceived Benefits of IFRS Adoption in Morocco and French Speaking Sub-
Saharan African Countries 183
    Azzouz Elhamma, Ibn Tofaîl University, Morocco

This chapter aims to study, by using a sample of 75 practitioners and researchers in accounting, the consequences of the International Financial Reporting Standards (IFRS) adoption on the qualitative characteristics of financial reporting in 12 African countries: Morocco and 11 French speaking Sub-Saharan African Countries. Two main findings can be highlighted in this research. Firstly, more than half of all Moroccan- and French-speaking Sub-Saharan African respondents consider that the adoption of IFRS improves "highly" or "very highly" the reliability (52%), the relevance (57.4%), and the comparability (54.7%) of their financial reporting. Secondly, Moroccan professionals and researchers in accounting are more concerned than their French-speaking Sub-Saharan African colleagues by the adoption of IFRS to improve the relevance and the understandability of the financial reporting. For the two other qualitative characteristics (reliability and comparability), the difference in means is not significant.

Chapter 8
Exploring the Matters by ESG Dimensions Disclosed Within the European Entities' Materiality Matrices: Are There Differences Explained by the Entities' Specific Characteristics? 211
    Miguel Gomes, ISCAL, Instituto Politécnico de Lisboa, Portugal
    Fábio Albuquerque, ISCAL, Instituto Politécnico de Lisboa, Portugal & CICF, IPCA, Barcelos, Portugal
    Maria Albertina Rodrigues, ISCAL, Instituto Politécnico de Lisboa, Portugal & CETRAD-Europeia, Centre for Interdisciplinary Development Studies, Universidade Europeia, Portugal

The concept of materiality is essential in the fields of accounting and auditing, enabling the identification of important issues from the entities' perspectives and those affected by it. This research focuses on the disclosure of materiality in non-financial information (NFI) reporting, assessing the topics disclosed within the entities' materiality matrix by ESG dimensions and considering their characteristics, such as size, profitability, debt, and gender diversity on the board of directors. The research uses archival research as a methodology and content analysis as an investigative technique, examining NFI reports for the year 2021 from companies listed on Euronext's main indices. The findings from the 69 NFI reports show the matters on the social aspect as the most disclosed, which is also the ESG dimension where those characteristics do not appear to be relevant when it comes to their disclosure levels. This study provides value to literature and practice by offering insights to standard-setter bodies, regulators, auditors, and various stakeholders involved in NFI reporting.

Chapter 9
Application of Governance, Risk Management, and Compliance Practices in the Public Service, in Light of the Tam Model: A Study at the Federal Institute of Bahia.. 245
    Rômulo Brito Oliveira, Universidade de Pernambuco, Brazil
    Luiz Carlos Miranda, Universidade de Pernambuco, Brazil
    Carlos Pinho, Universidade Aberta, Portugal

This work's main objective was to study the application of governance, risk management and compliance (GRC) practices at Federal Institute of Bahia (IFBA), based on COSO-ERM, ISO 31000, and PMBOK. The application was carried out from the perspective of the technology acceptance model (TAM) to investigate users' perception of using a GRC system. The study is based on a questionnaire graded on a seven-point Likert scale. This model, originating in studies by Davis in 1986, located a fundamental conceptual framework for understanding how people perceive and adopt new technologies. The results demonstrate the applicability of the TAM model to measure perceived usefulness and ease of use in relation to the use of new technologies. It is also concluded that managers perceive greater usefulness and ease of use than subordinates, in relation to the proposed system. Thus, this study contributes to the development of studies on the GRC theme by systematizing practical implementation guided by international models, evaluating the perception of servers using the system in light of the TAM model.

Chapter 10

Gender Diversity and Audit Fees Across Diverse Institutional Settings 297
    Kurt Desender, Universidad Carlos III de Madrid, Spain
    Mónica López Puertas-Lamy, Universidad Carlos III de Madrid, Spain

This Study examines whether and how gender diversity at the board and top management team (TMT) level, as well as commitment to the UN's Sustainable Development Goal on Gender Equality (SDG5), influences financial reporting quality by studying the independent auditors' assessment of the risk of material misstatement. Employing a large global dataset, they find a positive relationship between board gender diversity and audit fees, which is consistent with an active monitoring role by the board. In contrast, we do not find a significant effect of TMT gender diversity, nor for the firm's commitment to the SDG Goal on Gender Equality. In addition, we find that the relationship between board gender diversity and audit fees is mainly driven by firms in countries without mandatory board gender quotas, and that the results are especially strong in settings where there is a lower perception of corruption and a greater representation of females in parliament.

Compilation of References 331

About the Contributors 395

Index 399

Preface

In recent years, the fields of accounting and auditing have been challenged to evolve in response to complex and dynamic shifts across economic, political, social, and technological domains. The rapid pace of innovation requires not only adaptation within professional practices but also a critical expansion within accounting and auditing research. Yet, despite this, the literature has often remained constrained, overly conservative, and hesitant to embrace emerging interdisciplinary themes. Contemporary issues such as technological advancements, regulatory demands, and the integration of cultural, social, and ethical dimensions into accounting frameworks are yet to be fully explored within mainstream accounting and auditing scholarship.

Our intent in curating this volume, *Contemporary Innovations in Reporting and Analysis*, is to offer a comprehensive perspective on the modern landscape of accounting and auditing. This book seeks to bridge the gaps in existing research by addressing underexplored topics that have significant implications for the profession and its educational paradigms. By expanding beyond a purely technical view of accounting, we explore the field's role as a cultural, social, and moral practice that intersects with a range of global developments.

The chapters in this book cover pressing themes, from financial reporting and regulatory compliance to innovative practices in education and training. We delve into the specific challenges facing diverse entities—private, public, and non-profit organizations of varying sizes and across multiple industries, including financial, insurance, and non-financial sectors. This diversity ensures that our discussions are relevant and applicable to a wide audience, encompassing industry professionals, researchers, academics, instructors, and students.

Through this volume, we aim to inspire a more inclusive and forward-thinking approach to accounting and auditing research, encouraging the field to embrace emerging topics and interdisciplinary methodologies. We hope this work will contribute to a richer understanding of the contemporary accounting and auditing landscape and foster continued innovation within both professional and academic communities.

Organization of the Book

This edited volume, *Contemporary Innovations in Reporting and Analysis*, offers insights into the evolving landscape of accounting and auditing, bringing together perspectives on integrative approaches, technological advancements, regulatory implications, and the impact of social and environmental factors. Each chapter contributes to a broader understanding of the challenges and opportunities facing modern accounting and auditing professionals, providing theoretical insights, empirical findings, and practical applications.

Chapter 1 begins with a comprehensive look at *Integrative Approaches in Accounting and Auditing Education and Practice*. This chapter highlights how technological advancements such as AI and blockchain are reshaping accounting and auditing. It addresses the inclusion of social and ethical considerations, like sustainability, and explores how educational frameworks are adapting to integrate these dynamic fields into curricula.

Chapter 2 presents a *Success Story on Business Decision Making Using Artificial Intelligence*, emphasizing AI's potential to transform decision-making in accounting. By illustrating how AI tools aid in data analysis and forecasting, the chapter underscores AI's role in enhancing accountants' strategic impact, ultimately positioning them as critical drivers of a firm's growth.

Chapter 3 examines *The Potential Influences of Blockchain Technology in Financial Reporting*. Based on interviews with professionals, this chapter discusses blockchain's promise to increase transparency, security, and real-time data availability, offering an empirical perspective on blockchain's potential to revolutionize financial reporting reliability.

In Chapter 4, the authors analyze the *Use of Robotic Process Automation in Brazilian Accounting Firms*. This chapter explores how automation has optimized workflows in Brazilian accounting firms, freeing professionals for more strategic tasks. It also sheds light on the benefits and challenges encountered by professionals in adopting robotic process automation.

Chapter 5 discusses the *Digitalization of Financial Reporting* and its transformative effect on corporate transparency and efficiency. This chapter highlights the role of automation and data processing in enhancing reporting accuracy and regulatory compliance, alongside an exploration of emerging technologies and future trends.

In Chapter 6, the authors conduct an *Exploratory Analysis of IAS 37*, examining sentiment and thematic content within IASB standards. Using natural language processing, the study reveals a predominantly negative tone in the IAS 37 standard and provides valuable insights for interpreting the text's implications on financial reporting.

Chapter 7 explores the *Perceived Benefits of IFRS Adoption in Morocco and French-Speaking Sub-Saharan African Countries*. This chapter reveals that IFRS adoption has enhanced financial reporting reliability and comparability in these regions, with Moroccan professionals showing a particular emphasis on IFRS's impact on report relevance.

Chapter 8 investigates *Materiality Matrices in European Entities*, specifically examining ESG disclosures. Analyzing non-financial information reports, the authors identify social issues as the most disclosed, while noting that entities' characteristics, such as size and profitability, affect disclosure patterns within the environmental and governance dimensions.

In Chapter 9, the authors assess *Governance, Risk Management, and Compliance (GRC) Practices in the Public Sector* at the Federal Institute of Bahia. By applying the Technology Acceptance Model (TAM), this chapter explores user perceptions of GRC systems, uncovering a tendency for managers to perceive greater utility and ease of use than subordinates.

Chapter 10 analyzes *Gender Diversity and Audit Fees*. Using global data, the authors find that board-level gender diversity correlates with higher audit fees, particularly in countries without gender quotas. The study highlights the importance of gender diversity in reinforcing accountability, especially in low-corruption settings with greater female political representation.

Each chapter in this volume provides a unique perspective on the innovations transforming accounting and auditing, making this collection an essential resource for professionals, academics, and students seeking to understand and navigate these shifts in reporting and analysis.

CONCLUSION

In conclusion, this volume provides a comprehensive exploration of how contemporary advancements are reshaping accounting and auditing practices worldwide. The chapters within this book illustrate the profound influence of digitalization, artificial intelligence, blockchain, and other technological innovations on the financial reporting landscape. Together, they reflect the shifting expectations and standards that demand transparency, accountability, and agility in a rapidly evolving global economy.

Furthermore, this collection highlights the integration of social, cultural, and ethical dimensions within accounting and auditing—recognizing that financial stewardship today encompasses far more than technical skill. By examining emerging practices, challenges, and opportunities across diverse regions and institutional contexts, the contributors to this volume provide valuable insights for educators, practitioners, and policymakers. They underscore the importance of ongoing adaptation in professional education, regulatory compliance, and organizational governance, offering both theoretical foundations and practical implications.

As editors, we are grateful for the collective expertise and perspectives that each author has brought to this work. We believe that the insights shared here will not only enrich the reader's understanding but will also inspire continued innovation and responsible practices within the accounting and auditing fields. It is our hope that this book serves as a foundational resource for navigating the challenges and possibilities ahead in this dynamic and essential profession.

Fábio Albuquerque
Instituto Politécnico de Lisboa, Portugal

Paula Gomes dos Santos
Lisbon Accounting and Business School, Instituto Politécnico de Lisboa, Portugal & COMEGI, Portugal

Acknowledgment

This work was supported by the Instituto Politécnico de Lisboa, project IPL/IDI&CA2024/IAccount_ISCAL. This study was conducted at the Research Center on Accounting and Taxation (CICF) and was funded by the Portuguese Foundation for Science and Technology (FCT) through national funds (UIDB/04043/2020 and UIDP/04043/2020).

Chapter 1
Navigating New Frontiers:
Integrative Approaches in Accounting and Auditing Education and Practice

Muhammad Usman Tariq
https://orcid.org/0000-0002-7605-3040
Abu Dhabi University, UAE & University College Cork, Ireland

ABSTRACT

The chapter delves into the integrative approaches in accounting and auditing education and practice by addressing the revolutionary changes that have taken place in the accounting and auditing fields due to technology, the ever-changing nature of the regulations, and the expectations of the society. It further discusses the technologies, like AI, blockchain, and data analytics, which improve productivity and increase effectiveness and compliance in finance. The chapter also shows how accounting and auditing are no longer limited to only technical frameworks, but include cultural, social, and moral aspects, such as sustainability and social responsibility. By the means of case descriptions and best practices, it demonstrates new trends in educational approaches and effective integration of digital media and information, subject-area practices in curricula. In addition, it considers the issues that are connected with work-life imbalance, diversity, and minority issues in the occupation.

DOI: 10.4018/979-8-3693-5923-5.ch001

INTRODUCTION

This chapter aims to understand the ongoing changes in the discipline of accounting and auditing professions in light of emerging technologies, internationalization, and evolving legal requirements. The chapter elaborates on these radical changes and focuses on new educational paradigms and approaches to train new-generation professionals. This critical literature review focuses on scholarly articles, papers, and studies that identify the fundamental features of incorporating new technologies, teaching methodologies, and real-life experiences into accounting and auditing education. Technological advancement has been characterized by a high rate of change; this observation has not left accounting and auditing untouched. Some of the technologies arising as drivers of change in the profession include artificial intelligence, blockchain technology, and data analytics. In this study, Nicolau (2023) examines the effect of introducing artificial intelligence in internal audit and accounting practices, noting how it improves the efficiency of operations when conducting audits. Similarly, Odeyemi et al. (2024) presented a more extensive discussion on the adoption of AI in auditing worldwide to outline its value in students' training as accountants in the accounting education curriculum (Tariq, 2024).

Blockchain is another important field of study, specifically because of increasing interest in technology. According to Pimentel et al. (2021), numerous difficulties arise when auditing blockchain-based assets; therefore, auditors must appreciate the nature of blockchain systems for proper auditing. This is in concordance with the study carried out by Sarkar, Boss, and Gray 2021 that examines the technology-based pedagogy relating to AACSB curricula and called for the integration of Transcendental Blockchain technology with the accounting curriculum as the need intends to prepare students for future difficulty. These facts demonstrate the need for the implementation of new teaching strategies to provide accounting and auditing students with the knowledge and skills required to meet the challenges of the profession. Thus, Mustikarini and Adhariani (2022) emphasize that the auditor-client relationship is based on trust, and that there is a lack of educational methods to develop ethical thinking and a sufficient level of skeptical attitude among auditors. This is supported by Azambuja et al. (2023), who assert that multiple accountabilities arising from boundary work in PSFs must be managed; therefore, educational programs should incorporate realistic cases.

Special attention should be paid to Barac et al. (2021) to gain a better understanding of the nature of audit practices and the need to develop profound multifaceted knowledge. Thus, they recommend the use of case studies and other teaching approaches that expose students to interactions between different facets of the audit. Coelho and Menezes (2021) insist on the themes of USg and SL in accounting curricula by stating that combining lessons about citizenship and practical undertakings would be beneficial for students' personal and academic growth.

The systematic incorporation of STEM concepts into accounting education to enhance inclusiveness is progressing. To support this idea, Adebiyi et al. (2023) called for the implementation of STEM concepts for learning in a multicultural environment. It will be important to encourage and promote the adoption of STEM ideas and frameworks within the accounting educational curriculum because it will help students develop problem-solving skills and critical thinking capabilities that are essential for the present day and tomorrow's accounting professional.

LITERATURE/BACKGROUND

Handoyo (2024) conducted a bibliometric analysis to assess changes in the paradigms of the information technology effect on accounting education. This study calls for the curriculum to be frequently revised to incorporate new technologies and their use in accounting and auditing. Ethics and sustainability have emerged as core interests in accounting and audit education. Adaga et al. (2024) present a detailed analysis of ethics in banking and financial institutions and stress the importance of ethic courses in accounting discipline. He stated that students majoring in accounting should take ethical issues as core topics in their curriculum since they are bound to meet ethical challenges in the profession. With respect to the nature of accounting in the Anthropocene, Bebbington and Rubin (2022) outlined a map of stewardship based on ESG features. They believe that the information provided in accounting education programs must comprise topics related to sustainability and ESG reporting to meet society's requirements and expectations. Good teaching practices and curriculum development are central to the implementation of new technologies and improvement of methodologies in accounting education. According to Powell and McGuigan (2023), the accounting curriculum needs to be rewarded for crises which implies that the authors believe that the current rigidity of the accounting curriculum is undesirable, and that a more open approach will be more useful in today's complex world. They support the education of blended FESG accounting and reporting systems involving physical entities and disciplines.

Jejeniwa, Mhlongo, and Jejeniwa (2024) provide systematic literature on the effect of AI on contemporary accounting systems and financial reporting and argue about an accounting curriculum for current change. Based on this, accounting programs should incorporate AI applications of artificial intelligence and data analytics to prepare learners for the actual employment market.

Another factor that can explain why the use of case studies and other practical examples is crucial in accounting education revolves around the need to close the gap between classroom knowledge and field reality. In the work by Salleh, Moorthy, and Jasmon (2023), the authors analyzed scholarly discourses on accounting technical skills for Industry 4. 0; however, it is advisable that those learning such skills are required to apply them practically. They posit that the use of real and realistic problems and cases in teaching accounting improves students' understanding of hard technical content. Van der Merwe (2021) discusses the future of accounting and whether accountants will be replaced by robots, concluding that there is a continued need for people's skills, including critical thinking, creativity, and the daily ethical decisions made by mankind. Accordingly, the development of these skills along with technical skills should be part of the learning process in accounting education to produce a future workforce.

Cultural and social factors have major impacts on accounting practices as well as accounting education. Sivabalachandran and Gooneratne (2023) focused on the tensions and challenges in the delegation of management accountants' roles in the context of Sri Lanka and the impact of culture. They hold the opinion that debates over cultural and social issues should be incorporated into the accounting curriculum to increase students' awareness of the relevance of this context. Regarding how the existing conditions have changed in the context of the COVID-19 pandemic, Rinaldi (2023) shares information about changes in accounting practices and the ways that have been determined to solve the problems arising in the framework of the crisis. The study emphasizes the role of versatility in accounting curricula; in fact, it underlines the need to incorporate issues of managing crises and contingencies into the curricula. Therefore, the literature presented in this chapter underlines the necessity of applying new technologies along with innovative approaches to teaching accounting and auditing as well as the ethical and practical aspects of their implementation. Owing to the nature of the profession, the curricula being taught to students needs to be dynamically updated to accommodate the challenges and prospects of the future. Thus, by embracing such integrative approaches, accounting education can prepare future professionals in these new frontiers of the industry (Bhimani, 2020).

The field of accounting and auditing is still in the process of radical changes exerted by the development of new technologies, amendments to existing legislation, and alterations in people's perceptions of the role played by accountants and auditors. This chapter, Navigating New Frontiers: Integrative Approaches in Accounting and Auditing Education and Practice, is precisely designed to address these changes and ponder over integrative solutions based on both technical skills and culture, society, and ethics. Consequently, it brings out the fact that current employees require to familiarize themselves with such frontiers to become productive in the same (De

Villiers, 2021). New technologies such as the applications of artificial intelligence, blockchain, big data, and analytics have in turn transformed accounting and auditing. Specifically, the use of artificial intelligence in business has become apparent, especially in such spheres as the analysis of financial information where AI and machine learning are capable of processing much larger amounts of data as well as detecting patterns and data outliers which would otherwise remain unnoticed by analysts (Pasolo, 2024). This chapter explores the application of blockchain in the audit process to ascertain implications for the audit profession and the recording of transactions. Such advances imperatively call for a reconsideration of the courses taught in accounting schools of today and the general approach to the accounting profession in general, where workers are compelled to acquire new skills since the precedence of accounting information is increasingly being assumed by computers (Kunz & Kirstein, 2021).

In addition, analytical reviews have also attributed key roles to eradicating or modifying existing or established accounting and auditing systems through changes in regulations. Closely related to crises and scandals, many governments and other regulatory authorities have increased the criteria and overall stringency of rules and regulations both globally and domestically, with a focus on the objectives of transparency, accountability, and governance within corporations. Examples of such regulatory changes include The Sarbanes Oxley Act in the United States and the General Data Protection Regulation (GDPR) in the European Union. These developments require A&A professionals to be aware of the changing legal frameworks and incorporate compliance considerations into their daily practice to ensure that the organization's conduct is above reach regarding legal provisions (De Villiers, 2021). It can also be seen that as, with over a passage of time, cultural and social factors are also affecting the profession of accounting and auditing in today's world. The current world is characterized by globalization and an increasing number of multicultural workplaces which require knowledge of different cultures. As for job description, authorities here note that new technologies and processes mean accountants and auditors have to deal with numerous standards and practices introduced at the international level, which entails a deeper understanding of applicable business environments. For example, a global business company managing its business in several states is likely to follow the working practices and guidelines of each state, and this differs from one country to another. It establishes why having cultural skills is imperative in addition to technical abilities when it comes to the management of internationalization of accounts (Barac, Plant, Kunz, & Kirstein, 2021; Tariq, 2024).

In addition, one finds that the conceptual area of accounting not only evolved technically, but also contained social and moral elements. CSR and sustainability reporting have gained importance as a result of such social change. It is now a practice for organisations to provide information on their environmental and social responsibility, governance, ethical conduct, and financial position. For instance, most organisations have sustainability reports, which are well articulated, as seen in the case of Patagonia and Ben and Jerry's organisations. This has shown the need for ethical values to be incorporated into accounting courses so that professional accountants are ready to deal with the impacts of their work in society and the environment (Handoyo, 2024). Accounting and auditing education cannot remain passive observers in these new frontiers; hence, it has to be transformed to nurture future professionals. These are technician training interventions that include cultural, social, and ethical interventions that involve both strategies. In this way, the focus is not only on producing competent accountants and auditors in the field of financial reporting and analysis, but also on being aware of other implications of the task. For example, the use of ethical decision case material, sustainability issues, and cross-cultural financial considerations as part of the learning materials offers students a better view of the field (De Villiers, 2021; Tariq, 2024).

In summary, the emerging trends and practices of accounting and auditing require a problem-centered interrelated educational model. Therefore, through consciousness and awareness of these technological novelties, awareness and compliance with changes in the rules of the game, as well as grappling with culture, society, and morality issues, these new frontiers may be effectively managed by professionals. In this chapter, these trends will be explored in greater detail to provide a better understanding of how to build the foundations for a superior conceptual framework to guide accounting and auditing in contemporary society (Barac, Plant, Kunz, & Kirstein, 2021).

Digital Transformation in Accounting and Auditing

The digitalization process in the accounting and auditing profession is rather challenging, as it involves a radical transformation of the profession through the use of new technologies such as artificial intelligence, blockchain, and data analytics. These not only aid in the effectiveness and proper rendering of accounting chores but also contribute to an increase in transparency and compliance, making finance more reliable (Mustikarini & Adhariani, 2022).

Thus, Artificial intelligence is one of the pillars of digital transformation of accounting. AI tools can be applied for record keeping, scanning bills, and checking account balances, among many others, and this can greatly help in decreasing the time spent on such tasks. For example, machine learning can work with a large number of minutes of transactions and identify patterns and outliers with the help of which auditors stay in peculiar districts with a higher risk of fraud or mistakes. Some firms that have adopted the use of Artificial Intelligence include KPMG and Deloitte in their auditing service delivery. Common AI technologies are also used to apply predictive analytics that benefit organisations with strategic decision-making regarding their probable financial standing in the future (Olweny, 2024). Blockchain technology is a pivotal developmental change in the accounting and auditing profession. In terms of financial records, the decentralized and non-tamperable nature of the blockchain ensures that the transaction is transparent and cannot be forged or mistaken. Every transaction is recorded and connected to previous ones; thus, the record is highly transparent and cannot be altered. This will act as a dream tool in auditing, as it will give auditors access to different financial records, making auditing more efficient and accurate (Sarkar, Boss, & Gray, 2021).

For instance, IBM, in partnership with Maersk, has developed an online platform in the form of blockchain dubbed TradeLens, which increases the efficiency and accuracy of global trade transactions. In the accounting field, organisations are trying to adopt blockchain to maintain an efficient record system to minimize analysis and reconciliation activities (Handoyo, 2024). Data analytics is another useful technique with the potential to bring radical changes to the accounting and auditing fields. Big data analysis can work with billions of dollars to arrive at conclusions and find things that a layman analyst may not be able to easily see. It improves decision making as well as tactical planning since it presents a clearer view of business financials as well as risk. For instance, PwC's Halo suite of tools applies data analysis to complement the auditing method by presenting a financial data overview, along with the consideration of possible pattern anomalies and the adequacy of internal controls. Data analysis also contributes to predictive modelling, which helps an organization foresee future financial performance and adapt its consequent actions (Pontoppidan, 2024).

Thus, the effect of using these digital tools on efficiency, transparency, and compliance in accounting practices is significant. Applying AI decreases the amount of time and effort devoted to specific operations that can be charged to accountants and auditors, concentrating them on more vital actions. This has also led to increased efficiency, subordinated to the reduction of operating costs, and its impact is also seen in the improved accuracy and reliability of financial reports. For instance, AI application in the processing of invoices can minimize errors while simultaneously enhancing the payment cycle, which is key in cash flow (Bebbington & Rubin, 2022). One major gain achieved from the use of blockchain technology is its highly improved transparency. This makes it easier to record all transactions in full detail because the content of the records with regard to blockchains cannot be changed in the future. This enhances shareholders, regulators, and customers' trust, as it offers an open and factual account of trading activities. For instance, through blockchain, it is possible to provide evidence of the origin of products in supply chain management, since records of financial documentation portray the tracking of products and payments (Sarkar, Boss, & Gray, 2021).

Compliance is another core aspect that is significantly affected by the use of digital tools. This technology may prove beneficial in staying compliant with the regulations in the financial industry by analysing the transactions flowing through the organization and flagging problematic areas. They can identify certain actions or plans that may violate the law, regulatory requirements, or standards, thus enabling organisations to apprehend the issues before they occur. For instance, AI-based compliance products can scan a business's transactions for possible money laundering or any other unlawful activities to keep organisations in check according to anti-money laundering laws (Adebiyi et al., 2023). Finally, the extension of automation, application of AI technology, and the use of blockchain and analytic tools are the major trends of digitalization in accounting and auditing. Ancestor technologies increase effectiveness as they free labor for repetitive jobs, increase traceability because records are safe and cannot be modified, and promote compliance by frequently checking financial operations. Over time, these technologies will become unavoidable as the profession expands; it's imperative for accounting and auditing specialists to adapt to these technologies to be productive as the working environment advances (Ellili, Nobanee, Haddad, Alodat, & AlShalloudi, 2024).

Cyber Security in Digital Transformation

As computerized change advances quickly across ventures, bookkeeping and examining calls are going through massive changes. Arising advances such as man-made reasoning (computer-based intelligence), blockchain, and information examination are reshaping conventional works, improving effectiveness, and extending the extent of administrations presented by experts. However, these advancements are associated with increased risk, especially when it comes to protecting the financial data. Cybersecurity has emerged as an essential component of contemporary accounting and auditing, necessitating immediate attention in professional practice and education. The way financial information is managed, analyzed, and reported has changed because of the integration of digital technologies into accounting and auditing.

The accuracy and effectiveness of financial operations have been significantly enhanced by automated procedures, real-time access to data, and cutting-edge analytical tools. Nonetheless, these advantages have increased the weaknesses of digital dangers. Cyberattacks on monetary establishments, enterprises, and bookkeeping firms have become progressively modern, presenting dangers to the honesty, secrecy, and accessibility of monetary information (Azambuja et al., 2023). In the ongoing computerized scene, online protection is at this point not a fringe concern but a central part of bookkeeping and evaluating rehearses. The monetary aspect is an ideal objective for cybercriminals because of the touch and significant nature of the information it handles. Breaks in network safety can prompt serious outcomes, including monetary misfortune, reputational harm, legitimate liabilities, and the disintegration of partner trust.

Accordingly, basic bookkeeping and inspection experts are furnished with the information and abilities to safeguard against these dangers and guarantee the security of monetary data. Despite the significance of online protection, cybersecurity's Importance in Accounting and Auditing Education In often deficient in customary bookkeeping and reviewing schooling. The protection of digital assets and information systems has received less attention than that of technical and regulatory skills. However, there is a pressing need to incorporate cybersecurity into accounting and auditing curricula, as the profession becomes increasingly dependent on technology. Educators must understand cybersecurity as more than just a technical problem; it is also an essential part of digital ethics. Bookkeepers and examiners are overseers of delicate monetary data, and their capacity to safeguard this information is necessary to maintain public trust and honesty of the calling. Hence, bookkeeping and inspecting schooling should advance to remember the extensive preparation for network safety, covering subjects such as information security, risk of executives, moral hacking, and consistency with online protection guidelines (Van der Merwe, 2021). The rapid pace of technological change is one of the main obstacles in incorporating cybersecurity into accounting and auditing education. Digital dangers are continually developing, and new weaknesses are arising as innovation propels. Professionals must continuously learn and stay up-to-date on the most recent cybersecurity developments in this dynamic environment. Moreover, the intricacy of current data frameworks implies that network safety cannot be overseen by IT divisions alone; it requires cooperative exertion across all levels of an association, including bookkeeping and inspection groups (Michelon, 2021).

The intersection of cybersecurity with cultural and social factors in accounting practices is another obstacle. Accounting is influenced by cultural context, which can also influence how cybersecurity is perceived and implemented, as previously mentioned. For instance, in nations with solid lawful and administrative systems, such as the US, there might be a more noteworthy accentuation of severe consistency with network safety guidelines. Conversely, in nations where individual connections and organisations (e.g. guanxi in China) assume a huge part of deals, network protection practices might be more casual and dependent on trust (Powell and McGuigan, 2023).

These cultural differences emphasize the need for accounting and auditing education to incorporate a global cybersecurity perspective. Recognizing that what works in one country may not work in another, students must be taught how to navigate the complexities of implementing cybersecurity measures in different cultural contexts. This requires a comprehension of both worldwide network protection principles and the particular social and legitimate conditions in which they work (Nicolau, 2023). To address the difficulties of network protection in the computerized age, bookkeeping and reviewing training should embrace a comprehensive methodology that coordinates mechanical, social, and moral contemplation. Accompanying techniques can assist educators in integrating online protection into the educational plan.

Integrating Network Safety Into Center Bookkeeping Courses

Online protection should be incorporated into existing bookkeeping and reviewing courses as opposed to being treated as a different subject. For instance, seminars on monetary announcements and reviews can remember modules for information security, risk evaluation, and network protection control. According to Adebiyi et al. (2023), this method ensures that students comprehend the significance of cybersecurity in their potential careers in accounting and auditing. Creating Specific Network Protection Courses as well as coordinating network protection into center courses, particular courses zeroed in on network protection in bookkeeping and examining ought to be advertised. Risk management in cybersecurity, ethical hacking, cybersecurity regulations, and incident responses are some of the topics that might be covered in these courses. These courses prepare students for the specific challenges they face in the profession by providing an in-depth understanding of cybersecurity (Azambuja et al., 2023).

Stressing Moral and Social Elements of Online Protection

As examined previously, social variables play a critical role in bookkeeping practices, and this stretches out to network safety. Instructors ought to accentuate the moral ramifications of network safety, training understudies the adjustment of the requirement for information insurance with deference for social contrasts and moral norms. This approach assists understudies by fostering a nuanced comprehension of online protection taught by both specialised information and social mindfulness (Michelon, 2021). To guarantee that understudies get reasonable and cutting-edge preparations, bookkeeping and reviewing projects ought to work together with industry experts and network safety specialists. Visitor talks, studios, and temporary positions can furnish understudies with certifiable bits of knowledge about the difficulties and best acts of online protection in the monetary area. These organisations can also assist in overcoming any issues in the scholarly world and industry, guaranteeing that the educational plan remains pertinent to the necessities of the calling (Rinaldi, 2023).

Advancing Nonstop Learning and Expert Turning of Events

Given the rapid speed of mechanical change, it is fundamental for bookkeeping and examining experts to participate in consistent learning. Students should be encouraged to pursue professional certifications in cybersecurity and to stay up-to-date on the most recent developments in the field by educational institutions, which should foster a culture of lifelong learning. This can be accomplished through web-based courses, online classes, and expert associations that offer continuous preparation and accreditation potential (Liu and Ishak, 2023). The Fate of Network protection in Bookkeeping and Evaluating Cybersecurity will become increasingly important in the practice of accounting and auditing as the profession continues to develop.

Blockchain and artificial intelligence (AI) are two new technologies that have the potential to improve financial operations; however, they also introduce new risks that require careful management. The fate of bookkeeping and evaluating will rely upon experts who are capable and talented in safeguarding the computerized resources and data frameworks that support current monetary practices (Powell and McGuigan, 2023). To plan for this future, bookkeeping and inspection instruction should focus on network safety as a central part of the educational program. Educators can ensure that the next generation of professionals are prepared to face the challenges of the digital age by providing students with the knowledge and abilities necessary to navigate the complex cybersecurity landscape. This includes not only technical education, but also a comprehension of the ethical, cultural, and social facets of cybersecurity, which are necessary to preserve the profession's integrity and maintain public trust (Van der Merwe, 2021).

Thus, cybersecurity is a crucial component of contemporary accounting and auditing, which must be addressed in professional practice and education. As computerized change continues to reshape the call, the insurance of monetary information and data frameworks has become a basic concern. Teachers play a significant part in preparing understudies to explore these difficulties by coordinating network protection into bookkeeping and examining educational plans. This requires a comprehensive methodology that considers the mechanical, social, and moral elements of online protections. By doing this, teachers can provide students with the knowledge and skills they need to guard against cyberattacks and keep financial information safe.

PRACTICAL CHALLENGES IN IMPLEMENTING NEW TECHNOLOGIES IN ACCOUNTING AND AUDITING EDUCATION

Numerous opportunities exist to enhance learning outcomes and prepare students for the demands of the modern profession by incorporating new technologies into accounting and auditing education. However, this cycle is not without difficulties. When incorporating data analytics, blockchain technology, and artificial intelligence (AI) into the curriculum, educators face several practical challenges. These obstacles include a lack of resources, the requirement for ongoing professional development, and the need to align educational content with rapidly changing industrial standards. The lack of resources required to implement cutting-edge technologies in the classroom is one of the most significant practical obstacles educators faces. These assets remember not only monetary ventures for programming, equipment, and foundation but also the time and aptitude expected to coordinate these advances into the educational plan. According to Liu and Ishak (2023), many educational establishments, particularly those with limited budgets, cannot afford the most recent technological tools or provide sufficient training for faculty members. Expected answers to this challenge incorporate looking for associations with innovation organisations that can give programming licenses or prepare at diminished costs.

In addition, institutions may collaborate with other schools to share resources or to investigate grant opportunities. Another methodology is to integrate open-source programming and cloud-based apparatuses, which are much more reasonable and can be adjusted to different instructional settings (Van der Merwe, 2021). Another obstacle for educators is the rapid pace of their technological progress. Technologies for accounting and auditing are always changing, and what is cutting-edge today might be outdated tomorrow. This places a huge weight on instructors to consistently refresh their insight and educational plan content to stay up with industry improvements. Moreover, understudies should be educated to adjust to future innovations that may not yet exist, which requires an emphasis on creating decisive reasoning and critical thinking abilities as opposed to just dominating current devices (Azambuja et al., 2023). To address this test, instructors should underline an educational plan that offsets fundamental information with comprehension of the arising patterns. Students can develop the necessary adaptability to succeed in a rapidly changing environment by incorporating case studies and real-world projects that focus on the application of technology in accounting and auditing. Constant expert improvement open doors for teachers, such as studios, meetings, and online courses, are also vital in keeping employees refreshed with the most recent mechanical patterns (Michelon, 2021).

Another practical obstacle is the alignment of educational content with industrial standards. Standards and regulatory bodies that govern the accounting and auditing professions are subject to change as new technologies emerge. In addition to meeting the current regulatory requirements, educators must ensure that their curriculum prepares students for the profession's future. This necessitates a thorough comprehension of the regulatory environment and the technical aspects of new technologies (Powell & McGuigan, 2023). Engaging industry professionals and regulatory bodies in the curriculum development process is one approach to this problem. This should be possible through warning sheets, visitor talks, and associations that guarantee that the educational plan remains significant and aligned with industry needs. Additionally, students may be able to bridge the gap between academic learning and professional practice by incorporating professional certifications and credentials related to emerging technologies into the curriculum (Rinaldi, 2023).

Finally, faculty members' resistance to change may be a significant obstacle in the implementation of new technologies in accounting and auditing education. A few teachers might be reluctant to use new devices or show strategies because of the absence of commonality or trust in their capacity to utilize these advancements successfully. This obstruction can impede the combination cycle and breaking point of the expected advantages of new advancements in homeroom (Nicolau, 2023). Institutions should provide faculty members with comprehensive training and support to overcome these obstacles. This incorporates specialised preparation, as well as instructive direction, on the most proficient method to coordinate innovation into education. Faculty resistance to change can be reduced by cultivating a culture of innovation and collaboration (Liu & Ishak, 2023) and by encouraging the sharing of best practices. Thus, although there are several significant advantages to incorporating new technologies into accounting and auditing education, educators must also address the practical difficulties they face. Educational institutions can successfully navigate these obstacles and prepare students for the profession's future by looking for creative solutions to limited resources, staying up-to-date on technological advancements, aligning curricula with industry standards, and creating a supportive faculty environment.

INNOVATIVE EDUCATIONAL METHODS IN ACCOUNTING AND AUDITING

Apparently, the field of accounting and auditing education is dynamic and constantly developing owing to the ever-increasing demand to prepare future specialists for work in the world characterized by the use of advanced technologies. In addition, conventional paradigms of learning and teaching are constantly augmented and at times eliminated by new strategies and combined configurations of learning and material processes. These new strategies aimed to improve students' attention, build their skills in analysis, and help graduates meet the complex job situations they are going to encounter soon (Powell & McGuigan, 2023).

Another change that has received a massive boost in accounting education is the adoption of experiential learning instructional strategies. It entails the use of actual learning which involves the exposure of students to real-life accounting and auditing problems. For example, such scenarios have grown to include internships, cooperative education, and live cases where students tackle real-life financial problems with real-life organisations. This approach enables students to apply theories learned in the classroom environment and practice them in real-life situations, thus serving as a means of closing the theory practice gap among students. Therefore, institutions such as the University of Texas at Austin's McCombs School of Business have incorporated this approach into the accounting curriculum to prepare students for real-world performance (Azambuja et al., 2023).

Another can be implemented using the concept of flipped classrooms. In the case of a flipped classroom, activities that would normally be taught during lectures are conveyed online in the form of videos to students who can download and study them in their free time. In-person class time is then spent on experiential learning tasks, including class discussions, group and individual problem-solving activities, and case dissections. It also makes learning engaging, and students are likely to dig deeper into the content that is being delivered to them. Currently, the Gies College of Business of the University of Illinois Urbana-Champaign has incorporated the use of flipped classrooms in their accounting courses to the benefit of the students (De Villiers, 2021).

Other disruptive technologies are also immensely helpful in enhancing the learning and teaching of accounting. With the growing implementation of artificial intelligence in software and the analysis of large datasets in learning institutions, students must professionally apply state-of-the-art technologies in class. For instance, students could apply smart auditing tools and applications to identify outliers in financial statements or use financial intelligence to interpret large volumes of charts. The use of these tools in the curriculum not only sharpens technical competency, but also broadens students' perspectives on current accounting practices. The University of Southern California's Leventhal School of Accounting has put into practice the use of digital tools in courses, enabling students to acquire practical experience in the use of modern applications (Sarkar, Boss, & Gray, 2021).

Multidisciplinary techniques are also evident in the current trends in accounting education. Realising that accounting professionals are required to work in teams with specialists from other fields, many programs incorporate materials from IT, law, ethics, and so on. Thus, guaranteeing the acquisition of a sufficient number of skills is necessary for the complex work of accounting and audit workers. For instance, the University of Michigan-Flint's School of Management, which contains the Ross School of Business, presents courses in accounting, including accounting information analysis, legal aspects of accounting, and accounting ethics (Azambuja et al., 2023).

The real-life application of these methods in integration with traditional teaching learning strategies provides an understanding of the extent of change these methods produce in students' learning patterns. Bentley University's accounting program is one example that shows how the approaches to using technology and creating an experiential classroom change the learning process. The practical projects and assignments that students work on in their classes allow them to apply real-life data to the software used to solve real-life problems in their projects, thereby enhancing their problem-solving skills. Likewise, at D'Amore-McKim School of Business, Northeastern University, changes in the accounting education curriculum have also occurred in the form of courses in data science and business analytics, considering that accounting has evolved into a data-focused profession (Michelon, 2021).

In summary, the delivery of new strategies in the accounting and auditing education system is revolutionizing the field in terms of its dynamics, usefulness, and integration. With the help of incorporating more practical assignments, using flipped classrooms and digital resources, and integrating interdisciplinary materials, educational institutions are preparing students for the demands of a rapidly growing occupation. These approaches improve technical knowledge and skills as well as the aspects of critical thinking, cooperation, and versatility that result from the educational process preparing students for the accounting and auditing profession in the modern world characterized by high use of technologies (Rinaldi, 2023).

STRATEGIES AND SOLUTIONS

Cultural and Social Perspectives in Accounting

As we explore the rapidly developing scenes of bookkeeping and reviewing, it is apparent that innovative headways alone cannot address the intricacies of the calling. The interchange among innovation, social responsiveness, maintainability, and moral contemplations is crucial for a thorough way to deal with present-day bookkeeping rehearses. Teachers play an essential part in overcoming this issue by furnishing understudies with the abilities and mindfulness important to handle these multilayered difficulties. Bookkeeping is not simply a specialised field; it is profoundly impacted by social factors that shape its practices and schooling.

For accounting practices that are culturally sensitive and ethically sound, it is essential to understand these influences. For example, bookkeeping guidelines and practices have changed across nations, reflecting authentic, monetary, and social settings. In the US and the Unified Realm, which follow the Old English American bookkeeping custom, there are areas of strength for exposure and legitimate consistency because of their precedent-based regulation roots. In contrast, asset valuation and revenue recognition approaches differ in countries with code law systems, such as Germany and Japan, which place emphasis on creditor protection and long-term financial stability (Adebiyi et al., 2023). Japan's keiretsu system, in which interconnected businesses can obscure the financial standing of individual businesses and necessitate more liberal accounting standards, is a notable example of cultural influence.

This differentiations from the severe necessities of US GAAP and Sarbanes-Oxley, which implement severe consistency and revelation to safeguard financial backers (Powell and McGuigan, 2023). These models highlight the significance of grasping social settings in bookkeeping rehabilitation. Teachers assume a basic part in preparing understudies to explore these social and mechanical difficulties. Bookkeeping schooling should go past specialised preparations to incorporate social abilities and moral direction. To illustrate the country's centralized educational philosophy, Chinese accounting education traditionally emphasizes rote learning and mastery of the national curriculum. Western accounting education, on the other hand, emphasizes critical thinking, ethical reasoning, and the application of international standards such as IFRS, preparing students to deal with a variety of global issues (Nicolau, 2023). By integrating social mindfulness and moral contemplations into educational programs, instructors can assist understudies by fostering an all-encompassing comprehension of the calling. This includes acknowledging the ethical aspects of accounting such as the significance of fairness, accountability, and transparency. These values vary from society to society and include not only technical requirements but also cultural norms. For instance, the Chinese concept of guanxi, which emphasizes the significance of personal relationships in business, can have an impact on ethical decision making in ways that are distinct from Western concepts of impartiality and objectivity (Michelon, 2021).

The rising accentuation of corporate social obligation (CSR) and supportability further highlights the requirement for an incorporated way to deal with bookkeeping instructions. Today's accountants must be able to address not only financial performance, but also the effects of business practices on society and the environment. Organisations, such as Unilever and Patagonia, have set new principles by delivering complete manageability reports that detail their natural and social obligations close to their monetary outcomes. These reports delineate how bookkeeping practices can reflect more extensive cultural qualities and add to the moral business lead (Azambuja et al., 2023). Teachers can assist in understudies by understanding the meaning of these advancements by integrating manageability and moral contemplations into the bookkeeping educational plan. This approach guarantees that future bookkeepers are ready to meet the developing assumptions for partners and adds to the calling's honesty and public trust.

In conclusion, a comprehensive approach incorporating cultural, social, and ethical perspectives into education is necessary to address the technological challenges facing accounting and auditing. Thus, teachers can furnish under-studies with the abilities and mindfulness expected to explore the complex global business climate. Perceiving and regarding social contrasts, figuring out the moral components of bookkeeping, and embracing manageability are fundamental for keeping up with trust and honesty in the calling. Accounting practices must adapt to broader societal changes and meet the challenges of the current business environment from a comprehensive perspective (Van der Merwe, 2021).

Regulatory and Standardization Challenges

The global acceptance of the International Financial Reporting Standards (IFRS) is an important step towards accounting harmonization, but it also presents a number of challenges. The main purpose of IFRS is to harmonize accounting practices in different countries, which improves the comparability and transparency of financial reporting. However, the implementation of these standards can be difficult due to differences in local regulations, economic environments, and business practices. For example, countries such as the United States have not yet fully converged to IFRS, instead following generally accepted accounting principles (GAAP). This difference creates difficulties for international companies to reconcile the differences between IFRS and local standards, often resulting in increased compliance costs and complexity (Salleh et al., 2023).

Accounting harmonization under IFRS also faces resistance due to the cultural and economic differences between countries. For example, some countries may be reluctant to fully adopt IFRS for fear of losing control over their accounting standards. In addition, the transitioning costs to IFRS standards can make it difficult for smaller firms and developing countries, as they require the resources and expertise necessary for comprehensive implementation. These challenges showcased the need for a balanced approach that should be taken to understand the problems of of different jurisdictions and strives for global standardization (Jejeniwa, Mhlongo, & Jejeniwa, 2024

The implementation of accounting standards such as IFRS and regulatory frameworks is needed as they help to ensure a strong regulatory check which is mandatory to maintain the integrity of financial reporting and to monitor compliance as the number of bodies, such as the regulatory bodies, takes up the role of providing detailed guidance on compliance with accounting standards, as this assurance prevents financial misconduct and fraud as regulatory bodies such as the Securities and

Exchange Commission (SEC) in the United States and the European Securities and Markets Authority (ESMA) in the European Union (Michelon, 2021).

These frameworks ensure that the financial information produced by companies is accurate and reliable, as they ensure investor confidence in financial information and lead to the proper functioning of capital markets. However, the deficiency in regulatory frameworks varies considerably from country to country. In some countries, weak regulatory oversight may lead to the inconsistent application of accounting standards, undermining the purpose of transparency and comparability. For instance, in developing countries, companies may adopt practices that hide their true financial position, thus losing investors' trust and confidence in financial reporting (Azambuja et al., 2023). Therefore, Uniform standards are not sufficient to attain global accounting harmonization, as the establishment of an effective and strong regulatory framework is also needed to ensure consistent and transparent application of these standards. In short, although IFRS and accounting harmonization aim to improve global financial transparency and comparability, they face significant challenges related to local regulations, economic conditions, and cultural factors. Effective regulatory frameworks are essential for overcoming these challenges by ensuring the consistent application of standardized accounting practices across jurisdictions. By addressing these issues, accountants can move closer to true global harmonization, which will benefit investors, businesses, and economies around the world (Rinaldi, 2023).

Stakeholder Engagement and Reporting Innovations

In the present powerful business climate, partner commitment and revealing have developed past customary techniques driven by progressions in innovation and accentuation of straightforwardness and responsibility. Bookkeeping experts are progressively adopting new apparatuses and techniques to meet the developing requirements of different partners, improve correspondence, and cultivate trust. New strategies and instruments for partners revealing accentuated straightforwardness, openness, and intuitiveness. Advanced stages and manageability detailing programming empower organisations to give partners ongoing admittance to monetary and non-monetary information, including ecological, social, and administrative (ESG) measurements. For instance, coordinated detailing systems like the Worldwide Revealing Drive (GRI) and the Maintainability Bookkeeping Guidelines Board (SASB) norms permit associations to introduce a thorough perspective on their presentation and effect (Barr-Pulliam, Joe, Mason, & Sanderson, 2020).

These stages work with significant discourse among organisations and partners, advancing informed directions and exhibiting obligations to manageable practices. Online entertainment and advanced correspondence channels have likewise changed partner commitment. Organisations use stages such as LinkedIn, Twitter, and Facebook to draw in with financial backers, clients, workers, and the more extensive local area. These channels empower quick criticism and collaboration, encouraging a more comprehensive way of dealing with partner correspondence. For example, organizations might utilize online entertainment to share monetary updates, answer requests, feature corporate social obligation drives, upgrade straightforwardness, and build entrust with partners (Azambuja et al., 2023).

Bookkeeping experts can more readily meet the developing needs of different partners by embracing proactive and incorporated ways to deal with revealing. Past monetary measurements, partners progressively requested data on ecological effects, social obligations, and corporate administration rehearses. Bookkeeping experts assume a vital role in gathering, dissecting, and detailing this information precisely and straightforwardly. By utilizing advanced information examination and revealing devices, experts can furnish partners with more profound bits of knowledge into authoritative execution and dangers (Salleh et al., 2023).

Moreover, integrating partner viewpoints into dynamic cycles upgrades the pertinence and believability of detailed endeavors. Drawing in partners early and frequently permits organisations to distinguish and focus on issues that make the biggest difference to their assorted partner gatherings. For instance, directing partner studies, center gatherings, and counsels can provide important bits of knowledge into partner assumptions and concerns, illuminating vital drives, and revealing needs. All in all, partner commitment and revealing developments are fundamental for cultivating straightforwardness, responsibility, and confidence in the present corporate scene (Pimentel, Boulianne, Eskandari, & Clark, 2021). By embracing new strategies and devices for announcing and effectively captivating different partners, bookkeeping experts can improve correspondence, advance manageable practices, and meet the developing assumptions for partners around the world. This approach reinforces corporate standing and drives long-haul esteem creation and versatility in a rapidly changing business climate (Michelon, 2021).

Sustainability and Social Responsibility in Accounting

As corporations' social and environmental effects are more widely acknowledged, sustainability issues are being incorporated into accounting and auditing procedures. Accounting specialists are essential in determining and disclosing these effects and guaranteeing accountability and openness in company disclosures. Corporate reporting frameworks now heavily incorporate environmental, social, and governance

(ESG) criteria which impact how businesses assess and reveal their non-financial performance (van den Berg & Rothmann, 2024).

These standards cover a broad range of variables, such as carbon emissions diversity in the workplace, on-board community involvement, and moral business conduct. For instance, the Task Force on Climate-related Financial Disclosures (TCFD) promotes transparency and aids investors in evaluating long-term sustainability by encouraging businesses to disclose climate-related risks and opportunities. By giving stakeholders a complete picture of a company's effects on the environment and society, the inclusion of ESG criteria in reporting improves accountability (Shaleh, 2024). Companies exhibit their commitment to sustainable practices and responsible governance by publishing ESG metrics along with financial performance indicators. Building trust with consumer worker investors and the community at large is another benefit of this integrated approach to decision-making. Standards for auditing and accounting are changing to consider these sustainability factors. To create coherent corporate Organisations, such as the Sustainability Accounting Standards Board (SASB) and the International Integrated Reporting Council (IIRC) (Odeyemi et al., 2024). These frameworks push businesses to report in a way that takes a comprehensive view of their value-creation processes beyond just financial results. Furthermore, the requirement for the disclosure of ESG data by regulatory agencies is growing, emphasizing the significance of sustainability in corporate reporting. The SECs guidelines on climate-related disclosures and the EU Non-Financial Reporting Directive for example underscore the regulatory focus on ESG issues that is expanding (Olaniyi, Olabanji, & Adebiyi, 2023).

To maintain compliance and preserve the integrity of corporate reporting, accounting professionals must maneuver through these constantly changing regulatory environments. Social responsibility and sustainability are essential components of contemporary accounting and audit procedures. Accounting professionals support accountability transparency and long-term value creation by incorporating ESG criteria into their reporting frameworks. Accounting is critical for measuring disclosure and improving the environmental and social impacts that businesses adopt as they adopt sustainable practices. This contributes to the global development of a sustainable and ethical business environment (Adaga et al., 2024).

FUTURE DIRECTIONS IN THE PROFESSION

The main problem in the accounting and auditing profession is creating a balance between work and life, as this profession demands tight deadlines, excessive workloads, and administrative tensions. Accounting experts frequently face extended periods during the top seasons, for example, during the charge season and year-end reviews, which can strain individual connections and affect mental prosperity. Accomplishing a solid balance between serious and fun activities is essential for holding ability and generally advancing speaking position fulfilment in the calling (Coelho & Menezes, 2021). One of the latest things in balancing work and life activities is the execution of adaptable work plans. Many bookkeeping firms and associations currently offer choices such as remote work, adaptable hours, and packed work-filled weeks. These plans engage representatives to deal with their timetables all the more, taking into account more prominent independence and work-life incorporation. For instance, firms, such as PwC and Deloitte, have carried out adaptable work strategies that require different requirements and inclinations among their staff, advancing a more adjusted and practical way to deal with work (Powell & McGuigan, 2023).

Notwithstanding, challenges remain, especially with respect to the way of life of extended periods and the assumption of steady accessibility in bookkeeping calls. Splitting away from customary standards and advancing a culture that values work proficiency overstretched work hours are fundamental for further developing a balance between serious and fun activities (Sivabalachandran & Gooneratne, 2023). In addition, supporting emotional wellness drives and gives assets to push the board can assist in moderating the pessimistic effects of high-pressure workplaces. Inclusivity in bookkeeping and examining calling includes encouraging variety across all degrees of associations, including positions of authority, and creating a comprehensive work environment culture where people from different foundations feel esteemed and upheld. Drives to advance variety and inclusivity incorporate designated enrolment methodologies, mentorship programs for underrepresented gatherings, and an oblivious predisposition preparing for staff and the board (Shaleh, 2024). Best practices for advancing inclusivity additionally incorporate clear variety of objectives and measurements, considering authority responsible for a variety of results, and making liking gatherings or representative asset organizations to help minimize gatherings. For instance, firms such as EY and KPMG have executed a variety of incorporation programs that focus on enrolment, maintenance, and professional success open doors for women, minorities, and people from underrepresented networks (Powell & McGuigan, 2023).

Overall, tending to balance serious and fun activities and advancing inclusivity are essential for making a feasible and comprehensive bookkeeping and reviewing calling. By implementing adaptable work plans, supporting psychological wellness drives, and encouraging a culture of inclusivity, associations can draw in and hold different abilities while improving representative prosperity and efficiency. These endeavors benefit individual experts and add to a stronger and flourishing calling that mirrors the variety of society (Nicolau, 2023).

CONCLUSION

In conclusion, the advancement of bookkeeping and reviewing rehabilitation mirrors a powerful reaction to more extensive cultural changes, enveloping mechanical headways, social movements, and administrative turns of events. This chapter has investigated different aspects of these changes, featuring key experiences and suggestions for calling. Bookkeeping and inspecting have advanced past customary jobs as simple record managers of monetary exchanges. Today, these disciplines assume a basic role in giving straightforwardness, responsibility, and key bits of knowledge to partners in an undeniably complicated worldwide economy. The reconciliation of new advancements, such as computerized reasoning, blockchain, and information investigation, has upset how monetary data are handled, examined, and detailed. These advancements improve productivity and exactness as well as empower more proactive gambling of the board and direction. In addition, bookkeeping and examination have extended to encompass more extensive cultural aspects, including supportability, social obligation, and inclusivity. The reconciliation of ecological, social, and administration (ESG) models into announcing structures reflects the development of partner assumptions for straightforwardness and the moral corporate way of behaving. Drives to advance variety and inclusivity inside the calling encourage a more comprehensive work environment culture that values different points of view and ability.

Looking forward, the eventual fate of bookkeeping and reviewing will be molded by progress in innovation and continuous cultural assumptions for straightforwardness and responsibility. Future exploration ought to zero in improving the reconciliation of artificial intelligence and information examination in reviewing processes, guaranteeing the exactness and unwavering quality of monetary announcements in the midst of progressively complex business conditions.

Moreover, investigating the effect of social variables on bookkeeping practices can provide significant knowledge of worldwide varieties and administrative harmonization endeavors. In addition, the call should keep on adjusting to administrative changes and advancing accepted procedures to keep up with pertinence and confidence in monetary announcements. As organizations explore computerized change and globalization, bookkeeping experts play a significant role in directing key navigation and guaranteeing consistency with administrative principles.

Overall, by embracing mechanical advancement, advancing variety and inclusivity, and answering cultural requests for straightforwardness and supportability, bookkeeping and reviewing experts can explore the intricacies of the cutting-edge business scene. The excursion towards constant improvement and variation guarantees that bookkeeping remains the foundation of monetary soundness and corporate administration over a long period of time.

REFERENCES

Adaga, E. M., Egieya, Z. E., Ewuga, S. K., Abdul, A. A., & Abrahams, T. O. (2024). A comprehensive review of ethical practices in banking and finance. *Finance & Accounting Research Journal*, 6(1), 1–20. DOI: 10.51594/farj.v6i1.705

Adebiyi, O. O., Olabanji, S. O., & Olaniyi, O. O. (2023). Promoting inclusive accounting education through the integration of STEM principles for a diverse classroom. *Asian Journal of Education and Social Studies*, 49(4), 152–171. DOI: 10.9734/ajess/2023/v49i41196

Azambuja, R., Baudot, L., & Malsch, B. (2023). Navigating multiple accountabilities through managers' boundary work in professional service firms. *Accounting, Auditing & Accountability Journal*, 36(7/8), 1734–1762. DOI: 10.1108/AAAJ-08-2021-5407

Bakhtiyari, K., Salehi, H., Embi, M. A., Shakiba, M., Isfandyari-Moghaddam, A., Dadkhah, M., & Farhadi, M. (2014). Ethical challenges in academic research. *International Journal of High-Rise Buildings*, 3(4), 285–298.

Barac, K., Plant, K., Kunz, R., & Kirstein, M. (2021). Audit practice: A straightforward trade or a complex system? *International Journal of Auditing*, 25(3), 797–812. DOI: 10.1111/ijau.12249

Barr-Pulliam, D., Joe, J., Mason, S., & Sanderson, K. A. (2020). The auditor-valuation specialist coopetitive alliance in the fair value audit of complex financial instruments.

Bebbington, J., & Rubin, A. (2022). Accounting in the Anthropocene: A roadmap for stewardship. *Accounting and Business Research*, 52(5), 582–596. DOI: 10.1080/00014788.2022.2079780

Bhimani, A. (2020). Digital data and management accounting: Why we need to rethink research methods. *Journal of Management Control*, 31(1), 9–23. DOI: 10.1007/s00187-020-00295-z

Coelho, M., & Menezes, I. (2021). University social responsibility, service learning, and students' personal, professional, and civic education. *Frontiers in Psychology*, 12, 617300. DOI: 10.3389/fpsyg.2021.617300 PMID: 33716883

De Villiers, R. (2021). Seven principles to ensure future-ready accounting graduates–a model for future research and practice. *Meditari Accountancy Research*, 29(6), 1354–1380. DOI: 10.1108/MEDAR-04-2020-0867

Ellili, N., Nobanee, H., Haddad, A., Alodat, A. Y., & AlShalloudi, M. (2024). Emerging trends in forensic accounting research: Bridging research gaps and prioritizing new frontiers. *Journal of Economic Criminology*, 100065.

Handoyo, S. (2024). Evolving paradigms in accounting education: A bibliometric study on the impact of information technology. *International Journal of Management Education*, 22(3), 100998. DOI: 10.1016/j.ijme.2024.100998

Jejeniwa, T. O., Mhlongo, N. Z., & Jejeniwa, T. O. (2024). A comprehensive review of the impact of artificial intelligence on modern accounting practices and financial reporting. *Computer Science & IT Research Journal*, 5(4), 1031–1047. DOI: 10.51594/csitrj.v5i4.1086

Liu, X., & Ishak, N. N. B. M. (2023). Research on the application and development of RPA in accounting higher vocational education: A Chinese perspective. *International Journal of Education and Humanities*, 10(2), 178–182. DOI: 10.54097/ijeh.v10i2.11592

Michelon, G. (2021). Accounting research boundaries, multiple centers and academic empathy. *Critical Perspectives on Accounting*, 76, 102204. DOI: 10.1016/j.cpa.2020.102204

Mustikarini, A., & Adhariani, D. (2022). In auditor we trust: 44 years of research on the auditor-client relationship and future research directions. *Meditari Accountancy Research*, 30(2), 267–292. DOI: 10.1108/MEDAR-11-2020-1062

Nicolau, A. (2023). The impact of AI on internal audit and accounting practices. *Internal Auditing & Risk Management*, (Supplement), 38–56.

Odeyemi, O., Awonuga, K. F., Mhlongo, N. Z., Ndubuisi, N. L., Olatoye, F. O., & Daraojimb, A. I. (2024). The role of AI in transforming auditing practices: A global perspective review. *World Journal of Advanced Research and Reviews*, 21(2), 359–370. DOI: 10.30574/wjarr.2024.21.2.0460

Olaniyi, O. O., Olabanji, S. O., & Adebiyi, O. O. (2023). Promoting inclusive accounting education through the integration of STEM principles for a diverse classroom.

Olweny, F. (2024). Navigating the nexus of security and privacy in modern financial technologies. *GSC Advanced Research and Reviews*, 18(2), 167–197. DOI: 10.30574/gscarr.2024.18.2.0043

Pasolo, F. (2024). Understanding the interplay between accounting practices and organizational structures for strategic management. *Advances: Jurnal Ekonomi & Bisnis*, 2(3), 136–150.

Pimentel, E., Boulianne, E., Eskandari, S., & Clark, J. (2021). Systemizing the challenges of auditing blockchain-based assets. *Journal of Information Systems*, 35(2), 61–75. DOI: 10.2308/ISYS-19-007

Pontoppidan, C. A. (2024). Teaching the next generation of accountants: integrating financial, environmental, social and governance accounting and reporting practices. In *Business Education in the 21st Century* (pp. 371–385). Edward Elgar Publishing. DOI: 10.4337/9781802202694.00029

Powell, L., & McGuigan, N. (2023). Responding to crises: Rewilding accounting education for the Anthropocene. *Meditari Accountancy Research*, 31(1), 101–120. DOI: 10.1108/MEDAR-06-2021-1333

Rinaldi, L. (2023, July). Accounting and the COVID-19 pandemic two years on: Insights, gaps, and an agenda for future research. *Accounting Forum*, 47(3), 333–364. DOI: 10.1080/01559982.2022.2045418

Salleh, N. M. Z. N., Moorthy, K., & Jasmon, A. (2023). A review of scholarly discourses on accounting technical skills for IR 4.0. *Journal of Higher Education Theory and Practice*, 23(9).

Sarkar, S., Boss, S. R., & Gray, J. (2021). Pedagogical practices of accounting departments addressing AACSB technology requirements. *Issues in Accounting Education*, 36(4), 59–85. DOI: 10.2308/ISSUES-19-082

Shaleh, M. (2024). Advances in Management & Financial Reporting.

Sivabalachandran, T., & Gooneratne, T. (2023). Roles at crossroads: Complexities and conflicts surrounding management accountants' roles based on evidence from the Sri Lankan context. *Asian Journal of Accounting Research*, 8(1), 80–93. DOI: 10.1108/AJAR-11-2021-0242

Tariq, M. U. (2024). Harnessing Persuasive Technologies for Enhanced Learner Engagement and Motivation. In M. Sanmugam, D. Lim, N. Mohd Barkhaya, W. Wan Yahaya, & Z. Khlaif (Eds.), *Power of Persuasive Educational Technologies in Enhancing Learning* (pp. 30-62). IGI Global. DOI: 10.4018/979-8-3693-6397-3.ch002

Tariq, M. U. (2024). Smart Transportation Systems: Paving the Way for Sustainable Urban Mobility. In Munuhwa, S. (Ed.), *Contemporary Solutions for Sustainable Transportation Practices* (pp. 254–283). IGI Global. DOI: 10.4018/979-8-3693-3755-4.ch010

Tariq, M. U. (2024). Integration of IoMT for Enhanced Healthcare: Sleep Monitoring, Body Movement Detection, and Rehabilitation Evaluation. In Liu, H., Tripathy, R., & Bhattacharya, P. (Eds.), *Clinical Practice and Unmet Challenges in AI-Enhanced Healthcare Systems* (pp. 70–95). IGI Global. DOI: 10.4018/979-8-3693-2703-6.ch004

Tariq, M. U. (2024). Cybersecurity Risk Assessment Models and Theories in the Travel and Tourism Industry. In Thealla, P., Nadda, V., Dadwal, S., Oztosun, L., & Cantafio, G. (Eds.), *Corporate Cybersecurity in the Aviation, Tourism, and Hospitality Sector* (pp. 1–17). IGI Global. DOI: 10.4018/979-8-3693-2715-9.ch001

Tariq, M. U. (2024). Data Breach Incidents and Prevention in the Hospitality Industry. In Thealla, P., Nadda, V., Dadwal, S., Oztosun, L., & Cantafio, G. (Eds.), *Corporate Cybersecurity in the Aviation, Tourism, and Hospitality Sector* (pp. 181–199). IGI Global. DOI: 10.4018/979-8-3693-2715-9.ch010

Tariq, M. U. (2024). Navigating the Personalization Pathway: Implementing Adaptive Learning Technologies in Higher Education. In Minh Tung, T. (Ed.), *Adaptive Learning Technologies for Higher Education* (pp. 265–291). IGI Global. DOI: 10.4018/979-8-3693-3641-0.ch012

Tariq, M. U. (2024). Enhancing Students and Learning Achievement as 21st-Century Skills Through Transdisciplinary Approaches. In Kumar, R., Ong, E., Anggoro, S., & Toh, T. (Eds.), *Transdisciplinary Approaches to Learning Outcomes in Higher Education* (pp. 220–257). IGI Global. DOI: 10.4018/979-8-3693-3699-1.ch007

Van den Berg, E., & Rothmann, S. (2024). Twenty-first-century competencies and capabilities for financial accounting students. *Suid-Afrikaanse Tydskrif vir Ekonomiese en Bestuurswetenskappe*, 27(1), 11. DOI: 10.4102/sajems.v27i1.5535

Van der Merwe, N. (2021). The future of accounting: Will we be replaced by robots? Nico van der Merwe.

Chapter 2
Success Story on Business Decision Making Using Artificial Intelligence:
A Positive Vision of Disruptive Technologies

Flory Dieck-Assad
https://orcid.org/0000-0002-5002-4807
Tecnologico de Monterrey, Mexico

ABSTRACT

This chapter presents the advantages of using technological advancements such as artificial intelligence (AI) tools to enhance the traditional decision-making process of an accountant in the area of reporting and analysis. Throughout the chapter, the reader will discover a wide array of applications that the AI ecosystem (robo-advisors, virtual assistants, chatbots, etc.) offers to simplify data analysis and improve tactical decision-making for targeting new paths of growth for any company. It tells the success story of an accountant who was promoted to chief accounting officer (CAO) by enhancing the vision of the firm's path of growth through the use of AI tools, based on real data. AI will not replace professional accountants; on the contrary, with the help of AI, accountants can give strategic insights to improve the financial welfare of any firm by providing innovative data analysis faster and allowing the accountant more time to digest the analysis and provide better and informed tactical decision-making to target a newer vision of the company in the short and long term.

DOI: 10.4018/979-8-3693-5923-5.ch002

INTRODUCTION

This chapter introduces the reader to the use of Artificial Intelligence (AI) tools supporting every accountant with the data analysis of a firm towards better and faster decision making. It shows the struggle of a firm trying to cope with the latest wave of technological change and try to overcome its burden to reap potential benefits associated with the adoption of AI tools to increase profitability and remain competitive.

This case study tells the success story of Tracy Santos, an accountant who was promoted to Chief Accounting Officer (CAO) by enhancing the vision of the firm's path of growth using AI tools. It is written with the objective of promoting discussion about several Artificial Intelligence (AI) possibilities that an accountant can use to improve business results and increase profitability. The chapter is based on real data offered by a firm where the empirical study was researched. Some data has been changed to maintain confidentiality of the information. Tracy explored Data Analysis tools that allowed the use of the information of the firm without compromising information security. Tracy needed ample time to interpret and digest the data to provide a productive decision and proposal to improve the company's profitability and future market growth. Thus, she decided to use the combination of an existing software in the company (Excel) with an added AI function within the same software called 'Analyze Data', which has the benefit of using prompts with natural language to get the job done.

The main contribution of this chapter is to emphasize that AI will not replace professional accountants; on the contrary, with the help of AI, accountants can give strategic insights to improve the financial welfare of any firm. The second contribution is to inspire all accountants to navigate the AI ecosystem (Robo-Advisors, virtual assistants, chatbots, etc.) and discover the alternatives that this disruptive technology offers to improve business operations protecting the confidential information of the firm. After reading the chapter, accountants will be empowered to promote discussion about several AI possibilities to enhance the decision-making of their companies. AI tools will complement the accountant's role by providing a faster innovative data analysis and allowing the accountant more time to digest the analysis and provide better and informed tactical decision-making to target a newer vision of the company for increasing profitability in the short and long term.

This research presents the advantages of using technological advancements such as Artificial Intelligence (AI) tools to enhance the traditional decision-making process of an accountant in the area of reporting and analysis. Throughout the chapter, the reader will discover a wide array of applications that AI offers to simplify data analysis and improve tactical decision-making for targeting new paths of growth to increase profitability for any company. The breakthrough of the chapter is a new approach to the analysis of the data using conversational AI for the traditional profitability analysis of a firm choosing the right tool to minimize the risk to compromise the security and confidence of the data of the firm.

The structure of this chapter is as follows. The next section presents a background of the Mexican firm CelMex, S.A. de C.V. (CelMex), where the real case is researched. It presents the definition of the challenge and the hypothesis. The following section presents the literature review about how to increase profitability in a company, the challenge that accounting professionals must face, and the importance to master the use of information systems with AI tools to improve decision-making process toward the enhancement of the profitability of a company. It also presents the evolution of AI in business and in Data Analysis. The methodology is presented in the next section, where Tracy Santos, a member of CelMex's accounting team presents her selected profitability strategy and the AI tools for her analysis from the available technologies, with an emphasis in protecting sensitive data of the company. The next section presents the analysis and results of Tracy's proposal which led her to find a breakthrough in a firms' data analysis minimizing the risks for the company. The chapter continues with the discussion of the results. The last section presents the conclusions proving that indeed the knowledge of disruptive technologies as the AI tools improved Tracy's ability to present a strong analysis of the data in record time. She demonstrated that the participation of AI to improve business decision-making helped her to be promoted to the CAO position. At the end of the chapter, a references section is presented as well as key terms and definitions used throughout the chapter.

BACKGROUND

This section presents the description of the empirical case of Mexico based company CelMex, S.A. de C.V. (CelMex), the definition of the challenge, and the formulation of the hypothesis.

CelMex and Tom Diaz

CelMex is a firm that sells and distributes cellular phones in Mexico. The firm began operations in 1999 with a shocking growth process. CelMex has its legal, accounting, and financial operations spread across several states of Mexico. CelMex has influence and presence selling cellular phones through 35 distributors located in 4,556 sites across the country.

Tom Diaz is CelMex's Chief Accountant Officer (CAO) and has had an outstanding performance ever since he started working in 1999. He is knowledgeable of the legal and financial aspects of the firm. His vision, great talent, and responsibility helped him guide the expansion of the firm, participating in CelMex's growth to reach different locations of Mexico during the last 25 years. But now he is preparing for his retirement in one month.

Marcy Garza, Ph.D. and Chief Financial Officer (CFO) of CelMex, needed to find a fair process to select the next CAO of the firm among the current accountants working there. According to former US Secretary of Energy and Nobel Prize recipient Steven Chu *"the Stone Age did not end because we ran out of stones, it ended because we transitioned to better solutions"* (Drollette, 2023). Dr. Chu's hope of making this world a better place using better solutions (such as disruptive technologies) inspired Marcy Garza on the way to design a strategy to follow for the selection process to choose the new CAO of the firm. She decided to do this through a contest where the current candidates must offer the best proposal for using Artificial Intelligence to improve business operations and profitability for CelMex.

Definition of The Challenge

Marcy published the challenge in the company's bulletin: "As you know, our firm CelMex is not using Artificial Intelligence. You will have a test period of one week. You must do your jobs with enthusiasm and responsibility and solve the challenge of this task with creativity and innovation using disruptive technologies to formulate new paths to follow to improve the firm's operations and profitability. The proposal will be evaluated not only by the approach to profitability but also concerning the use of disruptive technologies. The time has come to introduce our business to the Artificial Intelligence wave. The one among you who presents the best proposal must provide us with a new vision to reinforce our market positioning, enhancing our profitability. Credibility is a requirement with a real proposal based on hard data and evidence. Let the challenge begin: 'The goal is to be always better than yesterday, not better than others'. I encourage you to begin your challenge envisioning possible strategies or innovations for the growth of the firm.".

Hypothesis

Tracy Santos, a member of CelMex's accounting team, showed eagerness to face the challenge after Marcy's bulletin announcement. Tracy started studying CelMex since its beginnings. She wanted to get acquainted with its growth process to identify the key elements for its expansion. She first researched the area where a company must pay attention to increase profitability, finding that the department of marketing and sales provides data which is the pivotal source of information to enhance the whole vision of the company and try to synchronize solutions from it to other departments of the firm. She was confident that knowing the market and sales history of the company could improve her vision of the future. Thus, she reflected on the challenge posed by Dr. Marcy and developed her own hypothesis to be tested and see if this could help her get promoted to CAO. Her hypothesis is that using the 'Analyze Data' AI feature in Microsoft Excel for data analysis will help her know more about the company's market history and performance faster and in record time without risking the confidentiality of the data. Thus, she will have more time to digest the analysis and provide better and informed tactical decision-making to target a newer vision of the company to increase profitability in the short and long term. If her hypothesis is not rejected, she envisions having great possibilities to earn her promotion as the new CAO of the firm. Thus, her research journey began.

LITERATURE REVIEW

Profitability

There are different strategies to increase the profitability of a company. It depends on the focus and viewpoint that the person in charge provides for achieving better results in a company and satisfying the interests of the stakeholders. The first and most obvious strategy for this task could be implemented through an increase in the prices of the products or after reviewing useless expenses and trying to reduce them. According to Amaresan (2024), this approach appears difficult in an intensely competitive environment and has the imminent danger of resulting in customer churn; thus, this strategy is not the one to follow on a short-term notice. The approach must include a debate of production and input costs, industry trends, and the possibility to offer extra benefits to existing customers to smooth the impact of a price increase. For this option to be effective, the firm must know its competitors. To reach an agreement of a price increase, there must be a synchronization with other departments of the firm such as the sales and customer service teams, to be sure that everybody is on the same page about a price increase, and it could be justified and be viewed as a riskless operation when communicating this change to customers.

An important metric for a profitable company is the KPI (Key Performance Indicator) because it measures what a company generates in net profits/benefits (Fitz-Gibbon, 1990). The person in charge of company profitability needs to satisfy the vision of investors, owners, bosses, and everyone in the company. Thus, to increase the profitability of a company it is important to choose the right approach: through an increase in the income or through a reduction of expenses.

According to Onsight (2024) the Pareto Law states that 80% of the profits come from 20% of the clients. This principle is sometimes referred to as the "80/20 Rule". The Pareto Principle has been found to apply to many situations, including sales. For example, 80% of your sales come from only 20% of your customers. Or even, 20% of your sales staff makes 80% of the company's overall sales. In essence, 20% of all input (effort, time, and resources) account for 80% of all output.

Another strategy could lead the decision makers to do a market analysis and focus on profitable customers and client retention. This could be done by conducting market research for these purposes. It could also be through an expansion of the market through developing a marketing and branding campaign, using promotions or offers that could increase and consolidate sales, enhancing the experience of the client with the brand and the product or service and finding new customers. There could be several approaches focusing on expanding the market: personalizing offers, building the loyalty of the customers, among others (Indeed Editorial Team, 2023).

The Sphere Group (2024) recommends analyzing financial statements of the company to monitor the financial health of the company through the analysis of income statements, balance sheets, and cash flows reports of several years in the life of the company. The analysis of financial health could guide the firm to identify potential problems and provide valuable insights of the business's finances and present ratios like profit margins and liquidity ratios to be compared throughout the years, for an evaluation of the evolution of them through the history of the company or against those of similar businesses. A good analysis of this data could help businesses to make more informed decisions about their finances and profitability.

A company may experience a rise in expenses that become unmanageable. A strategy to reduce expenses also sounds possible if a company wants to increase profitability and ensure long-term success. To define this strategy, the non-essential costs must be identified. This approach must also find ways to handle tasks more efficiently: this means to increase automatization and the optimization of supply chain operations. By identifying opportunities to reduce expenses and streamline workflow processes, businesses can be well-positioned for growth and profitability in the future (Business Gateway, 2024).

There are other strategies that could be followed: from investing in automation to smart investments in tools and technology, team engagement, inventory management, branding, improving the quality of customer services, waste reductions, and innovation, among others to increase profitability (SallyPort, 2021).

The Accounting Professional and Artificial Intelligence

Accounting professionals face their toughest challenge: master the use of information systems. How can it be possible to manage and analyze large volumes of data and, at the same time, automate and optimize their tasks? Indeed, they need to choose a digital platform and specialized software (Dell Technologies, 2024).

Artificial Intelligence (AI) arises as an ideal tool to face challenges. The objective would be to allow technology to oversee repetitive tasks like invoice processing, information offering, and prepare the accountant to evaluate the information and concentrate in the decision-making process that adds value to his/her profession (Bachinskiy, 2019).

With the use of AI, the activities of an accountant are changing because once the AI achieves the automatization of accountant's tasks, improve efficiency, accuracy, and decrease costs, then the accountant is ready to examine the report and take better decisions for the firm (Universidad de la Costa, 2024).

It is important to emphasize that AI will not replace accountants; on the contrary, with the help of AI accountants can give strategic insights to improve the financial welfare of any firm (Caruso, 2024). Thus, the accountant executives must develop analytical competences to work with the help of AI (Finerio Connect, 2024b).

In an interview with Sneha Revanur, the optimism about AI was emphasized: "Even as we are on the brink of potentially catastrophic threats, I remain grounded in the belief that if we act fast, we can get this right; we just need to move to set some rules on the road. If we do that, then AI still can be a force for good; it can open up realms of possibilities" (Drollette, 2024).

As Schreckinger (2023) states, AI must be regulated, but there is a generation of policymakers who are out of touch with contemporary disruptive technologies. He emphasizes the importance of improving technical literacy in government in order to decrease the fear to adopt these types of innovations. A new hope appeared on the horizon with the creation of the organization Encode Justice, a civil society group focused on AI issues, which mobilizes young people for human centered AI (Encode Justice, 2024b), hoping to deal with an AI aligned with human values (Encode Justice, 2024a).

The American business magazine Forbes published that 65% of the experts in finance expect positive changes with the use of AI in financial services (Finerio Connect, 2024a).

Ernst & Young, which has invested $1.4 billion in artificial intelligence, announced a new AI platform and its own large language model, and plans on teaching its 400,000 employees how to use AI in the workplace (Mok, 2023).

According to Enholm, et. al. (2022), organizations were struggling to adopt and leverage AI in their operations. They explain that due to the lack of a coherent understanding of how AI technologies create business value, and what type of business value is expected, they required a holistic understanding of how AI can generate a positive disruption in a firm.

Several reasons support that AI has positive implications of its use in the marketing, accounting, finance, and business fields. Every firm needs to focus on a new growth plan from an innovative point of view using AI. There are advantages and challenges derived from using AI as another way to analyze marketing, financial and accounting processes (Google Scholar, 2024).

The main advantages of using AI in accounting and financial processes are (IBN Technologies Limited, 2024):

- *Minimization of Human Errors*: If AI is used to automate various tasks and processes, it decreases the probability of human errors, emotional bad decisions, or the possibility to neglect certain details.
- *Accurate Analysis and Predictions*: AI has the possibility to analyze large amounts of financial data and identify useful patterns for decision making. Thus, the accountants and financial analysts improve their possibility to make more accurate decisions and forecasts about the market and consumer behavior in real time.
- *Process Acceleration*: The automatization that AI offers, makes it possible to have faster processes. As an example, the recollection and analysis of substantial large amounts of data do not need human intervention and help the accountants to take faster decisions (Berdiyeva, Umar Islam, and Saeedi, 2021).

Some innovative uses and applications of AI in accounting and financial processes which are revolutionizing the financial and accounting disciplines are (Cook, 2024):

- *Credit Analysis*: Using AI lets the accountant take better and informed decisions about the best candidates to take a credit through the analysis of huge amounts of information in real time (Sadok, Sakka, & El Maknouzi, 2022). The accountants call it the credit AI score as a credit worthiness assessment generated using AI algorithms and machine learning models to estimate the credit risk based on the financial history, transactions, income, employment, among other information analyzed. The AI models include data that is not considered in traditional credit scoring models, to predict a borrower's likelihood of repaying a loan (Datrics, 2024).

- *Robo-Advisors*: this is an automated financial advisor that offers algorithm-driven services to manage investments automatically. These systems can manage portfolios according to the preferences and risk wishes of a customer, make transactions, and adjust the strategy according to the market behavior, with lower commissions than those paid to human advisors (Hayes & Smith, 2023). The Best Robo-Advisors can be listed as follows (Hartley & Dammeyer, 2024):
- *Betterment*. Best Robo-Advisor for Everyday Investors.
- *SoFi Automated Investing*. Best Robo-Advisor for Low Fees.
- *Vanguard Digital Advisor*. Best Robo-Advisor for Beginners.
- *Vanguard Personal Advisor Services*. Best Robo-Advisor for High Balances.
- *Wealthfront*. Best Robo-Advisor for DIY (Do It Yourself) Financial Planning (Correct Capital, 2023).
- *Virtual Assistants and Chatbots*: These are the most common AI applications used in accounting and finance. They offer answers to customer inquiries, provide technical support and information about products and services in real time and in several languages, giving a comfortable experience to the accountant. (L & Alur, 2023).

AI has permeated the financial sector changing the process of decision making. However, important challenges have also emerged with the application and use of AI in accounting and financial processes. Some of them are:

- *Security and Data Protection*: The use of AI requires the administration of considerable amounts of data and sensitive information, such as personal and financial data. Thus, the use of AI should be accompanied by an increase in advance security measures to guarantee respect to privacy in this constant process of data interchange.
- *Education and Adaptation*: The *metathesiophobia* could manifest in humans; that is the fear of change, unwilling to accept change as part of life, that could trigger severe anxiety or panic attacks rooted in a human desire to keep life in a comfortable and consistent place (Calm, 2024). AI could be seen as a life threat, a possible job loss and distrust in automation, with the consequences of human responses such as depression and decrease in productivity. Employees should be educated with the eagerness to work with AI using technology as a tool that can complement human work, not substitute it.
- *Regulation and Ethics*: The use of AI in decision making also poses ethical and regulatory concerns (Hoffmann & Hann, 2019). The key to the success of the use of AI is to establish a clear regulatory framework with which the

accountant can face the risks and adapt technological changes to the firm (Carter, 2020).

ChatGPT is considered the fastest growing app in history with 100 hundred million active users just two months after its release (Aunoa, 2024). Soon, AI startups popped up everywhere as venture capitalists dumped billions of dollars into new players including the firm called Anthropic which was started by former OpenAI employees that raised $7.3 billion in its first year (a direct competitor to ChatGPT). As Caruso (2024) stated, "everyone was, and still seems to be, drinking the Kool-Aid and the AI innovation race is on". ChatGPT and Anthropic are the same but with one difference, the first one masters concepts with context and coherence. And the second one masters emotional sensibility with the ability to understand and emulate human emotions. ChatGPT is a better option for marketing, accounting and financial purposes.

There are several chatbots available to offer the firm an innovative point of view for decision making:

- ChatGPT: https://chat.openai.com/
- Copilot: https://copilot.microsoft.com/
- Claude: https://claude.ai/
- Gemini: https://gemini.google.com/
- Studio D-ID: https://studio.d-id.com/
- HeyGen: https://www.heygen.com/
- RunwayML: https://runwayml.com/
- PikaLabs: https://pika.art/

Some chatbots are free and some have a cost. However, even though some are free, they invade your privacy because they ask for personal information such as telephone numbers. The different chatbots present different risks for data confidentiality. Other chatbots require you to apply for a subscription, using a business account or a personal account or offer a free account with a limited capacity of interactions with the chatbot.

Artificial Intelligence in Business

Through the analysis of recently published literature on AI, Bahoo, et al. (2024) found that it has expanded considerably since the beginning of the XXI century, covering a variety of countries and different AI applications in finance. Some of the published research show how AI is applied to the stock market, trading models, volatility forecasting, portfolio management, performance, risk and default evaluation, cryptocurrencies, derivatives, credit risk in banks, investor sentiment analysis and foreign exchange management, among others.

According to Bahoo, et al. (2024), there is a rapid widespread of AI applications in the financial sphere and across a large variety of countries. Based on the growth rate exhibited by technological progress over time, they expect that the use of AI tools will further expand, both geographically, across sectors and across financial areas. This point of view coincides with the vision of Davenport & Ronanki (2018) when they surveyed 250 executives familiar with their companies' use of cognitive technology and a study of 152 projects show that companies do better by taking an incremental rather than a transformative approach to developing and implementing AI, and by focusing on augmenting rather than replacing human capabilities. Even though a company's AI projects encounter setbacks or fail, firms must understand which technologies perform what types of tasks, create a prioritized portfolio of projects based on business needs, and develop plans to scale up across the company. They suggested three important business needs where AI can support: automating business processes (typically back-office administrative and financial activities), gaining insight through data analysis, and engaging with customers and employees.

Bahoo, et al (2024) encouraged companies that have not adopted AI tools to introduce AI applications by providing training courses and funding to strengthen the complex skills required by employees dealing with these sophisticated systems and languages.

On the other hand, Surjadi (2024) states that college students in the United States are desperate to add a new skill to their resumes: AI literacy. There are universities that are changing the academic profile of a student. For example, Cornell University, among others, is designing curricular courses in AI literacy where professors prepare students to fill the AI talent gap in every academic field. This new approach is changing the role of universities and colleges with the objective of preparing their students on how to use AI and providing them with new skills that will be required as a must by headhunters in the future.

The research of Shanmugam, et al. (2023) present how the use of AI tools within the tourism sector through chatbots emerged as a pivotal element in the transformation of market structures and commercial paradigms.

Chui and Yee (2023) demonstrated that generative AI technologies like ChatGPT have taken the world by storm, thanks to their stunning ability to parse natural language and make decisions that are remarkably human.

McKinsey Global Institute finds that generative AI has the potential to generate value equivalent to $2.6 trillion to $4.4 trillion in global corporate profits annually. They analyzed 63 case studies in which they estimate that generative AI will raise productivity, including providing support interactions with customers, generating creative content for marketing and sales, and drafting software code based on natural-language prompts, among many other tasks. These findings would increase the value of productivity from artificial intelligence and analytics by 15% to 40% compared to previous generations of the technology—an amount that would roughly double as generative AI spreads more diffusely across the global workplace (Chui and Yee, 2023). They emphasized that about three-quarters of the value from generative AI would emerge from four areas of business: customer operations, marketing and sales, software engineering, and research and development. McKinsey Global Institute estimates that generative AI could increase labor productivity by 0.1% to 0.6% annually through 2040. They also estimated in 2017 that technologies available at that time could automate employees' activities that occupied half of their time. From 2017 to 2023 technologies evolved and combined with AI tools, allow the employees to use 60% to 70% of their time in analysis for decision making, rather than using the time for creating graphs, statistics, and visuals.

McKinsey Global Institute presented scenarios with the effects of generative AI, that suggest that half of today's work activities could be automated between 2030 and 2060. While adoption of AI might take decades across the global workforce, individual companies could transform their operations using generative AI much more quickly for a competitive advantage.

Gartner Research (2018) defines Hype Cycles that characterize the typical progression of innovation, from overenthusiasm through a period of disillusionment to an eventual understanding of the innovation's relevance and role in a market or domain. Since generative AI has been considered an innovation since 2014, through the years, it has passed through several expectations in the Hype Cycle. From 2014 to 2018, it started with the 'Innovation Trigger', where generative AI was considered a breakthrough, and public demonstrations were made in the press, generating industry interest in this technology innovation. From 2018 to 2024 it moved to a 'Peak of Inflated Expectations', where a wave of overenthusiasm builds and the expectations for this innovation rise above the current reality of its capabilities. However, this phase also implies that expectations may be unrealistic, and that some disillusionment is likely as limitations and challenges become more apparent (Gartner Research, 2024).

Goldman (2024) states that generative AI is viewed by several analysts like Goldman Sachs and a Venture Capitalist from Sequoia Capital to be "overhyped", "wildly expensive", "a bubble reaching a tipping point", and "a machine running on empty". The reasoning behind these viewpoints is because generative AI chatbots struggle to answer basic questions or hallucinate incorrect information. Also, the most sophisticated generative AI models are constantly hungry for data and computing power. Furthermore, generative AI startups with little to no revenue constantly ask for massive funding to stay afloat, and Fortune 500 companies cannot put generative AI analyzed cases into action because of concerns about accuracy, liability and security.

According to Goldman (2024), generative AI has already reached the 'Trough of Disillusionment', where impatience for results begins to replace the original excitement about potential value. Users start identifying problems with performance, a slower-than-expected adoption or a failure to deliver financial returns in the time anticipated. This leads to missed expectations, and disillusionment sets in. While generative AI has been a success by anyone's measure, the expectations around how quickly that would impact the bottom line of major organizations were not based in reality. Gartner's global chief of research, Chris Howard, stated his premise on generative AI being in the 'Trough of Disillusionment': "After an initial burst of excitement and enthusiasm by early adopters, new technology makes its way into the hands of mainstream users who find it doesn't live up their overinflated expectations. A retrenchment follows, during which the technology is refined, and expectations are reset. It's not this dark, dangerous place. It is where we figure out how to make something work–or not".

Artificial Intelligence in Data Analysis

There is an important distinction between data analysis and data science. Data analysis primarily involves extracting meaningful insights from existing data using statistical techniques and visualization tools. Whereas, data science encompasses a broader spectrum, incorporating data analysis as a subset while involving machine learning, deep learning, and predictive modeling to build data-driven solutions and algorithms (Simplilearn, 2024a). Data science involves a time-consuming process of preparing algorithms and programming (Google Workspace Learning Center, 2024).

Based on Datacamp (2023), Data Analysis (DA), whether on a small or large scale, can have a profound impact on business performance. It can drive significant changes, leading to improved efficiency, increased profitability, and a deeper understanding of market trends and customer behavior.

The business ecosystem is constantly evolving: every firm needs to exploit the power of DA to better adapt to changing market conditions, rising customer needs and continue the path of growth and profitability.

Regarding DA tools, there is a wide array of alternatives to choose from, depending on the complexity of the research and the required level of knowledge or expertise. According to Simplilearn (2024b), these tools range from programming languages like Python, R and SQL to visualization software (business analytics tool) like Power BI, Tableau, Excel, and Google Sheets. These can be defined as follows:

- **Python**: a high-level, general-purpose programming language that has become a favorite among data analysts and data scientists. Its simplicity and readability, coupled with a wide range of libraries like pandas, NumPy, and Matplotlib, make it an excellent tool for data analysis and data visualization.
- **R**: a programming language and free software environment specifically designed for statistical computing and graphics. It is widely used among statisticians and data miners for developing statistical software and data analysis. R provides a wide variety of statistical and graphical techniques, including linear and nonlinear modeling, classical statistical tests, time-series analysis, and more.
- **SQL**: Structured Query Language is a standard language for managing and manipulating databases. It is used to retrieve and manipulate data stored in relational databases. SQL is essential for tasks that involve data management or manipulation within databases.

These tools consider languages that need to be learned to master its process. Coding is also required, and this process requires a series of courses that can be time consuming. Also, the use of queries to manipulate the databases also requires taking additional courses as guidance into the functions for querying data, filtering data, aggregation, etc. These languages are mainly used by people who want to build a career as a data analyst or scientist.

- **Power BI**: a business analytics tool developed by Microsoft. It provides interactive visualizations with self-service business intelligence capabilities. Power BI is used to transform raw data into meaningful insights through easy-to-understand dashboards and reports.
- **Tableau**: a powerful data visualization tool used in the Business Intelligence industry. It allows you to create interactive and shareable dashboards, which depict trends, variations, and density of the data in the form of charts and graphs.
- **Google Sheets**: a business analytics tool used for data analysis and visualization. The process to analyze data is to import and clean data, sort and filter data, apply formulas and functions, create personalized charts and graphs, build pivot tables and slicers, and finally share the data (Akkio, 2024).
- **Excel**: Microsoft Excel is one of the most widely used tools for data analysis. It offers a range of features for data manipulation, statistical analysis, and visualization. Excel's simplicity and versatility make it a great tool for both simple and complex data analysis tasks.

Business analytics tools can transform data into graphs, visuals or even dashboards to better understand and digest the information for productive decision making. Even though Power BI and Tableau help enhance reports using exploratory data analysis functions, these basics still require a considerable amount of dedication and time to acquire the know how to develop attractive and useful visuals to aid in a company's decision making towards profitability for the company. These business intelligence tools require advanced and time-consuming skills to help clear, analyze, and visualize data to improve the user's analytics and visualizations. Google Sheets requires the user to create visuals and graphs, which could be time consuming (Google, 2024). Additionally, Google Sheets has a large library of formulas but lacks some statistical tests and functions that could be helpful for more complex data analysis (Guth, 2024). However, Excel has a new feature called 'Analyze Data' that incorporates the use of internal AI to clear, analyze, and visualize data in seconds and gives the user extra time to interpret and digest the data. Excel is considered a powerful tool for Data Analysis, with a wide range of functions and features.

The following section explains the methodology of Tracy, the accountant who was successfully promoted to Chief Accounting Officer (CAO) by enhancing the vision of the firm's path of growth through the use of AI tools.

METHODOLOGY

Selection of the Profitability Strategy

The first step was to choose the strategy to increase profitability for the company. Several strategies were analyzed and presented in the literature review, but some were not suited to implement in a short-term notice for the design of a project in only one week (Amaresan, 2024).

Even though the Sphere Group (2024) recommended the analysis of the financial statements of the company, Tracy decided that this vision should come after a thorough analysis of the market and the customers first. Another possible alternative for a presentation is an analysis of the productivity of the firm and a proposal to increase it. However, this strategy again should come after the initial analysis of the market, because it encompasses investing in business intelligence tools, technology, and enhance employee efficiency within the business.

Tracy decided to identify specific targets to allow the company to organize its priorities and operate accordingly. For a quick analysis of the firm, according to Pareto Law (Onsight, 2024), she decided to analyze the market data available from the sales and marketing department of the firm.

How can something like the 80/20 Rule help the company increase its profitability? If it could be possible to discover which customers fall into the 20% bracket that makes up 80% of the company sales, there could be a plan to focus on these valuable customers more accurately. If it were possible to identify the characteristics of the 20th percentile of customers and then find other customers who share those characteristics, the company could experience growth.

Therefore, Tracy thought it to be important to identify the key customers of the firm. Then, go look for more customers that are like them. A need to use innovative analysis tools arises, especially when the numbers are large enough.

From the four areas of business proposed by Chui and Yee (2023) to modernize with AI, Tracy found that marketing and sales are the key starting areas from where the company could synchronize the efforts of the all the business departments towards an increase in profitability.

A logical starting point could be to review the list of current/existing customers and analyze: who bought the different brands? And who spent the most money? The objective is to find the customers that fall in the 20% bracket; that is, the right targeted customers that are the key to increasing profitability of a firm.

Next step is to go geographical and determine where the 20% bracket of the customers are located; that is, identify the most prolific customers by identifying where they live. Thus, the first step is to analyze sales and propose a plan to guide future actions of the firm toward a possible increase in profit.

The target of Tracy's analysis for her presentation would be to narrow the focus of the firm to areas that are more likely to bring in the most profit and eliminating potentially unprofitable areas when designing the advertising and marketing campaigns.

Selection of the AI Tool

The adequate use of hard data, even though it could be too large, could help the firm to take decisions through the creation of formulas, statistics, graphs, and visuals to identify trends easier and find opportunities within the industry and business. Tracy needed to analyze this data, thus, according to Bahoo, et al. (2024), AI applications in business could help her achieve her purposes. However, the applications analyzed by Bahoo, et al (2024) fall out of the range for Tracy's purposes who needs to submit a proposal to guide the company towards a profitable future. She envisioned a plan to show how a simple AI data analysis could evolve in a synchronized company where all the departments could create a commitment to ensure the profit of the company.

Tracy's objective is to demonstrate the usefulness of AI Data Analysis features in her proposal but being cautious of what tools are adequate for the present state of the company where AI tools are not part of the applications followed in the company.

Since the data is too large, it is important to find techniques to efficiently analyze it and help with effective decision-making. A good start is to find how AI could help Tracy to design the best plan to offer the firm for future actions.

Of the possible alternatives to envision the future growth of the firm, the design of the presentation will be focused on the analysis and identification of the customers as a crucial step to increase profitability. This can be done with the help of AI.

Choosing an AI Tool for the Daily Operation of CelMex, S.A. de C.V. (CelMex)

Tracy concentrated and envisioned her main objective for the firm. If the firm wanted to continue growing, there should be a way to increase its sales and the number of its cell phone distributors to increase its profitability. Thus, she needed all the data about the firm's actual sales from all its distributors to take a tactical decision: how to change the budget of the firm to increase financial support to those geographic zones with the best potential for growth. Tracy should guide the firm about the best way to do the expansion with the highest probability of success.

Since Tracy only had a brief amount of time to prepare a market profitability proposal, she decided to use the Data Analysis (DA) alternative (Datacamp, 2023).

DA is an accurate tool to help the business make informed decisions based on facts, figures, trends, etc., rather than planning by intuition. Tracy wanted to present a plan with a strong foundation to help the strategic planning and policymaking of the firm. Her main objective was to trigger a synchronized effort within all the departments of the company unifying a global vision of efficient resource allocation looking to invest in areas that would provide benefits for the company. For example, analyzing sales data can help identify which products are performing well and which are not. This information can then be used to adjust marketing strategies, pricing, and inventory management, leading to increased sales and profitability. The synchronization of these efforts must be derived from the presentation of her proposal for the company.

The plan she has in mind for her proposal, should become a trigger to a deeper analysis in many areas through an even more profound analysis: discover complex patterns and trends to guide the company in the short run towards innovation and finding its business competitive edge. She wants to offer a pivotal key for future analysis that unleashes data analysis for the improvement of other activities of the company such as supply chain, cost reductions, improved product design, among others that could improve efficiency.

Tracy was convinced that in a data-driven world a good leader should master its capacity to analyze and interpret data in record time and minimize the time invested in collecting and administrating these data using the available modern disruptive technologies.

The next step was to decide which chatbot to choose as a tool to manage the large amounts of data about the distributors and its sales in all Mexico. She made some simulations to improve her idea of which chatbot to use and which one could give her better results.

Tracy tested chatbots such as Copilot and ChatGPT because they could suggest solutions to the market profitability analysis based on publicly available information. Chui and Yee (2023) state that chatbots, as the latest advance in artificial intelligence is speedily transforming business and work, leaving companies, governments, and individuals scrambling to assess its impact in real time. However, she rejected their use in her proposal because of the need of privacy in the management of sensitive information of the firm. Thus, she continued exploring other AI tools that could maintain the security of sensitive internal data. The privacy and security issue of sensitive market intelligence data could be in danger of being exposed outside the firm.

Loyal to her accounting profession, she chose a profitable and less expensive AI tool for CelMex. She remembered that the firm bought a business license for *Microsoft®Office 365*, thus, decided to use Copilot, a chatbot included in CelMex's business license. Microsoft Copilot is a chatbot developed by Microsoft and launched on February 7, 2023, and according to its web site:

'*Microsoft Copilot for Microsoft 365* combines Large Language Models (LLMs) with the data from the firm, everything in a flow of work to turn your words into one of the most powerful productivity tools on the planet. Copilot works with Microsoft *365's popular applications* like *Word*, *Excel*, *PowerPoint*, *Outlook*, *Teams* and more. *Copilot for Microsoft 365* offers intelligent assistance in real time, letting the users improve their creativity and boost their productivity and skills'.

Tracy began using Copilot by asking questions and using *'prompts'* on the Internet. However, the results were not what she was expecting. She needed to feed Copilot with CelMex´s confidential market data which cannot be obtained directly from internet. Tracy learned that Copilot could also help the users to analyze data in Microsoft Excel spreadsheets with the data formatting, drawing graphics, generating dynamic tables, identifying trends, and summarizing information. This can be done by helping the users with the Excel commands and suggesting formulas to do research from the questions asked to the program.

Thus, Tracy selected a combination of Microsoft Excel Spreadsheets with Copilot commands known in Excel as 'Analyze Data' in order to analyze market data.

That is why Tracy made a breakthrough in a company where the AI was not adopted yet. Tracy decided to make a proposal in record time by using the 'Analyze Data' feature obtained from the conversation (prompt) with the AI tool. That marked a difference from the effect of older artificial intelligence, which largely automated manual tasks without having a conversation with the user.

The next section presents the analysis of this empirical case.

ANALYSIS AND RESULTS

Tracy asked the marketing and sales department to share with her the excel file with the sensitive marketing information of the firm already formatted as a table with the following information: Distributor, Brand, State, Geographical Zone, Sales, Market Destination and Municipality. An extract of this table is shown in Figure 1.

Figure 1. CelMex's marketing information (own elaboration with the results from the empirical research)

Folio	Distributor	Brand	State	Geo ZONE	SALES	Market	Municipality
1	NOVACEL SA DE CV	Apple A	Sinaloa	1	23,800.00	Domestic	Culiacán
2	COMPUCEL SA DE CV	Apple A	Puebla	4	23,800.00	Domestic	Acatzingo
3	CELULARES Y ACCESORIOS SA DE CV	Apple A	Chiapas	5	43,660.00	Both	Tuxtla Gutiérrez
4	CELUALRES Y ACCESORIOS SA DE CV	Apple A	Chiapas	5	28,700.00	Both	La Trinitaria
5	EQUIPOS CELULARES SA DE CV	Apple A	México	4	45,325.00	Domestic	Tlalnepantla de Baz
6	CELULARES ECONOMICOS SA DE CV	Apple A	México	4	27,675.00	Domestic	El Oro
7	SMARTMOVILES SA DE CV	Apple A	Coahuila	2	40,515.00	Domestic	San Pedro
8	CELULARES Y MAS SA DE CV	Apple A	Jalisco	3	15,200.00	Domestic	Tlaquepaque
9	CELULARES Y MAS SA DE CV	Apple A	Jalisco	3	29,900.00	Domestic	Tlaquepaque
10	CELULARES Y MAS SA DE CV	Apple A	Jalisco	3	29,900.00	Domestic	Tlaquepaque

She received a table with the 35 customers (distributors) located in 4,556 branches, the cell phone's brands sold for each branch, including the sales, the location (state and municipality), and the geographical zone of the country where they are located, and the targeted market in each zone (domestic sales, export sales, or both).

The Creative Discovery

After some time invested in looking at Table 1, Tracy decided to do a 'Data Analysis' using Excel. She browsed through *Excel* and discovered that Excel's function of 'Analyze Data' uses Artificial Intelligence (AI) to help the user to understand the figures in a faster and easier way. She found out that she can ask questions about the data presented in the table with simple questions in a simple language, simulating a conversation (prompts), and Excel responds by generating graphics, tables, dynamic tables (*pivot tables*) to help the user better visualize the answers to the questions.

The function of 'Analyze Data' could also suggest the user new questions based on the data that is being analyzed.

The process is as follows:

1. Open the Excel spreadsheet which presents the data to be analyzed as a table (Home Menu)
2. Click on the Data Menu
3. Within the Data Menu, choose the Analyze Data option
4. A window will open on the right-hand side of the screen indicating that the AI is working on analyzing the data from the table
5. In the same window the AI opens a field that invites you to ask a question about your data
6. In that field you write your prompt (simple conversation with the AI). There could be several prompts according to the interest of the user.
7. The AI responds to your prompt by generating visuals that answer your questions such as: clustered bar charts, doughnut bars, tables, among others.
8. If the user does not know what prompts to create, the same AI offers suggested questions and possible visuals that the user may be interested in.

'Analyze Data' made an efficient data analysis to improve CelMex's future decision-making about a possible expansion and market growth in only 60 seconds. The data analyzed was summarized in graphics, tables, percentages, etc., valuable material to prepare a presentation of her proposal to CelMex's CFO, Marcy Garza, in an effective and efficient way.

One week later, Tracy had a meeting with Marcy Garza and handed in her presentation with her proposal. Tracy explained the objective of the firm and its short and long run growth objectives. She also presented a detailed study of the marketing and sales data of the firm, to justify the operative decision-making and the growth process of the firm.

Tracy explained Dr. Marcy Garza, that with the market data captured in an Excel worksheet, it is possible to show data analysis that supports her recommendations for the firm. Following the steps to use 'Analyze Data' in Excel, she presented her first prompt as follows:

- Prompt for Table 1 and Figure 2: Percentage of total sales by each state

Table 1 presents sales percentages by each state of Mexico, as follows, and Figure 2 orders the information by decreasing importance in participation of the market.

Table 1. Sales percentages by each state of Mexico

State	SALES
Jalisco	17.98%
Sinaloa	12.92%
Guanajuato	9.86%
Puebla	7.47%
Michoacán de Ocampo	5.19%
Sonora	4.40%
Veracruz	4.33%
Durango	3.36%
Coahuila	3.23%
Hidalgo	3.09%
Zacatecas	2.86%
Chihuahua	2.86%
México	2.69%
Distrito Federal	2.18%
Oaxaca	2.07%
Querétaro	2.07%
San Luis Potosí	1.94%
Nuevo León	1.63%
Nayarit	1.32%
Campeche	1.32%
Baja California	1.18%
Tamaulipas	0.99%
Aguascalientes	0.97%
Chiapas	0.83%
Colima	0.60%
Tlaxcala	0.58%
Guerrero	0.53%
Quintana Roo	0.45%
Morelos	0.41%
Tabasco	0.28%
Baja California Sur	0.28%
Yucatán	0.12%
Grand Total	**100.00%**

Source: Own elaboration with the use of Analyze Data AI feature within Excel

Figure 2. CelMex's Sales percentages by importance of each state of Mexico (Own elaboration with the use of Analyze Data AI feature within Excel)

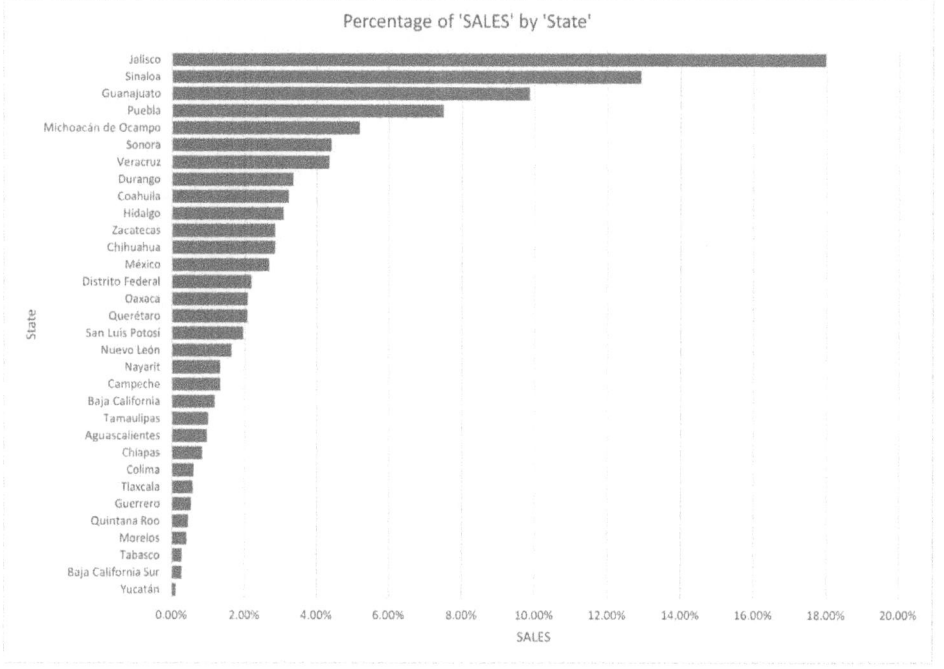

Tracy presented the following analysis according to the sales by each Mexican state shown in Figure 2. The best distributors are in the Mexican states of Jalisco, Sinaloa, Guanajuato, and Puebla. Her suggestion is first to talk with them to see if they can share with the company any additional petitions for their own plans of growth, following the Pareto Law. She also suggested having a meeting with the distributors of the Mexican states with the less market shares, to see if the firm could help them improve their services to increase sales in those areas and identify the reasons for these small market shares.

Tracy presented her second prompt as follows:

- Prompt for Table 2 and Figure 3: Graph the total sales by brand

With respect of the cell-phone brands, the AI helped Tracy identify the brands with the highest sales, as shown in Table 2 and in Figure 3.

Table 2. Cellphone's sales by brand

Brand	SALES
Apple A	130,197,335.40
Droid A	32,423,300.00
Droid B	385.00
Apple B	96.00
Grand Total	**162,621,116.40**

Source: Own elaboration with the use of Analyze Data AI feature within Excel

Figure 3. Cellphone's sales by brand (Own elaboration with the use of Analyze Data AI feature within Excel)

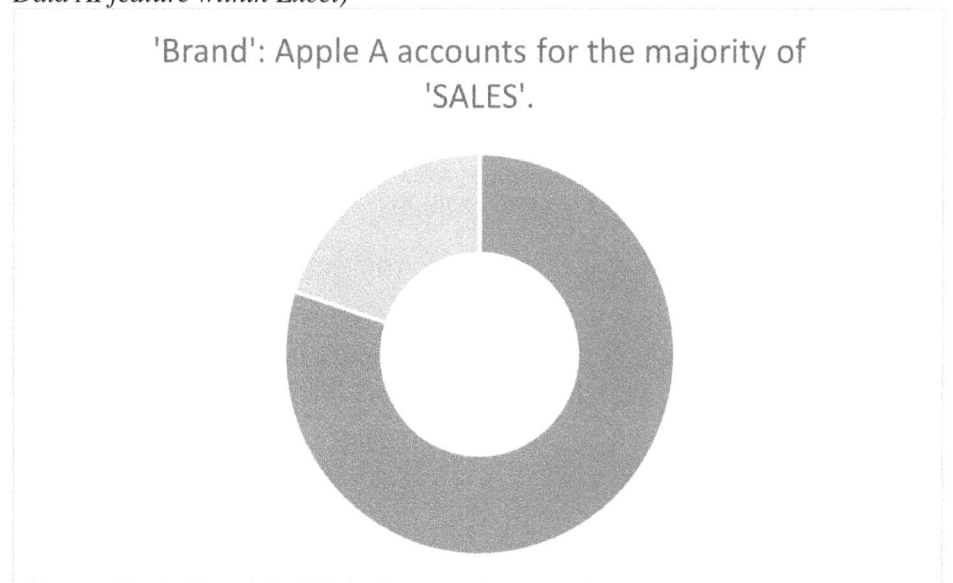

Figure 3 shows the distributors' preference to sell the brand Apple A. Tracy recommended reviewing newer models of this brand, with the vision that it is highly probable that the distributors will keep their preference for brand Apple A for the following years. However, because model Droid A also showed good sales numbers, she also recommended reviewing the new models of this brand as well. Sometimes, the first result offered by Analyze Data AI feature is not the ideal visual for the presentation. So, 'Analyze Data' creates several possible visual results to choose from. This was the case for the previous prompt.

Tracy pointed out another matter that caught her attention. There are distributors that only sell in the domestic market, some of them export, and others do both. Tracy showed the following information obtained with the AI in Table 3 and Figure 4, with the following prompt:
- Prompt for Table 3 and Figure 4: Total Sales by Market

Table 3. Cellphone's sales by destination: Domestic or export

Market Destination	SALES
Domestic	151,048,407.40
Both	7,132,786.00
Export	4,439,923.00
Grand Total	**162,621,116.40**

Source: Own elaboration with the use of Analyze Data AI feature within Excel

Figure 4. Cellphone's sales by destination: Domestic or export (Own elaboration with the use of Analyze Data AI feature within Excel)

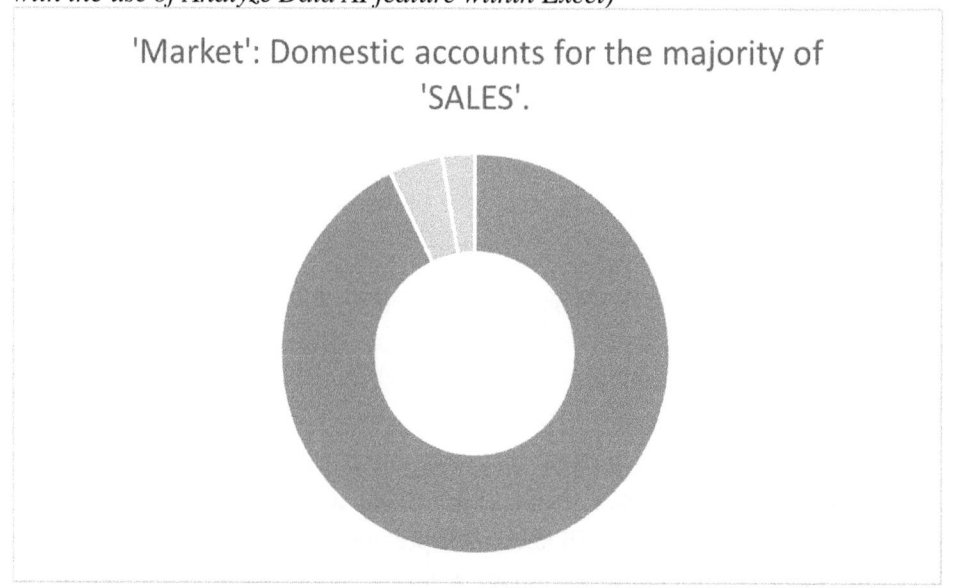

'Market': Domestic accounts for the majority of 'SALES'.

Tracy emphasized that the most important destination of the firm's sales is the domestic market. There could be an opportunity to expand sales to the export market. It would be advisable to talk to those in the export market to learn about their needs and ways of operations to decide about the company's possibilities to expand their markets to increase exports.

Using AI, Tracy also presented the sales of the firm by zones, as shown in Table 4 and Figure 5. The identified five zones are: Zone 1-Northwest, Zone 2-Northeast, Zone 3-Southwest, Zone 4-Center, and Zone 5-South. Tracy used the following prompt:

- Prompt for Table 4 and Figure 5: Sales by Geo Zone

Table 4. Cellphone's sales by zone

ZONE	SALES
3	69,589,953.10
1	30,539,040.00
4	26,710,649.10
2	19,616,058.10
5	16,165,416.10
Grand Total	**162,621,116.40**

Source: Own elaboration with the use of Analyze Data AI feature within Excel

Figure 5. Cellphone's sales by zone (Own elaboration with the use of Analyze Data AI feature within Excel)

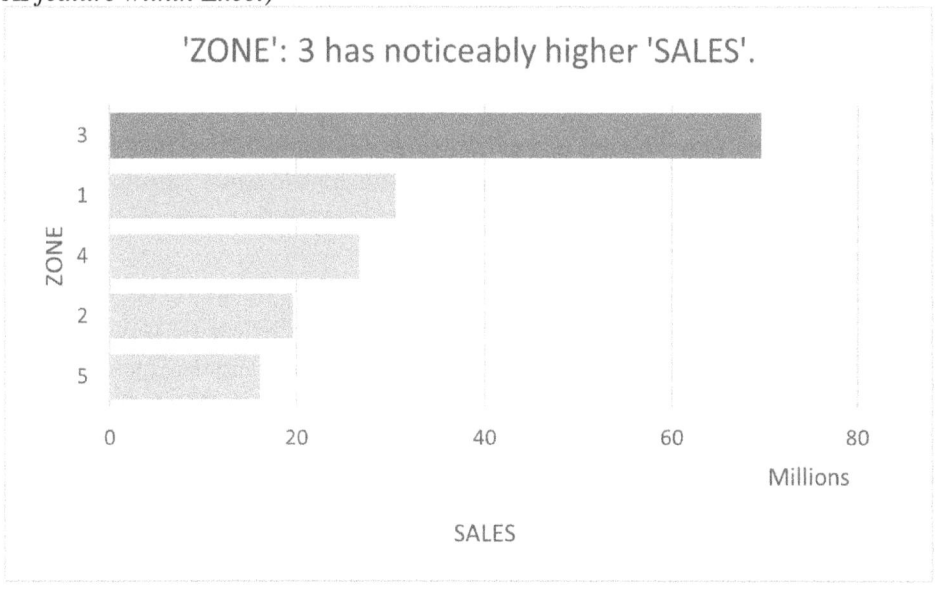

Using AI, Tracy could identify Mexico's zone with the highest sales. She explained that if Zone 3 presents sales more than double than the others, it should be recommended to do market research to investigate how can the company address the unattended zones to add more clients. This research could identify the competitive advantages of Zone 3 to replicate them in the zones with lower sales.

DISCUSSION

CelMex needed to fill the top position of the accounting leadership pyramid, the Chief Accountant Officer (CAO), because the current holder of the CAO position was in the process of retiring. For this task, Marcy Garza, the Chief Financial Officer (CFO) decided to fill the vacant position by selecting a candidate within the accounting department of the company. She proposed a contest, as a challenge, where the candidates must submit a proposal for using Artificial Intelligence to improve business operations and increase company profitability. In doing so, the candidate must show ethical and financial responsibility as the future leader of the accounting department. This individual must have the qualifications to motivate creative insight analysis, inspire excellence, and promote teamwork to reach a successful management of day-to-day operations.

Tracy achieved her analysis in record time using the right AI tools that presented no risk of a data security breach. She pointed out that this is a brief analysis and there is a considerable amount of additional data that can be managed with AI tools and use it to target the future objectives of the firm and provide time-efficient decision making. The operational challenge that she proposes implies the digital and accurate update of all financial statements of the firm and the data analysis, to reflect the profits from the sales of each distributor faster and efficiently. Using AI tools, the firm would be able to make financial decisions in a more precise and fast way. Financial ratios could also be generated for comparative analysis to support operational improvement initiatives by area.

After the analysis of all the proposals presented to Marcy Garza to decide which of the candidates would be the next Chief Accountant Officer (CAO), the final decision day arrived. Marcy called a meeting with all the candidates to make the announcement. Marcy stated that all the candidates have great talents to continue working in the firm. However, Tracy exceeded her expectations and was the one selected to take the position as our new Chief Accountant Officer (CAO).

Marcy Garza explained the reasoning behind her selection. Even as an accountant, she chose information from the marketing and sales department to create proposals that could be synchronized with all the departments of the firm in a holistic vision of the path to follow for the future profitability of the firm. She demonstrated that any firm must be cautious about choosing an AI tool, thinking about the cost and reliability of the tool to be chosen to protect confidentiality. She pointed out the importance and cautious use of AI tools to achieve an increase in the company's profitability, making the company aware of the need to learn how to use and choose them. She suggested the need for training courses for AI tools within all the firm's departments.

Tracy gave a new and fresh vision of the path the firm must take in a timely and efficient way to reach new targets for CelMex's growth, using AI tools with caution with the possibility to permeate it through all the departments of the firm. It is important to discover the use of Artificial Intelligence to improve the business operations of the firm in all the areas, giving a positive vision for the available disruptive technologies and use them with ethics in a legal framework. There are many more AI tools and it is crucial to keep learning to find those tools that help every executive of the firm to process data and leave them with ample time to make wiser and faster decisions with the available data. Thus, this presentation fulfills the goal to be better than yesterday, not better than others.

CONCLUSION

This chapter introduces the reader to the use of Artificial Intelligence (AI) tools supporting every accountant with the data analysis of a firm towards better and faster decision making. This is an empirical case in which Tracy Santos, a member of CelMex's accounting team, in a competition for obtaining the CAO position of the firm, proposed her hypothesis that using the 'Analyze Data' AI feature in Microsoft Excel for data analysis will help her know more about the company's market history and performance faster and in record time without risking the confidentiality of the data. She will have more time to digest the analysis and provide better and informed tactical decision-making to target a newer vision of the company in the short and long term. Indeed, her hypothesis was not rejected because through her presentation she earned the promotion as the new CAO of the firm.

The only limitation of Tracy's success story is that she only had a short period of time (one week) for her analysis, but there are no boundaries for the new applications that AI offers to professional accountants and every executive. Future research could include the results of the analysis of other accounting concepts, such as financial ratios, that could also be generated for comparative analysis to support operational improvement of the firm. As Bahoo, et al. (2024) suggested, AI could have different applications in finance: stock market, trading models, volatility forecasting, portfolio management, performance, risk and default evaluation, cryptocurrencies, derivatives, credit risk in banks, investor sentiment analysis and foreign exchange management, among others. The use of AI transforms the professional accountant's role in the firm from a routine activity of managing data to an active participant of managerial decision-making towards a higher profitability of the firm. Furthermore, the proposal opens the door for the firm's evolution to show how a simple AI data analysis could synchronize all the departments within the company to create a commitment to ensure its profitability.

Tracy stated in her proposal that the success of business analytics using AI tools could empower the company in the future, thus she suggests that employees will need support in learning new skills that help them work together with generative AI and, in some cases, in changing roles.

For the company to manage the transition to adopting AI tools, business leaders can begin by reexamining core business processes, and considering where best to apply Data Analysis and AI tools, and how employees can work with them, as well as determining what new skills and capabilities they may need.

Mastering the use of disruptive technologies such as AI tools helps the professional accountant and every executive to find creative discoveries through a more precise and faster analysis of data in real time, to improve the decision-making process. The knowledge of disruptive technologies as AI tools opens up an infinite number of possibilities.

The constant evolution of AI is leaving the available literature behind in a very short time, with the need to continue with future research to select those AI tools that are changing the face of doing business. One thing is totally clear, that AI is here to stay and as soon as the company understands which AI tools fulfill their interests, the firm will need them to increase productivity and efficiency to keep up the pace with innovation to secure a profitable place in the market.

The professional accountants and executives that will be navigating in an AI digital ecosystem must realize that it is always changing and that the AI tools are also evolving. Thus, this chapter has a wide span of time for its use with the flexibility of different AI tools applications, depending on the analysis approach of the accountant.

There is a long history of AI technologies that have become mature and gone on to contribute to other, newer AI disciplines, like the one presented by Tracy's success story: a chatbot like Copilot combined with Excel in 'Analyze Data'. So perhaps AI tools, pushed along by other newer AI technologies, can still reach their full potential.

It is expected that at the end of the analysis of this chapter, the reader should be capable to identify the impact of the use of AI tools for a more effective, faster, and efficient decision making in the business operation of every firm:

- Identify the AI tools available in the market.

- Choose those AI tools that would be the most useful for the firm depending on its objectives of growth and exercise its use.
- Evaluate ethical and financial implications of the use of AI tools and the seriousness of the practical consequences in the future of a firm.
- Make a cost-benefit analysis of the available AI tools for the firm.
- Take care of the confidentiality of the data. Avoid risks.

The reader will begin to learn how to manage contemporary terms such as Conversational Artificial Intelligence, Chatbots, Copilot, Spreadsheet (Excel), software packages for productivity, and collaboration, AI Business Administration, among others.

Every professional accountant as well as every executive must assess the following questions:

- What are the different AI tools available in the market and which could be applied to the firm?
- What are the threats that could be identified?
- What are the benefits that could be identified?
- What is the best AI tool that could be used for accounting and managerial decisions and analyzing its scope for the future of the firm?

Since Bahoo, et al (2024) encouraged companies that have not adopted AI tools to introduce AI applications by providing training courses and funding to strengthen the complex skills required by employees dealing with these sophisticated systems and languages, Tracy's proposal goes in the same way. In fact, as noted by Surjadi (2024) where universities are changing their academic programs to include courses in AI literacy, Tracy recommends the Human Resources department of the firm to consider AI literacy skills in the new candidates' resumes in the hiring process.

Tracy coincided with Goldman (2024) that the phase of 'Trough of Disillusionment' will be marked by small incremental progress in applications that deliver real benefits to businesses and to users. There is no magic button to see profitable results in AI tools. It is all about leveraging technologies and selecting the right tools to use as Tracy applied for the company: she used the best traits of generative AI through its application within the 'Analyze Data' feature in Excel.

REFERENCES

Akkio. (2024). Google Sheets Data Visualization: Comprehensive Guide. Retrieved from: https://www.akkio.com/post/google-sheets-data-visualization#:~:text= Google%20Sheets%20allows%20users%20to%20create%20bar%20charts%2C%20 histograms%20pie,many%20more%20for%20data%20visualization

Amaresan, S. (2024, May 30). How to Let Customers Know About a Price Increase (Without Losing Them), According to Pros Who've Done It. Retrieved from: https:// blog.hubspot.com/service/price-increase

Aunoa. (2024, March 5). Everything you need to know about Anthropic. Retrieved from: https://aunoa.ai/blog/todo-lo-que-debes-saber-sobre-anthropic/#:~:text= Comprensi%C3%B3n%20contextual%3A%20Anthropic%20puede%20entender,la %20tristeza%20y%20el%20miedo

Bachinskiy, A. (2019, February 21). Follow The Growing Impact of AI in Financial Services: Six Examples. Towards Data Science. Retrieved from: https:// towardsdatascience.com/the-growing-impact-of-ai-in-financial-services-six -examples-da386c0301b2

Bahoo, S., Cucculelli, M., Goga, X., & Mondolo, J. (2024). Artificial intelligence in Finance: A comprehensive review through bibliometric and content analysis. *SN Business & Economics*, 4(2), 23. DOI: 10.1007/s43546-023-00618-x

Berdiyeva, O., Umar Islam, M., & Saeedi, M. (2021). Artificial Intelligence in Accounting and Finance: Meta-Analysis. Nust Business Review, 3(1), 56-79. Retrieved from: https://www.researchgate.net/profile/Oguljan-Berdiyeva/publication/ 353641654_Artificial_Intelligence_in_Accounting_and_Finance_Meta-Analysis/ links/6107fe971e95fe241aa349ba/Artificial-Intelligence-in-Accounting-and- Finance-Meta-Analysis.pdf

Calm. (2024). How to overcome fear of change: 8 ways to navigate the unknown. Retrieved from: https://www.calm.com/blog/fear-of-change#:~:text=An%20intense %20fear%20of%20change,becoming%20a%20more%20debilitating%20fear

Capital, C. (2023, November 20). *DIY Financial Planning: How to Get Started* [Video]. YouTube. Retrieved from: https://www.youtube.com/watch?v=JObYz6u-_JU

Carter, D. (2020). Regulation and ethics in artificial intelligence and machine learning technologies: Where are we now? Who is responsible? Can the information professional play a role? *Business Information Review*, 37(2), 60–68. DOI: 10.1177/0266382120923962

Caruso, J. (2024, April 29). Drink the Kool-Aid all you want, but don't call AI an existential threat. *Bulletin of the Atomic Scientists*. Retrieved from: https://thebulletin.org/2024/04/drink-the-kool-aid-all-you-want-but-dont-call-ai-an-existential-threat/?utm_source=Newsletter&utm_medium=Email&utm_campaign=MondayNewsletter04292024&utm_content=DisruptiveTechnologies_AIExistentialThreat_04292024

Chui, M., & Yee, L. (2023, July 7). AI could increase corporate profits by $4.4 trillion a year, according to new research, *McKinsey Global Institute*. Retrieved from: https://www.mckinsey.com/mgi/overview/in-the-news/ai-could-increase-corporate-profits-by-4-trillion-a-year-according-to-new-research

Connect, F. (2024a). Artificial intelligence has arrived in financial services. Retrieved from: https://blog.finerioconnect.com/la-inteligencia-artificial-ha-llegado-a-los-servicios-financieros/

Connect, F. (2024b). Leading Open Finance Solutions for Latin America. Retrieved from: https://finerioconnect.com/

Cook, B. (2024). Navigating AI's Impact on Accounting: Uses, Trends and Tools, *Tipalti Accounting Hub*. Retrieved from: https://tipalti.com/accounting-hub/ai-accounting/

Datacamp. (2023, July). What is Data Analysis? An Expert Guide With Examples. Retrieved from: https://www.datacamp.com/blog/what-is-data-analysis-expert-guide

Datrics. (2024). AI Credit Scoring: The Future of Credit Risk Assessment. Retrieved from:_https://www.datrics.ai/articles/the-essentials-of-ai-based-credit-scoring#:~:text=A%20credit%20AI%20score%20is,likelihood%20of%20repaying%20a%20loan

Davenport, T. H., & Ronanki, R. (2018). Artificial intelligence for the real world. *Harvard Business Review*, 96(1), 108–116. https://hbr.org/2018/01/artificial-intelligence-for-the-real-world

Drollette, D., Jr. (2023, November 8). Charging ahead: Steven Chu, Nobel Prize-winner and former Energy Secretary, on today's battery research—and more. *Bulletin of the Atomic Scientists*. Retrieved from: https://thebulletin.org/premium/2023-11/charging-ahead-steven-chu-nobel-prize-winner-and-former-energy-secretary-on-todays-battery-research-and-more/#post-heading

Drollette, D., Jr. (2024, January 15). Interview with Sneha Revanur, "the Greta Thunberg of AI". *Bulletin of the Atomic Scientists*. Retrieved from: https://thebulletin.org/premium/2024-01/interview-with-sneha-revanur-the-greta-thunberg-of-ai/#post-heading

Enholm, I. M., Papagiannidis, E., Mikalef, P., & Krogstie, J. (2022). Artificial Intelligence and Business Value: A Literature Review. *Information Systems Frontiers*, 24(5), 1709–1734. DOI: 10.1007/s10796-021-10186-w

Fitz-Gibbon, C. (1990). *Performance indicators, BERA Dialogues (2)*. Taylor & Francis.

Gartner Research. (2018, August 20). Understanding Gartner's Hype Cycles. Retrieved from: https://www.gartner.com/en/documents/3887767

Gartner Research. (2024, July 31). Hype Cycle for Generative AI, 2024. Retrieved from https://www.gartner.com/en/documents/5636791

Gateway, B. (2024). Increase your profitability. Retrieved from: https://www.bgateway.com/resources/increase-your-profitability

Goldman, S. (2024, August 6). Generative AI is getting kicked off its pedestal — it will be painful but it's not a bad thing. *Fortune*. Retrieved from: https://fortune.com/2024/08/06/generative-ai-reality-check-tech-selloff-new-phase-less-hype-more-roi/

Google. (2024). Use Analytics with your site. Retrieved from: https://support.google.com/sites/answer/97459?hl=en

Google Workspace Learning Center. (2024). Switch from Excel to Sheets: What you'll learn. Retrieved from: https://support.google.com/a/users/answer/13189180?hl=en&visit_id=638585167896129518-2721732101&ref_topic=9296611&rd=1

Guth, C. (2024, April 17). Google Sheets VS. Excel: Complete Overview. Retrieved from: https://sada.com/blog/google-sheets-vs-excel/

Hartley, B. R., & Dammeyer, L. (2024, July 30). The Best Robo-Advisors Of April 2024. *Forbes*. Retrieved from: https://www.forbes.com/advisor/investing/best-robo-advisors/

Hayes, A., & Smith, A. (2023, September 1). Are Robo-Advisors Worth It? *Investopedia*. Retrieved from: https://www.investopedia.com/are-robo-advisors-worth-it-7568057#:~:text=Key%20Takeaways,investors%20seeking%20competent%20portfolio%20management

Hoffmann, C. H., & Hahn, B. (2020). Decentered ethics in the machine era and guidance for AI regulation. *AI & Society*, 35(3), 635–644. DOI: 10.1007/s00146-019-00920-z

IBN Technologies Limited. (2024, January 2). Advantages of AI Accounting: Unlocking Efficiency and Accuracy. Retrieved from: https://www.ibntech.com/blog/ai-accounting-benefits-and-challenges/

Indeed Editorial Team. (2023, March 10). 17 Strategies for Increasing the Profitability of a Business. Retrieved from: https://www.indeed.com/career-advice/career-development/increase-profitability

Justice, E. (2024a). Encode Justice is mobilizing communities for AI aligned with human values. Retrieved from: https://encodejustice.org/what-we-do/

Justice, E. (2024b). We're reimagining our generation's collective AI future. Retrieved from: https://encodejustice.org/#:~:text=Encode%20Justice%20is%20the%20world%27s,movement%20for%20safe%2C%20equitable%20AI

L.M. & Alur. (2023). Mapping the Research Landscape of Chatbots, Conversational Agents, and Virtual Assistants in Business, Management, and Accounting: A Bibliometric Review. *Qubahan Academic Journal*, 3(4), 502–513. Retrieved from: https://journal.qubahan.com/index.php/qaj/article/view/252

Mok, A. (2023, September 14). EY has created its own large-language model — and says it will train all 400,000 employees to use it as part of a $1.4 billion investment. *Business Insider*. Retrieved from: https://www.businessinsider.com/ey-ernst-young-consulting-invests-ai-strategy-training-model-tools-2023-9?r=MX&IR=T#:~:text=EY%20has%20created%20its%20own,of%20a%20%241.4%20billion%20investment&text=Ernst%20%26%20Young%20has%20invested%20%241.4,its%20own%20large%20language%20model

Onsight. (2024). What the heck is the Pareto Principle and how does it apply to sales? *Blog - Sales techniques and processes*. Retrieved from: https://www.onsightapp.com/blog/pareto-principle-how-it-applies-to-sales

Sadok, H., Sakka, F., & El Maknouzi, M. E. H. (2022). Artificial intelligence and bank credit analysis: A review. *Cogent Economics & Finance*, 10(1), 2023262. Advance online publication. DOI: 10.1080/23322039.2021.2023262

SallyPort. (2021, November 10). 10 Strategies to Increase Profitability in Small Business. Retrieved from: https://sallyportcf.com/10-strategies-to-increase-profitability-in-small-business/

Scholar, G. (2024). Retrieved from: https://scholar.google.com.mx/scholar?q= innovative+uses+and+applications+of+AI+in+accounting+and+financial+ processes&hl=en&as_sdt=0&as_vis=1&oi=scholart

Schreckinger, B. (2023, May 1). Meet the Greta Thunberg of AI. *POLITICO Global Playbook*. Retrieved from: https://www.politico.com/newsletters/digital-future-daily/ 2023/05/01/meet-the-greta-thunberg-of-ai-00094709

Shanmugam, G., Rajendran, D., Thanarajan, T., Murugaraj, S. S., & Rajendran, S. (2023). Artificial intelligence as a catalyst in digital marketing: Enhancing profitability and market potential. *Ingénierie des Systèmes d'Information*, 28(6), 1627–1636. DOI: 10.18280/isi.280620

Simplilearn. (2024a, July 31). What Is Data Analysis: A Comprehensive Guide. Retrieved from: https://www.simplilearn.com/data-analysis-methods-process-types -article

Simplilearn. (2024b, July 24). Top 24 Data Analysis Tools for 2024. Retrieved from: https://www.simplilearn.com/top-data-analysis-tools-article

Surjadi, M. (2024, August 5). Colleges Race to Ready Students for the AI Workplace. *The Wall Street Journal*. Retrieved from: https://www.wsj.com/us-news/education/ colleges-race-to-ready-students-for-the-ai-workplace-cc936e5b

Technologies, D. (2024, April 23). Human-AI Collaboration: The Key to Workplace Efficiency and Innovation. Retrieved from: https://www.businessinsider.com/events/ human-ai-collaboration?r=MX&IR=T

The Sphere Group. (2024). 6 strategies for increasing the profitability of a business. Retrieved from: https://thespheregroup.com.au/6-strategies-for-increasing-the -profitability-of-a-business/

Universidad de la Costa. (2024). How will Public Accounting be transformed with the arrival of artificial intelligence? Retrieved from: https://virtual.cuc.edu.co/ blog/inteligencia-artificial-contaduria-publica#:~:text=Contabilidad%20invisible &text=La%20IA%20puede%20realizar%20tareas,el%20riesgo%20de%20errores %20humanos

ADDITIONAL READING

Dieck-Assad, F. A. (2022). Disruptive Unicorn of Digital Innovations: A Challenge for University Professors. In Rivera-Trigueros, I., López-Alcarria, A., Ruiz-Padillo, D., Olvera-Lobo, M., & Gutiérrez-Pérez, J. (Eds.), *Handbook of Research on Using Disruptive Methodologies and Game-Based Learning to Foster Transversal Skills* (pp. 25–44). IGI Global. DOI: 10.4018/978-1-7998-8645-7.ch002

Infomineo. (2024). How CEOs Leverage Artificial Intelligence for Smarter Decision Making. Retrieved from: https://infomineo.com/blog/how-ceos-leverage-ai-for-smarter-decision-making/

Kitsios, F., & Kamariotou, M. (2021). Artificial Intelligence and Business Strategy towards Digital Transformation: A Research Agenda. *Sustainability (Basel)*, 13(4), 2025. DOI: 10.3390/su13042025

Kubatko, O., Ozims, S., & Voronenko, V. (2024). Influence of Artificial Intelligence on Business Decision-Making. Mechanism of Economic Regulation, 1(103), 17-23. DOI: 10.32782/mer.2024.103.03

Păvăloaia, V.-D., & Necula, S.-C. (2023). Artificial Intelligence as a Disruptive Technology—A Systematic Literature Review, Department of Accounting, Business Information Systems and Statistics, Faculty of Economics and Business Administration, Alexandru Ioan Cuza University of Iasi, 700506 Ia i, Romania. *Electronics (Basel)*, 12(5), 1102. DOI: 10.3390/electronics12051102

Prasanth, A., Vadakkan, D., Surendran, P., & Thomas, B. (2023). Role of Artificial Intelligence and Business Decision Making. *International Journal of Advanced Computer Science and Applications*, 14(6), 965–969. DOI: 10.14569/IJACSA.2023.01406103

Repsol. (2024). Disruptive Technologies: what they are, benefits and examples. Breakthroughs that change our lives, retrieved from: https://www.repsol.com/en/energy-and-the-future/technology-and-innovation/disruptive-technologies/index.cshtml

Zighan, S. (2022). Disruptive Technology from an Organizational Management Perspective. *2022 International Conference on Business Analytics for Technology and Security (ICBATS)*, Business Administration, University of Petra, Amman, Jordan. DOI: 10.1109/ICBATS54253.2022.9759055

KEY TERMS AND DEFINITIONS

AI (Artificial Intelligence): A type of digital disruptive innovation that tries to mimic the human mind and actions in machines. The objective is that a machine can learn and solve problems faster than a human being, allowing humans to have ample time for decision-making.

AI Chatbots: A form of artificial intelligence (AI), computer programs designed to help professionals get through those routine accounting tasks quickly so they can focus their attention on high-level, strategic, and engaging activities that require human capabilities that cannot be replicated by machines.

AI Ecosystem: A set of contemporary innovations that enhance traditional approaches for data analysis for an improved decision making in the accounting discipline.

AI Literacy: AI literacy is a range of skills that empower individuals to critically assess AI, communicate and collaborate efficiently with AI, and utilize AI as a tool in various settings such as online, at home, in school, and in the workplace. It is akin to skills used in the 1970s, such as typing or writing in shorthand, serving as a universal necessity for students entering any career field.

AI Prompts: AI prompting refers to the process of interacting with an artificial intelligence (AI) system by providing specific instructions or queries to achieve a desired outcome. The process begins with instructions given to AI to let it offer a specific result. An AI prompt could be keywords, or statements that require an answer from AI. The process is to get a useful response from the material provided to the AI.

AI Robo-Advisors: Digital platforms that provide automated, algorithm-driven financial planning and investment services with little to no human supervision. Their objective is to guide your investment, create portfolio management and goal planning for you, that is why other names for them are: "automated investment advisor", "automated investment management", and "digital advice platforms".

AI Virtual Assistant: An example of conversational AI. They follow automated rules and use capabilities called natural language processing (NLP), and machine learning. The most typical tasks they perform are scheduling appointments, making phone calls, making travel arrangements, and managing email accounts. But they can also offer graphic design, bookkeeping, and marketing services, among others.

Analyze Data in Excel: A command in Microsoft Excel that lets you understand your data through natural language by allowing you to ask questions about your data without having to write complicated formulas. In addition, Analyze Data provides high-level visual summaries, trends, and patterns.

Chief Accounting Officer (CAO): The top position of the accounting leadership pyramid. This person holds an ethical and financial responsibility to look out for an orderly process of organizational bookkeeping, budget and regulatory reporting, monitoring and analyzing finances relative to the budget or other metrics, among others. As the leader of the accounting department, this individual must have the qualifications to motivate creative insight analysis, inspire excellence, and promote teamwork to reach a successful management of day-to-day operations.

Conversational AI: Technologies that can have a conversation with humans such as virtual assistants, chatbots, robo-advisors, among others. They can process human language and use the conversation to solve questions and guide users to fulfill their objectives.

Data Analysis: A process to analyze the historical data of a firm to understand the behavior of the company through time. It is a process of digesting (inspect, cleanse, transform, etc.) data with the objective of discovering effective and creative ways of presenting the information to support tactical decision-making. A professional accountant can use this process to draw conclusions about specific data that could guide the company to a successful path of growth.

Disruptive Technology: A technology that changes the traditional way of doing things.

Financial Welfare: The status of a company that reflects economic stability and high profitability that triggers the company towards a growth path and market expansion. Achieving financial welfare involves ensuring creative and sustainable strategic decision-making enhanced by a responsible analysis of data. Financial welfare could be seen as a synonym for financial health.

Microsoft Excel: A program offered by Microsoft Office 365. It is a tool to store, sort, and manipulate data. It is often used in data analytics and finance to manage large amounts of information to better visualize them. It can be used for calculating averages and percentages, among others.

Professional Accountant: A professional who monitors the recording, analysis, and reporting of financial information. It is expected that this individual could provide analytical reports for strategic planning and decision making. Thus, this person should be part of the design of the corporate strategy, providing advice and help to guide the vision of the firm towards an effective path of growth. The professional accountant should assist management in setting its goals.

Chapter 3
Exploring the Potential Influences of Blockchain Technology in Financial Reporting

Pedro Pinheiro
https://orcid.org/0000-0003-3210-3963
ISCAL, Instituto Politécnico de Lisboa, Portugal & COMEGI, Portugal

Andreia Gomes
https://orcid.org/0009-0000-4977-5657
ISCAL, Instituto Politécnico de Lisboa, Portugal

Ana Isabel Dias
https://orcid.org/0000-0002-6503-4792
ISCAL, Instituto Politécnico de Lisboa, Portugal & CICF, IPCA, Barcelos, Portugal

ABSTRACT

This study aims to assess the influences that blockchain technology may have on financial reporting as the first presents unique characteristics that may contribute to transparency, immutability, security, and real-time availability of the latter. Hence, 11 interviews were conducted with professionals related to professors' professionals of accounting, and specialists in blockchain technology, to collect their perceptions on the subject. It was possible to conclude that blockchain technology may influence financial reporting mainly by enhancing its reliability, a qualitative characteristic referred to in the conceptual framework for financial reporting. In turn, reliability, associated with neutrality, ensures authenticity, transparency, and confidence in

DOI: 10.4018/979-8-3693-5923-5.ch003

the information derived from a blockchain system. This study contributes to the literature with new empirical evidence, so that the pros and cons of the adoption of this technology may change the paradigm of obtaining how financial information is analyzed in more detail.

1. INTRODUCTION

Blockchain technology and cryptocurrencies are concepts that usually appear together (McComb II & Smalt, 2018; Pugna & Duțescu, 2020), however, the concepts should not be confused, as blockchain was first invented for bitcoin (Institute of Chartered Accountants in England and Wales [ICAEW], 2018). A point in history that seems to be a significant mark for cryptocurrencies is the 2008 white paper of Satoshi Nakamoto (Hamilton, 2019; Reiff, 2022; Setiawan et al, 2021; Yu, Lin & Tang, 2018), when Nakamoto (2008) presented bitcoin and blockchain technology, and its popularity is undeniable. As the issues surrounding cryptocurrencies considered more problematic were decentralization and double-spending (Bonsón & Bednárová, 2018; Chohan, 2022; Nakamoto, 2008; Sheela et al., 2023), Nakamoto (2008) proposed a solution using blockchain technology, a peer-to-peer distributed timestamp server to generate computational proof of the chronological order of transactions. Later, in 2015, a bitcoin-independent blockchain network was launched by Vitalik Buterin, Ethereum, one of the biggest applications of blockchain technology (Mihus, 2022; Klinger & Szczeoanski, 2017). Through the novelty of smart contracts, it has been developed as the second largest open blockchain, whose application area has gone far beyond cryptocurrency transfer (Hamilton, 2019; Klinger & Szczeoanski, 2017).

Hence, although the appearance of blockchain technology is closely related to cryptocurrencies, nowadays, is feasible to be used for other purposes (Financial Executives Research Foundation Inc. [FERF], 2018); Mihus, 2022; Klinger & Szczeoanski, 2017). Financial executives expect blockchain will be used in other scenarios involving payments, like capital markets and contracts (FERF, 2018).

Its role in financial reporting implies that what makes blockchain unique is the innovation in organizing, recording, and validating the maintenance of financial information (Pimentel & Boulianne, 2020). Sheela et al. (2023) argue that blockchain technology can transform accounting and auditing practices by offering transparency, immutability, security, and decentralization, enhanced by triple-entry accounting. Through smart contracts, accounting information is recorded instantly and becomes available to all users (Bonsón & Bednárová, 2018; Hamilton, 2019). As such, it can be said that blockchain technology is a high-tech ledger (ALSaqa et al., 2019; Cardoso & Pinto, 2018; ICAEW, 2018; Pimentel & Boulianne, 2020; Yu et al., 2019). Also, for financial reporting and audit purposes, the main advantages of blockchain technology mentioned in the literature are having accounting information in real-time (Hamilton, 2019; ICAEW, 2018) and diminishing, or even eliminating, fraud (Garanina et al., 2021; Zheng, 2021; Pugna & Duțescu, 2020; and Tiron-Tudor et al., 2021), reducing the risk of malfeasance (Sheela et al., 2023). The process for inserting the data is faster and always up-to-date as blockchain technology can automate repetitive accounting tasks (Sheela et al., 2023). This will help enhance the accounting profession as with more time available, accountants can dedicate themselves to higher value-added tasks such as planning and evaluations, integrated analyses, and complex interpretations of results (Andersen, 2016; Garanina, Ranta & Dumay, 2021; Pugna & Duțescu, 2020). According to FERF (2018), currently, the model that is used is based on reporting past numbers annually, semi-annually, quarterly, or even, monthly, and the use of blockchain technology allows a ledger maintained daily (FERF, 2018) and decision-making, by company administrations and managers, much easier and more accurate (Borhani et al., 2021) because they do not have to wait for regular intervals stipulated for the delivery of accounting information to the respective states. ALSaqa, Hussein & Mahmood (2019) point out that timely disclosed financial reports are relevant to various stakeholders because they are expected to provide the most significant source of data on the financial health of companies and their prospects. ALSaqa, Hussein, and Mahmood (2019), Garanina, Ranta and Dumay (2021), ICAEW (2018), and Pugna and Duțescu (2020) reinforce that having real-time information allows audits to be conducted in multiple locations and organizations simultaneously.

Notwithstanding the possible advantages that using blockchain technology can bring to the professions surrounding corporate financial reporting, Zheng (2021) points out that trust in the information that technology brings is essential, to rely on the authenticity of the accounting records entered into the system. Yu, Lin, and Tang (2019) argue that the threat brought by the application is that firms could cheat on raw data, but once the technology is mature enough, it probably will bring fundamental changes to financial accounting and auditing. Sheela et al. (2023) state that the literature review that was made indicates limitations regarding the adoption of blockchain in accounting and auditing, such as regulatory issues, privacy concerns, scalability, interoperability, and technical complexities, only surpassed by joint efforts from regulators, legislators, industry leaders, and academics. Hence, the challenges to be overcome in fully implementing blockchain in accounting and auditing cannot be ignored (Tiron-Tudor, Deliu, Farcane & Dontu, 2021).

Due to these opportunities and challenges for the professionals, this study pretends to answer the following research question: 'What is the opinion of professionals regarding the impact of blockchain technology on the quality of financial information?

The interview technique was used to obtain the data to provide additional evidence on the opinion of professionals with experience in blockchain technology, and accounting professionals that have proximity to blockchain. An interview survey technique was used on 11 individuals, in October 2022, with specialists in blockchain technology, professionals of accounting, and accounting professors.

The main contribution of this study is to provide additional evidence on the pros and cons regarding the use of this technology, from the point of view of professionals for accounting-related professions.

This chapter is structured as follows: section 2 presents the literature review, section 3 the methodology, section 4 the results of the empirical study and the subsequent discussion, and section 5 the concluding remarks.

2. LITERATURE REVIEW

2.1. A Brief Historical Description of Blockchain Technology

Money hasn't always existed as it does today; it has evolved, taking on various forms over time (Bordo & Siklos, 2017; Brunnermeier et al., 2019; Liu et al., 2015; Santos, 2014; Vieira, 2017). Bank accounts have emerged with the main objective of providing a secure reserve of value, where central banks take on greater significance (Bordo, 2017). The more recent history of forms of payments shows a significant change toward more innovative and electronic means of payment (Sokołowska, 2015). In the literature, Antunes (2019), Liu, Kauffman, and Ma (2015) or Quinn and Roberds (2008), refer to the fast development of methods of payments, such as using plastic cards and Automated Teller Machines (ATMs), online banking, or bank applications, where all banking transactions begin to be possible via the internet. Nakamoto (2008) stated that Internet commerce relies almost exclusively on financial institutions, that serve as trusted third parties to process electronic payments. Haber and Stornetta (1991) discussed a technological solution for the problem of time-stamping to track the origin of digital assets and any attempt to modify them, with procedures that aimed to maintain the privacy of the documents and, therefore, no record-keeping by a third party was required.

The exponential growth of digitalization revolutionized cash and payment systems, which led to the appearance of new currencies, as the central lynchpins of large platforms, (Brunnermeier, James & Landau, 2019). These online currencies can be used for almost anything like any other currency (Setiawan et al., 2021). However, a digital currency, like cryptocurrency, is a means of payment, a financial asset, and a medium of exchange, that exists only in digital format and never in physical form, based on mathematics and cryptography (Antunes, 2019; Chohan, 2022; Nakamoto, 2008). A cryptocurrency is global, unlike any fiat money, and it does not require a bank to be transacted, as a decentralized protocol is used (Chohan, 2022; Yu, Lin & Tang, 2018), distinguished from traditional payment methods, which are centralized (Setiawan et al., 2021). Although the concept seems relatively recent, Reiff (2022) refers to eCash, developed in 1990 by DigiCash and the cryptographer David Chaum, as the first cryptocurrency; nevertheless, the author also recognizes that it took several years for the popular concept that it is today.

The 2008 paper of Satoshi Nakamoto presented "Bitcoin: A Peer-to-Peer Electronic Cash System" and introduced blockchain technology relating it to that cryptocurrency. Nakamoto (2008) stated that:

A purely peer-to-peer version of electronic cash would allow online payments to be sent directly from one party to another without going through a financial institution. Digital signatures provide part of the solution, but the main benefits are lost if a trusted third party is still required to prevent double-spending. We propose a solution to the double-spending problem using a peer-to-peer network.

Bitcoin, the most known and popular cryptocurrency (Setiawan, 2022), is sustained by blockchain technology, and although the concepts should not be mixed - bitcoin is the cryptocurrency and blockchain is the technology, the bitcoin does not exist without the blockchain (McComb II & Smalt, 2018) and was created as a method of proving the viability of the concept of blockchain (FERF, 2018).

Nakamoto (2008) stated that to make payments over a communications channel without a trusted party, like the role of banks, what is needed is a system for electronic payments based on cryptographic proof, using a peer-to-peer distributed timestamp server to generate computational proof of the chronological order of transactions. The author explained that the chain of digital signatures is the digital coin and that the payee can verify the signatures of who paid but cannot verify if this owner double-spend the coin. For this issue, Nakamoto (2008) stated:

The solution we propose begins with a timestamp server. A timestamp server works by taking a hash of a block of items to be timestamped and widely publishing the hash, such as in a newspaper (...)

(...) using proof-of-work to record a public history of transactions that quickly becomes computationally impractical for an attacker to change if honest nodes control a majority of CPU power. The network is robust in its unstructured simplicity (...)

With this proposal, the payee has proof that at the time of each transaction, the majority of nodes agreed it was the first received (Nakamoto, 2008).

Indeed, the name "blockchain" is descriptive of how the technology works (ICAEW, 2018): *transactions are gathered together into a block and added to a chain of all previous transactions, by a cryptographic process that is complex to perform, but which makes it easy to confirm that the history of all transactions is genuine.*

A development in blockchain technology, also worth mentioning, was achieved by Vitalik Buterin in 2015, with the launch of the Ethereum Frontier network (Mihus, 2022). The development of blockchain technology, smart contracts, take recourse to functionalities that perform virtually any calculations or store data, which remained unchanged after joining blockchain and continued to operate as originally programmed (Klinger & Szczeoanski, 2017).

Hence, blockchain is not just used to support Bitcoin as the cryptocurrency could disappear tomorrow, and it would not influence the future of blockchain technology (FERF, 2018; Pedreño et al., 2021). Zhao (2019) states that Blockchain offers a distributed and secure system for data storage and value transactions, which makes it possible to apply in multiple fields. Several entities are developing other uses of blockchain technology to create business opportunities or solve problems (McComb II & Smalt, 2018). Baba et al., (2021) and Mihus (2022) identify several companies in industries such as healthcare, auto industry, mining and oil, and pharmaceuticals, among others, that have used blockchain for business purposes.

2.2. Financial Information, the Qualitative Characteristics of Financial Reporting, and Accounting Quality

Information is based on data analysis, on what is communicated and understood, and what reduces uncertainty at the time of decision-making (Gouveia & Ranito, 2004). Information is increasingly important for decision-making, whatever the problem to be solved, and in companies where decisions are made daily, information has a particular and increased importance, and a bad decision can jeopardize the future (Almeida, 2018). Drucker (2001)[1], cited by Zucchi et al. (2008), states that the real function of the entity's administration is to transform information into knowledge and, subsequently, act by applying this same knowledge, reinforcing that the development of entities depends on the objectives set by their leaders. For Koehler and Bastos (2017), information is considered raw material for the creation of knowledge, which, in turn, adds value to organizations, provides them with innovation, and gives them prominence.

Financial information is the set of accounting information that is related to the activities of an entity, in whole or in part, and is the outcome of the transformation, through defined techniques and procedures, of operational and financial data on the entity's activities and processes into accounting facts (Alves, 2002). As stated by the IFRS Foundation (2018) Conceptual Framework for Financial Reporting, the general purpose of financial reporting is to provide financial information about the reporting entity that is useful to existing and potential investors, lenders, and other creditors in making decisions relating to providing resources to the entity, which makes it an essential tool in decision making and communication with the entity's stakeholders (Alves, 2002).

Although the conceptual framework does not present itself as a standard (IFRS, 2018), to do so, it identifies qualitative characteristics of useful financial information, applied to financial information provided in financial statements, as well as to financial information provided in other ways. Relevance and faithful representation are presented as fundamental qualitative characteristics and comparability, verifiability, timeliness, and understandability as enhancing qualitative characteristics.

Rodrigues and Albuquerque (2015) state that the main objective underlying the need for financial reporting standards is to increase reliability; that information that is relevant and reliable maintains its usefulness even if it is not readily comparable; and that comparable information is not useful if not relevant and may lead to error if it is not reliably represented. Notwithstanding, the authors conclude that despite the efforts made by the main international standardizing bodies, the disclosure of qualitative characteristics is intrinsically associated with the exercise of professional judgment and, therefore, may be influenced by cultural aspects, which may be in line with Fechner and Kilgore (1994) that suggested a conceptual framework based on culture.

The basis for the development of the characteristics of financial reporting begins with the joint project of the International Accounting Standards Board (IASB) and the US national standard-setter, the Financial Accounting Standards Board (FASB), to revise their conceptual frameworks started in 2004. Before, it existed the 1989 Framework for the Preparation and Presentation of Financial Statements, emitted by the IASB predecessor, the International Accounting Standards Committee (IASC). The 1989 Framework indicated four qualitative characteristics: relevance that was affected by its nature and materiality, reliability that included faithful representation, substance over form, neutrality, prudence and completeness, comparability, and comprehensiveness.

The European Commission assessed in 2003 that endorsing the Conceptual Framework was unnecessary because the IAS 1 Presentation of Financial Statements already stated the purpose of the financial statements. However, some jurisdictions adopted the 1989 Framework, mainly when national regulators transposed for the domestic legal order the Directive (EC) 2003/51 of the European Parliament and the Council, of 18 June, on the modernization of accounting directives. This was the case in Portugal.

Nobes and Stadler (2014), based on a sample of 514 large firms from 10 jurisdictions from 2005 to 2011, and thus, regarding the qualitative characteristics of the 1989 Framework, identified reasons for accounting policy changes mainly based on the relevance, faithful representation, comparability, and understandability, which indicates that decision makers such as managers are alert to its application.

However, the quality of financial reporting is not limited to the application of qualitative characteristics. Soderstrom and Sun (2007) state that accounting quality is a function of the firm's overall institutional setting, as capital structure, ownership, and tax system are incentives, including the legal and political system of the country in which the entity resides. Hence, the professionals' culture, institutional incentives, and legal systems may be influential factors in assessing the quality of financial reporting (Rodrigues & Albuquerque, 2015; Nobes & Stadler, 2014; Soderstrom & Sun, 2007), which may include the adoption of technologies and pre-disposition or acquired competences to use it in benefit of the organization.

2.3. The Potential Influence of Blockchain Technology on the Characteristics of Financial Reporting

At present time, accounting is mostly based on a double-entry system (Singh, 2022; Yu, Lin & Tang, 2018). The current system requires that information is manually input into the system or semi-manual with a combination of time scanning, which may result in leakages (Noor et al., 2019). In the preparation of financial reporting, blockchain technology may represent a radical change in how information is created, organized, updated, and validated (Cardoso & Pinto, 2018; ICAEW, 2018; Pimentel & Boulianne, 2020; Pugna & Duțescu, 2020) as it may function as a high-tech electronic ledger (ALSaqa, Hussein & Mahmood, 2019; Yu, Lin & Tang, 2019). ICAEW (2018) explains what may be the key terms that make blockchain different from the more familiar ledgers: 1) propagation, as all participants have access to a full copy, and no one has control; 2) permanence, as past transactions cannot be edited without the consent of the majority and each participant can inspect and verify, making records permanent; and 3) programmability, the "smart contracts" that creating automatic journal entries that execute automatically when triggered. Yu, Lin, and Tang (2018) state that the decentralized way of blockchain does not require any authority intermediaries, and guarantees the information to be transparent, secure, tamper-proof, and reliable through the distributed ledger technology, hash chaining, and proof-of-work mechanism.

Notwithstanding, Pimentel and Boulianne (2020) also present that many distributed ledger applications have blockchain characteristics, varying in their degree and operation. Zheng (2021) states that Blockchain, as a technology originating from an algorithm, is new to most accountants and is even described as a very "exotic" technology, mainly related to cryptocurrencies (Pugna & Duțescu, 2020). Desplebin et al., (2021), McComb II and Smalt (2018) and Tiron-Tudor, Deliu, Farcane, and Dontu (2021) warn about the challenges, complexity, and unbalanced reality of implementing blockchain technology in accounting. Tiron-Tudor, Deliu, Farcane, and Dontu (2021) state that how accountancy organizations might manage the technological changes and how they will impact companies' regular activities, is an open debate. McComb II and Smalt (2018) point out that the benefit of implementation may outweigh the cost, highlighting that replacing the legacy systems and processes is, currently, not practical. Bonsón and Bednárová (2018) also state that for those more skeptical of the potential for blockchain in accounting, the technology is not mature enough and there is a significant lack of regulation.

The literature also presents seems to be more incisive to point the potential benefits of introducing such technologies in accounting (ALSaqa, Hussein & Mahmood, 2019; Arnold, 2018; Borhani et al., 2021; Desplebin, Lux & Petit, 2021; Garanina, Ranta & Dumay, 2021; Hamilton, 2019; ICAEW, 2018; McComb II & Smalt, 2018; Pimentel & Boulianne, 2020; Pizzi et al., 2022; Pugna & Duțescu, 2020; Roszkowska, 2020; Serapicos, 2021; Sheela et al., 2023; Singh, 2022; Tiron-Tudor, Deliu, Farcane & Dontu, 2021; Yu, Lin & Tang, 2019; Zheng, 2021). Hamilton (2019) affirm that bookkeeping and financial reporting will utilize smart contracts and distributed ledgers to improve accuracy and transparency in financial data recording. FERF (2018) states that the primary benefit of blockchain technology for financial statements is to have information in real-time. This is in line with ICAEW (2018) and Hamilton (2019), as the ledger created receives immediate and secure data that can potentially be validated by external auditors.

ALSaqa, Hussein, and Mahmood (2019) studied the impact and benefit of the use of blockchain technology in accounting information systems, concluding that there is a need to fully transition in the design of accounting information systems to electronic sophisticated programs and applications developed and technologically advanced. But as accounting professionals will be fundamental in consulting for the design of Blockchain solutions (Roszkowska, 2020), such as advising companies and other stakeholders when dealing with blockchain and cryptocurrency and optimizing their processes and systems (Pugna & Duțescu, 2020). Accounting professionals do not need to understand all the details of the technology but will need to understand it to the point that they can use it to take advantage of the profession, for the benefit of their employer and their clients (Arnold, 2018). The accountant will have to ensure that blockchain technology evolves and becomes accessible, as most blockchain applications on corporate level are customized (Singh, 2022). Their work will change to a certain extent, but their efficiency will also change, as they will significantly save time (Desplebin, Lux & Petit, 2021). The accounting professions, with more time available, can dedicate themselves to higher-level activities like aligning competitive intelligence with business strategy and decision-making (Sheela et al., 2023), and assessing the real economic interpretation of blockchain records (ICAEW, 2018). Pizzi, Caputo, Venturelli, and Caputo (2022) based on the Idea Journey Framework, presented the case study of Banca Mediolanum in Italy in evaluating the blockchain's enabling role for sustainability reporting. For these tasks, new skills will be needed, specifically on technology, consulting, and providing value-added to clients (Pugna & Duțescu, 2020).

Described by Pugna and Duțescu (2020) as a "universal entry bookkeeping", the process for creating the data will be faster, always updated and verified by the parts (Cardoso & Pinto, 2018; Pimentel & Boulianne, 2020; Sheela et al., 2023), reducing the costs of maintaining and reconciling ledgers (ICAEW, 2018). By eliminating the need to enter and reconcile information in multiple locations, efficiency gains are a strong point of this technology (ALSaqa, Hussein, & Mahmood, 2019; Garanina, Ranta & Dumay, 2021). FERF (2018) states that implementation costs are perhaps be the biggest impediment to the advancement of Blockchain technology; Waidyaratne (2022) states that reducing transaction costs is the real motivation for banks to adopt Blockchain technology.

Garanina, Ranta, and Dumay (2021), Zheng (2021), Pugna and Duțescu (2020) and Tiron-Tudor, Deliu, Farcane, and Dontu (2021) reinforce that companies that incorporate Blockchain into their accounting processes can reduce the risk of fraud, as they improve the authenticity and reliability of the financial information produced. Also, by using both public key cryptography and network analysis the identification of an entity can be modeled as a place on a network, which with accounting recordkeeping techniques allows a balance of public access with privacy using a blockchain and can enhance the representational faithfulness of financial reporting systems (McCallig, Robb & Rohde, 2019).

The implementation of blockchain technology in companies can benefit most accounting professionals and auditors, but it can be perceived negatively by those who need to manipulate the appearance of illicit transactions (Garanina, Ranta & Dumay, 2021). Yermack (2015), states that accounting, as we know it today, places too much trust in the integrity of accountants and auditors, which Serapicos (2021) adds that the permanent registration of a Blockchain reduces the chances of financial crimes, making records more reliable.

Hence, the propagation of the information, the permanence of records, the programmability for "smart contracts", the reduction of human errors, the simplification and automation of processes, among others, help to improve financial reports, that is, improve the quality of financial reporting (Borhani et al., 2021). Some authors specifically mention the increase in meeting some qualitative characteristics. Reliability is mentioned by ALSaqa et al. (2019), Desplebin, Lux & Petit (2021), Pizzi, Caputo, Venturelli, and Caputo (2022); Roszkowska (2020), and Zheng (2021).

Given the above previous literature mentioned, the following specific objectives are formulated:

01. Understand whether it is important for accounting professionals to carry out activities with greater added value.

02. Define what other activities accounting professionals will undertake to add value to the their companies.

03. Assess the influence that Blockchain technology will have on the accounting profession.

04. Investigate the main positive impacts of Blockchain technology on accounting practice.

05. Assess whether Blockchain technology can effectively combat fraud and corruption.

06. Evaluate whether Blockchain technology allows meeting the qualitative characteristics of financial reporting.

07. Analyze whether, with Blockchain technology, the entities' financial reporting becomes more reliable.

08. Evaluate whether Blockchain technology reduces the risk of the financial reporting not achieving faithful representation.

09. Evaluate the improvements that Blockchain technology contributes to a better perception of financial reporting by its users.

10. Verify whether there are discrepancies when comparing the financial reporting of entities that use Blockchain technology and entities that do not.

3. METHODOLOGY

To accomplish the specific purposes of the study, an exploratory design was thought of as most papers in the literature according to Tiron-Tudor, Deliu, Farcane, and Dontu (2021). That was necessary to collect, and further analyze, qualitative data.

The interview technique was used to obtain the data and provide additional evidence on the opinions of professionals with experience in blockchain technology (Sander, Semeijn & Mahr, 2018), including accounting professionals with proximity to the use of blockchain. The interview technique is used to capture perceptions, as it allows the discovery of aspects to be considered, broadening the field of investigation of the readings, with the main objective being to reveal certain aspects of the phenomenon under study (Quivy & Campenhoudt, 2008; Tiron-Tudor, Deliu, Farcane, and Dontu, 2021). The interview will be supported by a script, which results in a semi-structured interview that allows a sufficient degree of openness, so it collects all the richness that the subjects put into their words and does not become an instrument that reduces information (Bogdan & Biklen, 1994; Sander, Semeijn & Mahr, 2018).

The script of the questionnaire, presented in Appendix A, has eight open-response questions, that may be augmented for ten questions depending on the positive answer to the first two questions. The questions are thought to provide answers regarding four main topics: a) the potential automation of the processes, b) the influence of Blockchain on the profession, c) the influence in combating fraud and corruption, and d) the influence of Blockchain in the qualitative characteristics of financial reporting. The focus on this last topic is due to what seems to be a lack in the literature, as few studied this perception (ICAEW, 2018, McCallig, Robb, & Rohde, 2019). Due to this, the profile of the interviewees was defined in line with Borhani et al. (2021): specialists in blockchain technology with notions of the influence on financial reporting, and preparers of financial reporting, with notions of the use of blockchain in the profession. The importance of including accounting professors as interviewees comes from the fact that academic professionals are also important in the mindset of future accountants. Hence, to be aware of the opinion of this type of professionals, is essential to a more detailed analysis, particularly accounting professors with research and other activities related to blockchain technology.

The interview survey technique was performed, during October 2022, with accounting professors, professionals in accounting, and specialists in blockchain technology. Also, according to the practice of Borhani et al. (2021), the interviewees were asked about other types of experts that could contribute to providing additional evidence on the use of blockchain technology in these areas.

Finally, 11 individuals were used in this study, as they completed all characteristics that the literature review indicated. When asked, the interviewees agreed that it covered the perspectives they believed to be significant.

The main language used during the interviews was Portuguese. Notwithstanding, 2 of the 11 interviewees did not speak the language (interviewee n.° 3 is South African and n.° 6 Dutch), in which case the English language was used. Table 1 presents the profiles of the different interviewees, listed in order of the interview dates.

Table 1. Summary of the profiles of the interviewees

	Profile of the interviewee
1	Bachelor's degree in Management from the Lisbon School of Economics and Management (ISEG); Postgraduate in Tax Law from the Faculty of Law, University of Lisbon; Master of Science (MSc) in International Management from the University of Liverpool; Certified Accountant in Portugal (CC); CEO and Founder of Mário Moura Contabilidade; Author of the Blog Mário Moura Contabilidade; Creator of the business organization app "Organize Your Office"
2	Professor at the Lisbon Accounting and Business School (ISCAL); Certified Auditor in Portugal (ROC); Bachelor's degree in Auditing, Accounting, and Finance from ISCAL; Master of Business Administration (MBA) from the Universidade Católica Portuguesa; Master's degree in Economic and Corporate Decision-making from ISEG; Financial Risk Manager
3	Professor at Stellenbosch University (South Africa); Bachelor's degree in Accounting; Master's degree in Blockchain Technologies from Zigurat Global Institute of Technology

continued on following page

Table 1. Continued

	Profile of the interviewee
4	*Head of Hybrid Cloud Services* at International Business Machines Corporation (IBM); Bachelor's degree in Computer Science from Universidade Autónoma de Lisboa
5	Professor at ISCAL and ISEG; ROC; Master's degree in Management from ISEG; President of the Registration Committee of the Portuguese professional Order of Certified Accountants (OCC).
6	*Blockchain and Digital Manager* at *Deloitte*; *Blockchain expert and consultant* for companies and other organizations; MSc in *Digital Business* from the University of Amsterdam; Thesis on *Blockchain* and its relationship with real estate.
7	President of the Portuguese Association of *Blockchain* and Cryptocurrencies; Lecturer in the Postgraduate program in Web 3.0, *Blockchain* and Criptoeconomics at the Instituto Superior de Administração e Gestão (ISAG); Lawyer at Cuatrecasas; Bachelor's degree in Law; Postgraduate in Taxation; Master's degree in Forensic Law from the Universidade Católica Portuguesa
8	President of the Portuguese Blockchain Alliance; International consultant; Guest professor at Porto Business School; Bachelor's degree in Business and Computing from the University of London; MBA in Management from the Institute for Management Development
9	Author of the Master's thesis "Crypto-currencies: Does sentiment play a role?"; Bachelor's degree in Management and Business Administration from Universidade Europeia and the London School of Economics; Master's degree in Management from Universidade Europeia and in Finance from the University of California; Founder of the first bitcoin mining company in Portugal (BitMasters)
10	Bachelor's degree in Finance and Accounting from the Instituto Superior de Ciências do Trabalho e da Empresa (Instituto Universitário de Lisboa) (ISCTE); Certified Financial Education Instructor (CFEI) from the National Financial Educators Council (NFEC); Manager of one of the largest financial education YouTube channels in Portugal (Workolic); Mentioned in Forbes Portugal; Partner of major brands such as X-Trade Brokers, Binance, and Trading212
11	Senior consultant at the OCC; Author of the manual "Cryptocurrency – Accounting and Tax Aspects" of the Order of Certified Accountants; Bachelor's degree in Economics from ISEG

In summary, of the 11 interviewees, 6 are specialists in blockchain technology with notions of the influence on financial reporting (interviewees 4, 6, 7, 8, 9, 10), 4 are preparers of financial reporting with notions of the use of blockchain in the profession (interviewees 1, 2, 5, 11), and 4 are accounting professors (interviewees 2, 3, 5). Interviewees 2 and 5 are accounting professionals and accounting professors, which enhances the possibility of better precepting how the academy could be aligned for the changes identified by the literature (automation of tasks, more analysis, more transparency, and prevention of fraud).

Afterward, the collected information was organized for subsequent content analysis, where the interviewees' responses were presented in summary form. Hence, the results are presented for a descriptive analysis.

4. RESULTS AND DISCUSSION

This section presents, one by one, the response and subsequent analysis to each of the questions posed to the interviewees.

The first question of the questionnaire was regarding the potential automation of the processes:

Question 1: According to the literature, it is suggested that if current accounting processes are no longer necessary due to automation, accounting professionals will be able to carry out activities with greater added value. Do you agree?

The analysis of the responses obtained from the interviewees shows that all agree that if current accounting processes are no longer necessary due to automation, accounting professionals will be able to carry out activities with greater added value (question 1). Indeed, there is also agreement that the way forward will be to have less mechanical and methodical work and move on to activities with greater added value. These results are in line with Borhani et al. (2021), ICAEW (2018), Noor, Isa, Anbarasan and Kin (2019), Pugna and Duțescu (2020), and Roszkowska (2020), who also concluded blockchain may contribute to accountants perform other tasks, less automated. However, the responses obtained also considered that in a simple organizational structure, automation is excellent for accounting but there will be no advantage in automating processes at the level of a Blockchain, simple automation is enough (interviewees n.º 4 and 5).

The positive answer to question 1 led to the following sub-question 1.1:

Question 1.1: If you answered yes to the previous question, through what activity or activities will this happen?

1) Analysis of transactions.
2) Internal controls.
3) Accounting consultancy.
4) Optimization and improvement of processes.
5) Increase the quality of reporting.
6) If another, which one?

Regarding which activities will emerge for accounting professionals in replacement of those that will be automated (question 1.1), 8 interviewees of the 11 (73%), responded "accounting consultancy" and "increase the quality of reporting", 7 interviewees (64%) mentioned "optimization and improvement of processes", 4 opted for the "analysis of transactions", and 4 mentioned "internal controls". Additionally, 2 interviewees considered activities related to "sustainability" and 1 suggested "automation of processes". Figure 1 presents the answers obtained and exposes well the choice for activities such as accounting consultancy and increasing the quality of financial reports.

Hence, the responses point to accountants having a new role if companies start incorporating blockchain technology, more as a consultant than a "to-do" professional. Regardless, the professionals might also dedicate more time to improving the quality of financial reporting, strengthening the systems of financial reporting as suggested by Sheela et al. (2023), and optimizing processes (Liu, Kauffman & Ma, 2015) related to financial information.

Figure 1. Accounting activities with greater value added due to the use of Blockchain technology

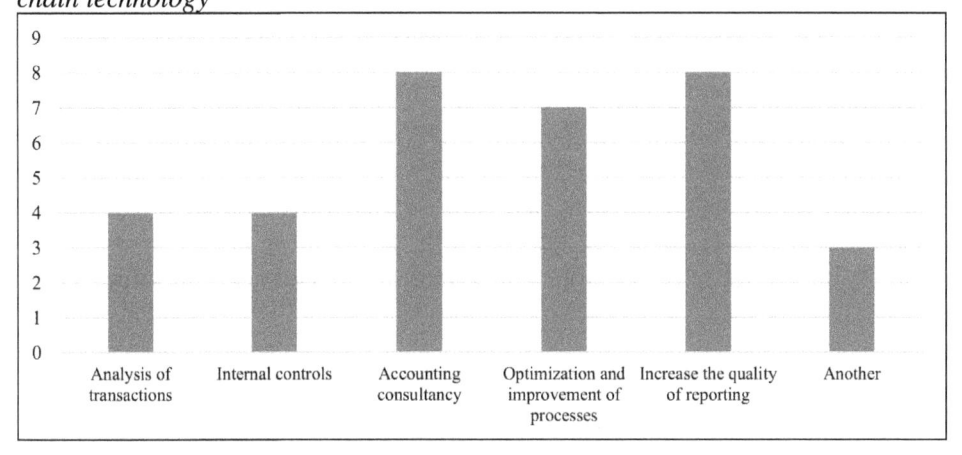

Activity	Count
Analysis of transactions	4
Internal controls	4
Accounting consultancy	8
Optimization and improvement of processes	7
Increase the quality of reporting	8
Another	3

Question 2 of the questionnaire was about the influence of Blockchain on the profession:

Question 2: The use of Blockchain technology will have a positive influence on the accounting profession?

When asked about the positive influence impact that the use of Blockchain technology may have on the accounting profession (question 2), 91% (10) of the interviewees responded affirmatively to the question, in line with Desplebin, Lux, and Petit (2021), ICAEW (2018), Pugna and Duțescu (2020) and Roszkowska (2020). Interviewee n.º 11 states that, at the present stage, it is premature to affirm that there will be a positive influence, as there are not yet enough studies on this topic (Tiron-Tudor, Deliu, Farcane & Dontu, 2021).

For ten of the eleven interviewees, the question 2.1 applied:

Question 2.1: If you answered yes to the previous question, what are the main positive impacts that you consider existing?

1) Lower costs of usage and transaction
2) Elimination of intermediaries
3) Shorter transaction time
4) Reliability in the authenticity of records
5) Elimination of tasks
6) Elimination of task duplication
7) Real-time information
8) Improvement of data analysis techniques
9) Safer and more secure information
10) Efficiency improvement

The main positive impacts that 82% (9 of the interviewees) referred to (question 2.2) are reliability in the authenticity of records and safer and more secure information. Real-time information was also pointed out by 73%, elimination of task duplication (64%), elimination of tasks and efficiency improvement (55%), shorter transaction time (45%), lower costs of usage and transaction, and elimination of intermediaries (36%), and finally, improvement of data analysis techniques (27%). Figure 2 shows the number of answers obtained for each task, highlighting reliability in the authenticity of records, safer and more secure information, and real-time information.

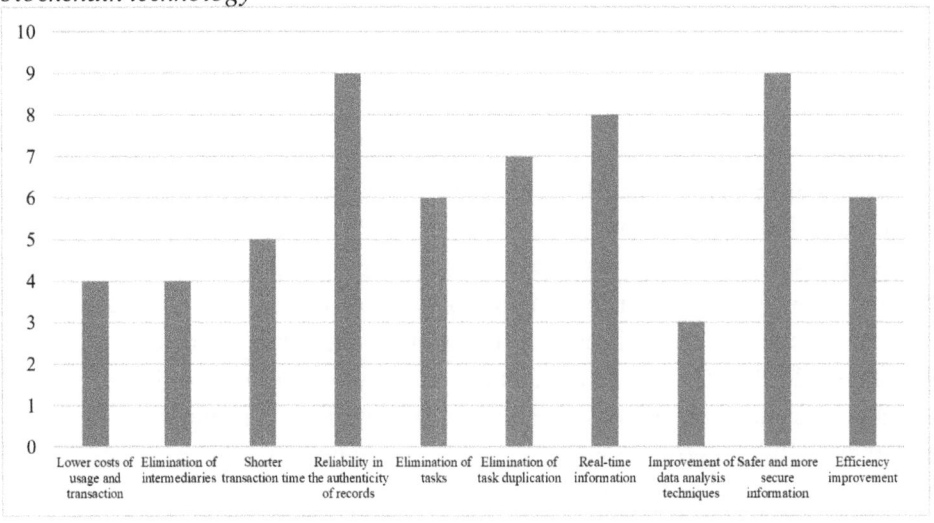

Figure 2. Main positive impacts on the accounting profession due to the use of blockchain technology

Question 3 incited the answers regarding fraud and corruption:

Question 3: Several authors argue Blockchain Technology can combat fraud and corruption. Do you agree with this statement?

The 11 interviewees believe Blockchain technology can combat fraud and corruption (question 3). This also is a point of large agreement in the literature (Garanina, Ranta, & Dumay, 2021; Zheng, 2021; Pugna & Duțescu, 2020; and Tiron-Tudor, Deliu, Farcane, & Dontu, 2021). Essentially, the interviewees point to the fact that this is the blockchains' purpose, making the records inserted immutable, public, and robust to attempted fraud, as this is the problem with traditional systems (ICAEW, 2018). Notwithstanding, interviewee n.º 2 highlights that blockchain technology may only be able to combat fraud and corruption to a certain extent, as financial reporting is still carried out by humans, very susceptible to fraud, which is something that Blockchain technology does not control.

Questions 4 to 8 concern the influence of Blockchain on the qualitative characteristics of financial reporting. Question 4 is about the perception of the interviewees on the validation of the characteristic(s) of financial reporting even when blockchain is used.

Question 4: Does Blockchain Technology reinforce the substantiation of which characteristic(s) of financial reporting?

Concerning the qualitative characteristics substantiation in financial reporting brought by blockchain use (question 4), 10 interviewees (91%) mentioned reliability, and 7 responded neutrality (64%). It was also referred: by 4 of the interviewees (36%), comparability and completeness; by 3 of the interviewees (27%) relevance; and by 2 interviewees, understandability (18%). Interviewee n.º 5 thinks Blockchain technology does not improve the quality of financial reporting at all. Figure 3 expresses the answers obtained.

As reliability continues to be a positive influence of blockchain, even when it is asked specifically in financial reporting, (ALSaqa et al., 2019; Desplebin, Lux & Petit, 2021, Pizzi, Caputo, Venturelli & Caputo, 2022; Roszkowska, 2020; and Zheng, 2021) some new characteristics are pointed, in this case, neutrality.

This may be linked to the concept of net neutrality (Agibalova, 2020; Muhamad & Demeter, 2021; Wogan & Kogan, 2018), when all data inserted is treated the same during its transport through the Internet, regardless of the sender, recipient, service, application or content. Wogan and Kogan (2018) argue that the blockchain ledger applies to different accounting treatments or even different accounting standards, which may succeed in achieving the neutrality characteristic that seeks a representation without bias in the selection or presentation of financial information (IFRS Conceptual Framework, 2018). Muhamad & Demeter (2021) present a solution to detect net neutrality breaches and incentivize collaborative contribution. The literature also shows that this relation should be a more discussed subject, even from the perspective of benefits and disadvantages, as when it comes to smart contracts it is essential to ensure that civil law regulation is applied (Agibalova, 2020).

Figure 3. Main reinforcement of qualitative characteristics due to the use of blockchain technology

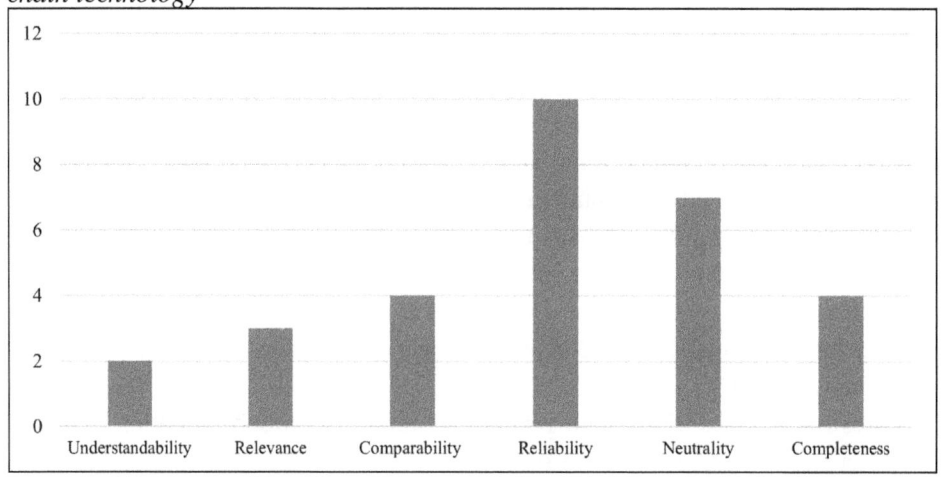

Characteristic	Value
Understandability	2
Relevance	3
Comparability	4
Reliability	10
Neutrality	7
Completeness	4

Question 5 specifically approaches the influence of blockchain on the reliability of financial reporting:

Question 5: Does the application of Blockchain Technology in accounting increase the level of reliability of financial statements?

When asked specifically about the increase in reliability of financial statements (question 5) all 11 interviewees answered affirmatively. Interviewee n.º 5, who in the previous question 4 had considered blockchain did not improve the quality of financial reporting explained his affirmative answer to question 5, arguing that it is the reliability related to fraud prevention that increases, and not that resulting from the error. The interviewee considers that in terms of reliability resulting from fraud, blockchain technology can be essential, as with Blockchain third parties are prevented from invading computer systems (prevents unauthorized access); the reliability resulting from the error, blockchain technology will not, at all, prevent, detect, nor eliminate it.

Question 6 addresses the influence of blockchain on faithful representation:

Question 6: Does the use of Blockchain Technology allow for a more faithful representation of the transactions?

About obtaining a more faithful representation of the transactions with the use of blockchain (question 6) the answers are divided, with 7 positive responses and 6 negative ones. Interviewees who state Blockchain technology allows for a more faithful representation of the transactions that occur present arguments that the information entered by blockchain is immutable and complete, with an absence of bias, which makes the process reliable, and allows for a guarantee of a faithful representation of the transaction as it occurred (as suggested by ICAEW, 2018 and Tiron-Tudor, Deliu, Farcane, & Dontu, 2021). The technicality of how blockchain may contribute to faithful representation is argued by McCallig, Robb, and Rohde (2019), requiring three ideas: shared data from independent entities, a transparent system, and open-access immutable storage. Interviewee n.º 10 explains that there are still many people skeptical about this technology, and as they don't understand it, they think it is something to reduce accounting (especially when everything that appears in the media is referred to in a derogatory way). Therefore, this interviewee assumes his answer to be no, since the faithful representation is related to the user's expectations.

Question 7 relates the precision of the information that is inserted with its understandability:

Question 7: The use of Blockchain Technology, in addition to safer access to data, allows for greater easiness in interpreting information by stakeholders, as the information is more precise and transparent. Does the use of this technology, by itself, make information more understandable?

Regarding blockchain technology making information more understandable (question 7), 91% of the interviewees (10) stated that information is not more understandable with it as whether using Blockchain or not, will be presented in the same ways, assuming that financial reports will be identical to the current ones, carried out using human interaction and not generated by Blockchain. Therefore, the overall perception is that Blockchain technology does not make financial information more understandable. Interviewee n.º 9 considered it was an arguable question as the information may be more understandable simply because of its increased transparency and accuracy, and everyone has access. However, is not more understandable as the information will be encrypted and only read by those who know cryptography.

Question 8 finishes the interview with the comparability that characterizes the financial reporting:

Question 8: Will the fact that entities are using Blockchain Technology in their accounting practice and others not, cause any constraints in terms of comparability of financial information?

Concerning the constraints that blockchain may cause in terms of comparability of financial information (question 8), 64% of the interviewees (7) considered that there are no constraints regarding comparability as financial reports will be the same, that is, the information is presented in the same way. However, 36% of the interviewees (n.º 1, n.º 3, n.º 7, and n.º 11) consider that there is a constraint because the data provided by Blockchain is reliable data and the others may have suffered some change.

Summarily, Table 2 presents a summary of the answers obtained from the interview.

Table 2. Summary of the answers to the questions of the interview

	Question 1	Question 2	Question 3	Question 4	Question 5	Question 6	Question 7	Question 8
Yes	11 (100%)	10 (91%)	11 (100%)	--	11 (100%)	7 (64%)	0	4 (36%)
No	0	0	0	--	0	4 (36%)	10 (91%)	7 (64%)
Premature answer / Maybe	0	1 (9%)	0	--	0	0	1 (9%)	0
Reliability	--	--	--	10 (91%)	--	--	--	--
Neutrality	--	--	--	7 (64%)	--	--	--	--
Comparability	--	--	--	4 (36%)	--	--	--	--
Completeness	--	--	--	4 (36%)	--	--	--	--
Relevance	--	--	--	3 (27%)	--	--	--	--
Comprehensibility	--	--	--	2 (18%)	--	--	--	--

There are important insights that should be considered when experienced professionals are heard. There seems to be no doubt about the potential of blockchain technology, but the structure of the entity must be considered, as another technology, of more simple use, may be sufficient. Reliability of the information, due to the safety and security of data inserted, is what most professionals point out as a positive influence of the use of technology, with the advantage that is real-time information.

In what concerns characteristics of the information, it is also a result of this study, that blockchain enhances neutrality in financial reporting, as proposed by IFRS and local conceptual frameworks for financial reporting. However, the preparers and stakeholders must be aware of the issues surrounding net neutrality, that may contribute positively or negatively to the "high-tech ledger" supported by blockchain. The influence of blockchain in faithful representation is discussed in an environment of doubt, as the bookkeeping is made with immutability and completeness, making the information faithfully represented; however, this might depend on the users' competencies on blockchain and expectations. Understandability and comparability were understood as enhancing qualitative characteristics that blockchain will not intend to bring to financial reporting.

5. CONCLUSION

Blockchain technology is a peer-to-peer distributed timestamp server that generates computational proof of the chronological order of transactions and proposes to solve issues surrounding Bitcoin, such as decentralization and double-spending. However, Blockchain technology characteristics make it possible to be used for other purposes, such as instantly organizing, recording, and validating the maintenance of financial information, which becomes available to all users in real-time. These features guarantee that financial reporting is transparent, secure, tamper-proof, and reliable through the distributed ledger. However, the literature also points out the challenges, complexity, and unbalanced reality of implementing blockchain technology in accounting. Hence, there is an open debate on how organizations will implement the technological changes and relate them to the regular activities recording.

This research resulted, among other aspects, from an existing gap in understanding how blockchain technology may create advantages and challenges in the professions surrounding financial reporting. The potential and interest in exploring how this disruptive technology might impact the quality of financial reporting also emerged, as there appears to be no existing study on this topic conducted in Portugal to date. The interviewees agreed that the reliability of the information, due to the safety and security of data inserted, is a positive influence of the technology use, with the advantage of real-time information. However, the immutability and completeness, that make information faithfully represented might depend on the users' competencies on blockchain and expectations. This study extends existing theoretical insights by exploring the opinions of experienced professionals in financial reporting and blockchain and how the latter can improve the first.

Regarding the limitations underlying this study, it is important to highlight the difficulty in obtaining previous studies regarding the influence of blockchain technology on the quality of financial reporting, due to the scarcity of research produced. Another limitation is related to the number of interviews carried out since a greater number of interviewees would bring a greater plurality of opinions and enrich the discussion. Additionally, most interviewees live in Portugal; a more international approach could proportionate further insights. Finally, the topic under study is also quite difficult to address, given the multiplicity of existing approaches, coming from different areas of knowledge.

REFERENCES

Agibalova, E. N. (2020). Blockchain Technology in Smart Contracts: Is It a Constitutive Attribute or a Technological Neutrality? In Popkova, E., & Sergi, B. (Eds.), *Scientific and Technical Revolution: Yesterday, Today and Tomorrow. ISC 2019. Lecture Notes in Networks and Systems* (Vol. 129). Springer. DOI: 10.1007/978-3-030-47945-9_19

Albuquerque, F., & Rodrigues, N. M. B. (2015). As características qualitativas da informação financeira: Uma análise ao relato das entidades cotadas nas principais bolsas europeias. *Congresso Dos TOC*. https://www.occ.pt/news/trabalhoscongv/pdf/73.pdf

ALSaqa, Z. H., Hussein, A. I., & Mahmood, S. M. (2019). The impact of blockchain on accounting information systems. *Journal of Information Technology Management*, 11(3), 62–80. DOI: 10.22059/jitm.2019.74301

Antunes, L. (2019). *Tecnologia blockchain e criptomoedas: o que é isto?* (1ª edição). Plátano Editora.

Arnold, A. (2018, August 28). Blockchain is not a threat to accounting, it's an opportunity. *Forbes*. https://www.forbes.com/sites/andrewarnold/2018/08/28/blockchain-is-not-a-threat-to-accounting-its-an-opportunity/

Baba, A. I., Neupane, S., Wu, F., & Yaroh, F. F. (2021). Blockchain in accounting: Challenges and future prospects. *International Journal of Blockchains and Cryptocurrencies*, 2(1), 44. DOI: 10.1504/IJBC.2021.117810

Barth, M. E., Landsman, W. R., & Lang, M. H. (2008). International accounting standards and accounting quality. *Journal of Accounting Research*, 46(3), 467–498. DOI: 10.1111/j.1475-679X.2008.00287.x

Bonsón, E., & Bednárová, M. (2018). Blockchain y los registros contables consensuados compartidos (RC3). XVIII Encuentro Internacional AECA, 20-21 de setembro. Lisboa, Portugal.

Bordo, M. D., & Siklos, P. L. (2017). *Central Banks: Evolution and Innovation in Historical Perspective* (Economics Working Papers, Issue April).

Borhani, S., Babajani, J., Vanani, I., Anaqiz, S., & Jamaliyanpour, M. (2021). Adopting Blockchain Technology to Improve Financial Reporting by Using the Technology Acceptance Model (TAM). *International Journal of Finance & Managerial Accounting*, 6(22), 155–171. http://www.ijfma.ir/article_17481.html

Brunnermeier, M. K., James, H., & Landau, J.-P. (2019). The Digitization of Money. *NBER Working Paper Series*.

Cardoso, J. A. A., & Pinto, J. de S. (2018). Blockchain e Smart Contracts: Um Estudo Sobre Soluções para Seguradoras. *2o. CONGENTI, October 2018*, 1–17.

Chohan, U. (2022). Cryptocurrencies: A Brief Thematic Review. In *Discussion Paper Series: Notes on the 21st Century*. https://doi.org/DOI: 10.2139/ssrn.3024330

Desplebin, O., Lux, G., & Petit, N. (2021). To be or not to be: Blockchain and the future of accounting and auditing. *Accounting Perspectives*, 20(4), 743–769. DOI: 10.1111/1911-3838.12265

Financial Executives Research Foundation Inc. [FERF] (2018). *Blockchain for Financial Leaders: Opportunity Vs. Reality*. https://www2.deloitte.com/content/dam/Deloitte/us/Documents/financial-services/us-fsi-fei-blockchain-report-future-hr.pdf

Garanina, T., Ranta, M., & Dumay, J. (2022). Blockchain in accounting research: Current trends and emerging topics. *Accounting, Auditing & Accountability Journal*, 35(7), 1507–1533. DOI: 10.1108/AAAJ-10-2020-4991

Haber, S., & Scott Stornetta, W. (1991). How to time-stamp a digital document. *Lecture Notes in Computer Science (Including Subseries Lecture Notes in Artificial Intelligence and Lecture Notes in Bioinformatics), 537 LNCS*, 437–455. DOI: 10.1007/3-540-38424-3_32

Hamilton, M. (2019). Blockchain distributed ledger technology: An introduction and focus on smart contracts. *Journal of Corporate Accounting & Finance*, 31(2), 7–12. DOI: 10.1002/jcaf.22421

Institute of Chartered Accountants in England and Wales [ICAEW] (2018). Blockchain And The Future Of Accountancy. *Icaew Thought Leadership*, 1–12. https://www.icaew.com/technical/technology/blockchain-and-cryptoassets/blockchain-articles/blockchain-and-the-accounting-perspective

Klinger, B., & Szczeoanski, J. (2017). Blockchain - History, Features and Main Areas of Application. *Człowiek W Cyberprzestrzeni, 1*(810), 7–20.

Liu, J., Kauffman, R. J., & Ma, D. (2015). Competition, cooperation, and regulation: Understanding the evolution of the mobile payments technology ecosystem. *Electronic Commerce Research and Applications*, 14(5), 372–391. DOI: 10.1016/j.elerap.2015.03.003

McCallig, J., Robb, A., & Rohde, F. (2019). Establishing the representational faithfulness of financial accounting information using multiparty security, network analysis and a blockchain. *International Journal of Accounting Information Systems*, 33, 47–58. DOI: 10.1016/j.accinf.2019.03.004

McComb, J. M.II, & Smalt, S. W. (2018). The rise of blockchain technology and its potential for improving the quality of accounting information. *Journal of Finance and Accountancy*, 23, 1–7. http://www.aabri.com/copyright.html

Mihus, I. (2022). Evolution of practical use of blockchain technologies by companies. *Economics. Finance and Management Review*, 1(1), 42–50. DOI: 10.36690/2674-5208-2022-1-42

Muhamad, L., & Demeter, D. (2021). *Design and Implementation of a Signaling Approach for the Detection of Net Neutrality Breaches using Blockchain-based Smart Contracts*. University of Zurich.

Nakamoto, S. (2022). Bitcoin: A Peer-to-Peer Electronic Cash System. SSRN *Electronic Journal*, 1–9. DOI: 10.2139/ssrn.3977007

Nobes, C. W., & Stadler, C. (2015). The qualitative characteristics of financial information, and managers accounting decisions: Evidence from IFRS policy changes. *Accounting and Business Research*, 45(5), 572–601. DOI: 10.1080/00014788.2015.1044495

Noor, S. A. M., Isa, M. M., Anbarasan, D., & Kin, G. W. (2019). Blockchain-Enabled Task and Time Sheet Management for Accounting Services Provision. *E-Proceeding of the International Conference on Social Science Research 2019*, 10–20. https://www.academia.edu/download/62083682/Syafiq20200212-29057-2jmukg.pdf

Pedreño, E. P., Gelashvili, V., & Nebreda, L. P. (2021). Blockchain and its application to accounting. *Intangible Capital*, 17(1), 1–16. DOI: 10.3926/ic.1522

Pimentel, E., & Boulianne, E. (2020). Blockchain in Accounting Research and Practice: Current Trends and Future Opportunities. *Accounting Perspectives*, 19(4), 325–361. DOI: 10.1111/1911-3838.12239

Pizzi, S., Caputo, A., Venturelli, A., & Caputo, F. (2022). Embedding and managing blockchain in sustainability reporting: A practical framework. *Sustainability Accounting. Management and Policy Journal*, 13(3), 545–567. DOI: 10.1108/SAMPJ-07-2021-0288

Pugna, I. B., & Duțescu, A. (2020). Blockchain – the accounting perspective. *Proceedings of the International Conference on Business Excellence, 14*(1), 214–224. DOI: 10.2478/picbe-2020-0020

Quinn, S., & Roberds, W. (2008). The Evolution of the Check as a Means of Payment: A Historical Survey. *Federal Reserve Bank of Atlanta Economic Review*, 93(4). Advance online publication. DOI: 10.1016/S1365-6937(04)00375-2

Reiff, N. (2022, July 23). What Was the First Cryptocurrency? There were cryptocurrencies before bitcoin. Investopedia. https://www.investopedia.com/tech/were-there-cryptocurrencies-bitcoin/

Roszkowska, P. (2020). Fintech in financial reporting and audit for fraud prevention and safeguarding equity investments. *Journal of Accounting & Organizational Change*, 17(2), 164–196. DOI: 10.1108/JAOC-09-2019-0098

Sander, F., Semeijn, J., & Mahr, D. (2018). The acceptance of blockchain technology in meat traceability and transparency. *British Food Journal*, 120(9), 2066–2079. DOI: 10.1108/BFJ-07-2017-0365

Santos, E. L. D. (2014). *Do escambo à inclusão financeira: a evolução dos meios de pagamento*. Linotipo Digital.

Serapicos. (2021). *Transformações digitais para financeiros - blockchain big data*. Lisboa: Ordem dos Contabilistas Certificados.

Setiawan, R., Cavaliere, L. P. L., Halder, S., Koti, K., Sarsengaliy, B., Ashok, K., Pallathadka, H., & Rajan, R. (2021). The concept of the cryptocurrency and the downfall of the banking sector in reflecting on the financial market. *RentgenologiyaiRadiologiya*, 60(S1), 17–33.

Sheela, S., Alsmady, A. A., Tanaraj, K., & Izani, I. (2023). Navigating the Future: Blockchain's Impact on Accounting and Auditing Practices. *Sustainability (Basel)*, 15(24), 16887. DOI: 10.3390/su152416887

Singh, A. (2022). Blockchain Technology: A Paradigm Shift in Accounting. *SMS Journal of Enterpreneurship & Innovation*, 8(1). Advance online publication. DOI: 10.21844/smsjei.v8i01.30006

Soderstrom, N. S., & Sun, K. J. (2007). IFRS adoption and accounting quality: A review. *European Accounting Review*, 16(4), 675–702. DOI: 10.1080/09638180701706732

Sokołowska, E. (2015). Innovations in the payment card market: The case of Poland. *Electronic Commerce Research and Applications*, 14(5), 292–304. DOI: 10.1016/j.elerap.2015.07.005

Supriadi, I., Harjanti, W., Suprihandari, M. D., Dwi Prasetyo, H., & Muslikhun, . (2020). Blockchain Innovation and Its Capacity to Enhance the Quality From Accounting Information Systems. *International Journal of Scientific Research and Management*, 8(02), 1590–1595. DOI: 10.18535/ijsrm/v8i02.em05

Tiron-Tudor, A., Deliu, D., Farcane, N., & Dontu, A. (2021). Managing change with and through blockchain in accountancy organizations: A systematic literature review. *Journal of Organizational Change Management*, 34(2), 477–506. DOI: 10.1108/JOCM-10-2020-0302

Vieira, J. P. (2017). *A história do dinheiro*. Academia das Ciências de Lisboa.

Wang, Y., & Kogan, A. (2018). Designing confidentiality-preserving Blockchain-based transaction processing systems. *International Journal of Accounting Information Systems*, 30(June), 1–18. DOI: 10.1016/j.accinf.2018.06.001

Yu, T., Lin, Z., & Tang, Q. (2018). Blockchain: The Introduction and Its Application in Financial Accounting. *Journal of Corporate Accounting & Finance*, 29(4), 37–47. DOI: 10.1002/jcaf.22365

Zhao, W. (2019). Blockchain technology: Development and prospects. *National Science Review*, 6(2), 369–373. DOI: 10.1093/nsr/nwy133 PMID: 34691875

Zheng, R. (2021). Applications Research of Blockchain Technology in Accounting System. *Journal of Physics: Conference Series*, 1955(1), 012068. Advance online publication. DOI: 10.1088/1742-6596/1955/1/012068

KEY TERMS AND DEFINITIONS

Blockchain Technology: A peer-to-peer distributed timestamp server to generate computational proof of the chronological order of transactions (Nakamoto, 2008).

High-Tech Ledger: A ledger that records information instantly and, at the same time, becomes available to all users.

Faithful Representation: Maximization of three concepts together, complete, neutral, and free from error.

Financial Reporting: A set of financial information provided in financial statements regarding a given reporting entity, that is considered useful.

Neutrality: Without bias in the introduction, selection or presentation.

Qualitative Characteristics: The characteristics that financial reporting should have to be considered useful.

Reliability: Free from material error and bias and represented faithfully.

ENDNOTE

[1] Drucker, P. F. (2001). melhor de Peter Drucker: a administração, O–Exame (Vol. 2). NBL Editora

APPENDIX I

Script for the Interviews

Question 1: According to the literature, it is suggested that if current accounting processes are no longer necessary due to automation, accounting professionals will be able to carry out activities with greater added value. Do you agree?

Question 1.1: If you answered yes to the previous question, through what activity or activities will this happen?
1) Analysis of transactions.
2) Internal controls.
3) Accounting consultancy.
4) Optimization and improvement of processes.
5) Increase the quality of reporting.
6) If another, which one?

Question 2: The use of Blockchain technology will have a positive influence on the accounting profession?

Question 2.1: If you answered yes to the previous question, what are the main positive impacts that you consider existing?
1) Lower costs of usage and transaction
2) Elimination of intermediaries
3) Shorter transaction time
4) Reliability in the authenticity of records
5) Elimination of tasks
6) Elimination of task duplication
7) Real-time information
8) Improvement of data analysis techniques
9) Safer and more secure information
10) Efficiency improvement

Question 3: Several authors argue Blockchain Technology can combat fraud and corruption. Do you agree with this statement?

Question 4: Does Blockchain Technology reinforce the substantiation of which characteristic(s) of financial reporting?

Question 5: Does the application of Blockchain Technology in accounting increase the level of reliability of financial statements?

Question 6: Does the use of Blockchain Technology allow for a more faithful representation of the transactions?

Question 7: The use of Blockchain Technology, in addition to safer access to data, allows for greater easiness in interpreting information by stakeholders, as the information is more precise and transparent. Does the use of this technology, by itself, make information more understandable?

Question 8: Will the fact that entities are using Blockchain Technology in their accounting practice and others not, cause any constraints in terms of comparability of financial information?

Chapter 4
The Use of Robotic Process Automation in Brazilian Accounting Firms:
A Study of the Perception of Accounting Professionals

João Marcelo Alves Macêdo
 https://orcid.org/0000-0002-6313-1759
Federal University do Paraíba, Brazil

Yanne Yasmim Gouveia Silva
 https://orcid.org/0009-0008-4865-769X
Federal University of Paraíba, Brazil

Ariane Silva Moura
 https://orcid.org/0000-0002-3364-5329
Federal University of Paraíba, Brazil

George Rogers Andrade Silva
 https://orcid.org/0000-0003-2843-7063
Federal University of Paraíba, Brazil

Gelyel Estevan dos Santos
 https://orcid.org/0009-0002-3778-9271
Federal University of Rio Grande do Norte, Brazil

DOI: 10.4018/979-8-3693-5923-5.ch004

Copyright © 2025, IGI Global. Scientific Publishing. Copying or distributing in print or electronic forms without written permission of IGI Global is prohibited.

ABSTRACT

Recently, there have been changes in the work processes of Brazilian accounting firms, with the implementation of systems automation, the integration of accounts payable and receivable systems, and payroll systems with accounting systems. The objective of this study was to analyze the perceptions of Brazilian accounting professionals about the implementation of robotic process automation (RPA) in their work routines. RPA was considered a strategic tool that aims to optimize time and expand business. A quantitative and descriptive approach was adopted, using an online questionnaire on Google Forms, which was answered virtually by 210 professionals. The participants' opinions regarding the use of RPA, their experiences, benefits, and challenges faced were considered. It was concluded that RPA automates repetitive tasks and frees accounting professionals for strategic and more complex activities. This study contributes to the management of accounting firms by optimizing processes and routines, especially their productivity.

1. INTRODUCTION

Over the years, accounting has established itself as an essential discipline for the functioning and transparency of economic activities and for the development of society. It has allowed organizations to be comparable and, above all, provides information to decision-makers: partners, government, stakeholders, employees, and society in general. Along with social relevance has come the need to adapt to cultural molds and the evolution of assets and business models, and one of the transformations experienced by accounting has been the digital transformation, involving the adoption of digital technologies and tools to optimize and modernize accounting practices.

The advent of the digital age has seen innovations in various spheres. Driven by the widespread availability of knowledge and ease of access, these transformations have affected professions, human interactions and even social values. Consequently, work management has come to demand mastery of digital technologies as an essential requirement in organizations, whether for hiring processes, keeping a job or seeking promotions (Pauleski, 2023).

According to Ferreira (2022), the use of the internet and computerized systems makes it possible to improve procedures, providing greater speed and security for both companies and accounting professionals. The evolution of technological tools has had a significant impact on corporate environments, restructuring social and professional practices.

In the context of accounting, the introduction of technology, with a focus on artificial intelligence (AI), has led to reflections on the continuity of the profession as we know it. As manual tasks and the use of paper documents decrease, there is an increase in operational activities aimed at monitoring, managing, structuring, automating, developing and optimizing tax environments (Braga; Colares, 2020).

Artificial intelligence has thus become a tool for automating manual processes. The trend is for accountants to spend less time on repetitive and routine tasks. This will allow professionals in the field to improve their activities, generating more agile information that will contribute to more effective decision-making (Oliveira, 2019).

One of the avenues for applying AI in accounting firms is Robotic Process Automation (RPA). RPA is driving a rapid transformation in the activities and tasks of accounting and other information professionals (Harrast, 2020). Fernandez & Aman (2018) show that several organizations have automated the technology used in finance and accounting (F&A) services to maximize productivity and reduce the operating expenses involved. In the new digital landscape of accounting and auditing services, not only RPA, but allied to other technologies, has been an important tool (Tiron-Tudor, et al. 2024).

In this way, RPA presents itself in the execution of repetitive, data input and stable tasks that overload the workday of accounting and information professionals, through bots, aimed at stable, repetitive processes that consume enough resources to generate a solid return on investment (Harrast, 2020). In this sense, the scope for automation by programmable software robots or bots is enormous and capable of generating opportunities for these companies.

Considering this, the following problem arises: What is the user's perception of the impact of incorporating automation robots into the processes and routines of accounting firms?

Based on this context, the general objective of this research is to investigate the perception of accounting professionals about the implementation of Robotic Process Automation (RPA) in their work routines. The aim is to gain insights into how this technology is perceived and how it can impact on the work of these professionals.

Therefore, this study is justified by the need to explore and analyze the adherence of accounting companies to digital transformation, with a focus on the scenario of implementing tools using process automation. The main focus of the research is to contribute to the services provided by accounting professionals. They will have an in-depth perspective on the use of automation for the development of their day-to-day activities, integration with clients and the results arising from implementation, particularly in the provision of contracted services and compliance with ancillary obligations.

In academia, this research is justified by providing students with a vision of how these routines can be automated, as well as new actions that will enable them to observe and develop more tools to support the accounting profession. This area of work was determined by the growing approach to the subject and the need to understand the scenario of professionals facing these changes and their perceptions of the opportunities in this scenario.

The methodological strategy for this research used a quantitative, descriptive approach, with online questionnaires for data collection. The respondents were accounting professionals and sought their perception of the use of automation in companies and RPA, including perceived benefits and the challenges faced.

This chapter is structured as an introduction and a theoretical framework that addresses the following issues: conceptualizing RPA, accounting and the use of RPA, discussing the implementation of RPA in accounting software, and the technology applied to accounting routines. After this contextualization, the choice of methodological route was presented, to support the results. Item four presents the results of the research, with descriptive statistics and other inferences. Finally, there are the final considerations, containing the study's conclusions, limitations, and suggestions for further research.

2. THEORETICAL BACKGROUND

2.1 Conceptualizing Robotic Process Automation (RPA)

The need to implement Robotic Process Automation (RPA) is a consequence of the need for organizations to provide consistent results to shareholders (Anagnoste, 2017). In this way, the use of RPA can, according to Anagnoste (2017) act to promote: (1) Cost reduction, (2) Increased quality and (3) Process agility. RPA is considered the great innovation for Shared Services Centers (SSC) and Business Process Outsourced (BPO) worldwide, especially in Central and Eastern Europe (Anagnoste, 2017).

The concept of Robotic Process Automation (RPA) is based on three main concepts: robot, process and automation. A robot is programmable software that performs an activity based on established criteria, such as sending emails with invoices for a specific service. In turn, a process refers to a set of tasks that culminate in the achievement of a specific result (Pauleski, 2023). Finally, automation represents the transformation of a previously manually executed activity into an automatic execution (Pedras & Oliveira, 2021).

Moffitt, Rozario, & Vasarhelyi (2018) point out that RPA has unique characteristics that distinguish it from other automation processes. Thus, RPA robots carry out their work in the same way as humans: running registers, reading and sending emails, carrying out analyses and creating predefined reports (Moffitt, Rozario, & Vasarhelyi, 2018). They can also perform well with data input, knowing that other functions are still being carried out and can be supervised by humans or other robots performing that function (Moffitt, Rozario, & Vasarhelyi, 2018).

Robotic process automation can be categorized into three distinct types: Attended RPA, Unattended RPA and Intelligent Process Automation. Attended RPA requires the robot to interact with a human, where the software partially performs the task. For example, in telecommunications companies, the attendant interacts with the robot to collect documents and information from the user on the other end of the line. Unattended RPA does not require human interaction, except for maintenance, and is triggered by a previously programmed trigger, such as receiving an email or detecting a specific element on the screen (Pedras & Oliveira, 2021). Finally, Intelligent Process Automation (IPA or cognitive RPA) is the most advanced form of RPA, which uses artificial intelligence in its programming and requires less human interaction, and can even carry out its maintenance, as its code is designed to identify usage patterns (Taulli, 2020).

RPA emerged from the convergence of technological advances and the constant search for efficiency in business processes. It emerged as a solution for dealing with repetitive, structured and rule-based tasks that were previously carried out by humans. Its origins go back to industrial automation, software development and artificial intelligence (Scheifler, 2016).

In the early days, industrial automation already played a key role in sectors such as manufacturing, where machines were employed to perform specific tasks according to schedules. In the field of software development, the automation of tests and processes was already an established practice to improve both efficiency and quality (Monma, 2023). Artificial intelligence and the development of software capable of reproducing human actions in graphical interfaces, triggered the creation of virtual robots capable of relating to digital systems in the same way as humans, performing functions such as filling in forms, extracting data and navigating web pages (Rozario, 2018).

Robotic process automation makes it possible to automate routine, simple and flexible tasks that are prone to errors and require a high administrative burden. This allows organizations to reduce costs and reallocate human resources from repetitive activities to control, analysis and decision-making support functions (Lopes, 2020).

Bot software makes it possible to carry out a workflow consisting of multiple steps and applications, covering various tasks such as reading and writing data, performing numerical calculations, and updating or modifying information (Issac, Muni & Desai, 2018).

Based on this contextualization, RPA can be considered a program that interacts with other programs, in most applications and interfaces, being perceived by the latter as the user, that is, as a human being (Cohen, Rozario & Zhang, 2019). As such, it is used to automate structured processes that are repetitive and previously defined with clear rules, as well as those with machine-visible data (Cohen, Rozario & Zhang, 2019).

Gotthardt et al. (2020) state that robotic process automation (RPA) and artificial intelligence (AI) are closely linked and have influenced accounting and auditing practices. For the authors, RPA and AI are at two ends of an intelligent automation continuum, one being process-oriented and the other data-oriented (Gotthardt et al., 2020).

2.2 Accounting and the Use of Robotic Process Automation (RPA)

The study by Cooper, Holderness, Sorensen & Wood (2019) shows that RPA has been ranked as the number one technology priority for global shared services and business services leaders. Being a pioneer, it mapped the impact of RPA on the accounting industry. From the perspective of the interviewees, it is observed that robots are implemented in all areas of the company, being more present in tax, consulting, and assurance services, increasing quality and efficiency (Cooper, Holderness, Sorensen & Wood, 2019).

The implementation of RPA still represents an initial scenario in accounting and financial tasks, however, when identifying tasks that can be automated and the improvement in organizational and individual performance that RPA provides, a considerable increase in the incorporation of the tool in accounting activities is projected (Kokina & Blanchette, 2019).

According to Pedras & Oliveira (2021), the use of RPA in the accounting environment does not yet have robust literature on this subject, which limited the research to this specificity.

The use of RPA in the area of Accounting manifests itself in various ways, and can be a solution created to address a specific issue independently or integrated with an accounting information system (ERP). According to Pedras & Oliveira (2021), specific solutions are sometimes made available by startups with the aim of reducing the time dedicated to a specific process. An example of this is importing customer bank statements into an accounting information system.

On the other hand, solutions that operate in an integrated manner with information systems are generally offered as part of the system contract and are intended to optimize the use of the accounting system, as they are native tools of the system itself. An example of RPA that integrates with the accounting system is the automatic and programmed search of government portals for tax documents, which are then included in the system's database.

Accounting tasks are known to have evolved with the implementation of enterprise resource planning (ERP) systems (Tiron-Tudor *et al.*, 2024). Its effect has been to unify tasks that were previously carried out in independent systems, which has eliminated much of the manual work associated with data processing and integration (Tiron-Tudor et al., 2024). However, this movement has not covered repetitive and low-value-added operations, which still require manual labor but can be incorporated into RPA processes (Kaya *et al.*, 2019).

Yoon (2020) points out that the technological evolution promoted in accounting processes has moved from the simple use of computers as a means of storing and recording data through manual inputs to the use of technologies such as AI, cloud computing, big data, and RPA. These changes represent the digital transformation of accounting and are being used to generate more meaningful and relevant accounting data for decision-making (Yoon, 2020).

2.3 Implementation of Robotic Process Automation (RPA) in Accounting Software

Feng (2015) describes the development of cloud accounting systems as an accounting information system based on cloud computing and the use of computers or other devices by the client to perform accounting and financial analysis functions. The author also projected that, with the development and popularization of cloud computing, there will be a major impact on the application of business accounting information and the model of its construction (Feng, 2015).

Currently, some accounting software is not limited to being standalone accounting systems but is integrated into platforms that fit into the concept of Enterprise Resource Planning (ERP). This means that they are part of integrated management systems, as they incorporate several essential modules for business administration, such as production, logistics, human resources management, invoicing and accounting.

Opting for integrated software (ERP) instead of a standalone accounting system makes it possible to generate value for the organization by integrating the company's data with the different modules, resulting in improvements in the analyses and reports produced, in internal communication and in planning and control. This, in turn, boosts user productivity and customer satisfaction (Pedras & Oliveira, 2021).

For this development, Yoon (2020) shows that the best-known cloud accounting systems are Enterprise Resource Planning (ERP) because they connect all areas of the company and are managed collectively. This is because accounting is the core of the ERP system, so accounting data and information are fundamental for managing all levels of the company in an integrated way (Yoon, 2020). In the experience of the Korean market, using Oracle ERP Cloud, companies that adopt it can draw up forecasts by identifying and using trends and patterns in financial and operational data, allowing for informed decisions (Yoon, 2020).

One of the applications of RPA is auditing processes, as Moffitt, Rozario and Vasarhelyi (2018) state that manual and repetitive auditing tasks, such as reconciliations, internal control tests, and detail tests, can be automated. By allowing auditors to allocate more resources to auditing areas of a complex nature, such as estimating fair value investments or investigating items that are potential anomalies, eventually leading to higher audit quality (Moffitt, Rozario, and Vasarhelyi, 2018), the following summary table is drawn from the authors' studies:

Table 1. A comparison between automation tools for audit tasks

Tools	Tool Execution	Audit Task
Excel Macros	Rules-Based Functions	Reconciliations
IDEA	Calculations	Analytical Procedures Internal Control Testing Detail Testing (Attribute Match)
Python	Rules-Based Functions	Reconciliations
R	Calculations Web Scraping	Analytical Procedures Internal Control Testing
RPA Vendor Tools, Such as UiPath and Blue Prism	Importing Data Exporting Data	Detail Testing (Attribute Match) Input: Collection of Data Output: Compilation of Audit Test Results

Font: Moffitt, Rozario, and Vasarhelyi (2018)

Table 1 describes the variety of tools that help automate audit tasks, some of which include RPA. According to Moffitt, Rozario and Vasarhelyi (2018), it is possible to complete all activities using RPA tools since, according to their suppliers, UiPath and Blue Prism2 robot automation offer similar features to Microsoft Excel, IDEA, Python, and R and does not require programming in the user-level interface.

For Huang and Vasarhelyi (2019), robotic process automation (RPA) has been widely adopted in many sectors, including the accounting industry. However, its application to auditing has lagged due to the unique nature of this sector. In this context, the authors present an RPA framework proposed to free auditors from doing repetitive and low-judgment audit tasks, allowing them to focus on tasks that require professional judgment (Huang and Vasarhelyi, 2019). Finally, it demonstrated the viability of RPA by implementing a pilot project that applies RPA to the confirmation process (Huang and Vasarhelyi, 2019).

Table 2. RPA applications

Applications
Opening, reading and sending emails and attachments.
Automated Internet application processing: Logging into web/enterprise applications or reading\entering\deleting or changing data in any web\enterprise.
Automating data cleansing: Moving, changing or deleting files and folders.
Automatically connecting to system APIs and uploading or downloading data
Automatically running batches.
Automatically followin "if/then" decisions and rules.
Automatically extracting and reformatting data into reports or dashboards.
Automatically extracting structured data from documents, formatting any data.
Automatically collecting and analyzing social media data.
Automatically collecting and processing data from multiple data resources, working with different data types, from structured and unstructured data.
Automatically making calculations and executing tasks or jobs due to the results of these calculations.
Automatically filling in forms.
Automatically connecting, reading and, writing to databases.
Automatically generating\sending\sharing reports.
Automatically generating early-warnings.
Making auto-corrections, block or stop transactions above the limit or threshold.
Automating fraudulent account closure process and fraud chargeback processing.
Making automatic bookings in accounting.
Making auto-monitoring and auto-corrections on accounts.
Executing, changing or correcting standing order details
Executing, changing or correcting direct debit details
Executing, changing or correcting address details
Auditing, blocking or correcting transaction duplications
Automating branch risk monitoring process
Automating personal loan application opening
Payment protection insurance claims processing
Automation of the administration of payment terms
Automated support for sale of insurance products
Automated marketing campaigns
Customer complaints automation
Compliance reporting automation
Insurance product administration automation
Automated risk analysis and automated execution due to this risk analysis
Automated direct debit cancellations
Automated personal account closures
Automated payment processing
Automated business account audit requests
Automated business account on boarding
Automatically excessing transaction approvals
Automatically excessing check approvals
Automatically excessing customer letters (Deloitte, 2017; IRPA, 2015)

Font: Kaya, Turkyilmaz & Birol (2019)

Kaya, Turkyilmaz & Birol (2019) presented, in Table 2, some of the most common applications of RPA, but emphasized that one should not limit oneself to these, but rather seek applications, starting from the premise of repetitive tasks that may have a low judgment.

2.4 Technology Applied to Accounting Routines

The search for control of asset information has always been pursued by mankind, and this is how accounting came about. Its main function is to organize data and generate information through reports and analyses of companies' assets. Its purpose is to provide support for decision-making, assisting in the effective management of resources and the strategic direction of organizations (Barros, 2020).

Based on this principle, the publication of the book Summa de Arithmetica, Geometria, Proportioni et Proportionalità in 1494, by the Italian author Luca Paciolli was a major milestone for accounting science, which presented techniques aimed at commercial mathematics, highlighting the double-entry method that still guides accounting today (Bonfim, 2023). However, because this method is part of the pillars of accounting, debit and credit are the essence of bookkeeping to this day, this represents only one side of the professional's reality, which is increasingly becoming a consultant and data analyst (Bomfim, 2020).

The introduction of robotics and the internet in the last century ushered in the third stage of the industrial revolution, which applies to business in an indistinct way. In this phase, there was a major impact on accounting, changes which led to the use of technology for bookkeeping, making typewriters obsolete, since data processing was left to computers and software, allowing agility in obtaining results (Silva, 2019).

The advance of information technology has changed the techniques used by accounting professionals to account for organizations. The digital age has brought about the computerization of practices and generated efficiency in the creation of documentation (Bomfim, 2020).

Sharma (2021) points out that technology has developed rapidly in recent decades, gaining relevance for accounting and auditing due to its potential discoveries. Thus, new technologies are becoming capable of simulating human behavior and performing repetitive activities faster and more accurately than humans. In this way, robotic process automation (RPA) is one of the branches that the author points to as one of the new technologies, which uses software bots to automate business processes and tasks, especially those that are repetitive, predictable, and based on rules (Sharma, 2021).

It can be seen that over the last few years, disruptive technologies have challenged accounting and auditing to reach the next level, especially given the need for Industry 4.0 (Hasan, 2022). The author also points out that this development requires interdisciplinary collaboration, bringing AI closer to accounting and auditing (Hasan, 2022). A wider application of AI in the accounting and auditing profession is expected to provide the benefits of greater efficiency, productivity, and accuracy while burdening it with the challenges of income and wealth inequality, the extinction of traditional jobs, and an unskilled workforce (Hasan, 2022).

Hasan (2022) shows the following focus areas for the application of AI in accounting & auditing:

Table 3. Application of AI in accounting & auditing

	Application	Descritive
1	Expert Systems (ES)	Among various AI technologies applied in the realm of Accounting, the most developed one is the application of Expert Systems (ES).
2	Continuous Auditing	Continuous Auditing is a thorough electronic auditing method that allows auditors to provide some level of assurance on continuous data while it is being disclosed or shortly after it is disclosed
3	Decision Support Systems	Decision Support System (DSS) is a computer-based system that assists in the decision-making process.
4	Neural Networks (NN)	A neural network is a machine learning system that replicates the organization of a human brain (composed of neurons and connections) and is capable of altering its structure to better accomplish the task it has learned.
5	Deep learning & Machine learning	Machine learning i(ML) s about computers learning to think and act with minimal human intervention. On the other hand deep learning is a subset of ML and is about computers learning to think using architecture modeled after the human brain.
6	Natural Language Processing (NLP)	Natural language processing is a field of study that focuses on teaching artificial models to understand and process human speech (Deloitte, 2018).
7	Fuzzy Logic	Fuzzy logic, according to artificial intelligence experts, is a technique of reasoning that resembles human thinking since its methodology mimics how humans make decisions.
8	Genetic Algorithm	Genetic algorithm is a search heuristic based on Charles Darwin's theory of natural selection. This algorithm mimics natural selection, in which the fittest individuals are chosen for reproduction in order to create the following generation's children.
9	Robotic Process Automation (RPA)	According to (PwC, 2017), RPA is a type of intelligent process automation (IPA) that depicts logic-driven robots that follow pre-programmed rules and work with primarily structured data. By redefining work and reassigning individuals to higher-value tasks, RPA takes productivity optimization to the next level. Process bots can execute rudimentary human-like operations such as interpreting, deciding, acting, and learning on their own. RPA is a technology solution that uses scripts to automate rule-based and standardized tasks.
10	Hybrid Systems:	All the audit tasks are not of the same nature i.e. some involve quantitative analysis, some involve qualitative judgment whereas some may involve both. Hybrid Systems may involve combination of any of the above discussed AI technologies.

Font: Hasan (2022, p. 451-454).

The table above shows the most frequently mentioned areas of application, which, among others, include the following.

3. METHODOLOGICAL PROCEDURES

This research was exploratory and descriptive in nature, using the inductive method, a quantitative approach, and data collection through the application of questionnaires in online Google Forms®, being part on a Likert scale.

Initially, a literature review was carried out to create a framework to support the analysis of the phenomenon of robotization in accounting firms. This theoretical background helped in the process of constructing the data collection instrument. The questionnaire was designed to investigate the perceptions of Brazilian accounting professionals about the implementation of robotic process automation (RPA) in their work routines, gaining insights into how this technology is perceived and how it can impact their work. In this context, we wanted to understand their experiences, opinions, perceived benefits, and challenges faced.

The questionnaire was designed with the specific aim of being answered virtually by professionals, based on their experience in the accounting routines of these organizations in Brazil. It was aimed at accounting professionals, students, and other professionals, including trainees.

The data was collected through a survey applied during the first semester of 2024, using an accessibility sample, and was distributed through social networks such as Facebook®, LinkedIn® and Instagram®, as well as instant messaging applications, such as WhatsApp®. In all, 210 (two hundred and ten) responses were obtained, providing a solid base of data for the analysis.

The data collected was analyzed using descriptive statistics, using statistical frequencies, and cross-tabulations so that we could obtain the most accurate analyses that could express and highlight their perceptions and why.

4. PRESENTATION AND ANALYSIS OF RESULTS

This topic deals with the analysis of the data collected in the research. This chapter was divided into three topics: Block I discuss the profile of the survey respondents; Block 2 exposes the respondents' knowledge of the subject; and Block 3 discusses the professionals' perceptions of the use of RPA and its implementation in offices.

4.1 Profile of the Profession and Respondents

Table 4 shows a diagnosis of the Brazilian accounting profession by region and gender, pointing to a male predominance, which in the northern region starts at 51.42% and reaches 59.31% in the central-west, reaching its highest level. Another piece of information we can glean from this study is that in Brazil there are more than 529,000 accountants registered and qualified to work in companies of all sizes. At country level, 56.23% are male and 43.77% are female.

Table 4. The accountancy profession in Brazil

Região	Masculino	%	Feminino	%
Center West	26.549	59,31	18.217	40,69
Northeast	50.075	57,69	36.720	42,31
North	16.301	51,42	15.399	48,58
Southeast	152.537	56,22	118.793	43,78
South	52.534	55,07	42.856	44,93
Brazil	297.996	56,23	231.985	43,77

Note: Federal Accounting Council (2024)

The following tables present the profile of the respondents, listing information on gender, age, education, length of time working in the area, position held and the sector in which they work in their respective offices. Table 5 illustrates the gender distribution of 210 respondents. It is clear that there is an almost equal proportion of men and women. This almost proportional distribution is indicative of the Brazilian market, which has evolved towards this ratio on a national level, which may guarantee the representativeness and relevance of the results.

Table 5. Gender of respondents

Gender	Absolute Frequency	Relative Frequency %
Male	112	53,3%
Female	98	46,7%
Total	210	100,0%

Source: Survey data (2024)

The proportion of male and female participants in the sample may indicate an inclusive approach in the selection of respondents. This symmetry allows for comparisons and varied perspectives. It is worth noting that the sample is non-probabilistic and was acquired through accessibility, which limits the extrapolation of the data. Table 6 shows the framing data by age group, to characterize the profile of the participants. As such, the largest group was made up of those in the 31 to 40 age bracket, representing 33.33% of the sample, the largest number of participants. Second was the 41 to 50 age group with 21.9%, and third was 13.81% of respondents. Finally, 12.86% were in the 51 to 60 age bracket, showing a frequency that includes age.

Table 6. Respondents' age range

age range	Absolute Frequency	Relative Frequency %
Up to 25 years old	22	10,48%
26 to 30 years old	29	13,81%
31 to 40 years old	70	33,33%
From 41 to 50 years old	46	21,90%
From 51 to 60 years old	27	12,86%
Over 60 years old	16	7,62%
Total	210	100,0%

Source: Survey data (2024)

Table 7 shows that 41.9% of the respondents have an undergraduate degree, 36.67% are specialists, 8.57% are students, 8.57% have a master's degree and 4.29% have a doctorate. This data shows that a large part of the sample is made up of people who have finished their undergraduate degree and specialized, which indicates a level of professional training capable of working with technological actions and processes beyond their undergraduate degree. Students in the process of training experience this activity as it happens, i.e., when the changes occur.

Table 7. Respondents' level of education

level of education	Absolute Frequency	Relative Frequency %
Student	18	8,57%
Graduate	88	41,90%
Specialist or MBA	77	36,67%
Master	18	8,57%
PhD	9	4,29%
Total	210	100,0%

Source: Survey data (2024)

Respondents were asked how long they had been working in the area, in particular trying to characterize their time in the profession. 62.38% of respondents had been working for an average of 10 years or more, while 14.76% had been working for between 6 and 9 years. Followed, respectively, by those who have been working for between 3 and 5 years, with 10.95%, and 11.91% who have been working for up to 2 years.

Table 8. Respondents' length of service

length of service	Absolute Frequency	Relative Frequency %
Less than 1 year	8	3,81%
1 to 2 years	17	8,10%
3 to 5 years	23	10,95%
6 to 9 years	31	14,76%
10 years or more	131	62,38%
Total	210	100,0%

Source: Survey data (2024)

Respondents were asked what position they held in the company, and it was initially noted that the position of Supervisor accounted for 4.3% of the sample, compared to Owner (5.7%) and Accountant (7.10%). The respondents also indicated that they worked as a manager (8.1%).

Table 9. Positions occupied by respondents

Positions	Absolute Frequency	Relative Frequency %
Lawyer, Professor and Programmer*	1	0,50%
Consultant, Coordinator and Expert*	2	1,00%
Assistant	3	1,40%
Trainee	6	2,90%
Supervisor	9	4,30%
Owner	12	5,70%
Accountant	15	7,10%
Manager	17	8,10%
Assistant	24	11,40%
Analyst	33	15,70%
Director	83	39,50%
Total	210	100,0%

Note: * These positions had the same frequency
Source: Survey data (2024)

The positions shown in Table 9 represent the diversity of occupations in the accounting world and account for the majority of existing cases. In this study, the position of director accounted for 39.5% of the sample, followed by assistant with 11.4% and analyst with 15.7%. We evaluated the relationship between the position and the respondent's age. It can be seen that the 26 to 39 age group is the most recurrent in most positions, with a proportion of 11 and 13 occurrences overall.

Despite the dominance of this age group, the sample showed a balanced distribution of positions across all age groups.

The positions of directors and analysts have a significant representation in the age groups, which indicates that these positions tend to be held by more experienced professionals. In the case of self-employed and proprietors, we see that the age group of 46 and over is also predominant, showing that entrepreneurship is more present in older professionals. This concludes the profile of the sample surveyed and we characterize the respondents in order to provide the reader with this horizon for their analysis.

4.2 Knowledge of Robotic Process Automation (RPA) and Professionals' Perceptions of the Use of RPA and Its Implementation in Offices

In this chapter, we will present the results of the statements made to the participants in order to assess their knowledge of RPA. The questions consisted of statements using a Likert scale, which provides an insight into the respondents' perceptions. In this way, respondents selected the option that best reflected their familiarity, with the alternatives being "I totally agree", "I partially agree", "I totally disagree", "I partially disagree" and "I don't know how to answer".

Table 10. Knowledge of RPA versus length of time working

Length of time working		RPA (Robotic Process Automation) is programmable software that performs an activity based on established criteria.					Total
		Totally agree	Partially Agree	Strongly Disagree	Partially Disagree	Don't know Answer	
Less than a year	Counting	5	1	0	0	2	8
	Rows	62,5%	12,5%	0,0%	0,0%	25,0%	100,0%
	Columns	3,8%	1,6%	0,0%	0,0%	15,4%	3,8%
1 to 2 years	Counting	12	4	0	0	1	17
	Rows	70,6%	23,5%	0,0%	0,0%	5,9%	100,0%
	Columns	9,2%	6,3%	0,0%	0,0%	7,7%	8,1%
3 to 5 years	Counting	15	7	0	1	0	23
	Rows	65,2%	30,4%	0,0%	4,3%	0,0%	100,0%
	Columns	11,5%	10,9%	0,0%	33,3	0,0%	11,0%
6 to 9 years	Counting	19	10	0	0	2	31
	Rows	61,3%	32,3%	0,0%	0,0%	6,5%	100,0%
	Columns	14,6%	15,6%	0,0%	0,0%	15,4%	14,8%

continued on following page

Table 10. Continued

Length of time working		RPA (Robotic Process Automation) is programmable software that performs an activity based on established criteria.					Total
		Totally agree	Partially Agree	Strongly Disagree	Partially Disagree	Don't know Answer	
10 years or more	Counting	79	42	0	2	8	131
	Rows	60,3%	32,1%	0,0%	1,5%	6,1%	62,4%
	Columns	60,8%	65,6%	0,0%	66,7%	61,5%	62,4%
Total	Counting	**130**	**64**	**0**	**3**	**13**	**210**
	Rows	61,9%	30,5%	0,0%	1,4%	6,2%	100,0%
	Columns	100,0%	100,0%	0,0%	100,0%	100,0%	100,0%

Source: Survey data (2024)

Table 10 shows the respondents' level of knowledge about the concept of RPA, with the majority (61.9%) and (30.5%) saying that they totally and partially agree with the concept, respectively, regardless of the length of time they have been working. This reflects a generalized distribution of the existence of this technology among professionals. Among professionals with less than a year's experience, 30.9% were unable to say whether the concept was correct, which may indicate a lack of contact with the technology.

The findings corroborate the definitions presented by Issac, Muni & Desai, (2018) and Sharma, (2021), when they confirm RPA as "programmable software that performs an activity based on established criteria".

Table 11. The use of robots in the accounting sector versus length of time working

Length of time working		The use of robots in accounting is increasingly present in the daily lives of accounting firms and companies.					Total
		Totally agree	Partially Agree	Strongly Disagree	Partially Disagree	Don't know Answer	
Less than a year	Counting	5	2	0	0	1	8
	Rows	62,5%	25,0%	0,0%	0,0%	12,5%	100,0%
	Columns	3,8%	15,4%	0,0%	0,0%	1,6%	3,8%
1 to 2 years	Counting	12	5	0	0	0	17
	Rows	70,6%	29,4%	0,0%	0,0%	0,0%	100,0%
	Columns	8,0%	9,4%	0,0%	0,0%	0,0%	8,1%
3 to 5 years	Counting	15	6	2	0	0	23
	Rows	65,2%	26,1%	8,7%	0,0%	0,0%	100,0%
	Columns	10,0%	11,3%	50,0%	0,0%	0,0%	11,0%

continued on following page

Table 11. Continued

Length of time working			The use of robots in accounting is increasingly present in the daily lives of accounting firms and companies.					Total
			Totally agree	Partially Agree	Strongly Disagree	Partially Disagree	Don't know Answer	
6 to 9 years		Counting	26	4	0	0	1	31
		Rows	83,9%	12,9%	0,0%	0,0%	3,2%	100,0%
		Columns	17,3%	7,5%	0,0%	0,0%	50,0%	14,8%
10 years or more		Counting	92	36	1	2	0	131
		Rows	70,2%	27,5%	0,8%	1,5%	0,0%	100,0%
		Columns	61,3%	67,9%	100,0%	50,0%	0,0%	62,4%
Total		Counting	**150**	**53**	**1**	**4**	**2**	**210**
		Rows	**71,4%**	**25,2%**	**0,5%**	**1,9%**	**1,0%**	**100,0%**
		Columns	**100,0%**	**100,0%**	**100,0%**	**100,0%**	**100,0%**	**100,0%**

Source: Survey data (2024)

In Table 12, we can see the relationship between length of service and the affirmation of growth in the use of RPA in accounting firms. The majority of respondents (96.6%) say they totally agree with the growth in the use of robots in the accounting environment, which indicates significant adherence or acceptance on the part of the professionals interviewed. The findings in Table 3 are similar to the statements by Huang and Vasarhelyi (2019), when they point to consolidated use in accounting firms and now its advancement in auditing.

Table 12. Use of robots in the accounting environment versus the use of robots brings efficiency to activities

			\multicolumn{6}{c}{The use of robots in the accounting routine brings efficiency to the reproduction of activities.}
			Totally agree	Partially Agree	Strongly Disagree	Partially Disagree	Don't know Answer	Total
The use of robots in accounting is increasingly present in the daily lives of accounting firms and companies.	Totally agree	Counting	125	24	0	0	1	150
		Rows	83,3%	16,0%	0,0%	0,0%	0,7%	100,0%
		Columns	86,8%	40,7%	0,0%	0,0%	25,0%	71,4%
	Partially Agree	Counting	18	32	3	0	0	53
		Rows	34,0%	60,4%	5,7%	0,0%	0,0%	100,0%
		Columns	12,5%	54,2%	100,0%	0,0%	0,0%	25,2%
	Strongly Disagree	Counting	0	2	0	0	2	4
		Rows	0%	50,0%	0%	0,0%	50,0%	100,0%
		Columns	0%	3,4%	0%	0,0%	50,0%	1,9%
	Partially Disagree	Counting	0	1	0	0	0	1
		Rows	0%	100,0%	0,0%	0,0%	0%	100,0%
		Columns	0%	1,7%	0,0%	0,0%	0%	0,5%
	Don't know Answer	Counting	1	0	0	0	1	2
		Rows	50,0%	0,0%	0,0%	0,0%	50,0%	100,0%
		Columns	0,7%	0,0%	0,0%	0,0%	25,0%	1,0%
	Total	Counting	144	59	3	0	4	210
		Rows	68,6%	28,1%	1,4%	0,0%	1,9%	100,0%
		Columns	100,0%	100,0%	100,0%	0,0%	100,0%	100,0%

Source: Survey data (2024)

In table 13, we compare the view of the use of robots and their contribution to bringing efficiency to the accounting process. We can see that the relationship between the two variables shows a high level of agreement and that accounting firms have a vision of the presence of robotization and its positive impact. The majority of respondents (96.7%) stated that they totally and partially agree with the use of robots, compared to 96.6% who totally and partially agree with the growth in the use of robots in the accounting environment, which indicates significant adherence or acceptance on the part of the professionals interviewed.

It can be seen that the majority of professionals partially agree (49%) with the statement, which indicates the need for prior IT/computer knowledge. On the other hand, 69% of respondents stated that their offices use RPA. Overall, the data shows that a large proportion of respondents have observed a growing implementation of robots in their offices.

Table 13. Use x applicability

<table>
<tr><th colspan="3"></th><th colspan="6">In order to use RPA (Robotic Process Automation), prior knowledge of IT/computing is required.</th></tr>
<tr><th colspan="3"></th><th>Totally agree</th><th>Partially Agree</th><th>Strongly Disagree</th><th>Partially Disagree</th><th>Don't know Answer</th><th>Total</th></tr>
<tr><td rowspan="9">Is RPA used in the office where you work?</td><td rowspan="3">No</td><td>Counting</td><td>18</td><td>33</td><td>4</td><td>1</td><td>2</td><td>58</td></tr>
<tr><td>Rows</td><td>31,0%</td><td>56,9%</td><td>6,9%</td><td>1,7%</td><td>3,4%</td><td>100,0%</td></tr>
<tr><td>Columns</td><td>35,3%</td><td>32,0%</td><td>9,1%</td><td>10,0%</td><td>100,00%</td><td>27,6%</td></tr>
<tr><td rowspan="3">I don't know</td><td>Counting</td><td>4</td><td>2</td><td>1</td><td>0</td><td>0</td><td>7</td></tr>
<tr><td>Rows</td><td>57,1%</td><td>28,6%</td><td>14,3%</td><td>0,0%</td><td>0,0%</td><td>100,0%</td></tr>
<tr><td>Columns</td><td>7,8%</td><td>1,9%</td><td>2,3%</td><td>0,0%</td><td>0,0%</td><td>3,3%</td></tr>
<tr><td rowspan="3">Yes</td><td>Counting</td><td>29</td><td>68</td><td>39</td><td>9</td><td>0</td><td>145</td></tr>
<tr><td>Rows</td><td>20,0%</td><td>46,9%</td><td>26,9%</td><td>6,2%</td><td>0,0%</td><td>100,0%</td></tr>
<tr><td>Columns</td><td>56,9%</td><td>66,00%</td><td>88,6%</td><td>90,0%</td><td>0,0%</td><td>69,0%</td></tr>
<tr><td colspan="2" rowspan="3">Total</td><td>Counting</td><td>51</td><td>103</td><td>44</td><td>10</td><td>2</td><td>210</td></tr>
<tr><td>Rows</td><td>24,3%</td><td>49,0%</td><td>21,0%</td><td>4,8%</td><td>1,0%</td><td>100,0%</td></tr>
<tr><td>Columns</td><td>100,0%</td><td>100,0%</td><td>100,0%</td><td>100,0%</td><td>100,0%</td><td>100,0%</td></tr>
</table>

Source: Survey data (2024)

Table 14 shows the cross-reference between the statement about the use of robots for efficiency and the application of RPA in the office where the respondent works. The majority of respondents, around 69%, said that RPA is implemented in the office where they work. Among the respondents, 68.6% partially agree and 28.1% totally agree that the use of robots in the accounting routine brings efficiency to the reproduction of activities.

Table 14. Use x efficiency

<table>
<tr><th colspan="3" rowspan="2">RPA in the work</th><th colspan="5">The use of robots in the accounting routine brings efficiency to the reproduction of activities.</th></tr>
<tr><th>Totally agree</th><th>Partially Agree</th><th>Strongly Disagree</th><th>Don't know Answer</th><th>Total</th></tr>
<tr><td rowspan="9">Is RPA used in the office where you work?</td><td rowspan="3">No</td><td>Counting</td><td>19</td><td>33</td><td>3</td><td>3</td><td>58</td></tr>
<tr><td>Rows</td><td>32,8%</td><td>56,9%</td><td>5,2%</td><td>5,2%</td><td>100,0%</td></tr>
<tr><td>Columns</td><td>13,2%</td><td>55,9%</td><td>100,0%</td><td>75,0%</td><td>27,6%</td></tr>
<tr><td rowspan="3">I don't know</td><td>Counting</td><td>7</td><td>0</td><td>0</td><td>0</td><td>7</td></tr>
<tr><td>Rows</td><td>100,0%</td><td>0,0%</td><td>0,0%</td><td>0,0%</td><td>100,0%</td></tr>
<tr><td>Columns</td><td>4,9%</td><td>0,0%</td><td>0,0%</td><td>0,0%</td><td>3,3%</td></tr>
<tr><td rowspan="3">Yes</td><td>Counting</td><td>118</td><td>26</td><td>0</td><td>1</td><td>145</td></tr>
<tr><td>Rows</td><td>81,4%</td><td>17,9%</td><td>0,0%</td><td>0,7%</td><td>100,0%</td></tr>
<tr><td>Columns</td><td>81,9%</td><td>44,1%</td><td>0,0%</td><td>25,0%</td><td>69,0%</td></tr>
</table>

continued on following page

Table 14. Continued

RPA in the work			The use of robots in the accounting routine brings efficiency to the reproduction of activities.				Total
			Totally agree	Partially Agree	Strongly Disagree	Don't know Answer	
	Total	Counting	59	144	3	4	210
		Rows	28,1%	68,6%	1,4%	1,9%	100,0%
		Columns	100,0%	100,0%	100,0%	100,0%	100,0%

Source: Survey data (2024)

Table 15 shows the cross-reference between the statement about the use of RPA in the office where the respondent works and perceived efficiency. The majority of respondents, around 81.5%, said that RPA is implemented in the office where they work. Among the respondents, 18.5%, 28.1% and 35.4%, representing the choices of agree, partially agree and totally agree, respectively, that the use of robots in the accounting routine brings efficiency to the reproduction of activities. In this question, 32 respondents did not answer because they do not work in an office that uses RPA.

Table 15. Effectiveness of RPA in automating tasks

Is RPA used in the office where you work?		If you or your office uses RPA, please answer: On a scale of 1 to 7, how would you rate the effectiveness of RPA (Robotic Process Automation) in automating tasks?							Total
		1	2	3	4	5	6	7	Total
No	Counting	5	2	2	7	4	3	5	28
	Rows	17,9%	7,1%	7,1%	25,0%	14,3%	10,7%	17,9%	100,0%
	Columns	83,3%	66,7%	50,0%	36,8%	12,1%	6,0%	7,9%	15,7%
I don't know	Counting	0	0	0	0	1	0	4	5
	Rows	0,0%	0,0%	0,0%	0,0%	20,0%	0,0%	80,0%	100,0%
	Columns	0,0%	0,0%	0,0%	0,0%	3,0%	0,0%	6,3%	2,8%
Yes	Counting	1	1	2	12	28	47	54	145
	Rows	0,7%	0,7%	1,4%	8,3%	19,3%	32,4%	37,2%	100,0%
	Columns	16,7%	33,3%	50,0%	63,2%	84,8%	94,0%	85,7%	81,5%
Overall Total	Counting	6	3	4	19	33	50	63	178
	Rows	3,4%	1,7%	2,2%	10,7%	18,5%	28,1%	35,4%	100,0%
	Columns	100,0%	100,0%	100,0%	100,0%	100,0%	100,0%	100,0%	100,0%
Lack of response due to not filing a report in an office that uses RPA									32

Source: Survey data (2024)

Table 16 sought to assess the impact of RPA on reducing errors in your firm's accounting processes. In this sense, respondents were asked to give their opinion on what contribution RPA (Robotic Process Automation) would make to improving operational efficiency in the accounting office? This evaluation resulted in a total of 67.2% partially or totally agreeing with this statement. Indicating a possible motivator for its implementation in accounting firms.

Table 16. Evaluation of the impact of RPA on reducing errors in accounting processes

Valid	Frequency	Percentage	Valid percentage	Cumulative percentage
1 (Strongly disagree)	2	1,0%	1,0%	1,0%
2 (Disagree)	2	1,0%	1,0%	2,1%
3 (More disagree than agree)	7	3,3%	3,6%	5,7%
4 (Indifferent)	15	7,1%	7,8%	13,5%
5 (More agree than disagree)	37	17,6%	19,3%	32,8%
6 (Partially agree)	67	31,9%	34,9%	67,7%
7 (Totally agree)	62	29,5%	32,3%	100,00%
Sub-total	182	91,4%		
Missing	18	8,6%		
Total	210	100,00%		

Source: Survey data (2024)

Table 17 shows the respondents' assessment of how easy it is to implement Robotic Process Automation in task automation. Among the respondents, the majority (31.9%) rated its ease at 5, i.e. they agree rather than disagree, but a further 16.7% and 18.1%, respectively, opted for 6 or 7, demonstrating a positive perception of the ease of RPA and thus choose to carry out the automation of activities satisfactorily.

Table 17. Ease of implementing RPA in the accounting office

Valid	Frequency	Percentage	Valid percentage	Cumulative percentage
1 (Strongly disagree)	3	1,4%	1,4%	1,4%
2 (Disagree)	9	4,3%	4,3%	5,7%
3 (More disagree than agree)	12	5,7%	5,7%	11,4%
4 (Indifferent)	46	21,9%	21,9%	33,3%
5 (More agree than disagree)	67	31,9%	31,9%	65,2%
6 (Partially agree)	35	16,7%	16,7%	81,9%
7 (Totally agree)	38	18,1%	18,1%	100,00%
Total	210	100,00%		

Source: Survey data (2024)

As for maximizing time for accounting professionals, we can see from table 18 that 73.4% of those surveyed gave a rating of 6 or 7, generating a positive result for this question. While (15.8%) rated it 5, not considering, although still agreeing, that the implementation has brought significant results in reducing obstacles and maximizing time for professionals. Overall, the data reveals a positive trend in the implementation, generating an optimization of activities.

Table 18. RPA has helped optimize time

Valid	Frequency	Percentage	Valid percentage	Cumulative percentage
1 (Strongly disagree)	2	1,0%	1,0%	1,0%
2 (Disagree)	1	0,5%	0,5%	1,4%
3 (More disagree than agree)	5	2,4%	2,4%	3,8%
4 (Indifferent)	14	6,7%	6,7%	10,5%
5 (More agree than disagree)	33	15,7%	15,8%	26,3%
6 (Partially agree)	69	32,9%	33,0%	59,3%
7 (Totally agree)	85	40,5%	40,7%	100,00%
Sub-total	209	95,5%		
Missing	1	0,5%		
Total	210	100,00%		

Source: Survey data (2024)

Thus, in relation to the implementation of RPA, only 3.8% classified this activity as not being able to help with optimization, creating difficulties. This data indicates that the main reason for non-adherence is not exclusively due to difficulties in implementation, but may be due to other variables. It can be concluded that those surveyed recognize the importance of using RPA to optimize time, allowing professionals to carry out other activities that cannot be done on a scheduled basis.

5. FINAL CONSIDERATIONS

The main objective of this research was to investigate the perceptions of Brazilian accounting professionals about the implementation of robotic process automation (RPA) in their work routines. In the course of the analysis, insights were gained into how this technology is perceived and how it has impacted the work of these professionals. It was possible to carry out a comparative analysis of the perceptions of accounting professionals regarding the adoption of RPA in their daily activities, considering it a strategic tool for optimizing time and expanding enterprises.

It was hoped that this study would contribute to improving the exploratory diagnosis, reinforcing existing knowledge about the benefits and challenges related to the implementation of APR in Brazilian accounting firms. From this study, it is possible to provide valuable insights and the information needed to devise increasingly effective strategies that can facilitate and improve the use of automation tools in the accounting field.

It can be seen that a significant proportion of offices (28.5%) have not yet adopted the use of robots in their operations, which raises important questions about the reasons behind this choice. This opens up a wide range of questions relating to possible technical, financial, or capacity difficulties that may be preventing these offices from pursuing this form of optimization. It was noted during the investigation that some professionals have limited knowledge of automation processes, although they recognize their potential to facilitate their activities.

On the other hand, there are those who believe it is necessary to have prior knowledge in areas such as IT to use this tool effectively. These findings highlight the importance of greater understanding and awareness of the capabilities and benefits of automation, as well as the need to offer adequate support and training to professionals who wish to adopt this technology.

It is concluded that RPA allows for the automation of repetitive tasks, providing time for accounting professionals to focus on more strategic and complex activities. According to the research, adoption can increase the office's operational efficiency, reducing the time spent on manual processes. It could reduce the occurrence of human errors, which are common in repetitive tasks, resulting in higher-quality deliveries, as well as eliminate manpower in these activities, which could also reduce the operating expenses of these organizations.

It is important to point out that throughout the study, there were limitations in terms of research into RPA in Portuguese or even in Brazil. This limitation had an impact on the national base, and international data were sought, exploring complementary data in relation to the application of the questionnaire. As a suggestion, one way forward could be to expand the study to include other respondents in other countries.

REFERENCES

Anagnoste, S. 2017. Robotic automation process: The next major revolution in terms of back office operations improvement. *Proceedings of the International Conference on Business Excellence, 11*(1), 676–86. DOI: 10.1515/picbe-2017-0072

Barros, V. D. M. (2005). O novo velho enfoque da informação contábil. *Revista Contabilidade & Finanças*, 16(38), 102–112. DOI: 10.1590/S1519-70772005000200009

Bomfim, V. C. (2020). Os avanços tecnológicos e o perfil do contador frente à era digital. *Revista Trevisan*, 18(173), 60.

Bonfim, M. P. (2023). A Contabilidade nas instituições Católicas nos Séculos XVII e XVIII. *Revista de Contabilidade da UFBA*, 17(1), e2319–e2319. DOI: 10.9771/rcufba.v17i1.49372

Braga, N. C. L.; Colares, A. C. V.(2020) Contabilidade digital: os desafios do profissional

Cohen, M., Rozario, A., & Zhang, C. (2019). Exploring the use of robotic process automation (RPA) in substantive audit procedures: Certified public accountant. *The CPA Journal*, 89(7), 49–53.

Cooper, L. A., Holderness, D. K.Jr, Sorensen, T. L., & Wood, D. A. (2019). Robotic process automation in public accounting. *Accounting Horizons*, 33(4), 15–35. DOI: 10.2308/acch-52466

da Silva, C. G., Eyerkaufer, M. L., & Rengel, R. (2019). Inovação tecnológica e os desafios para uma contabilidade interativa: estudo dos escritórios de contabilidade do estado de santa Catarina. Revista Destaques Acadêmicos, 11(1).

Feng, J. (2015). Cloud Accounting: The Transition of Accounting Information Model in the Big Data Background. *2015 International Conference on Intelligent Transportation, Big Data & Smart City (ICITBS)*, 207-211. DOI: 10.1109/ICITBS.2015.58

Ferreira, T. T. (2022). Evolução da contabilidade digital e seus desafios.

Gotthardt, M., Koivulaakso, D., Paksoy, O., Saramo, C., Martikainen, M., & Lehner, O. (2020). *Current state and challenges in the implementation of smart robotic process automation in accounting and auditing*. ACRN Journal of Finance and Risk Perspectives. DOI: 10.35944/jofrp.2020.9.1.007

Hasan, A. R. (2022). Artificial Intelligence (AI) in Accounting & Auditing: A Literature Review. *Open Journal of Business and Management*, 10(1), 440–465. DOI: 10.4236/ojbm.2022.101026

Huang, F., & Vasarhelyi, M. A. (2019). Applying robotic process automation (RPA) in auditing: A framework. *International Journal of Accounting Information Systems*, 35, 100433. DOI: 10.1016/j.accinf.2019.100433

Issac, R., Muni, R., & Desai, K. (2018, February). Delineated analysis of robotic process automation tools. In *2018 Second International Conference on Advances in Electronics, Computers and Communications (ICAECC)* (pp. 1-5). IEEE. DOI: 10.1109/ICAECC.2018.8479511

Kaya, C. T., Turkyilmaz, M., & Birol, B. (2019). Impact of RPA technologies on accounting systems. *Muhasebe ve Finansman Dergisi*, 82, 235–250. DOI: 10.25095/mufad.536083

Kokina, J., & Blanchette, S. (2019). Early evidence of digital labor in accounting: Innovation with Robotic Process Automation. *International Journal of Accounting Information Systems*, 35, 100431. DOI: 10.1016/j.accinf.2019.100431

Lopes, C. A. R. (2020). Automatização robótica de processos financeiros-automatização de processos financeiros SAP pela introdução de RPA (Doctoral dissertation).

Moffitt, K. C., Rozario, A. M., & Vasarhelyi, M. A. (2018). Robotic process automation for auditing. *Journal of Emerging Technologies in Accounting*, 15(1), 1–10. DOI: 10.2308/jeta-10589

Oliveira, E. D. (2019). Impacto do uso da inteligência artificial em sistemas de gestão empresarial no exercício da profissão contábil.

Pauleski, R. K. (2023). Impactos da inteligência artificial no trabalho do profissional que atua em escritório de contabilidade: um estudo de caso.

Pedras, S. R. G. (2020). Implementação do Robotic Process Automation em Pequenos Escritórios de Contabilidade: um Estudo Exploratório.

Scheifler, T., Faiz, E. B., Ludwig, J. P., & Drege, A. A. (2016). Automação como meio para aumento de produtividade e competitividade–Estudo de caso. Revista ESPACIOS, 37(28).

Sharma, R. (2021, October - December). A study of adoption & impact of robotic process automation in accounting and auditing. *International Journal of Innovations & Research Analysis*, 01(03), 31–36.

Taulli, T. (2020). The robotic process automation handbook. The Robotic Process Automation Handbook. https://doi. Org/10.1007/978-1-4842-5729-6

Tiron-Tudor, A., Lacurezeanu, R., Bresfelean, V. P., & Dontu, A. N. (2024). Perspectives on How Robotic Process Automation Is Transforming Accounting and Auditing Services. *Accounting Perspectives*, 23(1), 7–38. DOI: 10.1111/1911-3838.12351

Yoon, S. (2020). A study on the transformation of accounting based on new technologies: Evidence from Korea. *Sustainability (Basel)*, 12(20), 8669. DOI: 10.3390/su12208669

Chapter 5
Digitalization of Financial Reporting:
Its Role in Improving Corporate Efficiency and Transparency

María-Pilar Martín-Zamora
University of Huelva, Spain

João Miguel Capela Borralho
https://orcid.org/0000-0003-2860-0692
University Lusófona, Portugal

ABSTRACT

Digitalized financial processes are redefining 21st-century business landscapes. One area that has undergone significant transformation is financial reporting, which involves the preparation and presentation of essential reports that enhance strategic decision making and regulatory compliance. Automation and data processing play a crucial role in this context by enhancing the efficiency, accuracy, and transparency of the reports generated. This chapter explores in detail how advances in these two areas of digitalization are revolutionizing financial reporting and then analyzes the relevant technologies and their benefits and challenges, as well as best practices for their implementation. Regulatory guidelines are also examined in terms of their implications and future trends in digital financial reporting.

DOI: 10.4018/979-8-3693-5923-5.ch005

1. INTRODUCTION

Digital transformation has had a profound impact on the business world, producing "a change in how a firm employs digital technologies to develop a new digital business model that helps to create an appropriate . . . [added] value for the firm" (Schallmo et al., 2017; Verhoef et al., 2021). In this context, a substantial shift has been detected in consumers and other stakeholders' expectations and behaviors (Paul et al., 2024; Plekanov et al., 2023). Traditional companies are thus under increasing pressure to redesign their products, processes, and strategies (Kraus et al., 2022; Verhoef et al., 2021).

To avoid losing their market position (Saarikko et al., 2020; Tekic & Kiriteev, 2019), firms have been compelled to examine and reinvent most areas of their operations (Fernández-Vidal et al., 2019; Schiuma et al., 2021). This process includes supply chains and workflows (Aamer et al., 2023; Guo et al., 2023), employee skills (Schwarzmüller et al., 2018; Vuchkovski et al., 2023), interactions with stakeholders (Brunetti et al., 2020; Prebanić & Vukomanović, 2021), and information disclosure (Lombardi & Secundo, 2021). In the latter area, digitalization has not only significantly impacted the methods used to prepare information (Berikol & Killi, 2021; Gonçalves et al., 2022) but also the type of data made public (Lombardi & Secundo, 2021; Salvi et al., 2021) and the modes by which they become available to stakeholders (Bhimani & Willcocks, 2014; Pratama et al., 2023).

The literature on the preparation of accounting information highlights the changes in accounting driven by technological advances (Hasan, 2021; Leitner-Hanetseder et al., 2021). This transformation has specifically materialized as task automation (Eziefuele et al., 2022; Korhonen et al., 2021), improved accuracy (Fullana & Ruiz, 2021; Gonçalves et al., 2022), and the provision of real-time information (Manita et al., 2020). The digital revolution has had significant benefits for accounting (Agostino et al., 2022; Cagle, 2020; Kusumawardhani et al., 2024) as it saves time (Gonçalves et al., 2022) and resources (Gonçalves et al., 2022) and improves cash flow management (Avira et al., 2023) by automating billing procedures and payment management (Hofbauer & Sangl, 2019; Ulas, 2019).

However, significant challenges must be overcome before these advantages are obtained (Abhishek et al., 2024). Information security is probably the most significant issue (Gebremeskel et al., 2023) since digitalization and automated systems have increased organizations' exposure to cyber risks (Luo, 2022; Pandey et al., 2020), such as cyberattacks and fraud. Companies have been compelled to implement robust cybersecurity measures to protect the integrity and confidentiality of their financial data (Pansara, 2022), which requires continuous investment in technology and staff training (Furnell et al., 2017; He & Zhang, 2019).

A second challenge is the integration of old systems into new ones (Hoe, 2019; Urbach et al., 2019) as many firms still rely on traditional accounting tools that are incompatible with new digital technologies. The rapid pace of technological evolution also demands constant updates of accounting professionals' skills (Taib et al., 2022). These individuals must acquire competencies in areas such as data analysis and specialized software management, which implies ongoing training and thus a cultural shift within the accounting profession (Coman et al., 2022).

Communication with different users of accounting information is one of the many accounting tasks significantly affected by digitalization (Coman et al., 2022; Gulin et al., 2019). Company–client communication is generally carried out through the disclosure of reports (Adelberg, 1979; Merkl-Davies & Brennan, 2017). Firms seek to maintain and gain new competitive advantages (Leão & da Silva, 2021) by fulfilling their obligation to provide accounting information (Gordon et al., 2010; Lobschat et al., 2021). Companies also undergo digital transformation to broaden the range of their information (Kraus et al., 2021) and means of communication (Lombardi & Secundo, 2021).

This chapter explores the above scenario with the primary objective of analyzing how the digital revolution is affecting financial reporting and of highlighting what impact these changes have had on efficiency (Gupta et al., 2023) and organizations' transparency (Nicollaou, 2010). Technological innovations in accounting information are always accompanied by significant changes in regulations (Abhishek et al., 2024; Micheler & Whaley, 2020), so the main findings on this topic are also reviewed. The chapter ends by identifying the obstacles to the digital revolution of all accounting processes, as well as the trends in communication approaches in accounting that digitalization has triggered.

The remainder of this chapter is thus structured into four sections. The next section describes the scope of the digitalization of financial reporting from the perspective of corporate efficiency and transparency and analyzes the advantages derived from this process. The third section reviews the benefits of and obstacles to digital financial reporting. The fourth section discusses the changes made to financial report regulations due to this digital transformation. The fifth section and the conclusion present the implications and future trends in the digitalization of business information disclosure.

2. IMPROVING CORPORATE EFFICIENCY AND TRANSPARENCY THROUGH DIGITALIZATION OF FINANCIAL REPORTING

Digitalized financial reporting has emerged as crucial to the modernization and optimization of business processes (Chyzhevska et al., 2021; Tuan et al., 2021). Organizations exist in an increasingly competitive and regulated global environment, so they are constantly seeking ways to improve operational efficiency and enhance transparency (Ramírez & Tejada, 2018). The financial sector has adopted digital technologies to meet these needs (Gupta et al., 2023), thereby driving a profound transformation in how companies manage and communicate their financial information (Berikol & Killi, 2021; Bhimani & Willcocks, 2014), which has increased corporate efficiency and transparency.

2.1 Contribution of Digitalization to Corporate Efficiency

Efficient financial processes are a primary objective for all organizations (Arvelo et al., 2021; Handoyo et al., 2023) as these directly affect their profitability and responsiveness to the market (Arbelo et al., 2021). The digitalization of financial reporting significantly contributes to meeting this goal by automating routine tasks, integrating systems, and optimizing workflow (Broccardo et al., 2023).

The automation of financial processes is not a new concept, but the pace of its evolution has become much faster with the advent of digitalization and emerging technologies (Gulin et al., 2019; Kroon et al., 2021) such as artificial intelligence (AI), machine learning, and advanced analytics. These technologies have automated tasks that previously required significant human intervention (Jain & Ranjan, 2020; Rodríguez-Espíndola et al., 2022) including, among others, data entry, account reconciliation, and the generation of financial reports.

In its early stages, financial reporting automation was limited to the use of spreadsheets and basic accounting software (KPMG, 2019; Odonkor et al., 2024). These tools allowed firms to handle large volumes of financial data more efficiently than they had with traditional manual methods (Harrast, 2020; Wilson & Sangster, 1992). Although the new systems increased processing speed and reduced errors, their capacity to process and analyze data was limited (Odonkor et al., 2024).

The evolution toward more advanced tools began with the integration of enterprise resource planning (ERP) (Goldston, 2020), which allowed organizations to amalgamate their financial and operational data into a single system (AlMuhayfith & Shaiti, 2020; Suhaimi et al., 2016). Over time, digital platforms have further automated functions such as double-entry accounting, account reconciliation, and financial report production (Salim & Ferran, 2008).

More recently, AI and machine learning technologies have been incorporated to enable greater automation (Cho et al., 2020; Chowdhury, 2023; Hasan, 2021). These tools can both execute repetitive tasks (Adeyelu et al., 2024) and learn and adapt to data patterns (Odonkor et al., 2024), thereby allowing for smarter and more efficient automation (Adeyelu et al., 2024).

2.1.1 Intelligent Automation in Financial Reporting

Intelligent automation comprises integrating advanced technologies that computerize complex processes in financial reporting (Coombs et al., 2020). These tools automate everything from data extraction from financial documents (Jejeniwa et al., 2024) to predictive analysis (Bose et al., 2023) and the real-time generation of reports (Soori et al., 2023). Intelligent automation minimizes errors and improves efficiency (Al Najjar et al., 2024), as well as extracting valuable insights that facilitate strategic decision making (Antwi et al., 2024).

Therefore, one of the main benefits of digitalization is the automation of tasks that previously required manual intervention (Coombs et al., 2020), such as data entry, account reconciliation, and financial report creation. These activities were traditionally time- and labor-intensive, but they now can be executed more quickly and accurately through automated systems (Ayinla et al., 2024). The reduction of human errors is another key benefit (Yarmoliuk et al., 2024) because digital systems minimize the likelihood of mistakes that could have costly consequences for companies (Barchard & Pace, 2011).

In addition, automation frees up resources and redirects them toward higher-value activities (Ajayi-Nifise et al., 2024), for example, financial analysis and strategic decision making. In this way, firms not only optimize their daily operations but also enhance their ability to respond to changes in business environments (Wang et al., 2022).

In summary, data processing involves the collection, manipulation, and analysis of accounting and financial data to generate accurate, timely reports that comply with current regulations (Bose et al., 2022). Digitalization has made these procedures quicker and more accurate (Sujová et al., 2019) by using big data, data mining, and data analytics (Ahmed et al., 2022). For instance, the Oracle ERP cloud has increased organizations' efficiency and, as a result, their performance, contributing to cost reduction without requiring significant investment in infrastructure (Faccia & Petratos, 2021). Similarly, ChatGPT is an advanced natural language processing (NLP) model based on Generative Pre-trained Transformer 4 architecture, which demonstrates an exceptional ability to understand, interpret, and produce human-like writing. This tool can also remodel various accounting processes by automating repetitive tasks and thus improving financial and management reports and analyses (Zhao & Wang, 2024).

2.1.2 Systems and Data Integration

Digitalization facilitates the integration of various systems and data sources into a single cohesive platform (Hund et al., 2021). This transformation is especially important in large organizations whose financial data are generated across multiple departments and locations (Ritter & Pedersen, 2020). By centralizing their financial information, companies can reduce data redundancy, avoid inconsistencies, and improve the overall quality of information available for decision making (Bai et al., 2012).

Firms also need to integrate financial data with other types of data, such as operational or market data, in order to gain a more holistic view of their business performance (Abdul-Azeez et al., 2024). This integration improves operational efficiency and provides a solid foundation for deeper and more strategic analysis (Nik Abdullah et al., 2022). Digitalization enables the automatic extraction of data from varied sources (i.e., ERP systems, external databases, and social networks) that provide both traditional financial and non-financial information (Abhishek et al., 2024) that is increasingly important to decision makers (Avira et al., 2023). For example, big data tools allow the efficient handling and processing of large volumes of information (Almeida, 2017), thereby facilitating the gathering of data that are difficult to manage manually (Elgendy & Elragal, 2016).

Once the information is collected, it must be cleaned and prepared for analysis (Sivarajah et al., 2017) by removing duplicates, correcting errors, and normalizing the format (Aldoseri et al., 2023). At this stage, the role of algorithms becomes especially valuable as they can identify and correct mistakes without human intervention (Soori et al., 2023).

Data analysis thus emerges as a key component in the digitalization of information (Ritter & Pedersen, 2020). Technologies are used, such as data mining and analytics, to uncover patterns, trends, and relationships in the data that are not immediately apparent (Qatawneh, 2022). Predictive analysis is especially essential for planning and budgeting—and prescriptive analysis—to optimize financial decisions.

2.1.3 Real-Time Access to Information

The generation of reports is the final step in financial data processing (Tiwari & Khan, 2020). The digitalization of financial reporting enables real-time access to accurate compliance information (Manita et al., 2020), which is essential in dynamic business environments (JieWei et al., 2023). Digital systems can collect, process, and present data instantly (Riter & Pedersen, 2020), thereby allowing managers to make decisions based on the most up-to-date information available (Tagscherer & Carbon, 2023). Immediate access to data is also important in risk management (Rodríguez-Espíndola et al., 2022) as a way to identify and mitigate potential issues proactively (Ajayi-Nifise et al., 2024).

Digitalization also allows reports to be customized to meet different stakeholders' specific needs (Martínez-Peláez et al., 2023). Understanding financial information is additionally made easier by integrating data visualization tools, such as interactive dashboards. These technologies enable users to explore the data more deeply and gain valuable insights when making decisions (Khatri & Gupta, 2022).

2.2 Contribution of Digitalization to Corporate Transparency

Besides the benefits in terms of efficiency, corporate transparency is greatly improved by digitalized financial reporting (Gao, 2023). Transparency is a fundamental factor in maintaining the trust of investors, regulators, and other stakeholders (Schnackenberg & Tomlinson, 2016). Digitalization contributes to transparency by facilitating the disclosure of accurate, timely, and accessible information (Calderon-Monge & Ribeiro-Soriano, 2024).

Digitalizing procedures enhances the transparency of financial reporting by making detailed records of all transactions accessible (Abhishek et al., 2024). This availability strengthens confidence in the disclosed information (Pratama et al., 2023) and enables clearer and more precise communication with varied stakeholders (Kraus et al., 2021). Transparency is especially significant when trust and corporate reputation are crucial assets in business environments (Liu et al., 2023). More transparent companies are considered more trustworthy and accountable (Liu et al., 2023), which improves their reputation and relationships with stakeholders (Schnackenberg & Tomlinson, 2016).

2.2.1 Accurate and Consistent Information

As mentioned previously, the digitalization of accounting information significantly reduces errors in financial reports (Abhishek et al., 2024), thereby making the disclosed information more accurate and consistent (Salvi et al., 2021). Digital systems perform automatic checks and cross-reference data to ensure that accounting data are consistent and accurate before being disclosed (Han et al., 2023). Accuracy is essential to maintain shareholder trust (Schnackenberg & Tomlinson, 2016) and comply with current regulations (Urefe et al., 2024).

In addition, integrating technologies such as machine learning allows companies to detect anomalies and mistakes in their information (Alsoufi et al., 2021). These tools thus enhance the accuracy of the information disclosed (Nassif et al., 2021).

2.2.2 Transparency in Information Disclosure

Digitalization facilitates transparency by helping firms disclose clearer and more accessible data (Kraus et al., 2021). Financial reports can be distributed electronically to a broader audience, including investors, regulators, and other stakeholders (Han et al., 2023). Digital platforms also present information in interactive formats (Dilla et al., 2010) that ensure users can understand and analyze the data (JieWei et al., 2023).

The use of technologies (e.g., blockchain) further enhances transparency by providing an immutable, verifiable record of all transactions (Han et al., 2023). This information not only increases trust in the disclosed data (Secinaro et al., 2021) but also simplifies account auditing and regulatory compliance (Bakhshi & Ghita, 2021).

2.2.3 Regulatory Compliance and Auditing

The digitalization of financial reporting also increases transparency in terms of compliance information (Gao, 2023). Regulations have become increasingly complex and stringent, so legal compliance has become a constant challenge (Ameyaw et al., 2024). Digital systems incorporate automated controls that ensure all procedures and reports comply with current regulations (Jejeniwa et al., 2024).

Digitalized data also simplify the audit process by providing easier access (Lois et al., 2020), which in turn reduces the risk of non-compliance and the associated penalties (Abhishek et al., 2024). Technologies such as AI and machine learning can analyze large volumes of financial information to detect patterns and anomalies (Pattnaik et al., 2024), thereby identifying potential fraud or irregularities more efficiently than traditional methods do (Hilal et al., 2022) and ultimately improving transparency. Blockchain technology similarly facilitates regulatory compliance by providing transparent, permanent records of transactions (Dong et al., 2023) that can be easily verified by auditors and regulators.

2.3 Key Technologies Enhancing Corporate Efficiency and Transparency Through Digitalization of Financial Reporting

Digitalized financial reporting is gaining significant momentum thanks to a variety of advanced technologies including AI, machine learning, big data, robotic process automation, and blockchain, among others. AI and machine learning provide smarter and more adaptable reporting automation (Odonkor et al., 2024). More specifically, AI can analyze large volumes of data to identify patterns and make predictions (Soori et al., 2023), while machine learning allows systems to learn from past information and improve their accuracy over time (Sarker, 2021). For instance, machine learning algorithms can detect anomalies in accounting data (Ashtiani & Raahemi, 2021), which helps prevent fraud and ensure regulatory compliance. Concurrently, AI can automatically generate reports (Hasan, 2021) and use NLP to interpret and present information in ways that are easy to understand (Kang et al., 2020).

In the context of financial reporting, companies use big data to integrate information from various sources, such as financial, operational, and market data, in order to gain a more comprehensive view of their financial situation (Bose et al., 2022). Advanced big data analytics comprises techniques that include, among others, data mining and predictive and prescriptive analytics, which help organizations extract insights from the information available and make informed decisions (Bose et al., 2022). These tools are essential for financial planning, risk management, and financial performance optimization (Cerchiello & Giudici, 2016).

Robotic process automation, in turn, uses software robots to automate repetitive, rule-based tasks (Hazar & Toplu, 2023) such as data entry, account reconciliation, and report generation. This technology can handle large volumes of transactions and financial data quickly and accurately, freeing employees to focus on more strategic tasks (Balamurugan et al., 2022). Software robots can interact with different systems and applications, replicate human actions, and do tasks much faster without errors (Suri et al., 2017), thereby improving operational efficiency (Ayinla et al., 2024), reducing costs, and minimizing the risk of human mistakes (Sherif & Mohsin, 2021).

Finally, blockchain technology has the potential to transform financial reporting by offering a secure, transparent way to record and verify transactions (Danach et al., 2024). This technology has the potential to make financial data more transparent and ensure their integrity (Han et al., 2023), allowing auditors and regulators to verify transactions easily and ensure that reports are accurate and compliant with current regulations (Sheela et al., 2023). In addition, blockchain can automate account reconciliation and real-time financial reporting (Alkan, 2021).

3. BENEFITS AND OBSTACLES OF DIGITALIZING FINANCIAL REPORTING

The literature highlights that digitalization both improves corporate efficiency and transparency and contributes to the accuracy and timeliness of financial information (Antwi et al., 2024), which are all essential for organizations' long-term sustainability (Martínez-Peláez et al., 2023). Research has also shown that access to accurate and timely data is crucial for good decision making (Antwi et al., 2024). As Table 1 shows, the incorporation of digital financial reporting has resulted in significant benefits for companies' stakeholders (Troshani & Rowbottom, 2021).

Table 1. Benefits of digitalized financial reporting

Stakeholders	Benefits
Investors	• Automated data collection and reduced search costs • More efficient data processing • Reduced information asymmetry • Expanded number of possible global investment targets
Companies	• Increased analysts' coverage and access to capital, including international investment, which fosters a broad, stable investor base • More efficient and accurate benchmarking and peer analysis • Reduced burden in terms of submitting the same information to multiple organizations or government agencies
Regulators	• Increased capital formation • More efficient market oversight and enforcement reviews • Automated validation checks and technology-driven monitoring • Improved data sharing between regulators and government agencies

Source: International Financial Reporting Standards (IFRS), 2024

Despite these significant benefits, digitalizing financial reporting is also associated with challenges that can affect the accuracy and timeliness of reports (JieWei et al., 2023). Firms must overcome these obstacles to leverage the aforementioned technologies more fully (Antwi et al., 2024).

Implementing digital systems can be complex (Saarikko et al., 2020), so this process requires careful planning (Prasetianningrum & Sonjaya, 2024). Companies need to ensure that their current systems are compatible with new technologies (Attaran et al., 2020) and that the existing infrastructure can fully support digitalization (Sebastian et al., 2020). Preparations require a significant investment of time and resources (Prasetianningrum & Sonjaya, 2024), as well as hiring or training specialized personnel (Fetzer et al., 2023). The key to overcoming this challenge is meticulous planning and technology providers with experience in system integration (Gulin et al., 2019).

Resistance to change is another common issue in organizational transformation processes (Scholkmann, 2021). The digitalization of financial reporting necessitates a cultural shift within firms (JieWei et al., 2023). More specifically, employees may be accustomed to manual processes and resist adopting digital technologies (Odonkor et al., 2024), making the implementation of these tools difficult.

Organizations may show reluctance to change their working methods, especially companies with rigid hierarchical structures and established traditions (De Long & Fahey, 2000). Workers and managers are often used to manual or traditional processes, so these individuals perceive AI tools as a threat to their work routines and, in some cases, fear they will lose their jobs or role within their organization. Resistance can take the form of staff and managers who fail to cooperate actively during implementations and remain passively detachment from the transformation (Potosky & Azan, 2023) because they fear AI-derived automation will result in a loss of control over specific aspects of organizational management.

Organizations may have highly centralized decision-making processes and strict hierarchies, which makes approval and change procedures slow and bureaucratic (Meier & Krause, 2003). This rigidity contributes to slowing down the adoption of AI and thus limits its potential to transform organizational procedures effectively. Conversely, AI can be more easily integrated when firms promote a culture of cross-functional collaboration and allow different departments to explore together how AI can improve their management practices (Lin et al., 2024).

To overcome resistance to change, organizations need to provide adequate training, namely, encourage continuous learning and clearly communicate the benefits of digitalization (Vuchkovski et al., 2023). Effective communication and employee involvement in the change process ensure the success of digitalization (Ullrich et al., 2023). The staff must understand that AI tools are being implemented to improve efficiency and support decision making rather than lessen the value of human capital (Perez & de Pablos, 2023). Thus, organizational culture should foster innovation, learning, and experimentation, as well as committed leadership, to provide the internal support needed to implement AI in an enduring, sustainable manner (Ahmed et al., 2022).

Data security and privacy is another challenge that arises when digitalizing financial reporting (Avira et al., 2023). The integration of multiple systems and automation of processes can exacerbate security vulnerabilities that malicious actors may seek to exploit (Kaur et al., 2023). In addition, digitalization entails managing large volumes of sensitive data that require robust security measures to protect financial information (Zhyvko et al., 2022).

Companies' increased reliance on technology produces other important problems related to digitalizing financial reporting (Prasetianingrum & Sonjaya, 2024). Organizations should make sure their digital systems are reliable and up to date to avoid disruptions in reporting processes (Plekhanov et al., 2023). Firms further need to be prepared to manage potential technical failures or infrastructure issues (Corkern et al., 2015) that could affect the accuracy and timeliness of reports.

Technology migration is the process of updating computing systems to take full advantage of AI technologies (Bedushi, 2021), which both provides tangible benefits and raises obstacles that must be carefully removed before these new tools are implemented. The main challenge can be compatibility with existing infrastructure as many companies rely on legacy systems developed decades ago. These technologies were robust in their time but may now be incompatible with newer systems, and their integration with AI platforms can be complicated. In these cases, migration requires firms to restructure their technological infrastructure completely, which results in greater costs and time losses.

Thus, companies must carry out a detailed analysis of current and future needs before technology migration. All areas of the organization may not require AI tools (Jöhnk et al., 2021), so identifying where their impact will be greater is an essential step. Gradual migration is also an option since this minimizes the risk of interrupted operations (Chamie, 2000). In any case, firms should collaborate with specialized companies that facilitate the process and ensure implementations are carried out correctly (Shao et al., 2021).

Compliance with regulations is a critical aspect of digitalizing financial reporting (Gullin et al., 2019), especially since regulatory environments are constantly evolving (Reier Forradellas & Garay Gallastegui, 2021). Organizations need to confirm that their new digital systems can adapt to these changes (Mihu et al., 2023). Evolving regulations may require software updates or process changes (Gullin et al., 2019) that can be costly and time-consuming and may require periodic internal audits (Gotthardt et al., 2020) to ensure compliance with current legislation. Companies must also ensure that their digital systems comply with current data privacy regulations (Quach et al., 2022).

4. REGULATORY CONSIDERATIONS RELATED TO DIGITAL FINANCIAL REPORTING

The digitalization process has revolutionized how organizations prepare, present, and analyze their financial statements (Meraghni et al., 2021). Firms adopt advanced technologies such as big data, AI, and automation to achieve greater accuracy, efficiency, and transparency in their reporting (Antwi et al., 2024). However, this shift presents significant challenges in terms of legal compliance (Alqodsi & Gura, 2023). The relevant regulatory guidelines are essential to ensure that digitalization avoids compromising the integrity and accuracy of financial information (González Páramo, 2017).

Currently, various regulatory frameworks govern financial reporting, establishing the standards and requirements organizations have to meet in order to guarantee the transparency, precision, and veracity of their financial information (Harshitha et al., 2023). These legal guidelines vary depending on the area of jurisdiction, but they are generally designed to protect investors, shareholders, and other stakeholders' interests by ensuring financial reports are clear and reliable (Mähönen, 2020).

At the international level, the digitalization of financial reporting must respect the IFRS (Nassar & Kamal, 2021). The technologies that collect, process, and present accounting information thus need to make sure that reports comply with these standards (Mannapova, 2023).

In the United States, the guidelines issued by the Financial Accounting Standards Board include the integration of analytical tools and software that help companies comply with the rules governing the recognition, measurement, and presentation of financial data (Tarca, 2020). The digitalization of reports arguably enhances transparency and efficiency in capital markets, enabling firms to raise capital at lower costs and take advantage of more investment opportunities (Roszkowska, 2021).

In 2009, the United States Securities and Exchange Commission (SEC) also began to require publicly traded companies to file their financial statements in eXtensible Business Reporting Language (XBRL), a structured data format that computers can read (Du et al., 2013). From 2019 onward, the SEC asked that financial statements be filed in Inline XBRL (iXBRL), which both computers and humans can comprehend (Luo et al., 2023). Any user can use the SEC's application to access all public digital filings submitted to the Commission through its Electronic Data Gathering, Analysis, and Retrieval system.[1] This application thus allows investors to integrate and automate real-time company information into their investment tools and portfolio management systems (IFRS, 2024).

In Europe, digitalized financial reporting has become a priority (Ionaşcu et al., 2022) for two reasons. First, investors, regulators, and other stakeholders' increasing demands for transparency have driven organizations to adopt technologies that provide easier and faster access to financial information (European Investment Bank, 2021). In particular, the 2008 financial crisis triggered regulatory reforms, such as the Transparency Directive and the Markets in Financial Instruments Directive II, that highlight the importance of accurate, timely financial information to prevent similar crises in the future (Saboni et al., 2024).

Second, digitalization is considered a key tool for improving European companies' competitiveness in globalized markets (Galindo-Martín et al., 2023). Regulatory initiatives have been adopted, including the European Single Electronic Format (ESEF), as the European Union's mandatory standards for financial reports presented by publicly listed companies (Szymanek & Wiśniewski, 2023). Since January 2020, firms listed in regulated European markets have had to submit their annual financial reports in an electronic XHTML format, using the iXBRL standard for accounting tags.

This requirement ensures human readability and automated processing by software systems (ERICA Working Group, 2023). The ESEF not only facilitates cross-border comparison and analysis of financial data but also enhances the accessibility of information for retail investors and regulators (Szymanek & Wiśniewski, 2023). This standard format is a key step toward harmonizing financial reporting across Europe, which reduces administrative barriers and increases market transparency (Kinderman, 2020).

In parallel, the General Data Protection Regulation (GDPR) was implemented in 2018 to establish a clear framework for how to protect sensitive financial information (European Parliamentary Research Service, 2020). As a result, organizations must confirm that their digital systems comply with the GDPR's strict privacy and security requirements (Hoofnagle et al., 2019). These standards have pushed firms to adopt advanced encryption and cybersecurity technologies as part of their financial reporting digitalization process (Oyewole et al., 2024).

In short, the legal aspects of digitalizing financial reporting are crucial features that safeguard the integrity, transparency, and security of financial information (Anyanwu et al., 2024). Important requirements have been established to protect sensitive data (Stach et al., 2022), and reports have to be submitted in standard electronic formats (Ghani et al., 2009) to facilitate comparability and compliance with accounting guidelines (Rowbottom et al., 2021). Regulations ensure that digitalization avoids any missteps that might compromise the accuracy or accessibility of financial information (González Páramo, 2017) while simultaneously promoting transparency and trust in the markets (Udeh et al., 2024).

5. FUTURE TRENDS AND IMPLICATIONS

Digital financial reporting is reshaping the way organizations prepare, present, and manage their reports (Prasetianingrum & Sonjaya, 2024). Firms are adopting advanced technologies, such as AI, big data, and automation, that have produced profound changes in how financial reporting is conducted (Antwi et al., 2024). This section explores future trends in the digitalization of financial reporting and the implications these developments have for organizations, investors, and regulatory environments.

5.1 Future Trends in Digital Financial Reporting

As mentioned previously, AI and machine learning have emerged as key tools in the digitalization of financial reports (Pattnaik et al., 2024). These technologies enable advanced analyses of large volumes of data, the identification of patterns, and the automation of repetitive tasks (Ajayi-Nifise et al., 2024).

More specifically, AI can be used in financial reporting to perform financial forecasting, detect anomalies, and optimize audit processes (Adelakun, 2023). AI also automates account reconciliation and report generation (Ajayi-Nifise et al., 2024), reducing the time and effort required for either task (Hussin et al., 2024) and minimizing the risk of human error (Al Najjar et al., 2024). Machine learning, in turn, can improve the accuracy of forecasting models by continuously adjusting algorithms to reflect new data (Ahamed et al., 2023).

The proliferation of big data tools is transforming financial reporting by giving organizations access to an unprecedented volume and variety of information (Ibrahim et al., 2021). Companies are thus using big data to gain more detailed insights into their operations and business environments (Bose et al., 2023). These firms are integrating external information (e.g., market conditions and economic trends) with internal company data to enable more comprehensive, accurate analyses (Ibrahim et al., 2021).

Predictive analytics further use statistical models and machine learning algorithms to forecast future trends, a practice that is gaining traction in financial planning and risk management (Panda & Agrawal, 2021). As a result, predictive analytics has become a powerful tool for anticipating market changes, managing risks, and making informed decisions based on more robust data (Aljohani, 2023).

In addition, automated financial reporting is on the rise (Jędrzejka, 2019) because of the implementation of tools and technologies that facilitate the automatic generation of reports (Szmajser et al., 2022). These solutions more specifically integrate financial data from multiple sources (Samuelsen et al., 2019), perform complex calculations (Odonkor et al., 2024), and generate real-time reports (Antwi et al., 2024). Automation is thus enhancing efficiency (Ajayi-Nifise et al., 2024) by reducing manual workloads (Matthies, 2020) and increasing the accuracy of reports by minimizing human mistakes (Eziefule et al., 2022). Automation further provides greater flexibility and speed in terms of report presentations (Jędrzejka, 2019) and different report formats (Matthies, 2020), as well as meeting regulatory requirements (Ajayi-Nifise et al., 2024).

Blockchain technology offers easily distributed, immutable ledgers of transactions (Ballamudi, 2016) and promising solutions that improve transparency and security in financial reporting (Tripathi et al., 2023). This technology can be used to record transactions securely and transparently (Pascual Pedreño et al., 2021) and to guarantee the integrity and auditability of financial data (Wibowo & Christian, 2021). Incorporating blockchain tools into financial reporting facilitates account reconciliation (Han et al., 2023), transaction verification (Pascual Pedreño et al., 2021), and fraud prevention (Oladejo & Jack, 2020). This technology provides a permanent record of all operations (Ballamudi, 2016), which enhances trust in financial information (Van Thanh Le et al., 2019) and reduces the risk of manipulation or errors (Han et al., 2023).

Data visualization and interactivity advances are revolutionizing the way financial reports are shared (Dilla et al., 2010). New visualization tools present financial data more clearly and comprehensibly (Korkut & Surer, 2023) using charts, dashboards, and interactive analyses. These technologies help diverse stakeholders explore data dynamically (Perkhofer et al., 2019) and thus identify trends and patterns more effectively (Dilla et al., 2010), which expedites deeper analyses (Dilla et al., 2010). Interactivity in financial reports additionally facilitates decision making by providing more detailed and accessible financial information (Ozili, 2018).

5.2 Implications of Digitalizing Financial Reporting

This digitalization process has already had a significant impact on business decisions (Kusumawardhani et al., 2024). Integrating AI and predictive analytics enables organizations to reach decisions based on more accurate and comprehensive data (Farayola et al., 2024), which boosts strategic planning (Jejeniwa et al., 2024), risk management (Fritz-Morgenthal et al., 2022), and the identification of growth opportunities (Cho, 2024; Peng et al., 2023).

Automation and advanced data visualization also enhance managers' ability to interpret and use financial information (Ajayi-Nifise et al., 2024). More informed and agile decision-making processes ensue when information appears in more accessible formats and interactive analysis becomes easier (Dilla et al., 2010; Intezari & Gressel, 2017).

Digitalization is additionally transforming accounting professionals and auditors' roles (Gonçalves et al., 2022) by introducing new technologies into financial reporting procedures (Miaoquan et al., 2023). A shift is occurring from manual tasks to more strategic functions (Mujiono, 2021) that include data analysis, risk assessment, and advice given to decision makers (Jejeniwa et al., 2024; Khaled AlKoheji & Al-Sartawi, 2022). Overall, accounting and auditing tasks are changing (Ebirim et al., 2024) so that professionals can focus on higher value-added activities (Hussin et al., 2024). For example, auditors can use data analytics tools to identify patterns and anomalies that may indicate financial or compliance issues (Dempsey & van Dyk, 2023).

Digital financial reporting has further changed organizations' regulatory obligations (Ageeva et al., 2020). More specifically, companies that integrate new technologies must constantly update their processes and systems to comply with current regulatory requirements (Marotta & Madnick, 2021). Data protection and privacy become critical issues when financial reporting is digitalized (Mujtaba, 2024). Firms have to ensure that their digital systems comply with privacy regulations in order to protect sensitive financial information (Adelakun, 2022).

In addition, advanced financial reporting tools require accounting professionals to train and develop their skills continuously (JieWei et al., 2023). Organizations must invest in employee training (Whitehead, 2022) to guarantee proficiency in the latest applications and techniques, including data analysis, visualization tools, and the use of emerging technologies (e.g., blockchain and AI) (Qasim & Kharbat, 2020).

Finally, the digitalization of financial reporting can strengthen transparency and trust in this information (Gao, 2023). Implementing technologies such as blockchain increases transparency by providing immutable transaction records (Nassar & Kama, 2021), while data visualization tools facilitate users' understanding and analysis of financial information (Kothakota & Kiss, 2020).

In summary, more accurate and transparent financial reports strengthen investors and other stakeholders' confidence in organizations' financial data (Barth & Schipper, 2008). This increased trust contributes to greater stability in financial markets (Cagle, 2020) and better reputations for the companies that effectively adopt cutting edge technologies (Lombardi & Cagle, 2021).

6. CONCLUSION

The digital revolution has recently transformed all aspects of the business world, including financial reporting. Digital financial reports have significantly improved corporate efficiency and transparency (Gao, 2023). Firms have automated procedures, integrated systems, and facilitated real-time access to information (Prasetianingrum & Sonjaya, 2024), thereby optimizing their operations (Avira et al., 2023) and decision-making processes (JieWei et al., 2023). Digitalization specifically makes large volumes of data more accessible (Plekhanov et al., 2023) and advanced analytical tools easier to use (Abhishek et al., 2024) by those seeking to interpret information more accurately and efficiently (JieWei et al., 2023).

This deeper understanding of accounting information allows organizations to identify trends (Verhoef et al., 2021), predict future outcomes (Bhumani & Villcocks, 2014), and make decisions that improve company profitability and sustainability (Grabski et al., 2011). Digital financial reporting has also enhanced corporate transparency (Gao, 2023) as digitalization ensures the accuracy, consistency, and accessibility of disclosed data (Antwi et al., 2024).

To leverage these advantages, firms must address a set of challenges including, among others, information security (JieWei et al., 2023), organizational change management (Bhimani & Willcocks, 2014), and regulatory compliance (Abhishek et al., 2024). Today's ever-evolving business environments are characterized by an increasing demand for information from varied stakeholders (Jeffery, 2009). The digitalization of financial reporting has thus become an essential tool for achieving corporate success (Prasetianingrum & Sonjaya, 2024) and ensuring companies' long-term survival (Gupta et al., 2023).

Automated data processing will continue to evolve as new technologies emerge (Cascio & Montealegre, 2016) and businesses adopt more rigorous standards regarding the content and format of digital information disclosure (Rowbottom et al., 2021). More specifically, the growing use of AI, blockchain, and advanced analytics means these tools will soon become major drivers of the ongoing transformation of financial reporting (Han et al., 2023). This trend will not only improve decision-making processes but also optimize companies' financial performance and provide them with significant competitive advantages.

Firms that can act on their financial data faster than their competitors can better position themselves to capitalize on opportunities, mitigate risks, and adapt to market changes (Knudsen et al., 2021). Timely disclosures of accurate, detailed reports will enhance these organizations' corporate reputation (Xiao & Shailer, 2022) and thus attract lower-cost financing (Liu & Zhang, 2023). In addition, digitalization can enable greater customization of analyses of accounting information (Gonçalves et al., 2022) so that they meet different stakeholders' specific needs (Plekhanov et al., 2023).

REFERENCES

Aamer, A., Sahara, C. R., & Al-Awlaqi, M. A. (2023). Digitalization of the supply chain: Transformation factors. *Journal of Science and Technology Policy Management*, 14(4), 713–733. DOI: 10.1108/JSTPM-01-2021-0001

Abdul-Azeez, O., Ihechere, A. O., & Idemudia, C. (2024). Enhancing business performance: The role of data-driven analytics in strategic decision-making. *International Journal of Management & Entrepreneurship Research*, 6(7), 2066–2081. DOI: 10.51594/ijmer.v6i7.1257

Abhishek, N., Suraj, N., Rahiman, H. U., Nawaz, N., Kodikal, R., Kulal, A., & Raj, K. (2024). Digital transformation in accounting: elevating effectiveness across accounting, auditing, reporting and regulatory compliance. *Journal of Accounting & Organizational Change*, (ahead-of-print). DOI: 10.1108/JAOC-01-2024-0039

Adelakun, B. O. (2022). Ethical Considerations in the Use of AI for Auditing: Balancing Innovation and Integrity. *European Journal of Accounting. Auditing and Finance Research*, 10(12), 91–108. DOI: 10.37745/ejaafr.2013/vol10n1291108

Adelakun, B. O. (2023). AI-Driven Financial Forecasting: Innovations and Implications for Accounting Practices. *International Journal of Advanced Economics*, 5(9), 323–338. DOI: 10.51594/ijae.v5i9.1231

Adelberg, A. H. (1979). Narrative disclosures contained in financial reports: Means of communication or manipulation? *Accounting and Business Research*, 9(35), 179–190. DOI: 10.1080/00014788.1979.9729157

Adeyelu, O. O., Ugochukwu, C. E., & Shonibare, M. A. (2024). The impact of artificial intelligence on accounting practices: Advancements, challenges, and opportunities. *International Journal of Management & Entrepreneurship Research*, 6(4), 1200–1210. DOI: 10.51594/ijmer.v6i4.1031

Ageeva, O., Karp, M., & Sidorov, A. (2020). The application of digital technologies in financial reporting and auditing. In Popkova, E. G., & Sergi, B. S. (Eds.), *Smart Technologies" for Society, State and Economy* (pp. 1526–1534). Springer International Publishing. DOI: 10.1007/978-3-030-59126-7_167__

Agostino, D., Saliterer, I., & Steccolini, I. (2022). Digitalization, accounting and accountability: A literature review and reflections on future research in public services. *Financial Accountability & Management*, 38(2), 152–176. DOI: 10.1111/faam.12301

Ahamed, S. F., Vijayasankar, A., Thenmozhi, M., Rajendar, S., Bindu, P., & Rao, T. S. M. (2023). Machine learning models for forecasting and estimation of business operations. *The Journal of High Technology Management Research*, 34(1), 100455. Advance online publication. DOI: 10.1016/j.hitech.2023.100455

Ahmed, R., Shaheen, S., & Philbin, S. P. (2022). The role of big data analytics and decision-making in achieving project success. *Journal of Engineering and Technology Management*, 65, 101697. DOI: 10.1016/j.jengtecman.2022.101697

Ajayi-Nifise, A. O., Odeyemi, O., Mhlongo, N. Z., Ibeh, C. V., Elufioye, O. A., & Awonuga, K. F. (2024). The future of accounting: Predictions on automation and AI integration. *World Journal of Advanced Research and Reviews*, 21(2), 399–407. DOI: 10.30574/wjarr.2024.21.2.0466

Al Najjar, M., Gaber Ghanem, M., Mahboub, R., & Nakhal, B. (2024). The Role of Artificial Intelligence in Eliminating Accounting Errors. *Journal of Risk and Financial Management*, 17(8), 353. DOI: 10.3390/jrfm17080353

Aldoseri, A., Al-Khalifa, K. N., & Hamouda, A. M. (2023). Re-thinking data strategy and integration for artificial intelligence: Concepts, opportunities, and challenges. *Applied Sciences (Basel, Switzerland)*, 13(12), 7082. DOI: 10.3390/app13127082

Aljohani, A. (2023). Predictive analytics and machine learning for real-time supply chain risk mitigation and agility. *Sustainability (Basel)*, 15(20), 15088. DOI: 10.3390/su152015088

Alkan, B. Ş. (2021). Real-time Blockchain accounting system as a new paradigm. *Muhasebe ve Finansman Dergisi*, 41-58. DOI: 10.25095/mufad.950162

Almeida, F. L. (2017). Benefits, challenges and tools of big data management. *Journal of Systems Integration*, 8(4). http://dx.doi.org/DOI: 10.20470/jsi.v8i4.311

AlMuhayfith, S., & Shaiti, H. (2020). The impact of enterprise resource planning on business performance: With the discussion on its relationship with open innovation. *Journal of Open Innovation*, 6(3), 87. DOI: 10.3390/joitmc6030087

Alqodsi, E. M., & Gura, D. (2023). High tech and legal challenges: Artificial intelligence-caused damage regulation. *Cogent Social Sciences*, 9(2), 2270751. DOI: 10.1080/23311886.2023.2270751

Alsoufi, M. A., Razak, S., Siraj, M. M., Nafea, I., Ghaleb, F. A., Saeed, F., & Nasser, M. (2021). Anomaly-based intrusion detection systems in IoT using deep learning: A systematic literature review. *Applied Sciences (Basel, Switzerland)*, 11(18), 8383. DOI: 10.3390/app11188383

Ameyaw, M. N., Idemudia, C., & Iyelolu, T. V. (2024). Financial compliance as a pillar of corporate integrity: A thorough analysis of fraud prevention. *Finance & Accounting Research Journal*, 6(7), 1157–1177. DOI: 10.51594/farj.v6i7.1271

Antwi, B. O., Adelakun, B. O., & Eziefule, A. O. (2024). Transforming Financial Reporting with AI: Enhancing Accuracy and Timeliness. *International Journal of Advanced Economics*, 6(6), 205-223. DOI: 10.51594/ijae.v6i6.1229

Anyanwu, A., Olorunsogo, T., Abrahams, T. O., Akindote, O. J., & Reis, O. (2024). Data confidentiality and integrity: A review of accounting and cybersecurity controls in superannuation organizations. *Computer Science & IT Research Journal*, 5(1), 237–253. DOI: 10.51594/csitrj.v5i1.735

Arbelo, A., Arbelo-Pérez, M., & Pérez-Gómez, P. (2021). Profit efficiency as a measure of performance and frontier models: A resource-based view. *Business Research Quarterly*, 24(2), 143–159. DOI: 10.1177/2340944420924336

Ashtiani, M. N., & Raahemi, B. (2021). Intelligent fraud detection in financial statements using machine learning and data mining: A systematic literature review. *IEEE Access : Practical Innovations, Open Solutions*, 10, 72504–72525. DOI: 10.1109/ACCESS.2021.3096799

Attaran, M., Attaran, S., & Kirkland, D. (2020). Technology and organizational change: Harnessing the power of digital workplace. In Idemudia, E. C. (Ed.), *Handbook of Research on Social and Organizational Dynamics in the Digital Era* (pp. 383–408). IGI Global., DOI: 10.4018/978-1-5225-8933-4.ch018

Avira, S., Setyaningsih, E., & Utami, S. S. (2023). Digital transformation in financial management: Harnessing technology for business success. *Influence: International Journal of Science Review*, 5(2), 336–345. DOI: 10.54783/influencejournal.v5i2.161

Ayinla, B. S., Atadoga, A., Ike, C. U., Ndubuisi, N. L., Asuzu, O. F., & Adeleye, R. A. (2024). The Role of Robotic Process Automation (RPA) in Modern Accounting: A Review-Investigating how Automation Tools are Transforming Traditional Accounting Practices. *Engineering Science & Technology Journal*, 5(2), 427–447. DOI: 10.51594/estj.v5i2.804

Bai, X., Nunez, M., & Kalagnanam, J. R. (2012). Managing data quality risk in accounting information systems. *Information Systems Research*, 23(2), 453–473. DOI: 10.1287/isre.1110.0371

Bakhshi, T., & Ghita, B. (2021). Perspectives on Auditing and Regulatory Compliance in Blockchain Transactions. In Rehman, M. H., Svetinovic, D., Salah, K., & Damiani, E. (Eds.), *Trust Models for Next-Generation Blockchain Ecosystems* (pp. 37–65). Springer International Publishing. DOI: 10.1007/978-3-030-75107-4_2

Balamurugan, A., Krishna, M. V., Bhattacharya, R., Mohammed, S., Haralayya, B., & Kaushik, P. (2022). Robotic Process Automation (RPA) in Accounting and Auditing of Business and Financial Information. *British Journal of Administrative Management*, 58(157), 127–142.

Ballamudi, K. R. (2016). Blockchain as a Type of Distributed Ledger Technology. *Asian Journal of Humanity. Art and Literature*, 3(2), 127–136. DOI: 10.18034/ajhal.v3i2.528

Barchard, K. A., & Pace, L. A. (2011). Preventing human error: The impact of data entry methods on data accuracy and statistical results. *Computers in Human Behavior*, 27(5), 1834–1839. DOI: 10.1016/j.chb.2011.04.004

Barth, M. E., & Schipper, K. (2008). Financial reporting transparency. *Journal of Accounting, Auditing & Finance*, 23(2), 173–190. DOI: 10.1177/0148558X0802300203

Berikol, B. Z., & Killi, M. (2021). The effects of digital transformation process on accounting profession and accounting education. In Caliyurt, K. T. (Ed.), *Ethics and Sustainability in Accounting and Finance* (Vol. II, pp. 219–231). Springer Nature. DOI: 10.1007/978-981-15-1928-4_13

Bhimani, A., & Willcocks, L. (2014). Digitisation, 'Big Data' and the transformation of accounting information. *Accounting and Business Research*, 44(4), 469–490. DOI: 10.1080/00014788.2014.910051

Bose, S., Dey, S. K., & Bhattacharjee, S. (2023). Big data, data analytics and artificial intelligence in accounting: An overview. In Akter, S., & Wamba, S. F. (Eds.), *Handbook of Big Data Research Methods* (pp. 32–51). Edward Elgar Publishing. DOI: 10.4337/9781800888555.00007

Broccardo, L., Zicari, A., Jabeen, F., & Bhatti, Z. A. (2023). How digitalization supports a sustainable business model: A literature review. *Technological Forecasting and Social Change*, 187(6-7), 122146. DOI: 10.1016/j.techfore.2022.122146

Brunetti, F., Matt, D. T., Bonfanti, A., De Longhi, A., Pedrini, G., & Orzes, G. (2020). Digital transformation challenges: Strategies emerging from a multi-stakeholder approach. *The TQM Journal*, 32(4), 697–724. DOI: 10.1108/TQM-12-2019-0309

Cagle, M. N. (2020). Reflections of digitalization on accounting: the effects of industry 4.0 on financial statements and financial ratios. In Hacioglu, U. (Ed.), *Digital Business Strategies in Blockchain Ecosystems: Transformational Design and Future of Global Business* (pp. 473–501). Springer International Publishing. DOI: 10.1007/978-3-030-29739-8_23

Calderon-Monge, E., & Ribeiro-Soriano, D. (2024). The role of digitalization in business and management: A systematic literature review. *Review of Managerial Science*, 18(2), 449–491. DOI: 10.1007/s11846-023-00647-8

Cascio, W. F., & Montealegre, R. (2016). How technology is changing work and organizations. *Annual Review of Organizational Psychology and Organizational Behavior*, 3(1), 349–375. DOI: 10.1146/annurev-orgpsych-041015-062352

Cerchiello, P., & Giudici, P. (2016). Big data analysis for financial risk management. *Journal of Big Data*, 3(1), 1–12. DOI: 10.1186/s40537-016-0053-4

Cho, O. H. (2024). Analysis of the Impact of Artificial Intelligence Applications on the Development of Accounting Industry. *Nanotechnology Perceptions*, 20(S1), 74–83. DOI: 10.62441/nano-ntp.v20iS1.7

Cho, S., Vasarhelyi, M. A., Sun, T., & Zhang, C. (2020). Learning from machine learning in accounting and assurance. *Journal of Emerging Technologies in Accounting*, 17(1), 1–10. DOI: 10.2308/jeta-10718

Chowdhury, E. K. (2023). Integration of Artificial Intelligence Technology in Management Accounting Information System: An Empirical Study. In Abedin, M. Z., & Hajek, P. (Eds.), *Novel financial applications of machine learning and deep learning: algorithms, product modeling, and applications* (pp. 35–46). Springer International Publishing. DOI: 10.1007/978-3-031-18552-6_3

Chyzhevska, L., Voloschuk, L., Shatskova, L., & Sokolenko, L. (2021). Digitalization as a vector of information systems development and accounting system modernization. *Studia Universitatis Vasile Goldi Arad. Seria tiin e Economice*, 31(4), 18–39. DOI: 10.2478/sues-2021-0017

Coman, D. M., Ionescu, C. A., Duică, A., Coman, M. D., Uzlau, M. C., Stanescu, S. G., & State, V. (2022). Digitization of accounting: The premise of the paradigm shift of role of the professional accountant. *Applied Sciences (Basel, Switzerland)*, 12(7), 3359. DOI: 10.3390/app12073359

Coombs, C., Hislop, D., Taneva, S. K., & Barnard, S. (2020). The strategic impacts of Intelligent Automation for knowledge and service work: An interdisciplinary review. *The Journal of Strategic Information Systems*, 29(4), 101600. DOI: 10.1016/j.jsis.2020.101600

Corkern, S. M., Kimmel, S. B., & Morehead, B. (2015). Accountants need to be prepared for the big question: Should I move to the cloud? *International Journal of Management & Information Systems*, 19(1), 13. DOI: 10.19030/ijmis.v19i1.9085

Danach, K., Hejase, H. J., Faroukh, A., Fayyad-Kazan, H., & Moukadem, I. (2024). Assessing the Impact of Blockchain Technology on Financial Reporting and Audit Practices. *Asian Business Research*, 9(1), 30. DOI: 10.20849/abr.v9i1.1427

De Long, D. W., & Fahey, L. (2000). Diagnosing cultural barriers to knowledge management. *The Academy of Management Perspectives*, 14(4), 113–127. DOI: 10.5465/ame.2000.3979820

Dempsey, K., & van Dyk, V. (2023). The Role of Data Analytics in Enhancing External Audit Quality. In Moloi, T., & George, B. (Eds.), *Towards Digitally Transforming Accounting and Business Processes* (pp. 399–423). Springer Nature Switzerland. DOI: 10.1007/978-3-031-46177-4_22

Dilla, W., Janvrin, D. J., & Raschke, R. (2010). Interactive data visualization: New directions for accounting information systems research. *Journal of Information Systems*, 24(2), 1–37. DOI: 10.2308/jis.2010.24.2.1

Dong, S., Abbas, K., Li, M., & Kamruzzaman, J. (2023). Blockchain technology and application: An overview. *PeerJ. Computer Science*, 9, e1705. DOI: 10.7717/peerj-cs.1705 PMID: 38077532

Du, H., Vasarhelyi, M. A., & Zheng, X. (2013). XBRL mandate: Thousands of filing errors and so what? *Journal of Information Systems*, 27(1), 61–78. DOI: 10.2308/isys-50399

Ebirim, G. U., Unigwe, I. F., Oshioste, E. E., Ndubuisi, N. L., Odonkor, B., & Asuzu, O. F. (2024). Innovations in accounting and auditing: A comprehensive review of current trends and their impact on US businesses. *International Journal of Science and Research Archive*, 11(1), 965–974. DOI: 10.30574/ijsra.2024.11.1.0134

Elgendy, N., & Elragal, A. (2016). Big data analytics in support of the decision making process. *Procedia Computer Science*, 100, 1071–1084. DOI: 10.1016/j.procs.2016.09.251

ERICA Working Group. (2023). *XBRL in European CBSO*. Brussels: European Committee of Central Balance Sheet Data Offices. https://www.bde.es/wbe/en/areas-actuacion/central-balances/colaboracion-con-otras-instiuciones/comite-europeo-centrales-balances

European Investment Bank. (2021). *Artificial intelligence, blockchain and the future of Europe: How disruptive technologies create opportunities for a green and digital economy*. Brussels: European Commission. https://www.eib.org/en/publications/artifical-intelligence-blockchain-and-the-future-of-europe-report

European Parliamentary Research Service. (2020). *The impact of the General Data Protection Regulation (GDPR) on artificial intelligence*. Brussels: European Parliament. https://www.europarl.europa.eu/RegData/etudes/STUD/2020/641530/EPRS_STU(2020)641530_EN.pdf

Faccia, A., & Petratos, P. (2021). Blockchain, enterprise resource planning (ERP) and accounting information systems (AIS): Research on e-procurement and system integration. *Applied Sciences (Basel, Switzerland)*, 11(15), 6792. DOI: 10.3390/app11156792

Farayola, O. A., Adaga, E. M., Egieya, Z. E., Ewuga, S. K., Abdul, A. A., & Abrahams, T. O. (2024). Advancements in predictive analytics: A philosophical and practical overview. *World Journal of Advanced Research and Reviews*, 21(3), 240–252. DOI: 10.30574/wjarr.2024.21.3.2706

Fernandez-Vidal, J., Perotti, F. A., Gonzalez, R., & Gasco, J. (2022). Managing digital transformation: The view from the top. *Journal of Business Research*, 152, 29–41. DOI: 10.1016/j.jbusres.2022.07.020

Fetzer, T. H., Gibson, Y. S., & Kuhn, J. R. (2023). Technological Transformation of Accounting–Need for Firms to add Technology Training Employee Skill Sets. *International Journal of Professional Business Review*, 8(12), e03858–e03858. DOI: 10.26668/businessreview/2023.v8i12.3858

Fritz-Morgenthal, S., Hein, B., & Papenbrock, J. (2022). Financial risk management and explainable, trustworthy, responsible AI. *Frontiers in Artificial Intelligence*, 5, 779799. DOI: 10.3389/frai.2022.779799 PMID: 35295866

Fullana, O., & Ruiz, J. (2021). Accounting information systems in the blockchain era. *International Journal of Intellectual Property Management*, 11(1), 63–80. DOI: 10.1504/IJIPM.2021.113357

Furnell, S., Fischer, P., & Finch, A. (2017). Can't get the staff? The growing need for cyber-security skills. *Computer Fraud & Security*, 2017(2), 5–10. DOI: 10.1016/S1361-3723(17)30013-1

Galindo-Martín, M. A., Castaño-Martínez, M. S., & Méndez-Picazo, M. T. (2023). Digitalization, entrepreneurship and competitiveness: An analysis from 19 European countries. *Review of Managerial Science*, 17(5), 1809–1826. DOI: 10.1007/s11846-023-00640-1

Gao, X. (2023). Digital transformation in finance and its role in promoting financial transparency. *Global Finance Journal*, 58, 100903. DOI: 10.1016/j.gfj.2023.100903

Gebremeskel, B. K., Jonathan, G. M., & Yalew, S. D. (2023). Information security challenges during digital transformation. *Procedia Computer Science*, 219, 44–51. DOI: 10.1016/j.procs.2023.01.262

Ghani, E., Laswad, F., & Tooley, S. (2009). Digital reporting formats: Users' perceptions, preferences and performances. *The International Journal of Digital Accounting Research*, 9(1), 45–98. DOI: 10.4192/1577-8517-v9_3

Goldston, J. (2020). The evolution of ERP systems: A literature review. *International Journal of Research Publications*, 50(1), 21–37.

Gonçalves, M. J. A., da Silva, A. C. F., & Ferreira, C. G. (2022). The future of accounting: How will digital transformation impact the sector? *Informatics (MDPI)*, 9(1), 1–17. DOI: 10.3390/informatics9010019

González Páramo, J. M. (2017). Financial innovation in the digital age: Challenges for regulation and supervision. *Revista de Estabilidad Financiera/Banco de España*, 32, 9-37. https://repositorio.bde.es/handle/123456789/11293

Gordon, L. A., Loeb, M. P., & Sohail, T. (2010). Market value of voluntary disclosures concerning information security. *Management Information Systems Quarterly*, 34(3), 567–594. DOI: 10.2307/25750692

Gotthardt, M., Koivulaakso, D., Paksoy, O., Saramo, C., Martikainen, M., & Lehner, O. (2020). Current state and challenges in the implementation of smart robotic process automation in accounting and auditing. *ACRN Journal of Finance and Risk Perspectives*, 91(1), 90–102. DOI: 10.35944/jofrp.2020.9.1.007

Grabski, S. V., Leech, S. A., & Schmidt, P. J. (2011). A review of ERP research: A future agenda for accounting information systems. *Journal of Information Systems*, 25(1), 37–78. DOI: 10.2308/jis.2011.25.1.37

Guo, C., Ke, Y., & Zhang, J. (2023). Digital transformation along the supply chain. *Pacific-Basin Finance Journal*, 80, 102088. DOI: 10.1016/j.pacfin.2023.102088

Gupta, S., Tuunanen, T., Kar, A. K., & Modgil, S. (2023). Managing digital knowledge for ensuring business efficiency and continuity. *Journal of Knowledge Management*, 27(2), 245–263. DOI: 10.1108/JKM-09-2021-0703

Han, H., Shiwakoti, R. K., Jarvis, R., Mordi, C., & Botchie, D. (2023). Accounting and auditing with blockchain technology and artificial Intelligence: A literature review. *International Journal of Accounting Information Systems*, 48, 100598. DOI: 10.1016/j.accinf.2022.100598

Handoyo, S., Suharman, H., Ghani, E. K., & Soedarsono, S. (2023). A business strategy, operational efficiency, ownership structure, and manufacturing performance: The moderating role of market uncertainty and competition intensity and its implication on open innovation. *Journal of Open Innovation*, 9(2), 100039. DOI: 10.1016/j.joitmc.2023.100039

Harrast, S. A. (2020). Robotic process automation in accounting systems. *Journal of Corporate Accounting & Finance*, 31(4), 209–213. DOI: 10.1002/jcaf.22457

Harshitha, T. N., Sudha, M., Ramachandran, M., & Ramu, K. (2023). A Review on Regulations of Financial Reporting. *Recent trends in Management and Commerce*, 4(2), 144-156. http://dx.doi.org/DOI: 10.46632/rmc/4/2

Hasan, A. R. (2021). Artificial Intelligence (AI) in accounting & auditing: A Literature review. *Open Journal of Business and Management*, 10(1), 440–465. DOI: 10.4236/ojbm.2022.101026

Hazar, H. B., & Toplu, C. (2023). The use of robotic process automation in accounting. *Prizren Social Science Journal*, 7(3), 45–50. DOI: 10.32936/pssj.v7i3.481

He, W., & Zhang, Z. (2019). Enterprise cybersecurity training and awareness programs: Recommendations for success. *Journal of Organizational Computing and Electronic Commerce*, 29(4), 249–257. DOI: 10.1080/10919392.2019.1611528

Hilal, W., Gadsden, S. A., & Yawney, J. (2022). Financial fraud: A review of anomaly detection techniques and recent advances. *Expert Systems with Applications*, 193, 116429. DOI: 10.1016/j.eswa.2021.116429

Hodge, F. D., Kennedy, J. J., & Maines, L. A. (2004). Does search-facilitating technology improve the transparency of financial reporting? *The Accounting Review*, 79(3), 687–703. DOI: 10.2308/accr.2004.79.3.687

Hoe, S. L. (2019). Digitalization in practice: The fifth discipline advantage. *The Learning Organization*, 27(1), 54–64. DOI: 10.1108/TLO-09-2019-0137

Hofbauer, G., & Sangl, A. (2019). Blockchain technology and application possibilities in the digital transformation of transaction processes. *Forum Scientiae Oeconomia*, 7(4), 25–40. DOI: 10.23762/FSO_VOL7_NO4_2

Hoofnagle, C. J., Van Der Sloot, B., & Borgesius, F. Z. (2019). The European Union general data protection regulation: What it is and what it means. *Information & Communications Technology Law*, 28(1), 65–98. DOI: 10.1080/13600834.2019.1573501

Hund, A., Wagner, H. T., Beimborn, D., & Weitzel, T. (2021). Digital innovation: Review and novel perspective. *The Journal of Strategic Information Systems*, 30(4), 101695. DOI: 10.1016/j.jsis.2021.101695

Hussin, N. A. K. M., Bukhari, N. A. N. M., Hashim, N. H. A. N., Bahari, S. N. A. S., & Ali, M. M. (2024). The Impact of Artificial Intelligence on the Accounting Profession: A Concept Paper. *Business Management and Strategy*, 15(1), 34–50. DOI: 10.5296/bms.v15i1.21620

Ibrahim, A. E. A., Elamer, A. A., & Ezat, A. N. (2021). The convergence of big data and accounting: Innovative research opportunities. *Technological Forecasting and Social Change*, 173, 121171. DOI: 10.1016/j.techfore.2021.121171

IFRS. (2024). *Digital Financial Reporting. Facilitating digital comparability and analysis of financial reports*. London: International Accounting Standards Board. https://www.ifrs.org/digital-financial-reporting/

Intezari, A., & Gressel, S. (2017). Information and reformation in KM systems: Big data and strategic decision-making. *Journal of Knowledge Management*, 21(1), 71–91. DOI: 10.1108/JKM-07-2015-0293

Ionaşcu, I., Ionaşcu, M., Nechita, E., Săcărin, M., & Minu, M. (2022). Digital transformation, financial performance and sustainability: Evidence for European Union listed companies. *Amfiteatru Economic*, 24(59), 94–109. DOI: 10.24818/EA/2022/59/94

Jain, A., & Ranjan, S. (2020). Implications of emerging technologies on the future of work. *IIMB Management Review*, 32(4), 448–454. DOI: 10.1016/j.iimb.2020.11.004

Jędrzejka, D. (2019). Robotic process automation and its impact on accounting. *Zeszyty Teoretyczne Rachunkowości*, 105(161), 137–166. DOI: 10.5604/01.3001.0013.6061

Jeffery, N. (2009). Stakeholder engagement: A road map to meaningful engagement. *Doughty Centre, Cranfield School of Management, 2*, 19-48. http://hdl.handle.net/1826/3801

Jejeniwa, T. O., Mhlongo, N. Z., & Jejeniwa, T. O. (2024). A comprehensive review of the impact of artificial intelligence on modern accounting practices and financial reporting. *Computer Science & IT Research Journal*, 5(4), 1031–1047. DOI: 10.51594/csitrj.v5i4.1086

JieWei, W., JianQiang, C., Li, L., YuZheng, L., Zhenhong, G. U., & Loang, O. K. (2023). The Impact of Digital Transformation on Financial Reporting and Analysis in the Accounting Industry. *The International Journal of Accounting*, 8(50), 290–309. DOI: 10.55573/IJAFB.085021

Kang, Y., Cai, Z., Tan, C. W., Huang, Q., & Liu, H. (2020). Natural language processing (NLP) in management research: A literature review. *Journal of Management Analytics*, 7(2), 139–172. DOI: 10.1080/23270012.2020.1756939

Kaur, R., Gabrijelčič, D., & Klobučar, T. (2023). Artificial intelligence for cybersecurity: Literature review and future research directions. *Information Fusion*, 97, 101804. DOI: 10.1016/j.inffus.2023.101804

Khaled AlKoheji, A., & Al-Sartawi, A. (2022). Artificial intelligence and its impact on accounting systems. In Al-Sartawi, A., Razzque, A., & Kamel, M. M. (Eds.), *From the Internet of Things to the Internet of Ideas: The role of Artificial Intelligence* (pp. 647–655). Springer International Publishing. DOI: 10.1007/978-3-031-17746-0_51

Khatri, A., & Gupta, N. (2022). Impact of Data Visualization on Management Decisions. *London Journal of Research in Management and Business*, 22, 53–62.

Kinderman, D. (2020). The challenges of upward regulatory harmonization: The case of sustainability reporting in the European Union. *Regulation & Governance*, 14(4), 674–697. DOI: 10.1111/rego.12240

Knudsen, E. S., Lien, L. B., Timmermans, B., Belik, I., & Pandey, S. (2021). Stability in turbulent times? The effect of digitalization on the sustainability of competitive advantage. *Journal of Business Research*, 128, 360–369. DOI: 10.1016/j.jbusres.2021.02.008

Korhonen, T., Selos, E., Laine, T., & Suomala, P. (2021). Exploring the programmability of management accounting work for increasing automation: An interventionist case study. *Accounting, Auditing & Accountability Journal*, 34(2), 253–280. DOI: 10.1108/AAAJ-12-2016-2809

Korkut, E. H., & Surer, E. (2023). Visualization in virtual reality: A systematic review. *Virtual Reality (Waltham Cross)*, 27(2), 1447–1480. DOI: 10.1007/s10055-023-00753-8

Kothakota, M. G., & Kiss, D. E. (2020). Use of Visualization Tools to Improve Financial Knowledge: An Experimental Approach. *Financial Counseling and Planning*, 31(2), 193–208. DOI: 10.1891/JFCP-18-00070

KPMG. (2019). Automation of financial reporting and technical accounting. Amstelveen: KMPG International. https://assets.kpmg.com/content/dam/kpmg/uk/pdf/2019/09/automation-of-financial-reporting-and-technical-accounting.pdf

Kraus, S., Durst, S., Ferreira, J. J., Veiga, P., Kailer, N., & Weinmann, A. (2022). Digital transformation in business and management research: An overview of the current status quo. *International Journal of Information Management*, 63(4), 102466. DOI: 10.1016/j.ijinfomgt.2021.102466

Kraus, S., Jones, P., Kailer, N., Weinmann, A., Chaparro-Banegas, N., & Roig-Tierno, N. (2021). Digital transformation: An overview of the current state of the art of research. *SAGE Open*, 11(3), 1–15. DOI: 10.1177/21582440211047576

Kroon, N., do Céu Alves, M., & Martins, I. (2021). The impacts of emerging technologies on accountants' role and skills: Connecting to open innovation—a systematic literature review. *Journal of Open Innovation*, 7(3), 163. DOI: 10.3390/joitmc7030163

Kusumawardhani, F., Ratmono, D., Wibowo, S., Darsono, D., Widyatmoko, S., & Rokhman, N. (2024). The impact of digitalization in accounting systems on information quality, cost reduction and decision making: Evidence from SMEs. *International Journal of Data and Network Science*, 8(2), 1111–1116. DOI: 10.5267/j.ijdns.2023.11.023

Leão, P., & da Silva, M. M. (2021). Impacts of digital transformation on firms' competitive advantages: A systematic literature review. *Strategic Change*, 30(5), 421–441. DOI: 10.1002/jsc.2459

Leitner-Hanetseder, S., Lehner, O. M., Eisl, C., & Forstenlechner, C. (2021). A profession in transition: Actors, tasks and roles in AI-based accounting. *Journal of Applied Accounting Research*, 22(3), 539–556. DOI: 10.1108/JAAR-10-2020-0201

Lin, J., Zeng, Y., Wu, S., & Luo, X. R. (2024). How does artificial intelligence affect the environmental performance of organizations? The role of green innovation and green culture. *Information & Management*, 61(2), 103924. DOI: 10.1016/j.im.2024.103924

Liu, Y., Heinberg, M., Huang, X., & Eisingerich, A. B. (2023). Building a competitive advantage based on transparency: When and why does transparency matter for corporate social responsibility? *Business Horizons*, 66(4), 517–527. DOI: 10.1016/j.bushor.2022.10.004

Liu, Z., & Zhang, N. (2023). The productivity effect of digital financial reporting. *Review of Accounting Studies*, 29(3), 1–41. DOI: 10.1007/s11142-022-09737-6

Lobschat, L., Mueller, B., Eggers, F., Brandimarte, L., Diefenbach, S., Kroschke, M., & Wirtz, J. (2021). Corporate digital responsibility. *Journal of Business Research*, 122, 875–888. DOI: 10.1016/j.jbusres.2019.10.006

Lois, P., Drogalas, G., Karagiorgos, A., & Tsikalakis, K. (2020). Internal audits in the digital era: Opportunities risks and challenges. *EuroMed Journal of Business*, 15(2), 205–217. DOI: 10.1108/EMJB-07-2019-0097

Lombardi, R., & Secundo, G. (2021). The digital transformation of corporate reporting–a systematic literature review and avenues for future research. *Meditari Accountancy Research*, 29(5), 1179–1208. DOI: 10.1108/MEDAR-04-2020-0870

Luo, X., Wang, T., Yang, L., Zhao, X., & Zhang, Y. (2023). Initial evidence on the market impact of the iXBRL adoption. *Accounting Horizons*, 37(1), 143–171. DOI: 10.2308/HORIZONS-2020-023

Luo, Y. (2022). A general framework of digitization risks in international business. *Journal of International Business Studies*, 53(3), 344–361. DOI: 10.1057/s41267-021-00448-9 PMID: 34075261

Mähönen, J. (2020). Comprehensive approach to relevant and reliable reporting in Europe: A Dream impossible? *Sustainability (Basel)*, 12(13), 5277. DOI: 10.3390/su12135277

Manita, R., Elommal, N., Baudier, P., & Hikkerova, L. (2020). The digital transformation of external audit and its impact on corporate governance. *Technological Forecasting and Social Change*, 150, 119751. DOI: 10.1016/j.techfore.2019.119751

Mannapova, R. (2023). Application of IFRS in the conditions of digital technologies. *Science and Innovation*, 2(A11), 301–307. DOI: 10.5281/zenodo.10113335

Marotta, A., & Madnick, S. (2021). Convergence and divergence of regulatory compliance and cybersecurity. *Issues in Information Systems*, 22(1), 10–50. DOI: 10.48009/1_iis_2021_10-50

Martínez-Peláez, R., Ochoa-Brust, A., Rivera, S., Félix, V. G., Ostos, R., Brito, H., Félix, R. A., & Mena, L. J. (2023). Role of digital transformation for achieving sustainability: Mediated role of stakeholders, key capabilities, and technology. *Sustainability (Basel)*, 15(14), 11221. DOI: 10.3390/su151411221

Matoušková, D. (2022). Digitalization and Its Impact on Business. *Theory Methodology Practice*, 18(2), 51–67. DOI: 10.18096/TMP.2022.02.03

Matthies, B. (2020). Assessing the automation potentials of management reporting processes. *The International Journal of Digital Accounting Research*, 20, 75–101. DOI: 10.4192/1577-8517-v20_4

Meier, K. J., & Krause, G. A. (2003). The scientific study of bureaucracy: An overview. *Politics, Policy, and Organizations: Frontiers in the Scientific Study of Bureaucracy*, 1-19.

Meraghni, O., Bekkouche, L., & Demdoum, Z. (2021). Impact of digital transformation on accounting information systems–evidence from Algerian firms. *Economics and Business*, 35(1), 249–264. DOI: 10.2478/eb-2021-0017

Merkl-Davies, D. M., & Brennan, N. M. (2017). A theoretical framework of external accounting communication: Research perspectives, traditions, and theories. *Accounting, Auditing & Accountability Journal*, 30(2), 433–469. DOI: 10.1108/AAAJ-04-2015-2039

Miaoquan, X., Yu, K. W., Xuewen, L., Yi, W., Jun, Y., & Loang, O. K. (2023). The Impact of Digital Transformation on Financial Reporting and Analysis in the Accounting Industry. *The International Journal of Accounting*, 8(50), 324–336. DOI: 10.55573/IJAFB.085021

Micheler, E., & Whaley, A. (2020). Regulatory technology: Replacing law with computer code. *European Business Organization Law Review*, 21(2), 349–377. DOI: 10.1007/s40804-019-00151-1

Mihu, C., Pitic, A. G., & Bayraktar, D. (2023). Drivers of digital transformation and their impact on organizational management. *Studies in Business and Economics*, 18(1), 149–170. DOI: 10.2478/sbe-2023-0009

Mujiono, M. N. (2021). The shifting role of accountants in the era of digital disruption. *International Journal of Multidisciplinary: Applied Business and Education Research*, 2(11), 1259–1274. DOI: 10.11594/10.11594/ijmaber.02.11.18

Mujtaba, B. G. (2024). Cybercrimes and safety policies to protect data and organizations. *Journal of Crime and Criminal Behavior*, 4(1), 91–112. DOI: 10.47509/JCCB.2024.v04i01.04

Nassar, A., & Kamal, M. (2021). Ethical dilemmas in AI-powered decision-making: A deep dive into big data-driven ethical considerations. *International Journal of Responsible Artificial Intelligence*, 11(8), 1–11. https://neuralslate.com/index.php/Journal-of-Responsible-AI/article/view/43

Nassif, A. B., Talib, M. A., Nasir, Q., & Dakalbab, F. M. (2021). Machine learning for anomaly detection: A systematic review. *IEEE Access : Practical Innovations, Open Solutions*, 9, 78658–78700. DOI: 10.1109/ACCESS.2021.3083060

Nicolaou, A. I. (2010). Integrated information systems and transparency in business reporting. *International Journal of Disclosure and Governance*, 7(3), 216–226. DOI: 10.1057/jdg.2009.27

Nik Abdullah, N. H., Krishnan, S., Mohd Zakaria, A. A., & Morris, G. (2022). Strategic management accounting practices in business: A systematic review of the literature and future research directions. *Cogent Business & Management*, 9(1), 2093488. DOI: 10.1080/23311975.2022.2093488

Odonkor, B., Kaggwa, S., Uwaoma, P. U., Hassan, A. O., & Farayola, O. A. (2024). The impact of AI on accounting practices: A review: Exploring how artificial intelligence is transforming traditional accounting methods and financial reporting. *World Journal of Advanced Research and Reviews*, 21(1), 172–188. DOI: 10.30574/wjarr.2024.21.1.2721

Oladejo, M. T., & Jack, L. (2020). Fraud prevention and detection in a blockchain technology environment: Challenges posed to forensic accountants. *International Journal of Economics and Accounting*, 9(4), 315–335. DOI: 10.1504/IJEA.2020.110162

Oyewole, A. T., Oguejiofor, B. B., Eneh, N. E., Akpuokwe, C. U., & Bakare, S. S. (2024). Data privacy laws and their impact on financial technology companies: A review. *Computer Science & IT Research Journal*, 5(3), 628–650. DOI: 10.51594/csitrj.v5i3.911

Ozili, P. K. (2018). Impact of digital finance on financial inclusion and stability. *Borsa Istanbul Review*, 18(4), 329–340. DOI: 10.1016/j.bir.2017.12.003

Panda, K. C., & Agrawal, S. (2021). Predictive Analytics: An Overview of Evolving Trends and Methodologies. *Journal of Scientific and Engineering Research*, 8(10), 175–180. DOI: 10.5281/zenodo.11232896

Pandey, S., Singh, R. K., Gunasekaran, A., & Kaushik, A. (2020). Cyber security risks in globalized supply chains: Conceptual framework. *Journal of Global Operations and Strategic Sourcing*, 13(1), 103–128. DOI: 10.1108/JGOSS-05-2019-0042

Pansara, R. R. (2022). Cybersecurity Measures in Master Data Management: Safeguarding Sensitive Information. *International Numeric Journal of Machine Learning and Robots*, 6(6), 1-12. https://injmr.com/index.php/fewfewf/article/view/35

Pascual Pedreño, E., Gelashvili, V., & Pascual Nebreda, L. (2021). Blockchain and its application to accounting. *Intangible Capital*, 17(1), 1–16. DOI: 10.3926/ic.1522

Pattnaik, D., Ray, S., & Raman, R. (2024). Applications of artificial intelligence and machine learning in the financial services industry: A bibliometric review. *Heliyon*, 10(1), e23492. DOI: 10.1016/j.heliyon.2023.e23492 PMID: 38187262

Paul, J., Ueno, A., Dennis, C., Alamanos, E., Curtis, L., Foroudi, P., Kacprzak, A., Kunz, W. H., Liu, J., Marvi, R., Nair, S. L. S., Ozdemir, O., Pantano, E., Papadopoulos, T., Petir, O., Tyagi, S., & Wirtz, J. (2024). Digital transformation: A multidisciplinary perspective and future research agenda. *International Journal of Consumer Studies*, 48(2), e13015. DOI: 10.1111/ijcs.13015

Peng, Y., Ahmad, S. F., Ahmad, A. Y. B., Al Shaikh, M. S., Daoud, M. K., & Alhamdi, F. M. H. (2023). Riding the waves of artificial intelligence in advancing accounting and its implications for sustainable development goals. *Sustainability (Basel)*, 15(19), 14165. DOI: 10.3390/su151914165

Perez, J. R., & de Pablos, P. O. (2003). Knowledge management and organizational competitiveness: A framework for human capital analysis. *Journal of Knowledge Management*, 7(3), 82–91. DOI: 10.1108/13673270310485640

Perkhofer, L. M., Hofer, P., Walchshofer, C., Plank, T., & Jetter, H. C. (2019). Interactive visualization of big data in the field of accounting: A survey of current practice and potential barriers for adoption. *Journal of Applied Accounting Research*, 20(4), 497–525. DOI: 10.1108/JAAR-10-2017-0114

Plekhanov, D., Franke, H., & Netland, T. H. (2023). Digital transformation: A review and research agenda. *European Management Journal*, 41(6), 821–844. DOI: 10.1016/j.emj.2022.09.007

Potosky, D., & Azan, W. (2023). Leadership behaviors and human agency in the valley of despair: A meta-framework for organizational change implementation. *Human Resource Management Review*, 33(1), 100927. DOI: 10.1016/j.hrmr.2022.100927

Prasetianingrum, S., & Sonjaya, Y. (2024). The Evolution of Digital Accounting and Accounting Information Systems in the Modern Business Landscape. *Advances in Applied Accounting Research*, 2(1), 39–53. DOI: 10.60079/aaar.v2i1.165

Pratama, A. H., Dwita, S., & Sum, R. M. (2023). Digitalization Disclosure and Accounting Information Quality. *Wahana Riset Akuntansi*, 11(2), 109–123. DOI: 10.24036/wra.v11i2.124490

Prebanić, K. R., & Vukomanović, M. (2021). Realizing the need for digital transformation of stakeholder management: A systematic review in the construction industry. *Sustainability (Basel)*, 13(22), 12690. DOI: 10.3390/su132212690

Qasim, A., & Kharbat, F. F. (2020). Blockchain technology, business data analytics, and artificial intelligence: Use in the accounting profession and ideas for inclusion into the accounting curriculum. *Journal of Emerging Technologies in Accounting*, 17(1), 107–117. DOI: 10.2308/jeta-52649

Qatawneh, A. (2022). The influence of data mining on accounting information system performance: A mediating role of information technology infrastructure. *Journal of Governance and Regulation*, 11(1), 141–151. DOI: 10.22495/jgrv11i1art13

Quach, S., Thaichon, P., Martin, K. D., Weaven, S., & Palmatier, R. W. (2022). Digital technologies: Tensions in privacy and data. *Journal of the Academy of Marketing Science*, 50(6), 1299–1323. DOI: 10.1007/s11747-022-00845-y PMID: 35281634

Ramírez, Y., & Tejada, Á. (2018). Corporate governance of universities: Improving transparency and accountability. *International Journal of Disclosure and Governance*, 15(1), 29–39. DOI: 10.1057/s41310-018-0034-2

Reier Forradellas, R. F., & Garay Gallastegui, L. M. (2021). Digital transformation and artificial intelligence applied to business: Legal regulations, economic impact and perspective. *Laws*, 10(3), 70. DOI: 10.3390/laws10030070

Ritter, T., & Pedersen, C. L. (2020). Digitization capability and the digitalization of business models in business-to-business firms: Past, present, and future. *Industrial Marketing Management*, 86, 180–190. DOI: 10.1016/j.indmarman.2019.11.019

Rodríguez-Espíndola, O., Chowdhury, S., Dey, P. K., Albores, P., & Emrouznejad, A. (2022). Analysis of the adoption of emergent technologies for risk management in the era of digital manufacturing. *Technological Forecasting and Social Change*, 178, 121562. DOI: 10.1016/j.techfore.2022.121562

Roszkowska, P. (2021). Fintech in financial reporting and audit for fraud prevention and safeguarding equity investments. *Journal of Accounting & Organizational Change*, 17(2), 164–196. DOI: 10.1108/JAOC-09-2019-0098

Rowbottom, N., Locke, J., & Troshani, I. (2021). When the tail wags the dog? Digitalisation and corporate reporting. *Accounting, Organizations and Society*, 92, 101226. DOI: 10.1016/j.aos.2021.101226

Saarikko, T., Westergren, U. H., & Blomquist, T. (2020). Digital transformation: Five recommendations for the digitally conscious firm. *Business Horizons*, 63(6), 825–839. DOI: 10.1016/j.bushor.2020.07.005

Saboni, K., Bennis, L., & Anguer, N. E. (2024). A retrospective on the 2008 financial crisis: In-depth analysis. *International Journal of Accounting, Finance, Auditing. Management and Economics*, 5(5), 619–632. DOI: 10.5281/zenodo.11269142

Salim, R., & Ferran, C. (2008). From Ledgers to ERP. In Ferran, C., & Salim, R. (Eds.), *Enterprise Resource Planning for Global Economies: Managerial Issues and Challenges* (pp. 1–22). IGI Global. DOI: 10.4018/978-1-59904-531-3.ch001

Salvi, A., Vitolla, F., Rubino, M., Giakoumelou, A., & Raimo, N. (2021). Online information on digitalisation processes and its impact on firm value. *Journal of Business Research*, 124, 437–444. DOI: 10.1016/j.jbusres.2020.10.025

Samuelsen, J., Chen, W., & Wasson, B. (2019). Integrating multiple data sources for learning analytics—Review of literature. *Research and Practice in Technology Enhanced Learning*, 14(1), 11. DOI: 10.1186/s41039-019-0105-4

Sarker, I. H. (2021). Machine learning: Algorithms, real-world applications and research directions. *SN Computer Science*, 2(3), 160. DOI: 10.1007/s42979-021-00592-x PMID: 33778771

Schallmo, D., Williams, C. A., & Boardman, L. (2017). Digital transformation of business models—Best practice, enablers, and roadmap. *International Journal of Innovation Management*, 21(08), 1740014. DOI: 10.1142/S136391961740014X

Schiuma, G., Schettini, E., & Santarsiero, F. (2021). How wise companies drive digital transformation. *Journal of Open Innovation*, 7(2), 122. DOI: 10.3390/joitmc7020122

Schnackenberg, A. K., & Tomlinson, E. C. (2016). Organizational transparency: A new perspective on managing trust in organization-stakeholder relationships. *Journal of Management*, 42(7), 1784–1810. DOI: 10.1177/0149206314525202

Scholkmann, A. B. (2021). Resistance to (digital) change: Individual, systemic and learning-related perspectives. In Ifenthaler, D., Hofhues, S., Egloffstein, M., & Helbig, C. (Eds.), *Digital Transformation of Learning Organizations* (pp. 219–236). Springer. DOI: 10.1007/978-3-030-55878-9_13

Schwarzmüller, T., Brosi, P., Duman, D., & Welpe, I. M. (2018). How does the digital transformation affect organizations? Key themes of change in work design and leadership. *Management Review*, 29(2), 114–138. DOI: 10.5771/0935-9915-2018-2-114

Sebastian, I. M., Ross, J. W., Beath, C., Mocker, M., Moloney, K. G., & Fonstad, N. O. (2020). How big old companies navigate digital transformation. In Galliers, R. D., Leidner, D. E., & Simenova, B. (Eds.), *Strategic Information Management* (pp. 133–150). Routledge. DOI: 10.4324/9780429286797-6

Secinaro, S., Dal Mas, F., Brescia, V., & Calandra, D. (2021). Blockchain in the accounting, auditing and accountability fields: A bibliometric and coding analysis. *Accounting, Auditing & Accountability Journal*, 35(9), 168–203. DOI: 10.1108/AAAJ-10-2020-4987

Sheela, S., Alsmady, A. A., Tanaraj, K., & Izani, I. (2023). Navigating the Future: Blockchain's Impact on Accounting and Auditing Practices. *Sustainability (Basel)*, 15(24), 16887. DOI: 10.3390/su152416887

Sherif, K., & Mohsin, H. (2021). The effect of emergent technologies on accountants ethical blindness. *The International Journal of Digital Accounting Research*, 21, 61–94. DOI: 10.4192/1577-8517-v21_3

Sivarajah, U., Kamal, M. M., Irani, Z., & Weerakkody, V. (2017). Critical analysis of Big Data challenges and analytical methods. *Journal of Business Research*, 70, 263–286. DOI: 10.1016/j.jbusres.2016.08.001

Soori, M., Arezoo, B., & Dastres, R. (2023). Artificial intelligence, machine learning and deep learning in advanced robotics, a review. *Cognitive Robotics*, 3, 54–70. DOI: 10.1016/j.cogr.2023.04.001

Stach, C., Gritti, C., Bräcker, J., Behringer, M., & Mitschang, B. (2022). Protecting sensitive data in the information age: State of the art and future prospects. *Future Internet*, 14(11), 302. DOI: 10.3390/fi14110302

Suhaimi, N. S. A., Nawawi, A., & Salin, A. S. A. P. (2016). Impact of Enterprise Resource Planning on Management Control System and Accountants' Role. *International Journal of Economics & Management*, 10(1), 93–108.

Sujová, E., Čierna, H., & Żabińska, I. (2019). Application of digitization procedures of production in practice. *Management Systems in Production Engineering*, 27(1), 23–28. DOI: 10.1515/mspe-2019-0004

Suri, V. K., Elia, M., & van Hillegersberg, J. (2017). Software bots-the next frontier for shared services and functional excellence. In *Global Sourcing of Digital Services: Micro and Macro Perspectives,* 81-94. Cham: Springer International Publishing. DOI: 10.1007/978-3-319-70305-3_5

Szmajser, R., Kędzior, M., Andrzejewski, M., & Świetla, K. (2022). Implementation of new technologies in accounting and financial processes: An effectiveness assessment. *International Entrepreneurship Review*, 8(3), 7–21. DOI: 10.15678/IER.2022.0803.01

Szymanek, A., & Wiśniewski, T. (2023). Digitalization of reporting standards on the capital markets. In Gasiorkiewicz, L., & Monkiewicz, J. (Eds.), *The Digital Revolution in Banking, Insurance and Capital Markets* (pp. 236–251). Routledge. DOI: 10.4324/9781003310082-20

Tagscherer, F., & Carbon, C. C. (2023). Leadership for successful digitalization: A literature review on companies' internal and external aspects of digitalization. *Sustainable Technology and Entrepreneurship*, 2(2), 100039. DOI: 10.1016/j.stae.2023.100039

Taib, A., Awang, Y., Shuhidan, S. M., Rashid, N., & Hasan, M. S. (2022). Digitalization in accounting: Technology knowledge and readiness of future accountants. *Universal Journal of Accounting and Finance*, 10(1), 348–357. DOI: 10.13189/ujaf.2022.100135

Tarca, A. (2020). The IASB and comparability of international financial reporting: Research evidence and implications. *Australian Accounting Review*, 30(4), 231–242. DOI: 10.1111/auar.12326

Tekic, Z., & Koroteev, D. (2019). From disruptively digital to proudly analog: A holistic typology of digital transformation strategies. *Business Horizons*, 62(6), 683–693. DOI: 10.1016/j.bushor.2019.07.002

Tiwari, K., & Khan, M. S. (2020). Sustainability accounting and reporting in the industry 4.0. *Journal of Cleaner Production*, 258, 120783. DOI: 10.1016/j.jclepro.2020.120783

Tripathi, G., Ahad, M. A., & Casalino, G. (2023). A comprehensive review of blockchain technology: Underlying principles and historical background with future challenges. *Decision Analytics Journal*, 9(1), 100344. DOI: 10.1016/j.dajour.2023.100344

Troshani, I., & Rowbottom, N. (2021). Digital corporate reporting: Research developments and implications. *Australian Accounting Review*, 31(3), 213–232. DOI: 10.1111/auar.12334

Udeh, E. O., Amajuoyi, P., Adeusi, K. B., & Scott, A. O. (2024). The role of Blockchain technology in enhancing transparency and trust in green finance markets. *Finance & Accounting Research Journal*, 6(6), 825–850. DOI: 10.51594/farj.v6i6.1181

Ulas, D. (2019). Digital transformation process and SMEs. *Procedia Computer Science*, 158, 662–671. DOI: 10.1016/j.procs.2019.09.101

Ullrich, A., Reißig, M., Niehoff, S., & Beier, G. (2023). Employee involvement and participation in digital transformation: A combined analysis of literature and practitioners' expertise. *Journal of Organizational Change Management*, 36(8), 29–48. DOI: 10.1108/JOCM-10-2022-0302

Urbach, N., Ahlemann, F., Böhmann, T., Drews, P., Brenner, W., Schaudel, F., & Schütte, R. (2019). The impact of digitalization on the IT department. *Business & Information Systems Engineering*, 61(1), 123–131. DOI: 10.1007/s12599-018-0570-0

Urefe, O., Odonkor, T. N., & Agu, E. E. (2024). Enhancing financial reporting accuracy and compliance efficiency in legal firms through technological innovations. *International Journal of Management & Entrepreneurship Research*, 6(8), 2549–2560. DOI: 10.51594/ijmer.v6i8.1386

Van Thanh Le, C. P., El Ioini, N., & D'Atri, G. (2019). Enabling financial reports transparency and trustworthiness using blockchain technology. *International Journal on Advances in Security*, 12(3-4), 236–247. https://hdl.handle.net/10863/12122

Verhoef, P. C., Broekhuizen, T., Bart, Y., Bhattacharya, A., Dong, J. Q., Fabian, N., & Haenlein, M. (2021). Digital transformation: A multidisciplinary reflection and research agenda. *Journal of Business Research*, 122, 889–901. DOI: 10.1016/j.jbusres.2019.09.022

Vuchkovski, D., Zalaznik, M., Mitręga, M., & Pfajfar, G. (2023). A look at the future of work: The digital transformation of teams from conventional to virtual. *Journal of Business Research*, 163, 113912. DOI: 10.1016/j.jbusres.2023.113912

Wang, X., Lin, X., & Shao, B. (2022). How does artificial intelligence create business agility? Evidence from chatbots. *International Journal of Information Management*, 66, 102535. DOI: 10.1016/j.ijinfomgt.2022.102535

Whitehead, T. A. (2022). Training and Development: Investing in Employees Through Assessment. *Scholar Chatter*, 3(1), 1–6. DOI: 10.47036/SC.3.1.1-6.2022

Wibowo, T., & Christian, Y. (2021). Usage of blockchain to ensure audit data integrity. *Equity*, 24(1), 47–58. DOI: 10.34209/equ.v24i1.2357

Wilson, R. A., & Sangster, A. (1992). The automation of accounting practice. *Journal of Information Technology*, 7(2), 65–75. DOI: 10.1177/026839629200700202

Xiao, X., & Shailer, G. (2022). Stakeholders' perceptions of factors affecting the credibility of sustainability reports. *The British Accounting Review*, 54(1), 101002. DOI: 10.1016/j.bar.2021.101002

Yarmoliuk, O., Abramov, A., Mulyk, T., Smirnova, N., & Ponomarova, N. (2024). Digital technologies in accounting and reporting: Benefits, limitations, and possible risks. *Amazonia Investiga*, 13(74), 323–333. DOI: 10.34069/AI/2024.74.02.27

Zhao, J., & Wang, X. (2024). Unleashing efficiency and insights: Exploring the potential applications and challenges of ChatGPT in accounting. *Journal of Corporate Accounting & Finance*, 35(1), 269–276. DOI: 10.1002/jcaf.22663

Zhyvko, Z., Nikolashyn, A., Semenets, I., Karpenko, Y., Zos-Kior, M., Hnatenko, I., Klymenchukova, N., & Krakhmalova, N. (2022). Secure aspects of digitalization in management accounting and finances of the subject of the national economy in the context of globalization. *Journal of Hygienic Engineering and Design*, 39, 259–269.

KEY TERMS AND DEFINITIONS

Artificial Intelligence (AI): Technology that enables machines to perform tasks that typically require human intelligence, such as recognizing voices, understanding texts, or making decisions, namely, allowing computers to "think" and solve problems in a human-like manner.

Big Data: Large volumes of data generated en masse and at high speed, whose complexity requires advanced technologies to store, analyze, and extract needed information (e.g., behavioral patterns).

Blockchain: Technology that stores information securely and transparently in a chain of interconnected blocks that each contain data and are linked to the previous block, making altering the information difficult and producing digital ledgers that enable secure transactions without the need for intermediaries.

Corporative Efficiency: Companies' ability to use their resources optimally and achieve their objectives with the least possible cost and effort.

Corporative Transparency: Firm practices that share clear, complete, and accessible information about company activities, decisions, and finances, thereby allowing multiple stakeholders to understand how organizations operate and to trust their actions.

Deep Learning: Branch of AI that teaches computers to learn from large amounts of data typically by using neural networks to recognize patterns, identify images, or understand language, without needing to be programmed for each specific task.

Digitalization: Process of converting information, procedures, and physical or manual services into digital formats, which allows them to be managed by and accessed through computers and other electronic devices, thereby improving efficiency and facilitating access to information.

Digitalization of Financial Reporting: Process of transforming traditional financial reports into digital formats that allow companies to generate, share, and analyze financial information more quickly and accurately and that enhance transparency and facilitate decision making.

Machine Learning: AI technology that enables computers to learn from data and improve on their own instead of being programmed to do specific tasks, allowing these machine systems to analyze patterns in the information and make predictions or decisions autonomously.

Robotic Process Automation: Technology that uses software to perform repetitive tasks automatically and thus act as a virtual robot, for example, handling tasks such as entering data, generating reports, or sending emails in order to save time and reduce human errors.

ENDNOTE

[1] This application is available at https://www.sec.gov/edgar/sec-api-documentation.

Chapter 6
An Assessment of the Sentiments Behind the IASB's Standards:
An Exploratory Analysis of IAS 37

Fábio Albuquerque
https://orcid.org/0000-0001-8877-9634
ISCAL, Instituto Politécnico de Lisboa, Lisboa, Portugal & CICF, IPCA, Barcelos, Portugal

Paula Gomes dos Santos
https://orcid.org/0000-0003-2192-8855
ISCAL, Instituto Politécnico de Lisboa, Portugal & COMEGI, Portugal

ABSTRACT

This exploratory study aims to assess the aspects related to the message tone, magnitude, subjective-objective distinction, and thematic area behind the text collected from the International Accounting Standards Board (IASB) standard that outlines the accounting for provisions, contingent liabilities and contingent assets, i.e., International Accounting Standard (IAS) 37 - Provisions, Contingent Liabilities and Contingent Assets. The study uses archival research as a method and content analysis as a technique. The analysis is supported by an application programming interface, which uses text analytics based on natural language processing and machine learning. The findings show a most predominant negative approach underlying the message, regardless of the aspects under assessment, which also have a higher level of magnitude on average. Furthermore, messages are mostly subjective or of an unknown nature, particularly for those related to more technical aspects of IAS 37. Finally, those aspects present reduced scores of their classification within the "Business and Finance."

DOI: 10.4018/979-8-3693-5923-5.ch006

INTRODUCTION

Mining text documents, namely regarding sentiment analysis, have been receiving increasing attention from the literature due to their wide applicability in several areas (e.g., Fakalou, 2024; Hajek & Munk, 2023; Hamed et al., 2020; Kearney & Liu, 2014; Krishnamoorthy, 2018).

Sentiment analysis or opinion mining involves extracting and assessing information from textual data to capture the sentiment or opinion expressed (Pagliarussi et al., 2016). Two main types of classification are commonly found: subjectivity, which intends to differentiate subjective from objective opinions in a given text; and sentiment, which captures whether the message tone is positive, negative, or neutral (Bochkay et al., 2023; Pagliarussi et al., 2016).

Deep learning models to study sentiment analysis have been applied in several areas, namely in the behavioural finance field (Gandía & Huguet, 2021), where sentiment analysis and speech emotion recognition have the potential to capture the intentions and opinions of corporate stakeholders (Hajek & Munk, 2023). Also, research on sentiment analysis in financial reporting and market prediction has shown that the sentiment expressed in financial news, earnings calls, and reports can provide valuable predictive indicators for market trends and company performance, and frequently influences investor decisions (Faccia et al., 2024).

Those methodologies have a great potential for application in accounting research (Fisher et al., 2016; Gandía & Huguet, 2021; Loughran & McDonald, 2016). This is due to the volume of documents used for communicating qualitative information as a complement to financial statements (such as Management Discussion and Analysis (MD&A) reports, earnings press releases, or corporate social responsibility reports), and to the growth in the use of digital tools and social media (Gandía & Huguet, 2021).

Furthermore, sentiment analysis techniques can help researchers investigate if the tone behind the companies' disclosures contains implicit clues not evident in numerical data, whether information on the analysts' reports contains data beyond their ratings or opinions, and if the sentiment attempts to influence users' decision-making processes (Gandía & Huguet, 2021). In this context, researchers have been studying several topics, such as fraud detection (Bhattacharya & Mickovic, 2024; Faccia et al., 2024), non-financial disclosures (Mućko, 2021), financial condition (Hajek & Munk, 2023; Pagliarussi et al., 2016; Zhong & Ren, 2022), or the tone at the top (Patelli & Pedrini, 2015).

Nevertheless, compared with quantitative methods traditionally employed in accounting, auditing, and finance, textual analysis is less precise (Loughran & McDonald, 2016). Besides, despite the potential to complement traditional numerical analysis (Faccia et al., 2024), the use of textual analysis and sentiment analysis techniques in finance, accounting, and auditing is still relatively scarce (Gandía & Huguet, 2021).

According to Fisher et al. (2010), textual documents are widespread in accounting practice, and various groups rely on written guidance for making financial decisions. The International Accounting Standards (IAS) and the International Financial Reporting Standards (IFRS), issued by the International Accounting Standards Board (IASB), in addition to annual corporate financial statements and other reporting narratives, are relevant sources of such guidance and information (Fisher et al., 2010).

The IASB standards are instrumental in establishing global accounting standards and ensuring transparency and comparability in financial reporting (O Cualain & Tawiah, 2023; Tarca, 2020). Notwithstanding, those standards are acknowledged for their principle-based nature, requiring considerable professional judgment and estimations in their implementation (Coram & Wang, 2021). Therefore, acknowledging the sentiments behind IASB standards may provide insights into stakeholders' perceptions and regulatory impacts.

A few studies can be mentioned as a research application of sentiment analysis within the accounting standards process. For instance, within the scope of IASB, Shields et al. (2019) analysed the potential for influencing the IASB through the submission of comment letters during the standards formulation, by assessing whether the use of arguments can be identified through a negative tone and whether this serves as a better predictor of lobbying success compared to direct disagreement. Despite that, there are no studies which assessed the sentiment behind IASB standards as far as it is the authors' knowledge.

Therefore, this exploratory study aims to assess the aspects related to the message tone, magnitude, subjective-objective distinction and thematic area behind the text collected from the IASB standard that outlines the accounting for provisions, contingent liabilities and contingent assets, i.e., IAS 37 - Provisions, Contingent Liabilities and Contingent Assets.

This chapter is structured in four sections, in addition to this introduction. The next section presents the theoretical framework underlying the proposed study. The third section identifies the materials and methods underlying the exploratory analysis proposed for this chapter and is followed by the results section. Finally, the last section presents the conclusions, as well as the limitations and suggestions for future avenues.

THEORETICAL FRAMEWORK

Although the IASB standards have been developed to minimize accounting practices across countries, as principle-based standards they require significant professional judgment to be applied (Coram & Wang, 2021; Maradona et al., 2024), which may compromise the intended comparability (Gierusz et al., 2022; Hellmann et al., 2021; Hellmann & Patel, 2021).

Professional judgment and comparability are major issues in accounting research, as the worldwide adoption of IASB standards does not ensure their consistent understanding and application (Gierusz et al., 2022). For instance, the interpretation of key accounting concepts may be biased by professionals' characteristics such as the language used, as those standards are developed in English and translated into local languages (Hellmann et al., 2021; Hellmann & Patel, 2021; Zhang et al., 2020), or by their national culture (Gierusz et al., 2022).

Also, some standards include subjective uncertainty expressions which are subject to professional interpretation and judgment (Gierusz et al., 2022; Zhang et al., 2019). For instance, Monica and Stefan (2019) highlighted that stakeholders considered IFRS 9 difficult to understand and involved a high degree of professional judgment. The use of subjective uncertainty expressions has raised concerns about information quality and communication efficiency, which drove researchers to assess their effects in financial reporting, as well as in the context of judgment and decision-making behaviour (Gierusz et al., 2022; Zhang et al., 2019, 2020).

Within the set of IASB's standards, the IAS 37 have been pointed out as a standard in which professional judgment leads to significant differences in financial reporting (Langa & Albuquerque, 2024; Marcelino et al., 2016), namely by using expressions such as "probable" relating to judgments on accounting disclosures (Gierusz et al., 2022).

IAS 37 was issued by the International Accounting Standards Committee (IASC) in 1998, effective from the following year, and was adopted by the IASB in 2001. This standard prescribes the accounting and disclosure of matters relating to provisions, contingent liabilities, and contingent assets, except those resulting from non-onerous enforceable contracts and those covered by other rules (§§ 1 and 5).

Enforceable contracts are understood as contracts for which neither party has fulfilled any of its obligations or both parties have only partially fulfilled their obligations to the same extent (§ 3), whereas non-onerous contracts are contracts in which the inevitable costs of meeting the obligations of the contract do not exceed the economic benefits expected to be received under them (§ 10).

A provision is defined in IAS 37 as a liability of uncertain timing or uncertain amount (§ 10), which should only be recognised when the following conditions are cumulatively met (§ 14):

a. an entity has a present obligation (legal or constructive) because of a past event.
b. an outflow of resources will probably be required to settle the obligation;
c. a reliable estimate of the amount of the obligation can be made.

All provision is, consequently, a liability, but it is related to characteristics (greater uncertainty than other liabilities as to the amount or timing). It is also important to observe the definition of a liability, identified as a present obligation (legal or constructive) of an entity arising from past events, from which settlement is expected to result in an outflow of resources (§ 10).

The legal obligation should be understood as an obligation deriving from a contract (explicit or implicit), legislation or other operation of the law (§ 10), while the constructive obligation must have the meaning of an obligation that derives from the actions of an entity in which:

a. by an established model of past practices, published policies or a sufficiently specific current statement, the entity has indicated to other parties that it will accept certain responsibilities (§ 10); and
b. consequently, the entity has created a valid expectation in those other parts that it will discharge those responsibilities (§ 10).

Also in this context, it should be noted that the uncertainty and the greatest risk about the timing or amount of future expenditure necessary for its liquidation, present in the provisions, distinguishes them from other liabilities since in the liabilities the time of settlement and the amount of the obligation are established legally or constructively (§ 11).

In turn, contingent liabilities are defined as:

a. a possible obligation that derives from past events and whose existence will only be confirmed by the occurrence or not of one or more uncertain future events not entirely under the control of the entity (§ 10); or
b. a present obligation which stems from past events, but which is not recognised because:
    i. It is not likely that an outflow of resources embodying economic benefits will be necessary to settle the obligation (§ 10); or
    ii. the amount of the obligation cannot be measured with sufficient reliability (§ 10).

Similarly, a contingent asset must be understood as a possible asset arising from past events and whose existence will only be confirmed by the occurrence or absence of one or more uncertain future events not fully under the control of the entity (§ 10).

As a common point between liabilities and contingent assets are, in summary, issues related to either the reliability of measurement, or with the lowest level of probability of outflow (in the case of liabilities) or inflow (in the case of the asset) or, furthermore, dependence on future events (uncertain and outside the control of the entity) for their confirmation.

Finally, it should be noted that an entity should not recognise a contingent liability (or an asset), and should disclose this unless the possibility (probability) of the outflow (inflow) of resources (§§ 28, 33 and 34) is remote.

Sentiment analysis has been used in accounting, auditing and finance research for several purposes. For instance, it has been used in fraud detection, exploring, for example, how textual contents from financial reports help in detecting accounting fraud by analysing the Management Discussion and Analysis (MD&A) (Bhattacharya & Mickovic, 2024), and introducing a novel approach to detecting financial statement fraud by applying sentiment analysis to analyse the textual data within financial reports (Faccia et al., 2024).

In this context, natural language processing (NLP) techniques have also addressed the firms' financial condition, by focusing, for instance, on the association between the tone of annual reports and market variables (Pagliarussi et al., 2016), the relationship between subjective expression in financial reports and company performance (Zhong & Ren, 2022), and on the role of managerial emotions in predicting financial distress (Hajek & Munk, 2023).

NLP applications have also been used to mine several documents in the accounting, auditing, and finance domains, such as corporate disclosures, management's assessment of current and future firm performance, analysts' reports, domain standards and regulations as well as evidence of compliance with relevant standards and regulations (Gandía & Huguet, 2021; Fisher et al., 2016), the internet and social media, and press news (Gandía & Huguet, 2021).

In auditing, the top management tone has also been studied, as leadership responsibilities are an element of a strong quality control system within a firm, often referred to as tone at the top (Transnational Auditors Committee, 2007). According to Patelli and Pedrini (2015), a relevant determinant of tone at the top is the corporate narrative language, since it is a fundamental way in which the chief executive officer enacts leadership.

Accounting researchers have often used textual analysis to measure disclosure sentiment and readability, to count words, sentences, or articles that contain keywords as a proxy for the quantity of textual information, to compare disclosures to determine similarities or differences, to identify forward-looking information, and to detect disclosure topics (Bochkay et al., 2023). However, newer NLP techniques can offer opportunities to address new research questions (Bochkay et al., 2023), as it is proposed for this research by assessing a novelty research object in accounting.

Due to the use of uncertainty expressions in IAS 37, which are subjective and rely on professional judgment to be applied, it is useful to understand how that standard can be interpreted or understood by their stakeholders, which underlies the aim of this research by the use of sentiment analysis tools and classification.

The next section presents the research questions, material and methods underlying this research.

RESEARCH QUESTIONS, MATERIAL, AND METHODS

This study aims to assess the aspects related to the message tone, magnitude, subjective-objective distinction, and thematic area behind the standard, from an exploratory perspective. To achieve its purpose, this study uses archival research as a method and content analysis as a technique. Specifically, it uses the sentiment analysis of IAS 37 content provided by the IASB.

Then, the excerpts (paragraphs) gathered from the IAS 37 were selected as the research object, considering the level of inherent subjectivity that is usually attributed to its underlying content, requiring professional judgment to be properly applied (e.g., Coram & Wang, 2021; Maradona et al., 2024). Consequently, the following research questions (RQs) have emerged as relevant for this analysis, based on the objective proposed for this research, as follows:

- RQ1. What are the message tones (positive, neutral or negative) found for those excepts?
- RQ2. What are the message magnitudes found for those excerpts?
- RQ3. Can the messages within those excerpts be interpreted as being of a subjective or objective nature?
- RQ4. Which thematic area can be predominantly found for those excerpts?

This analysis is supported by an application programming interface (API) available on the platform text2data, which uses text analytics based on NLP and machine learning.

Regarding RQ1, the API tool assesses the negativity or positivity of a message's tone, with a score that ranged from -1 to 1, respectively, with scores closer to zero (between -0.25 and 0.25) indicating a neutral tone.

For RQ2, the magnitude can be interpreted as the volume of sentiment expressed throughout the message, regardless of sentiment polarity, which can be used to detect the strength of emotions or fine-tune sentiment polarity, ranging from 0 to ∞.

Concerning the RQ3, the tool identifies the likely mode of how the discourse can be interpreted by readers, namely if it expresses opinions, feelings or doubts, conversely to those based on facts, providing three possible classifications or categories for it: objective, subjectivity and unknown.

Finally, RQ4 identifies the inclusion of the text within a given thematic area, based on the Interactive Advertising Bureau (IAB) - Quality Assurance Guidelines (QAG) taxonomy, providing a classification between 0 to 1 for a given area and also for the sum of all areas found, which can not be higher than 1 at a total.

Each one of the 101 paragraphs of the IAS 37, plus the objective, was individually assessed. Nonetheless, the analysis was also performed by gathering sets of paragraphs that cover the different aspects of IAS 37, as follows:

- Objective;
- Scope (paragraphs 1 to 9, except the 4 and 6, which were deleted);
- Definitions (paragraphs 10 to 13);
- Recognition (paragraphs 14 to 35);
- Measurement (paragraphs 36 to 52);
- Reimbursements (paragraphs 53 to 58);
- Changes in provisions (paragraphs 59 and 60);
- Use of provisions (paragraphs 61 and 62);
- Application of the recognition and measurement rules (paragraphs 63 to 83, including the 68A);
- Disclosures (paragraphs 84 to 92);
- Transitional provisions (paragraphs 93 and 94A);
- Effective date (paragraphs 95 to 105, excluding paragraphs 96, 97 and 98, which were deleted).

The next section provides the findings.

RESULTS

This section presents the findings of each of the four RQs mentioned in the previous one.

The figures for **RQ1** analysis indicate that the excerpts from the IAS 37 have mostly a negative tone (53%), followed by a neutral tone (29%). The average score for each one of the subgroups of excerpts with negative and positive tone is about 0.6 in absolute values for both. The subgroup of excerpts with neutral tones had 0.08 on average.

Table 1 provides further details by providing those figures for the set of paragraphs that represent the different aspects covered by the IAS 37.

Table 1. Message tones of the excerpts within the aspects covered by the IAS 37

Aspects covered by the IAS 37	Negative (number; percentage; score)	Neutral (number; percentage; score)	Positive (number; percentage; score)	Total (number; percentage; score)
Objective	1; **100**; -0.61			1; **100**; -0.61
Scope	5; **71**; -0,61	2; **29**; 0.01		7; **100**; -0.43
Definitions	2; **50**; -0.61	1; **25**; 0.18	1; **25**; 0.99	4; **100**; -0.01
Recognition	14; **64**; -0.61	3; **14**; 0.16	5; **23**; 0.56	22; **100**; -0.24
Measurement	9; **53**; -0.59	5; **29**; 0.15	3; **18**; 0.65	17; **100**; -0.15
Reimbursements	1; **17**; -0.52	3; **50**; 0.02	2; **33**; 0.51	6; **100**; 0,09
Changes in provisions	1; **50**; -0.55	1; **50**; 0.15		2; **100**; -0,20
Use of provisions	1; **50**; -0.64	1; **50**; 0.22		2; **100**; -0,21
Application of the recognition and measurement rules	12; **55**; -0.61	6; **27**; 0,11	4; **18**; 0.61	22; **100**; -0.19
Disclosure	4; **44**; -0.56	3; **33**; -0,02	2; **22**; 0.54	9; **100**; -0.14
Transitional provisions	2; **100**; -0.60			2; **100**; -0.60
Effective date	2; **25**; -0.60	5; **63**; 0.02	1; **13**; 0.63	8; **100**; -0.06
Total	54; **53**; -0.60	30; **29**; 0,09	18; **18**; 0.60	102; **100**; -0.19

Figures from Table 1 indicate that negative messages are the most observed across the aspects under assessment, except for those related to reimbursements and the IAS 37 effective date, which are mostly neutral in both cases. For some aspects, the neutral or positive tones were not found at all. Nonetheless, it's worth stressing that the total number of paragraphs related to those cases, i.e., whenever neither the neutral nor positive tones occur, is reduced (equal to or lower than two paragraphs), except those for the IAS 37 scope (mostly negative).

Regarding the magnitude underlying the messages (**RQ2**), the average value found is 1.36, which is not significantly high, ranging between 0.64 at a minimum and 2.37 at a maximum. The messages with a negative tone present a higher level of magnitude on average (1.60).

Table 2 presents the average magnitudes by the several aspects covered by the IAS 37, with a further breakdown by the message tones.

Table 2. Magnitudes by message tones of the excerpts within the aspects covered by the IAS 37

Aspects covered by the IAS 37	Negative	Neutral	Positive	Total
Objective	0.86			0.86
Scope	1.81	0.69		1.49
Definitions	2.02	0.30	5.15	2.37
Recognition	1.81	1.46	1.24	1.63
Measurement	1.94	0.60	1.51	1.47
Reimbursements	0.65	1.18	0.99	1.03
Changes in provisions	1.30	0.69		1.00
Use of provisions	1.17	0.10		0.64
Application of the recognition and measurement rules	1.31	0.96	1.36	1.22
Disclosure	0.75	0.88	0.89	0.82
Transitional provisions	1.97			1.97
Effective date	2.01	0.93	1.04	1.22
Total	**1.60**	**0.88**	**1.45**	**1.36**

The highest magnitudes can be found in Table 2 for the messages related to the definitions under IAS 37, particularly for the single positive message identified, which also reaches the maximum value from an overall assessment. Conversely, the aspects related to the disclosures present lower levels of magnitude, regardless of the tone of the messages (below 1.00 in all cases). Globally, the messages with neutral tones are also those for which the magnitudes are commonly low (below 1.00, except for the aspects related to recognition and reimbursements).

Concerning the subjective or objective nature underlying the messages (**RQ3**), the findings indicate a lower level of objective messages across the paragraphs of IAS 37 (17%). The remaining are divided between the subjective (40%) and unknown nature (43%).

Table 3 provides the figures for the several aspects covered by the IAS 37 for this classification.

Table 3. Subjective versus objective nature of the message for the excerpts within the aspects covered by the IAS 37

Aspects covered by the IAS 37	Objective (number; percentage)	Subjective (number; percentage)	Unknown (number; percentage)	Total (number; percentage)
Objective			1; **100**	1; **100**
Scope		4; **57**	3; **43**	7; **100**
Definitions	2; **50**	2; **50**		4; **100**
Recognition	5; **23**	10; **45**	7; **32**	22; **100**
Measurement	3; **18**	6; **35**	8; **47**	17; **100**
Reimbursements	1; **17**	2; **33**	3; **50**	6; **100**
Changes in provisions		1; **50**	1; **50**	2; **100**
Use of provisions			2; **100**	2; **100**
Application of the recognition and measurement rules	5; **23**	6; **27**	11; **50**	22; **100**
Disclosure	1; **11**	5; **56**	3; **33**	9; **100**
Transitional provisions		2; **100**		2; **100**
Effective date		3; **38**	5; **63**	8; **100**
Total	17; **17**	41; **40**	44; **43**	102; **100**

Figures in Table 3 enable the identification that the excerpts related to the scope and effective date, to mention those with more than 7 paragraphs at least, are not classified as objective in any case. This classification was also not predominantly found in any aspects covered by the IAS 37. Furthermore, the more technical aspects of this standard, such as recognition, measurement and application rules are mostly classified as either subjective or unknown.

Finally, regarding the thematic area that can be found for those excerpts (**RQ4**), the "Business and Finance" area emerged as the most predominant as expected, considering the scope, objective, and users of IAS 37. On average, it scores of 0.685 but it ranges differently depending on the aspect covered by the IAS 37 under assessment.

Table 4 provides those scores for the "Business and Finance" area, on average and by ranges (R), for the several aspects covered by the IAS 37 for this classification.

Table 4. Thematic area of the message for the excerpts within the aspects covered by the IAS 37

Aspects covered by the IAS 37	R1 (number; percentage)	R2 (number; percentage)	R3 (number; percentage)	R4 (number; percentage)	Total (number; percentage, average)
Objective				1; **100**	1; **100**; 0.81
Scope		3; **43**	2; **29**	2; **29**	7; **100**; 0.64
Definitions				4; **100**	4; **100**; 0.99
Recognition	4; **18**	2; **9**	4; **18**	12; **55**	22; **100**; 0.69
Measurement	2; **12**	4; **24**	3; **18**	8; **47**	17; **100**; 0.69
Reimbursements			2; **33**	4; **67**	6; **100**; 0.81
Changes in provisions	1; **50**			1; **50**	2; **100**; 0.52
Use of provisions	1; **50**	1; **50**			2; **100**; 0.14
Application of the recognition and measurement rules	3; **14**	5; **23**	4; **18**	10; **45**	22; **100**; 0.65
Disclosure		2; **22**	1; **11**	6; **67**	9; **100**; 0.80
Transitional provisions				2; **100**	2; **100**; 0.98
Effective date	1; **12**	3; **37**	2; **25**	2; **25**	8; **100**; 0.51
Total	12; **12**	20; **20**	18; **18**	52; **51**	102; **100**; 0.68

Legend: R1 for scores equal to or lower than 25%; R2 for scores higher than 25% and equal to or lower than 50%; R3 for scores higher than 50% and equal to or lower than 75%; R1 for scores higher than 75%.

Table 4 shows that more than two-thirds of the excerpts were classified in the "Business and Finance" area at a level higher than 50%, with about half of them scoring even higher than 75%. Nonetheless, it should be noted that some excerpts related to technical issues provided by IAS 37 were also classified in this area at a reduced level (lower than 50%), which includes relevant matters related, for instance, to recognition, measurement, and application rules. Those, besides the IAS 37 scope and effective date, also present the most reduced level on average (between 0.51 and 0.69, which means below or close to the total average), to mention those with at least seven paragraphs.

The last section provides the conclusions from this study, including its limitations and suggestions for future research.

CONCLUSION

From an exploratory perspective, this study aims to assess the message tone, magnitude, subjective-objective distinction, and thematic area behind the text collected from the IASB's standards. A combination of archival research and content analysis is used for this purpose. It relies on the sentiment analysis of IAS 37 content provided by IASB.

The analysis covered different aspects, namely the message tones (positive, neutral, or negative), message magnitudes, whether messages can be seen as subjective or objective, as well as their thematic area. The excerpts were assessed individually and by the different aspects (set of paragraphs) covered by the IAS 37.

The findings show a most predominant negative approach underlying the message, regardless of the aspects under assessment, with a few exceptions. The messages with a negative tone present a higher level of magnitude on average. The highest magnitudes were found for the message within the paragraphs related to the definitions under IAS 37, conversely to the aspects related to the disclosures. Furthermore, messages are mostly subjective or of an unknown nature, particularly for those related to more technical aspects of IAS 37. Finally, despite the higher level of identification of the messages within the "Business and Finance" area, relevant technical matters, as well as those related to the IAS 37 scope and effective date, present reduced scores in this regard.

Together, those findings may indicate that the messages behind the IAS 37 are commonly proposed by exclusion (particularly the IAS 37 scope) or from the perspective of what should not be done or why certain requirements are not necessary, required or indicated in a given circumstance. It also provides insights that corroborate some criticism regarding its non-assertive approach occasionally as well as its higher level of subjectivity, which requires the use of professional judgment (Coram & Wang, 2021; Langa & Albuquerque, 2024; Maradona et al., 2024; Marcelino et al., 2016). Because of this, the entities' financial reporting can be more discretionary, which means that their comparability among providers can be reduced to a level that, to a final extent, can be non-relevant for users to make their decisions based on it (Gierusz et al., 2022; Zhang et al., 2019, 2020).

This research, despite still exploratory, can contribute to standard-setter bodies, regulatory bodies, and other relevant interested parties, such as local policymakers involved in the process of accounting harmonisation or national convergence to the IASB's standards, to acknowledge the relevance of understanding how those documents can be interpreted or understood by their stakeholders. Since it is the first study that assesses the sentiment analysis behind a document of such nature, as far as it is the authors' knowledge, it also contributes to the literature by proposing some viewpoints of sentimental analysis that can be used in future investigations.

In this path, future researchers can also derive the analysis behind this study from diverse but related perspectives. For instance, studies can compare the findings from those tools of sentiment analysis with the perception of readers with a reasonable understanding of the language and the matters underlying accounting and reporting standards. The analysis of the effects of this understanding, and its properness concerning the preparers' interpretations and application, which includes the analysis of possible judgment bias, can also be relevant in this research field. Experimental studies can be used to achieve this research purpose, also providing a significant contribution to standard-setter bodies to achieve their goals when proposing future standards or amending the existing ones.

Also, researchers can compare the findings from this research with similar ones that may result from the assessment of other standards also issued by IASB covering different aspects other than those provided by IAS 37. In a similar sense, the comparison between older standards, such as IAS 37, with the latest ones, such as those from IFRS 15 – Revenues onwards, can be of interest to identify whether there is a different pattern underlying the messages within them, which may be an indication of a possible change of attitude or position regarding their stakeholders by the IASB. Finally, the findings from this study can be compared with those using standards of a similar nature but issued by other standard-setter bodies, such as the International Public Sector Accounting Standards (IPSAS) issued by the International Public Sector Accounting Standards Board (IPSASB), to compare if they have a similar pattern or if there is a difference that can be attributed to their specific profile, goals or stakeholders.

Despite the likely interest behind this research, a broader understanding of these findings requires acknowledging its limitations, which can be summarised in a set of two-fold main restrictions. The first is related to the size of the paragraphs, which cannot be, ideally, too short or too large for a proper analysis of the characteristics assessed by the tool used. The second is related to the analysis performed by these tools, which still presents some inherent restrictions mostly derived from a focus on the text (for instance, keywords that are classified as expressing negative sentiments) over the context, despite the growing and rapid evolution over the last few years, considering the increasing machine learning developments.

ACKNOWLEDGMENT

This work was supported by Instituto Politécnico de Lisboa (IPL/IDI&CA 2024/IAccount_ISCAL).

REFERENCES

Bhattacharya, I., & Mickovic, A. (2024). Accounting fraud detection using contextual language learning. *International Journal of Accounting Information Systems*, 53, 100682. DOI: 10.1016/j.accinf.2024.100682

Bochkay, K., Brown, S. V., Leone, A. J., & Tucker, J. W. (2023). Textual Analysis in Accounting: What's Next? *Contemporary Accounting Research*, 40(2), 765–805. DOI: 10.1111/1911-3846.12825

Coram, P. J., & Wang, L. (2021). The effect of disclosing key audit matters and accounting standard precision on the audit expectation gap. *International Journal of Auditing*, 25(2), 270–282. DOI: 10.1111/ijau.12203

Cualain, O. (2023). Review of IFRS consequences in Europe: An enforcement perspective. *Cogent Business & Management*, 10(1), 1–19. DOI: 10.1080/23311975.2022.2148869

Faccia, A., McDonald, J., & George, B. (2024). NLP Sentiment Analysis and Accounting Transparency: A New Era of Financial Record Keeping. *Computers*, 13(1), 5. DOI: 10.3390/computers13010005

Fakalou, C. (2024). The Sociolinguistics of Asylum Decision-Writing in the Context of the Greek Appeals Authority. *International Journal for the Semiotics of Law*, 37(2), 305–328. DOI: 10.1007/s11196-023-10039-6

Fisher, I. E., Garnsey, M. R., Goel, S., & Tam, K. (2010). The Role of Text Analytics and Information Retrieval in the Accounting Domain. *Journal of Emerging Technologies in Accounting*, 7(1), 1–24. DOI: 10.2308/jeta.2010.7.1.1

Fisher, I. E., Garnsey, M. R., & Hughes, M. E. (2016). Natural Language Processing in accounting, auditing, and finance: A synthesis of the literature with a roadmap for future research. *International Journal of Intelligent Systems in Accounting Finance & Management*, 23(3), 157–214. DOI: 10.1002/isaf.1386

Gandía, J. L., & Huguet, D. (2021). Textual analysis and sentiment analysis in accounting. *Revista de Contabilidad-Spanish Accounting Review*, 24(2). DOI: 10.6018/rcsar.386541

Gierusz, J., Kolesnik, K., Silska-Gembka, S., & Zamojska, A. (2022). The influence of culture on accounting judgment – Evidence from Poland and the United Kingdom. *Cogent Business & Management*, 9(1), 1993556. Advance online publication. DOI: 10.1080/23311975.2021.1993556

Hajek, P., & Munk, M. (2023). Speech emotion recognition and text sentiment analysis for financial distress prediction. *Neural Computing & Applications*, 35(29), 21463–21477. DOI: 10.1007/s00521-023-08470-8

Hamed, S., Ezzat, M., & Hefny, H. (2020). A Review of Sentiment Analysis Techniques. *International Journal of Computer Applications*, 176(37), 20–24. DOI: 10.5120/ijca2020920480

Hellmann, A., & Patel, C. (2021). Translation of International Financial Reporting Standards and implications for judgments and decision-making. *Journal of Behavioral and Experimental Finance*, 30, 100479. DOI: 10.1016/j.jbef.2021.100479

Hellmann, A., Patel, C., & Tsunogaya, N. (2021). Foreign-language effect and professionals' judgments on fair value measurement: Evidence from Germany and the United Kingdom. *Journal of Behavioral and Experimental Finance*, 30, 100478. DOI: 10.1016/j.jbef.2021.100478

Kearney, C., & Liu, S. (2014). Textual sentiment in finance: A survey of methods and models. *International Review of Financial Analysis*, 33, 171–185. DOI: 10.1016/j.irfa.2014.02.006

Krishnamoorthy, S. (2018). Sentiment analysis of financial news articles using performance indicators. *Knowledge and Information Systems*, 56(2), 373–394. DOI: 10.1007/s10115-017-1134-1

Langa, E., & Albuquerque, F. (2024). Conservatism as a cultural accounting value: An empirical study from the perspective of chartered accountants and auditors in Mozambique. *Contaduría y Administración*, 69(1), 1–22. DOI: 10.22201/fca.24488410e.2024.4682

Loughran, T., & McDonald, B. (2016). Textual analysis in accounting and finance: A survey. *Journal of Accounting Research*, 54(4), 1187–1230. DOI: 10.1111/1475-679X.12123

Maradona, A. F., Chand, P., & Lodhia, S. (2024). Professional skills required by accountants for applying international financial reporting standards: Implications from Indonesia. *Meditari Accountancy Research*, 32(2), 269–293. DOI: 10.1108/MEDAR-02-2022-1591

Marcelino, M. M., Albuquerque, F., Justino, M. D. R., & Quirós, J. T. (2016). The influence of culture and professional judgment on Accounting: An analysis from the perspective of financial information preparers in Portugal. *Journal of Education and Research in Accounting*, 10(1), 63–87. DOI: 10.17524/repec.v10i1.1214

Monica, M., & Stefan, B. (2019). Ifrs 9 benchmarking test: Too complicated to worth doing it? *Economic Computation and Economic Cybernetics Studies and Research*, 53(1), 217–230. DOI: 10.24818/18423264/53.1.19.14

Mućko, P. (2021). Sentiment analysis of CSR disclosures in annual reports of EU companies. *Procedia Computer Science*, 192, 3351–3359. DOI: 10.1016/j.procs.2021.09.108

Pagliarussi, M.S., Aguiar, M.O., & Galdi, F.C. (2016). Sentiment analysis in annual reports from Brazilian companies listed at the BM&FBOVESPA. *BASE - Revista de Administração e Contabilidade da Unisinos*, 13(1). DOI: 10.4013/base.2016.131.04

Patelli, L., & Pedrini, M. (2015). Is Tone at the Top Associated with Financial Reporting Aggressiveness? *Journal of Business Ethics*, 126(1), 3–19. DOI: 10.1007/s10551-013-1994-6

Shields, K., Clacher, I., & Zhang, Q. (2019). Negative Tone in Lobbying the International Accounting Standards Board. *The International Journal of Accounting*, 54(03), 1950010. DOI: 10.1142/S1094406019500100

Tarca, A. (2020). The IASB and comparability of international financial reporting: Research evidence and implications. *Australian Accounting Review*, 30(4), 231–242. DOI: 10.1111/auar.12326

Transnational Auditors Committee. (2007). Tone at the Top and Audit Quality. Forum of firms. https://www.iasplus.com/en/binary/ifac/0712toneatthetop.pdf

Zhang, Y., De Zoysa, A., & Cortese, C. (2019). Uncertainty expressions in accounting: Critical issues and recommendations. *Australasian Accounting Business and Finance Journal*, 13(4), 4–22. DOI: 10.14453/aabfj.v13i4.2

Zhang, Y., De Zoysa, A., & Cortese, C. (2020). The directionality of uncertainty expressions and the foreign language effect: Context and accounting judgement. *Meditari Accountancy Research*, 28(3), 543–563. DOI: 10.1108/MEDAR-09-2018-0377

Zhong, N., & Ren, J. (2022). Using sentiment analysis to study the relationship between subjective expression in financial reports and company performance. *Frontiers in Psychology*, 13, 949881. DOI: 10.3389/fpsyg.2022.949881 PMID: 35936313

ADDITIONAL READING

Azmi Shabestari, M., & Romero, J. A. (2024). Textual Analysis and Future Performance: Evidence From Item 1A and Item 7. *Journal of Accounting, Auditing & Finance*, 39(3), 931–948. DOI: 10.1177/0148558X221107849

Bennani, H., Couharde, C., & Wallois, Y. (2024). The effect of IMF communication on government bond markets: Insights from sentiment analysis. *Review of World Economics*, 160(2), 615–656. DOI: 10.1007/s10290-023-00509-1

Kirtac, K., & Germano, G. (2024). Sentiment trading with large language models. *Finance Research Letters*, 62, 105227. DOI: 10.1016/j.frl.2024.105227

Yang, S., Tai, Y., Cao, Y., Chen, Y., & Zhang, Q. (2024). Underwriter Discourse, IPO Profit Distribution, and Audit Quality: An Entropy Study from the Perspective of an Underwriter–Auditor Network. *Entropy (Basel, Switzerland)*, 26(5), 393. DOI: 10.3390/e26050393 PMID: 38785641

Yao, X., Wu, D., Li, Z., & Xu, H. (2024). On the prediction of stock price crash risk using textual sentiment of management statement. *China Finance Review International*, 14(2), 310–331. DOI: 10.1108/CFRI-12-2022-0250

KEY TERMS AND DEFINITIONS

Liability: Is a present obligation of the entity arising from past events, the settlement of which is expected to result in an outflow from the entity of resources embodying economic benefits (§ 10, IAS 37).

Obligating Event: Is an event that creates a legal or constructive obligation that results in an entity having no realistic alternative to settling that obligation.

Onerous: Contract is a contract in which the unavoidable costs of meeting the obligations under the contract exceed the economic benefits expected to be received under it (§ 10, IAS 37).

Provision: Is a liability of uncertain timing or amount (§ 10, IAS 37).

Chapter 7
Perceived Benefits of IFRS Adoption in Morocco and French Speaking Sub-Saharan African Countries

Azzouz Elhamma
Ibn Tofaîl University, Morocco

ABSTRACT

This chapter aims to study, by using a sample of 75 practitioners and researchers in accounting, the consequences of the International Financial Reporting Standards (IFRS) adoption on the qualitative characteristics of financial reporting in 12 African countries: Morocco and 11 French speaking Sub-Saharan African Countries. Two main findings can be highlighted in this research. Firstly, more than half of all Moroccan- and French-speaking Sub-Saharan African respondents consider that the adoption of IFRS improves "highly" or "very highly" the reliability (52%), the relevance (57.4%), and the comparability (54.7%) of their financial reporting. Secondly, Moroccan professionals and researchers in accounting are more concerned than their French-speaking Sub-Saharan African colleagues by the adoption of IFRS to improve the relevance and the understandability of the financial reporting. For the two other qualitative characteristics (reliability and comparability), the difference in means is not significant.

DOI: 10.4018/979-8-3693-5923-5.ch007

INTRODUCTION

Over the past two decades, especially after the adoption of IFRS (International Financial Reporting Standards) in 2005 by the European Union for consolidated accounts and the financial crisis of 2008, IFRS has been the subject of many research studies around the world. Most of these studies have been conducted in European and Asian countries (Tawiah and Boolaky, 2020). In Africa, this type of research is still rare and dominated by Anglophone African countries such as South Africa (Coetzee and Schmulian, 2013; Sellami and Fendri, 2017; etc.), Ghana (Aboagye-Otchere and Agbeibor, 2012; Appiah et al., 2016; Coffie and Bedi, 2019; etc.), Kenya (Bova and Pereira, 2012), Nigeria (Osinubi, 2020; Oluwagbemiga, 2021; etc.), Zimbabwe (Chamisa, 2000; Kenneth and Grazyina, 2013; etc.), Zambia (Kabwe et al. 2021); etc. These researches studied the adoption, the compliance and the consequences of IFRS.

Unfortunately, very few studies have been done in Africa on the consequences of the IFRS adoption. Tawiah and Boolaky (2020) found "four ranked papers specifically on the consequences of IFRS in Africa and 19 articles that included some African countries. Of these 19 articles, only four included more than three African countries in their sample. Most of the studies that claimed to include Africa only considered South Africa". In addition, the results obtained of empirical studies are generally mixed (Tawiah and Boolaky, 2020). In Zimbabwe, Chamisa (2000) showed the conclusion that the IASC standards (IFRS now) are relevant to Zimbabwe and similar capitalistic developing countries. Also, the study of Hessayri and Saihi (2018) done in Morocco, South Africa and Turkey found an increase in equity investment following the IFRS adoption. On the other hand, the study of 34 African countries, Nnadi and Soobaroyen (2015) confirmed a negative relationship between IFRS adoption and FDI.

In addition, in North Africa and French speaking Sub-Saharan African Countries, the international of financial reporting standards are very rarely studied. It is true, according to the study done by Akisik et al. (2020) between 1997 and 2017, that Anglophone and common-law African countries adopt IFRS more than French-speaking countries. Degos et al. (2019) explain this situation by "the significance of the interaction between the ex-colonization and the indigenous accounting standards, the importance of key actors and the level of the educational institutions". Certainly, this situation changed with the IFRS adoption of OHADA countries in 2019.

In this context, this article aims to study, with a sample of 75 practitioners and researchers in accounting, the consequences of the IFRS adoption on the qualitative characteristics of financial reporting in 12 African countries in two different regions: North Africa represented by Morocco and 11 French speaking Sub-Saharan African Countries. We will try to answer three main questions:

- How do professionals and researchers in Morocco and in French speaking Sub-Saharan African Countries assess the improvement levels of the four qualitative characteristics of financial reporting through the IFRS adoption?
- Which professions in Morocco and French speaking Sub-Saharan African prioritize the enhancement of the four qualitative characteristics of accounting and financial information through the IFRS adoption more than others?
- Are there significant differences between the perceptions of Moroccan respondents and those of their sub-Saharan African colleagues regarding to the improvement of qualitative characteristics of financial reporting through the adoption of IFRS?

A literature review (§ 1) and a presentation of our choices of research methodology (§ 2) are necessary to conduct the statistical analysis and to present the main results (§ 3).

1. LITERATURE REVIEW

1.1. IFRS adoption in Africa: adoption and challenges

International Financial Reporting Standards (IFRS), previously called International Accounting Standard (IAS), are developed and published by the International Accounting Standards Board (IASB). IFRS are published in order to obtain a better financial understanding of all companies. Nowadays, out of 167 jurisdictions, 159 have declared adopting IFRS, accounting for 95% of the total number of jurisdictions (Table 1).

Table 1. Status of global IFRS adoption

Status of IFRS adoption	No. of jurisdictions
Require	145
Permit but not require	14
Neither require nor permit	8
Total jurisdictions	167

Source: Effah, (2024), p. 194.

In Africa, out of 54 countries, 44 countries require or permit IFRS adoption (adoption rate is 81 per cent) (Table 2). These countries can be classified as follows:

- 61 per cent of African countries require IFRS for all listed companies (these countries include OHADA countries which adopted IFRS since January 1, 2019);
- 9 per cent require IFRS for some companies;
- and 11 per cent permit IFRS. Generally, these countries do not have national accounting standards (Tawiah, 2019).

In Africa, we should note that seven countries (Kenya, Lesotho, Malawi, Mauritius, Tanzania, Uganda and Zimbabwe) required IAS/IFRS reporting before the mandatory IFRS adoption by the EU companies in 2005. The most recent countries to adopt IFRS are located within the OHADA region. For these countries, "as of 1 January 2019, IFRS Standards are required for all listed companies and companies making a public call for capital" (IFRS Foundation's official website, www.ifrs.org).

Table 2. Status of IFRS adoption in Africa (listed companies)

Required for all companies	Required for some companies	Permitted	Not permitted
Benin (2019)	Eritrea (2008)	Cape Verde	Algeria
Botswana (2004)	Gambia (2013)	Djibouti	Angola
Burkina Faso (2019)	Liberia (2012)	Ethiopia	Burundi
Cameroon (2019)	Morocco (2008)	Libya	Central Africa
Chad (2019)	Seychelles (2004)	Madagascar	Egypt
Comoros (2019)		South Sudan	Mauritania
Congo DR (2019)			Sao Tome
Congo Republic (2019)			Somalia
Cote D'ivoire (2019)			Sudan
Equatorial Guinea (2019)			Tunisia
Gabon (2019)			
Ghana (2007)			
Guinea (2019)			
Guinea Bissau (2019)			
Kenya (1999)			
Lesotho (2002)			
Malawi (2002)			
Mali (2019)			
Mauritius (2002)			
Mozambique (2011)			
Namibia (2005)			
Niger (2019)			
Nigeria (2012)			
Rwanda (2009)			
Sénégal (2019)			
Sierra Leone (2009)			
South Africa (2005)			
Swaziland (2010)			
Tanzania (2004)			
Togo (2019)			
Uganda (1998)			
Zambia (2005)			
Zimbabwe (1996)			

Source: www.ifrs.org and www.iasplus.com

The mandatory or voluntary adoption of IFRS in Africa has been the subject of some research studies to understand why some countries have adopted IFRS while others have not. Elhamma (2024) examined the main determinants of the national IFRS adoption in 14 MENA countries (5 North African countries and 9 Middle Eastern countries). By using a panel data from 2005 to 2020, the study showed that total external debt, openness of the economy to the outside world and educational level are significant in their positive association with national IFRS adoption. However, "these relationships are more significant in Middle Eastern countries than those in North African countries". Boolaky et al. (2020), by studying all 54 African countries during the period 2010-2015, showed that the influence of international organizations like the World Bank and the International Monetary Fund on IFRS adoption is significant. They also found that "the presence of global audit firms and the years of membership in the International Federation of Accountants are strongly associated with a country's decision to adopt IFRS" (Boolaky et al. 2020, p. 1). In addition, they highlighted that "countries with a more structured and active professional accounting organization are more likely to adopt IFRS" (Boolaky et al. 2020, p. 1). Akisik et al. (2020) found that "FDI, openness, schooling, and control of corruption have a positive effect of countries' decisions to adopt IFRS." The study's findings revealed also that "Anglophone and common law African countries adopt IFRS more than Francophone countries".

1.2. Local Accounting Standards and IFRS in Morocco and French Speaking Sub-Saharan African Countries

Morocco is located in Northern Africa just south of Europe. Spain is only 8.6 miles away from the Moroccan border and has a population of 36 million (World Bank, 2020). It has been under both French and Spanish protectorates from 1912 until 1956. The Moroccan economy is considered the most competitive economy in North Africa. According to the World Bank's 2020 Doing Business report, Morocco is ranked 53th, among 190 countries around the world. It is the first in the North Africa, third in Africa, behind Mauritius (13th) and Rwanda (38th). According to World Bank projections, the GDP growth rate will reach only 4.6% in 2021 and 3.4% in 2022.

French protectorate has influenced Moroccan Business managerial practices. The financial accounting in Morocco is largely drawn on the French model (Elhamma and Moalla, 2015). However, in recent years, Moroccan companies have begun to adopt modern management tools, including international accounting standards (IFRS) (Elhamma, 2023, 2024), modern management control tools (Elhamma, 2012, 2014; Elhamma and Zhang, 2013; Achibane and Elhamma, 2016)), and new sources of financing such as Islamic finance (Bennani and Elhamma, 2015). The general code of accounting standardization of 1992 that governs Moroccan financial accounting is largely drawn on the French General Chart of Accounts of 1982. Morocco that has chosen liberalization, globalization and the opening on the international market became pushed to adopt and use IFRS international standards. In Morocco, the CNC (National Accounting Council) and the Central Bank of Morocco (Bank Al Maghrib) required, since 2007, the IFRS adoption for listed companies on the stock exchange; banks and financial institutions (listed or unlisted) and public institutions, and allowed other entities to apply either the IFRS or the Moroccan accounting (Elhamma, 2023).

Only a few researches in IFRS have been done in North African countries in general and in Morocco in particular. Hessayri and Saihi (2018), in their research on publicly listed firms in Morocco, South Africa and Turkey, confirmed that the "institutional investors and institutional blockholders (both domestic and foreign) invest more heavily in the stocks of the firms that have committed to IFRS". Alnaas and Rashid (2019) studied the influence of firm characteristics on harmonization of companies listed on the Egypt, Morocco and Tunisia Stock Exchanges. They showed that the level of compliance with IFRS increases with company size, institutional ownership, industry and language of disclosure. Recently, Khlif et al. (2020) demonstrated that the convergence of the national accounting standards with IFRS in Morocco, Algeria and Tunisia is confronted especially by the prevailing SMEs, difficulty in fair-value measurement and the cost of convergence for companies.

According to the United Nations, sub-Saharan Africa consists of all African countries that are located south of the Sahara. In this research, we focus on French-speaking sub-Saharan countries (Benin, Burkina Faso, Burundi, Cameroon, Central African Republic, Chad, Comoros, Congo (Republic), Democratic Republic of Congo (DRC), Ivory Coast (Cote d'Ivoire), Djibouti, Gabon, Guinea, Madagascar, Mali, Mauritania, Niger, Senegal and Togo).

In its first years of independence (1960s), French-speaking sub-Saharan African countries used a system inherited from its colonizers, essentially the French accounting systems of 1947 and 1957 (Dicko and Fortin, 2014). In January 1970, the first African accounting system was adopted by the Joint African and Malagasy Organization in Yaoundé (Cameroon). It was dubbed the OCAM accounting plan (Fortin and Dicko, 2009). In 1998, a new West African accounting system *(SYSCOA)* was adopted in the West African Economic and Monetary Union (*WAEMU*). According to Gouadain and Wade (2009), this system later evolved into the OHADA accounting system (SYSCOHADA) and was implemented in all OHADA member countries (Tawiah, 2019). There are currently 17 OHADA Member States: Benin, Burkina Faso, Cameroon, Central African Republic, Chad, Comoros, Congo, the Democratic Republic of the Congo, Equatorial Guinea, Gabon, Guinea, Guinea Bissau, Cote d'Ivoire, Mali, Niger, Senegal, and Togo.

At its 43rd session, on January 26, 2017 in Brazzaville, the Council of Ministers of the OHADA adopted the new Uniform Act on Accounting Law and Financial Reporting (*l'Acte uniforme relatif au droit comptable et à l'information financière-AUDCIF*), partially transposing the IFRS corpus. It also contains the revised OHADA accounting system (SYSCOHADA revised). The updated AUDIF and SYSCOHADA will be the only accounting reference in all OHADA Member States and will enter into force on January 1st, 2018 for personal accounts, and on January 1st, 2019 for consolidated accounts, combined accounts and financial statements prepared in accordance with IFRS.

1.3. Benefits of IFRS Adoption in the World and in Africa

1.3.1. Benefits of IFRS Adoption in the World

Certainly, the impact of IFRS adoption on the quality of accounting information remains one of the most controversial topics in international accounting. Barth et al. (2008) and Bartov et al. (2005) argue that there is no conclusive evidence that IFRS adoption contribute to improvements in accounting quality. However, the most of the empirical studies conducted in both developed and developing countries have shown that IFRS adoption plays an important role in improving the quality of financial information. Bartov et al. (2005) investigate the comparative value relevance of earnings reported under German GAAP, US GAAP and IFRS. The research sample included 417 German companies listed on local stock markets during the period 1998–2000. They conclude that US GAAP and IFRS are more value relevant than German GAAP. In Chinese context, Liu and Liu (2007) state that the accounting amounts reported under IFRS were more relevant than those reported under Chinese GAAP. In the same sense, Barth et al. (2008), based on a study conducted in 21 countries, indicate that the voluntary adoption of IFRS by European companies is associated with a decrease in earnings management and hence with an increase in the quality of financial reporting. Gordon (2008) highlight the different benefits from IFRS adoption over the world: better financial information for shareholders; better financial information for regulators; enhanced comparability; improved transparency of results; increased ability to secure cross-border listing; better management of global operations; and decreased cost of capital.

The study conducted by Armstrong et al. (2010) to examine European stocks market reactions to 16 events associated with the adoption of IFRS in Europe suggests that the investors of European companies perceived the adoption of IFRS as beneficial. In France, Lenormand and Touchais (2009) conducted a study from 160 French firms to compare the value relevance for investors between IAS/IFRS and French GAAP. Thy have found that "even if the two standards seem value relevant, we show IAS/IFRS bring more information" (p. 145-146). In the United Kingdom, Iatridis (2010) states that the application of IFRS has increased the relevance of accounting information published by British companies. According to this author, the study "indicates that the implementation of IFRSs generally reinforces accounting quality. The findings show that the implementation of IFRSs reduces the scope for earnings management, is related to more timely loss recognition and leads to more value relevant accounting measures" (p.193). Chai et al. (2010) compares the accounting quality of publicly listed companies in 15 member states of the European Union (EU) before and after the full adoption of IFRS in 2005. They found that the majority of accounting quality indicators improved after IFRS adoption.

In the case of Turkish companies, Kargin (2013) investigates the value relevance of accounting information in pre- and post-financial periods of IFRS adoption by Turkish listed firms from 1998 to 2011. He found that value relevance of financial reporting has improved in the post-IFRS period. Yrisandi and Puspitasari (2015) analyze whether the IFRS adoption is associated with increasing in financial reporting quality in listed companies at Indonesian Stock Exchange (IDX). The findings showed that "the qualitative characteristics of relevance, understandability and comparability level increased after IFRS adoption" (p. 650). Mita et al. (2018), based on a study of companies listed in 18 countries in Europe, Asia, Africa and Australia, showed that the level of IFRS adoption has a positive effect on the comparability of financial statements. Recently, based on a sample of nine MENA countries over a period of ten years (2006–2015), Klish et al. (2022) studied the impact of the IFRS adoption on the quality of MENA region firms' financial reporting. The main findings reveal that "firms that adopted IFRS, in both the rentier (oil-dependent states) and non-rentier states, have a higher financial reporting quality than non-IFRS adopters" (Klish et al., 2022, p.570). More recently, Elhamma (2023) examined the impact of mandatory IFRS adoption on economic growth in 30 developing countries (15 MENA countries and 15 SSA countries) during the period 2017–2020. The study's results showed that "the impact of mandatory IFRS adoption on economic growth is positive and statistically significant for the full sample".

All these results must be interpreted carefully. Several other empirical studies have not found the same results. Tendeloo and Vanstraelen (2005), using a sample of 636 firms, found that "IFRS-adopters do not present different earnings management behavior compared to companies reporting under German GAAP" (p.155). Schiebel (2007) examines the value relevance of IFRS and German GAAP of 24 German companies listing on the Frankfurt Stock Exchange and publishing exclusively either IFRS or German GAAP consolidated financial reports over the period 2000-2004. The results of the study show that German GAAP are significantly more value relevant than IFRS. In the same sense, Hung and Subramanyam (2007) analyze the financial statement effects of IAS adoption during 1998 through 2002 in German firms. The finding showed that the "book value and income are no more value relevant under IAS than under HGB" (p.623). Morais and Curto (2008), by using a sample of 34 Portuguese listed firms before (1995-2004) and after (2004-2005) the IFRS adoption, demonstrated that "the value relevance of accounting information decreases with the adoption of IASB standards" (p.103). Dobija and Klimczak (2008) stated that financial market efficiency and relevance of accounting information have not improved with the adoption of IFRS by 2005. Recently, Suadiye (2017) highlighted that the switching to IFRS does not improve financial reporting quality expect value relevance in Turkey.

1.3.2. Benefits of IFRS Adoption in Africa

In Africa, some research studies demonstrate that the IFRS adoption is beneficial. According to Chamisa (2000), the impact of the IASC standards on the reporting practices of listed Zimbabwe companies is significant. The IASC standards are relevant to Zimbabwe and similar capitalistic developing countries. In the Kenyan context, Bova and Pereira (2012) find a positive and significant association between share return and the level of IFRS compliance. Recently, using a data of two African countries (Morocco and South Africa) and Turkey, Hessayri and Saihi (2018) found a significant increase in equity investment following the adoption of IFRS. Recently, Akisik and Mangaliso (2020) studied the relationships between IFRS, types of FDI and economic growth in 49 African countries. The results provide evidence that the effect of FDI on growth is significantly and positively influenced by IFRS. On the other hand, Nnadi and Soobaroyen (2015), using data of 34 Anglophone and French African countries, provided empirical evidence that the IFRS adoption has a negative impact on the net FDIs.

The study of Osasere and Ilaboya (2018) aims to investigate the change in financial reporting quality after the IFRS adoption in the Nigeria Money Deposit Banks (MDBs). The researchers showed that the financial reporting quality increased in the post-IFRS adoption across the five qualitative characteristics of accounting and financial information: relevance, faithful representation, comparability, understandability and timeliness. Recently, Oluwagbemiga (2021), based on a sample of 162 companies listed on the Nigerian Stock Exchange, investigated whether the IFRS adoption improve the quality of financial reporting that was measured by using the fundamental qualitative characteristics such as relevance, faithful representation, understandability, comparability, verifiability, and timeliness. From both univariate and multivariate analysis, the author confirmed "strong evidence suggesting that accounting standard used in the preparation of financial statement have significant influence on the quality of financial report of the reporting entity".

Recently Ajibade et al. (2022) studied the impact of IFRS adoption and corporate governance on the faithful representation of the financial reporting quality in Nigeria's development banks. The stud's results revealed that "IFRS adoption and corporate governance significantly affect the faithful representation of financial reporting of Nigeria's Development Banks. The study concluded that IFRS adoption and corporate governance significantly affect the faithful representation of the financial reporting quality in Nigeria's development banks". More recently, Gowry et al. (2023) examined the evolution of the value relevance of book value, earnings and its components in Mauritius. The study used a data set of 567 firm-year observations (2001–2018) and revealed that "the combined importance of IFRS adoption with institutional and enforcement reforms to improve value relevance" (Gowry et al., 2023).

2. METHODOLOGY

2.1. Sample

This study is based on a questionnaire survey conducted among Moroccan and French speaking sub-Saharan African professionals and academician researchers in accounting. In front of the impossibility of obtaining exact information about our total population (practitioners and academicians in accounting in the chosen countries), we have choose the simple random sampling. We retained 38 Moroccan respondents and 37 French speaking sub-Saharan African respondents. The following table summarizes the composition of our sample.

Table 3. The sample according to the nationalities of respondents

Countries		N	%	Professions	N	%
Morocco		38	50.7%	Academicians Researchers in Accounting	12	12
French speaking Sub-Saharan African Countries	Cameroon	6	8%	Accountants	16	21.3%
	Gabon	2	2.7%	Auditors	23	30.7%
	Senegal	5	6.7%	Consolidators	3	4%
	Togo	3	4%	Management controllers	7	9.3%
	Ivory Coast (Côte d'Ivoire)	4	5.3%	Chief Financial officers (CFO)	4	5.3%
	Mali	2	2.7%	Charted accountants (liberal profession)	10	13.3%
	Niger	2	2.7%			
	Congo	4	5.3%			
	Benin	2	2.7%			
	Central African republic	2	2.7%			
	The democratic republic of Congo	5	6.7%			
Total		75	100%	Total	75	100%

Our sample consists of 12 African countries belonging to two different regions: Morocco in the North Africa (38 respondents: 50.7%) and 11 countries in French speaking sub-Saharan Africa: Cameroon, Gabon, Senegal, Togo, Ivory Coast (Cote d'Ivoire), Mali, Niger, Congo, Benin, Central African republic and the democratic republic of Congo (37 respondents: 49.3%).

We have ensured that our sample is made up only of people who have a direct relationship with accounting: auditors (30.7%), accountants (21.3%), academician researchers in accounting (16%), charted accountants (liberal profession) (13.3%), management controllers (9.3%), CFOs (5.3%) and consolidators (4%).

2.2. Measurement of Variables: Benefits of IFRS Adoption

To measure the perceived benefits of the adoption of IFRS, we have retained four qualitative characteristics of financial reporting: reliability, relevance, comparability and understandability. We have proposed to the respondent a five-point scale (ranging from "very low improvement" to "very high improvement") to precise the average contribution of the adoption of IFRS in the improvement the four qualitative characteristics of accounting and financial information.

3. RESULTS AND DISCUSSION

3.1. The Main Results for Both African Regions

The main results of our survey are summarized in the following table.

Table 4. Perceived benefits of the IFRS adoption of Moroccan and French speaking sub-Saharan African respondents

	Reliability	Relevance	Comparability	Understandability
Very low improvement	1 (1.3%)	1 (1.3%)	4 (5.3%)	2 (2.7%)
Low improvement	12 (16%)	7 (9.3%)	8 (10.7%)	7 (9.3%)
Moderate improvement	23 (30.7%)	24 (32%)	22 (29.3%)	33 (44%)
High improvement	35 (46.7%)	32 (42.7%)	38 (50.7%)	29 (38.7%)
Very high improvement	4 (5.3%)	11 (14.7%)	3 (4%)	4 (5.3%)
Total	75 (100%)	75 (100%)	75 (100%)	75 (100%)

More than half of the all respondents consider that the adoption of IFRS improves "highly" or "very highly" the reliability (52%), the relevance (57.4%) and the comparability (54.7%) of their accounting and financial information. This rate is only 44% for the understandability of financial reporting. The majority of respondents from the both African areas prefer the IFRS adoption to improve the qualitative characteristics of their accounting and financial information. These results agree with those of some studies around the world. In Anglophone African countries, the ROSC (AA) (The Report on the Observance of Standards and Codes) report on Ugandan and South Africa indicated that the IFRS adoption has improved accounting reporting for investors' relevance and reliability (Tawiah, 2019). In Indonesia, Yurisandi and Puspitasari (2015) demonstrated that the IFRS adoption improve the relevance, the understandability and the comparability of financial reporting. By using a sample of 46 bankrupt firms and 46 non-bankrupt, Bodle et al. (2016) confirmed that the IFRS adoption improves significantly the quality of information contained in the financial statements for predicting bankruptcy. In Canada, Okafor et al. (2016) proved empirically, by using several statistical tests, that the accounting information prepared and disclosed by adopting IFRS enhance the price and the returns value relevance the accounting information prepared and disclosed under local GAAP.

To have more details on the collected responses, we will present our results according to the professions of the respondents (Table 5, Table 6, Table 7 and Table 8).

Table 5. Perceived improvement of the reliability of the accounting and financial information according to the professions of respondents

	Very low improvement	Low improvement	Moderate improvement	High improvement	Very high improvement	Total
Academicians researchers in accounting	00%	00%	33.3%	66.7%	00%	100%
Accountants	00%	18.8%	12.5%	56.3%	12.5%	100%
Auditors	00%	21.7%	43.5%	34.8%	00%	100%
Consolidators	00%	00%	00%	100%	00%	100%
Management controllers	00%	14.3%	57.1%	00%	28.6%	100%
Chief Financial officers (CFO)	00%	50%	00%	50%	00%	100%
Charted accountants (liberal profession)	10%	10%	30%	50%	00%	100%

Table 6. Perceived improvement of the relevance of the accounting and financial information according to the professions of respondents

	Very low improvement	Low improvement	Moderate improvement	High improvement	Very high improvement	Total
Academicians researchers in accounting	00%	00%	33.3%	41.7%	25%	100%
Accountants	00%	12.5%	31.3%	43.8%	12.5%	100%
Auditors	00%	21.7%	39.1%	26.1%	13%	100%
Consolidators	00%	00%	00%	100%	00%	100%
Management controllers	00%	00%	71.4%	00%	28.6%	100%
Chief Financial officers (CFO)	00%	50%	00%	75%	25%	100%
Charted accountants (liberal profession)	10%	00%	10%	80%	00%	100%

Table 7. Perceived improvement of the comparability of the accounting and financial information according to the professions of respondents

	Very low improvement	Low improvement	Moderate improvement	High improvement	Very high improvement	Total
Academicians researchers in accounting	00%	8.3%	25%	66.7%	00%	100%
Accountants	00%	18.8%	12.5%	56.3%	12.5%	100%
Auditors	8.7%	4.3%	47.8%	39.1%	00%	100%
Consolidators	00%	00%	00%	100%	00%	100%
Management controllers	00%	14.3%	57.1%	28.6%	00%	100%
Chief Financial officers (CFO)	25%	00%	00%	75%	00%	100%
Charted accountants (liberal profession)	10%	20%	20%	40%	10%	100%

Table 8. Perceived improvement of the understandability of the accounting and financial information according to the professions of respondents

	Very low improvement	Low improvement	Moderate improvement	High improvement	Very high improvement	Total
Academicians researchers in accounting	00%	8.3%	58.3%	33.3%	00%	100%
Accountants	6.3%	12.5%	37.5%	31.3%	12.5%	100%
Auditors	00%	417.4%	52.2%	30.4%	00%	100%
Consolidators	00%	00%	00%	100%	00%	100%
Management controllers	00%	00%	71.4%	28.6%	00%	100%
Chief Financial officers (CFO)	00%	00%	25%	25%	50%	100%
Charted accountants (liberal profession)	10%	00%	20%	70%	10%	100%

All consolidators of our sample (100%) judge that the IFRS adoption improves "highly" or "very highly" the reliability of the accounting and financial information. this rate is in descending order 68.% of accountants, 66.7% of academician researchers in accounting, 50% of CFOs and charted accountants (liberal profession), 34.8% of auditors and 28.6% of management controllers. Regarding to the relevance of financial reporting, all consolidators and CFOs (100%) declare that the IFRS adoption improves "highly" or "very highly" this qualitative characteristic of accounting information. This rate is 66.7% of academician researchers in accounting, 56.3% of accountants, 39.1% of auditors and 28.6% of management controllers. Regarding to the third qualitative characteristic of accounting information, all consolidators of the sample (100%) consider that the IFRS adoption improves "highly" or "very highly" the comparability of the accounting and financial information. This rate is 75% of CFOs, 68.8% of accountants, 66.7% of academician researchers in accounting, 50% of charted accountants (liberal profession), 39.1% of auditors and 28.6% of management controllers. 100% of the interviewed consolidators confirm that the IFRS adoption improves "highly" or "very highly" the understandability of the financial reporting. This rate is in descending order 80% of charted accountants (liberal profession), 75% of CFOs, 43.8% of accountants, 33.3% of academician researchers in accounting, 30.4% of auditors and finally 28.6% of management controllers.

In general, consolidators, CFOs and accountants are the most attracted by the adoption of IFRS. They confirmed that these accounting standards improve significantly the qualitative characteristics of accounting and financial information. On the other hand, management controllers are less motivated for the adoption of IFRS.

3.2. Comparison Between Morocco and French-Speaking Sub-Saharan African Countries

The results obtained concerning the improvement of the qualitative characteristics of financial reporting by the adoption of IFRS in Morocco and in French-speaking sub-Saharan African countries are summarized in Tables 9, 10, 11 and 12.

Table 9. Perceived improvement of reliability of information accounting by adoption of IFRS

	Very low improvement	Low improvement	Moderate improvement	High improvement	Very high improvement
Morocco	00%	18.4%	21.1%	50%	10.5%
French speaking Sub-Saharan African Countries	2.7%	13.5%	40.5%	43.2%	00%
All countries	1.3%	16%	30.7%	46.7%	5.3%

52% of all respondents declared that the IFRS adoption improve "highly" or "very highly" the reliability of the accounting and financial information. This rate is 60.5% for professionals and academicians researchers in accounting in Morocco and 43.2% for their colleagues in French speaking Sub-Saharan African Countries. However, only 18.4% of Moroccan respondents judge that the IFRS adoption improves "lowly" or "very lowly" the reliability of financial reporting, this rate is 16.2% in French speaking Sub-Saharan African Countries. These results show the great importance given to the adoption of IFRS for improving the reliability of accounting and financial information for the both African regions.

Table 10. Perceived improvement of relevance of information accounting by adoption of IFRS

	Very low improvement	Low improvement	Moderate improvement	High improvement	Very high improvement
Morocco	00%	5.3%	31.6%	39.5%	23.6%
French speaking Sub-Saharan African Countries	2.7%	13.5%	32.4%	45.9%	5.4%
All countries	1.3%	9.3%	32%	42.7%	14.7%

63.1% of Moroccan respondents consider that the IFRS adoption improve "highly" or "very highly" the relevance of the accounting and financial information. This rate is 51.3% in French speaking Sub-Saharan African Countries. In addition, only 10.6% of all respondents declare that the adoption of IFRS improve just "lowly" or "very lowly" this qualitative characteristic of financial reporting. This rate is 5.3% in Morocco and 16.2% in French speaking Sub-Saharan African Countries. From these results, we can conclude that Moroccan respondents are more concerned than their French speaking sub-Saharan counterparts about IFRS adoption to improve the relevance of their accounting and financial information. Nevertheless, to decide in this result, we must wait for the verdict of the statistical test.

Table 11. Perceived improvement of comparability of accounting and financial information by adoption of IFRS

	Very low improvement	Low improvement	Moderate improvement	High improvement	Very high improvement
Morocco	2.6%	10.5%	26.3%	52.6%	7.9%
French speaking Sub-Saharan African Countries	8.1%	10.8%	32.4%	48.6%	00%
All countries	5.3%	10.7%	29.3%	50.7%	4%

More than half of our sample (54.7%) consider that the adoption of IFRS improves "highly" or "very highly" the comparability of the accounting and financial information. This rate is respectively 60.5% and 48.6% for Moroccan and French speaking sub-Saharan African respondents. However, only 13.1% of Moroccan professionals and researchers in accounting judge a "low" or "very low" improvement of this qualitative characteristic of information accounting by the IFRS adoption. Also, this rate is only 18.9% in French speaking Sub-Saharan African Countries.

From these results, we notice that the majority of respondents from the both African regions prefer the adoption of IFRS to improve the comparability of their financial reporting.

Table 12. Perceived improvement of understandability of information accounting by adoption of IFRS

	Very low improvement	Low improvement	Moderate improvement	High improvement	Very high improvement
Morocco	2.6%	5.3%	39.5%	42.1%	10.5%
French speaking Sub-Saharan African Countries	2.7%	13.5%	48.6%	35.1%	00%
All countries	2.7%	9.3%	44%	38.7%	5.3%

44% of our sample consider that the IFRS adoption improves "highly" or "very highly" the understandability of financial reporting. This rate is 52.6% in Morocco and 35.1% in French speaking Sub-Saharan African Countries. From these results, we can have a preliminary idea according to which Moroccan respondents prefer, more than their French speaking sub-Saharan African colleagues, the IFRS adoption to improve the understandability of their accounting and financial information. Nevertheless, this finding will be confirmed or rejected by the statistical test.

To confirm statistically the results obtained above, we will code the collected responses (from: 1 "very low improvement" to 5: "very high improvement") and then we will calculate a mean value of these responses for each qualitative characteristic, and we will use the Student's t-test for a difference in means. The main results of this test are shown in the table below.

Table 13. Test of difference in means of qualitative characteristics of accounting information between Morocco and French speaking Sub-Saharan African Countries

Qualitative characteristics	Morocco	French speaking Sub-Saharan African Countries	Difference	t-value	Sig.
Reliability	3.5263	3.2432	0.28307	1.421	0.159[ns]
Relevance	3.8158	3.3784	0.20303	2.154	0.035*
Comparability	3.5263	3.2162	0.31010	1.460	0.149[ns]
Understandability	3.5263	3.1622	0.36415	1.934	0.057**

* Significant at the 5% ** Significant at the 10% [ns] Not Significant

Regarding to the relevance of the financial reporting, the mean of responses of Moroccan professionals and researchers in accounting (3.8158) exceed that of their colleagues from French-speaking sub-Saharan African countries (2.8636). The difference between the two means (0.203) is positive and statistically significant at the 5% level. These results confirm those obtained above. Moroccan professionals and researchers in accounting are more attracted by the adoption of IFRS to improve this qualitative characteristic of financial reporting. The difference in means is also positive (+0.36) and statistically significant at the 10% level for the understandability of financial reporting. These results are consistent with those obtained above. The Moroccan respondents value the adoption of IFRS to improve this qualitative characteristic of accounting and financial information more than their colleagues in French-speaking sub-Saharan African countries.

For the other two qualitative characteristics (reliability and comparability) the difference in means is not significant between Moroccan and sub-Saharan African responses. More than half of all respondents declared that the IFRS adoption improves the reliability and the comparability of financial reporting. The both categories of respondents (Moroccan and French speaking sub-Saharan African) are with the adoption of IFRS to improve these two qualitative characteristics of accounting and financial information.

These results can be explained by the presence in Morocco of an accounting system largely attached to the Franco-Germanic model (continental Europe model) characterized by a strong presence of the accounting principle of prudence and historical cost and by its very high relationship with taxation. In North African countries, Khlif et al. (2020) found that the extent of convergence with IFRS in Morocco is lower compared to other countries. On the other hand, the revised SYSCOHADA, adopted by French speaking sub-Saharan African countries, is inspired by IFRS standards.

CONCLUSION

The research studies that have examined the effects of IFRS adoption in Africa have obtained mixed results. According to some African studies, the adoption of IFRS has positive impact on the accuracy and reliability of accounting data (Boolaky et al., 2018, 2020; Odoemelam et al., 2019). On the other hand, other researchers have not found this positive relationship (Nnadi and Soobaroyen, 2015; Houqe, 2018). In this context, this study aimed to highlight the impact of the adoption of IFRS on the qualitative characteristics of financial information.

In this research, based on a survey of 38 professionals and academicians researchers in accounting in Morocco and 37 of their colleagues in 11 French speaking Sub-Saharan African Countries, we found the following results:

- More than half of the all respondents (Moroccan and sub-Saharan African) consider that the adoption of IFRS improves "highly" or "very highly" the relevance (57.4%) and the comparability (54.7%) and the reliability (52%) of their financial reporting.
- Consolidators, CFOs and accountants are the most concerned by the IFRS adoption to improve significantly the qualitative characteristics of accounting and financial information. On the other hand, management controllers are less motivated for the adoption of IFRS.
- Moroccan professionals and researchers in accounting are more concerned than their colleagues Sub-Saharan African by the adoption of IFRS to improve the relevance and the understandability of the financial reporting. For the two other qualitative characteristics (reliability and comparability), the difference in means is not statistically significant.

This research work makes important contributions at both the theoretical and managerial levels. On the theoretical level, this study will add new knowledge about the effects of mandatory adoption of IFRS in French-speaking Africa on the quality of financial information. On the managerial level, this study shows the positive effects of adopting IFRS and therefore constitutes a practical guide for decision-makers in African countries that have not yet adopted this international accounting language.

However, our results must be interpreted with caution given some limitations of our present research. Generally, two main methodological limitations should be highlighted. First, the modest size of the study's sample. Second, the use of a perceptual approach via questionnaires to collect data.

To complete our present research work, we propose introducing the cultural variable to explain the adoption of IFRS and their benefits in countries with different cultures. According to Borker (2013), cultural theory dimensions can explain the success or failure of IFRS adoption in different countries.

REFERENCES

Aboagye-Otchere, F., & Agbeibor, J. (2012). The International Financial Reporting Standard for Small and Medium-sized Entities (IFRS for SMES): Suitability for small businesses in Ghana. *Journal of Financial Reporting and Accounting*, 10(2), 190–214. DOI: 10.1108/19852511211273723

Achibane, M., & Elhamma, A. (2016). Balanced Scorecard Et Incertitude Environnementale: Cas Des Entreprises Au Maroc. *European Scientific Journal*, 12(7), 459–469. DOI: 10.19044/esj.2016.v12n7p459

Ajibade, A. T., Okutu, N., Akande, F., Kwarbai, J. D., Olayinka, I. M., & Olotu, A. (2022). IFRS adoption, corporate governance and faithful representation of financial reporting quality in Nigeria's development banks. *Cogent Business and Management*, 9(1), 2139213. Advance online publication. DOI: 10.1080/23311975.2022.2139213

Akisik, O., Gal, G., & Mangaliso, M. P. (2020). IFRS, FDI, economic growth and human development: The experience of Anglophone and Francophone African countries. *Emerging Markets Review*, 45, 45. DOI: 10.1016/j.ememar.2020.100725

Akisik, O., & Mangaliso, M. P. (2020). How IFRS influence the relationship between the types of FDI and economic growth: An empirical analysis on African countries. *Journal of Applied Accounting Research*, 21(1), 60–76. DOI: 10.1108/JAAR-02-2018-0025

Alnaas, A., & Rashid, A. (2019). Firm characteristics and compliance with IAS/IFRS: Evidence from North African companies. *Journal of Financial Reporting and Accounting*, 17(3), 383–410. DOI: 10.1108/JFRA-06-2018-0052

Appiah, K., Awunyo-Vitor, D., Mireku, K., & Ahiagbah, C. (2016). Compliance with international financial reporting standards: The case of listed firms in Ghana. *Journal of Financial Reporting and Accounting*, 14(1), 131–156. DOI: 10.1108/JFRA-01-2015-0003

Armstrong, S. C., Barth, M. E., Jagolinzer, A. D., & Riedl, E. J. (2010). Market Reaction to the Adoption of IFRS in Europe. *The Accounting Review*, 85(1), 31–61. DOI: 10.2308/accr.2010.85.1.31

Barth, M., Landsman, W., & Lang, M. (2008). International accounting standards and accounting quality. *Journal of Accounting Research*, 46(3), 467–498. DOI: 10.1111/j.1475-679X.2008.00287.x

Bartov, E., Goldberg, S. R., & Kim, M. (2005). Comparative value relevance among German, US and International Accounting Standards: A German stock market perspective. *Journal of Accounting, Auditing & Finance*, 20(2), 95–119. DOI: 10.1177/0148558X0502000201

Bennani, S., & Elhamma, A. (2015). *La comptabilité en finance islamique selon les normes AAOIFI*. Editions Universitaires Européennes.

Bodle, K. A., Cybinski, P. J., & Monem, R. (2016). Effect of IFRS adoption on financial reporting quality: Evidence from bankruptcy prediction. *Accounting Research Journal*, 29(3), 292–312. DOI: 10.1108/ARJ-03-2014-0029

Boolaky, P. K., Omoteso, K., Ibrahim, M. U., & Adelopo, I. (2018). The development of accounting practices and the adoption of IFRS in selected MENA countries. *Journal of Accounting in Emerging Economies*, 8(3), 327–351. DOI: 10.1108/JAEE-07-2015-0052

Boolaky, P. K., Tawiah, V., & Soobaroyen, T. (2020). Why do African countries adopt IFRS? An institutional perspective. *The International Journal of Accounting*, 55(1), 1–40. DOI: 10.1142/S1094406020500055

Borker, D. R. (2013). Accounting and Cultural Values: IFRS in 3G Economies. *The International Business & Economics Research Journal*, 12(6), 671. DOI: 10.19030/iber.v12i6.7872

Bova, F., & Pereira, R. (2012). The determinants and consequences of heterogeneous IFRS compliance levels following mandatory IFRS adoption: Evidence from a developing country. *Journal of International Accounting Research*, 11(1), 83–111. DOI: 10.2308/jiar-10211

Chai, H., Tang, Q., Jiang, Y., & Lin, Z. (2010). The Role of International Financial Reporting Standards in Accounting Quality, Evidence from the European Union. *Journal of International Financial Management & Accounting*, 21(3), 220–278. DOI: 10.1111/j.1467-646X.2010.01041.x

Chamisa, E. (2000). The relevance and observance of the IASC standards in developing countries and the particular case of Zimbabwe. *The International Journal of Accounting*, 35(2), 267–286. DOI: 10.1016/S0020-7063(00)00049-2

Coetzee, S., & Schmulian, A. (2013). The Effect of IFRS Adoption on Financial Reporting Pedagogy in South Africa. *Issues in Accounting Education*, 28(2), 243–251. DOI: 10.2308/iace-50386

Coffie, W., & Bedi, I. (2019). The effects of IFRS adoption and firm size on audit fees in financial institutions in Ghana. *Accounting Research Journal*, 32(3), 436–453. DOI: 10.1108/ARJ-07-2017-0114

Degos, J.-G., Levant, Y., & Touron, P. (2019). The history of accounting standards in French-speaking African countries since independence: The uneasy path toward IFRS. *Accounting, Auditing & Accountability Journal*, 32(1), 75–100. DOI: 10.1108/AAAJ-03-2016-2459

Dicko, S., & Fortin, A. (2014). IFRS adoption and the opinion of OHADA Accountants. *Afro-Asian J. Finance and Accounting*, 4(2), 141–162. DOI: 10.1504/AAJFA.2014.063746

Dobija, D., & Klimczak, K. M. (2008). Development of accounting in Poland: Market efficiency and the value relevance of reported earnings. *The International Journal of Accounting*, 45(3), 356–374. DOI: 10.1016/j.intacc.2010.06.010

Effah, N. A. A. (2024). A bibliometric review of IFRS adoption and compliance research in Africa. *Journal of Business and Socio-economic Development*, 4(3), 193–209. DOI: 10.1108/JBSED-01-2023-0001

Elhamma, A. (2012). The activity based costing in morocco: Adoption and diffusion. *Arabian Journal of Business and Management Review*, 1(6), 33–45. DOI: 10.12816/0002111

Elhamma, A. (2014). Performance du Balanced Scorecard: Perception des responsables d'entreprises. *Revue Internationale de Management et de Stratégie*, 5(2), 1–9.

Elhamma, A. (2023), Cinquante ans des normes comptables internationales IAS/IFRS: adoption, conséquences et où en est-on au Maroc? Ouvrage Collectif: « 50 ans de Management: regards croisés d'un demi-siècle du management », sous la direction de M'Rabet R. et Issami M.A., édition EDISCA, pp. 121-136.

Elhamma, A. (2023). Impact of mandatory IFRS adoption on economic growth: The moderating role of Covid-19 crisis in developing countries. *Journal of Accounting and Management Information Systems*, 22(3), 554–568. DOI: 10.24818/jamis.2023.03007

Elhamma, A. (2023). Impact of mandatory IFRS adoption on foreign direct investment: the moderating role of conflict of interest regulation. *Journal of Financial Reporting and Accounting*, Vol. ahead-of-print No. ahead-of-print. DOI: 10.1108/JFRA-04-2022-0145

Elhamma, A. (2024). Determinants of national IFRS adoption: Evidence from the Middle East and North Africa region. International Journal of Accounting. *Auditing and Performance Evaluation*, 20(1/2), 69–90. DOI: 10.1504/IJAAPE.2024.135535

Elhamma, A., & Moalla, H. (2015). Impact of uncertainty and decentralization on activity-based costing use. *International Journal of Accounting and Economics Studies*, 3(2), 148–155. DOI: 10.14419/ijaes.v3i2.4817

Elhamma, A., & Zhang, Yi. (2013). The relationship between activity-based costing, business strategy and performance in Moroccan enterprises. *Journal of Accounting and Management Information Systems*, 12(1), 22–38.

Fortin, A., & Dicko, S. (2009). The impact of the new OHADA accounting system on the judgments and decisions of Cameroonian bankers. *Advances in Accounting, Incorporating. Advances in Accounting*, 25(1), 89–105. DOI: 10.1016/j.adiac.2009.02.006

Gordon, E. A. (2008). Sustainability in global financial reporting and innovation in institutions. *Accounting Research Journal*, 21(3), 231–238. DOI: 10.1108/10309610810922486

Gouadain, D., & Wade, E. B. (2009). 'SYSCOA/OHADA'. In *Encyclopédie de-Comptabilité, Contrôle de gestion et Audit*. Économica.

Gowry, Y., Subadar Agathee, U. & Soobaroyen, T. (2023). IFRS and the evolution of value relevance: evidence from an African developing country. *Journal of Financial Reporting and Accounting*, Vol. ahead-of-print No. ahead-of-print. DOI: 10.1108/JFRA-07-2022-0252

Hessayri, M., & Saihi, M. (2018). Ownership dynamics around IFRS adoption: Emerging markets context. *Journal of Accounting in Emerging Economies*, 8(1), 2–28. DOI: 10.1108/JAEE-01-2016-0002

Houqe, N. (2018). A review of the current debate on the determinants and consequences of mandatory IFRS adoption. *International Journal of Accounting and Information Management*, 26(3), 413–442. DOI: 10.1108/IJAIM-03-2017-0034

Hung, M., & Subramanyam, K. (2007). Financial Statement Effects of Adopting International Accounting standards: The case of Germany. *Review of Accounting Studies*, 12(4), 623–657. DOI: 10.1007/s11142-007-9049-9

Iatridis, G. (2010). International Financial Reporting Standards and the Quality of Financial Statement Information. *International Review of Financial Analysis*, 19(3), 193–204. DOI: 10.1016/j.irfa.2010.02.004

Kabwe, M., Mwanaumo, E., & Chalu, H. (2021). Effect of corporate governance attributes on IFRS compliance: Evidence from a developing country. *Corporate Governance (Bradford)*, 21(1), 1–22. DOI: 10.1108/CG-03-2020-0103

Karğin, S. (2013). The impact of IFRS on the value relevance of accounting information: Evidence from Turkish firms. *International Journal of Economics and Finance*, 5(4), 71–80. DOI: 10.5539/ijef.v5n4p71

Kenneth, M., & Grazyina, M. (2013). The Adoption of International Financial reporting Standards for small and medium enterprises in Zimbabwe. *International Journal of Asian Social Science*, 3(11), 2315–2349.

Khlif, H., Kamran, A., & Manzurul, A. (2020). Accounting Regulations and IFRS Adoption in Francophone North African Countries: The Experience of Algeria, Morocco, and Tunisia. *The International Journal of Accounting*, 55(1), 2050004. DOI: 10.1142/S1094406020500043

Klish, A. A., Shubita, M. F. S., & Wu, J. (2022). IFRS adoption and financial reporting quality in the MENA region. *Journal of Applied Accounting Research*, 23(3), 570–603. DOI: 10.1108/JAAR-08-2020-0155

Lenormand, G. & Touchais, L. (2009). Les IFRS améliorent-elles la qualité de l'information financière ? Approche par la value relevance. *Comptabilité- Contrôle- Audit*, 15(2), 145 – 164.

Liu, J., & Liu, C. (2007). Value relevance of accounting information in different stock market segments: The case of Chinese A-, B-, and H-shares. *Journal of International Accounting Research*, 6(2), 55–81. DOI: 10.2308/jiar.2007.6.2.55

Mita, A. F., Utama, S., Fitriany, F., & Wulandari, E. R. (2018). The adoption of IFRS, comparability of financial statements and foreign investors' ownership. *Asian Review of Accounting*, 26(3), 391–411. DOI: 10.1108/ARA-04-2017-0064

Morais, A. I., & Curto, J. D. (2008). Accounting quality and the adoption of IASB standards: Portuguese evidence. *Revista Contabilidade & Finanças*, 19(48), 103–111. DOI: 10.1590/S1519-70772008000300009

Nnadi, M., & Soobaroyen, T. (2015). International financial reporting standards and foreign direct investment: The case of Africa. *Advances in Accounting*, 31(2), 228–238. DOI: 10.1016/j.adiac.2015.09.007

Odoemelam, N., Okafor, R. G., & Ofoegbu, N. G. (2019). Effect of international financial reporting standard (IFRS) adoption on earnings value relevance of quoted Nigerian firms. *Cogent Business and Management*, 6(1), 1–22. DOI: 10.1080/23311975.2019.1643520

Okafor, O. N., Anderson, M., & Warsame, H. (2016). IFRS and value relevance: Evidence based on Canadian adoption. *International Journal of Managerial Finance*, 12(2), 136–160. DOI: 10.1108/IJMF-02-2015-0033

Oluwagbemiga, O. E. (2021). The Influence of IFRS Adoption on the Quality of Financial Reporting in Nigerian Listed Companies. In Advances in Pacific Basin Business, Economics and Finance. Emerald Publishing Limited.

Osasere A.O. & Ilaboya O.J. (2018). IFRS Adoption and Financial Reporting Quality: IASB Qualitative Characteristics Approach. *Accounting & Taxation Review*, 2(3).

Osinubi, I. S. (2020). The three pillars of institutional theory and IFRS implementation in Nigeria. *Journal of Accounting in Emerging Economies*, 10(4), 575–599. DOI: 10.1108/JAEE-07-2019-0139

Schiebel, A. (2006). Empirical value relevance of German GAAP and IFRS. *Journal of Economic and Financial Sciences*, 1(2), 141–170. DOI: 10.4102/jef.v1i2.365

Sellami, Y., & Fendri, H. (2017). The effect of audit committee characteristics on compliance with IFRS for related party disclosures: Evidence from South Africa. *Managerial Auditing Journal*, 32(6), 603–626. DOI: 10.1108/MAJ-06-2016-1395

Suadiye, G. (2017). Does mandatory IFRS adoption improve financial reporting quality? Empirical evidence from an emerging economy. *European Journal of Business and Social Sciences*, 6(5), 63–80.

Tawiah, V. (2019). The state of IFRS in Africa. *Journal of Financial Reporting and Accounting*, 17(4), 635–649. DOI: 10.1108/JFRA-08-2018-0067

Tawiah, V., & Boolaky, P. (2020). A review of literature on IFRS in Africa. *Journal of Accounting & Organizational Change*, 16(1), 47–70. DOI: 10.1108/JAOC-09-2018-0090

Tendeloo, B., & Vanstraelen, A. (2005). Earnings Management under German GAAP versus IFRS. *European Accounting Review*, 14(1), 155–180. DOI: 10.1080/0963818042000338988

World Bank. (2020). World Bank's 2020 Doing Business Report.

Yurisandi, T., & Puspitasari, E. (2015). Financial reporting Quality – Before and After IFRS Adoption Using NiCE Qualitative Characteristics Measurement. *Procedia: Social and Behavioral Sciences*, 211, 644–652. DOI: 10.1016/j.sbspro.2015.11.091

KEY TERMS AND DEFINITIONS

Comparability: Comparability of financial information refers to the ability of users to identify similarities and differences between the financial statements of different companies or across different periods.

French-Speaking Sub-Saharan African Countries: French-speaking Sub-Saharan African countries include several nations where French is either an official language or widely spoken like: Senegal, Côte d'Ivoire (Ivory Coast), Cameroon, Democratic Republic of the Congo, Republic of the Congo, Gabon, etc.

IFRS (International Financial Reporting Standards): IFRS (International Financial Reporting Standards) are accounting standards developed and published by the IASB (International Accounting Standards Board) that address the measurement, recognition, and presentation of company financial statements. Prior to 2001, these standards were known as IAS (International Accounting Standards).

Morocco: Morocco (officially the Kingdom of Morocco) is a country located in northwestern Africa and is part of the Maghreb region. It is bordered by the Atlantic Ocean to the west, the Mediterranean Sea to the north, Algeria to the east, and Mauritania to the south. The capital of Morocco is Rabat.

Relevance: The relevance of financial information refers to its ability to influence the decisions of users, such as investors, creditors, and managers.

Reliability: The reliability of financial information refers to the extent to which the financial information presented by a company can be considered accurate and complete.

Understandability: The understandability of financial information refers to the importance of presenting financial data in a clear and accessible manner.

Chapter 8
Exploring the Matters by ESG Dimensions Disclosed Within the European Entities' Materiality Matrices:
Are There Differences Explained by the Entities' Specific Characteristics?

Miguel Gomes
https://orcid.org/0009-0005-4829-1462
ISCAL, Instituto Politécnico de Lisboa, Portugal

Fábio Albuquerque
https://orcid.org/0000-0001-8877-9634
ISCAL, Instituto Politécnico de Lisboa, Portugal & CICF, IPCA, Barcelos, Portugal

Maria Albertina Rodrigues
https://orcid.org/0000-0002-7858-5358
ISCAL, Instituto Politécnico de Lisboa, Portugal & CETRAD-Europeia, Centre for Interdisciplinary Development Studies, Universidade Europeia, Portugal

ABSTRACT

The concept of materiality is essential in the fields of accounting and auditing, enabling the identification of important issues from the entities' perspectives and

DOI: 10.4018/979-8-3693-5923-5.ch008

those affected by it. This research focuses on the disclosure of materiality in non-financial information (NFI) reporting, assessing the topics disclosed within the entities' materiality matrix by ESG dimensions and considering their characteristics, such as size, profitability, debt, and gender diversity on the board of directors. The research uses archival research as a methodology and content analysis as an investigative technique, examining NFI reports for the year 2021 from companies listed on Euronext's main indices. The findings from the 69 NFI reports show the matters on the social aspect as the most disclosed, which is also the ESG dimension where those characteristics do not appear to be relevant when it comes to their disclosure levels. This study provides value to literature and practice by offering insights to standard-setter bodies, regulators, auditors, and various stakeholders involved in NFI reporting.

INTRODUCTION

Materiality is an elementary concept in the preparation and subsequent assessment of both financial and non-financial information (NFI), helping to identify the information considered relevant (Baumuller & Sopp, 2022). One of the main problems in terms of materiality is its subjective nature, with multiple definitions of the concept and the need to resort to judgments (Lai et al., 2017).

Historically, the first definitions of the concept of materiality were developed by entities involved in the standardization of financial reporting and the auditing of this information, namely the International Accounting Standards Board (IASB) and the International Auditing and Assurance Standards Board (IAASB), respectively (Chong, 2015), since the first reports contained information of a mostly financial nature (Mio & Fasan, 2013). Given the continuing difficulties in operationalising the concept of materiality, the IASB and IAASB have made recent efforts to clarify the concept of materiality and its application, through the revision of standards or the development of guidance guides (Sousa, 2017). Materiality is a concept of a flexible and changing nature (Edgley, 2014), realigning, and adapting to changing priorities and new challenges. However, the concept of materiality has traditionally been addressed in the field of financial reporting (Gibassier, 2019; Moroney & Trotman, 2016).

On the other hand, NFI has achieved great relevance due to the increased importance of data on performance evaluation, value creation, and sustainability in social, environmental, governance, ethical, and economic aspects (Green & Cheng, 2019; Torelli et al., 2020). In the face of growing awareness of environmental, social and governance (ESG) issues, entities must adapt their business practices and strategies to the needs and interests of stakeholders (Kolk & Van Tulder, 2010).

The growing relevance of NFI disclosure has led to new developments in the European Union (EU), as well as in the sphere of other international bodies, such as the International Financial Reporting Standards (IFRS) Foundation (IFRS Foundation) (Arif et al., 2021; Opferkuch et al., 2021; Carmo & Simões, 2021; Ferreira, 2022). More specifically, the EU recently issued Directive 2014/95 of 22 October 2014, known as the Non-Financial Reporting Directive (NFRD), as well as a new proposal for a Directive in 2021, called the Corporate Sustainability Reporting Directive (CSRD), dedicated to the disclosure of NFI, privileging the transparency of information on ESG dimensions provided by certain entities (European Parliament, 2014; European Parliament, 2021).

Consequently, the discussion regarding the definition and framing of materiality in the NFI report is increasingly relevant. The issues regarding ESG topics were initially allocated to materiality from a mostly financial perspective (Delgado-Ceballos et al., 2023). However, relevant stakeholders, such as non-governmental organizations and regulators, warned that this notion of materiality focused on financial aspects was restricted, and it was necessary to complement it with information on social and environmental impacts to ensure the achievement of sustainability in a broader perspective (Delgado-Ceballos et al., 2023). ESG issues address multiple and varied topics (GRI, 2023). For example, issues related to climate change, biodiversity, and waste are addressed for environmental issues, while topics related to diversity, inclusion, and employee well-being can be mentioned for social matters, and, finally, those related to cybersecurity and data privacy, corruption, and business ethics are within the governance ones (GRI, 2023).

In this context, the materiality matrix (MM) is presented as a tool developed by the Global Reporting Initiative (GRI) that allows demonstrating the prioritization of topics considered material through a graph, considering the perspective of both the entity and its stakeholders (De Cristofaro & Raucci, 2022). As such, the disclosure of MM is relevant, as it allows the identification and prioritization of sustainability issues (Calabrese et al., 2017). In addition, the MM affecting ESG practices is central to the business strategy of entities, as its awareness allows the entity and its stakeholders to direct efforts and resources to the topics that generate the greatest value, prioritizing their interests (Madison & Schiehll, 2021; Rodrigues, 2023).

Thus, the present study aims to analyze the content of the comparable MM of the entities, identifying the relative importance of the material topics across ESG dimensions. The study adopts archival research as a method and content analysis as an investigation technique, using as a source different consolidated NFI reports (reports and accounts, sustainability report and integrated report) for the year 2021. The population respects the entities that are part of the main indices of the countries that are members of Euronext. More specifically, it includes the entities belonging to the indices of the regulated securities markets of Amsterdam, Brussels, Dublin,

Lisbon, Oslo and Paris. A total of 69 consolidated reports of NFI were assessed, after excluding entities that did not present MM. For statistical analysis, descriptive analyses and non-parametric tests were used.

The results identified that there is no balance between the disclosure of material topics in the ESG dimensions, since the social dimension has higher disclosure indices (DI) compared to the others, although there is no considerable difference concerning the amount of material topics disclosed by the ESG dimension.

This research is distinguished from the others by its broader analysis of the disclosure of materiality in the NFI report and the content of the MM, covering multiple countries, industries of activity and entities' specific characteristics. In addition, the proposed analysis of the content of the MM allows us to identify the relevance attributed by entities and stakeholders across ESG dimensions, as well as to the material topics associated with them.

The subjectivity of the concept of materiality and the lack of an NFI reporting structure makes it difficult to harmonize the implementation and application of this concept in NFI reporting today (León & Salesa, 2023). As such, the study is pertinent in the context of the discussion about both the content and the form of disclosure of materiality in the NFI report. In addition, the study assumes particular importance due to the diversity of topics addressed related to materiality in NFI reporting, making it relevant for standardization bodies, regulators, auditors, and different stakeholders of NFI reporting.

The study consists of five sections, including this introduction. The second section is dedicated to the theoretical framework. The third section concerns the materials and methods used to achieve the objective proposed in this study. The fourth section is dedicated to the presentation and discussion of the findings. Finally, in the last section, the conclusions, limitations, as well as proposals for future research related to the subject of this study.

THEORETICAL FRAMEWORK

The MM is proposed by the GRI G4 guidelines as a way of illustrating the results of the materiality analysis. It is a special techno-rational tool, represented through a graph that identifies, through Cartesian axes (Adams et al., 2021), the importance of sustainability issues, namely the ESG dimensions (Puroila & Mäkelä, 2019), in the spheres of stakeholders (y-axis of MM) and entity (x-axis of MM), in terms of the potential impact on business. Consequently, MMs are specific to each entity, potentially considering the activity developed, the environment (cultural, legal, regulatory, among others) in which it operates, and the needs of stakeholders.

Some elements that differentiate the MM approach between different entities are, for example, the items considered material, the description of the Cartesian axes, the evaluation of the importance of the different quadrants, the presentation models (dimension, colours, schematization, illustration, legend, among others). Although it is not possible to quantify the importance of material topics in MM (Jones et al., 2016), several entities try to overcome these drawbacks through different presentation proposals, namely through the representation of each material item with circles, of different colours, according to the dimension to which it relates, in which the diameter varies considering its importance.

Among the multiple hypotheses of MM, the 2x2 and 3x3 types stand out. The difference between these is related to the level of presentation of the relative importance of a given topic considered material for stakeholders and for the entity. Thus, the 2x2 type highlights only two levels of importance, namely, low, or high, while the 3x3 type adds one more level, commonly referred to as low, moderate, and high importance. As an example, the upper right quadrant will present the most significant material issues that substantially influence the evaluations and decisions of both entities and their stakeholders, as opposed to those in the lower left quadrant (Wee et al., 2016).

MM allows the identification of a large amount of information in a concise way, identifying the relative importance of several items (Wee et al., 2016). Although it is a requirement required by the GRI G4 guidelines, it is also presented in the integrated report (Ferrero-Ferrero et al., 2021; Lai et al., 2017; Rashed, 2022), although it is inconsistent with its structure (Mio et al., 2020). More recently, the GRI has changed its approach to materiality, modifying both its prioritization and its visualization, and the presentation of MM is no longer required (De Cristofaro & Raucci, 2022; GRI, 2021).

Figure 1 shows an example of the MM analysis conceived in a 3x3 model, subdivided between the different quadrants.

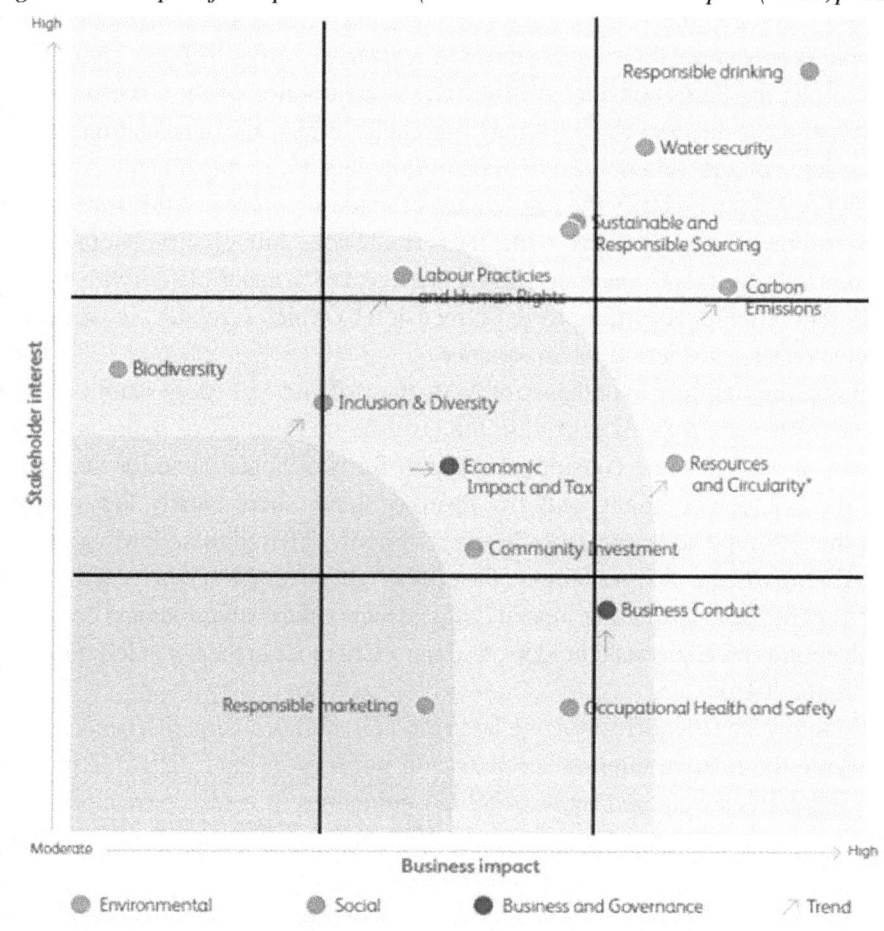

Figure 1. Example of MM presentation (Heineken N.V. Annual Report (2021, p. 128))

The GRI G4 guidelines do not provide approaches that allow for the analysis of materiality (Calabrese et al., 2017), and the literature also refers to the difficulties faced by entities in the use of MM (Calabrese et al., 2017; Jones et al., 2016; Guix et al., 2018). In addition to the adversities associated with the subjectivity of the concept of materiality, the fact that the GRI recommends the opinion of several stakeholders can sometimes make the task more arduous, considering the potentially distinct and conflicting opinions (Bellantuono et al., 2016).

The lack of information presented in the NFI reports concerning materiality has also been an obstacle to their perception since the entities do not present why certain topics are considered material to the detriment of others (Calabrese et al., 2017; Ferrero-Ferrero et al., 2021). In this sense, some authors argue for the existence of a threshold that would allow quantifying the materiality of the topics and, thus, defining their inclusion, or not, within the scope of the topics considered material (Puroila & Mäkelä, 2019).

The MM demonstrates the entity's commitment to sustainable issues (Beske et al., 2020). However, for it to be useful, the quality of the analysis and interaction with stakeholders must be high (Sardianou et al., 2021; Torelli et al., 2020). As such, the process of engaging with stakeholders is crucial, as it allows reporting information more efficiently, enabling value creation (Torelli et al., 2020).

In the literature, there is a diversity of studies that have as their object the materiality in the report of NFI, being, however, quite divergent in terms of approaches and proposals for analysis and not yet presenting references to potential underlying theories.

Table 1 presents a summary of the studies on materiality in the NFI reporting from the literature.

Table 1. Summary of studies on materiality in NFI reporting

Study	Methods (research techniques)	Source and sample	Research objectives
Formisano et al. (2018)	Archival research (content analysis)	Report of 56 entities in the banking industry in Italy	Compare the relevance of the elements that Italian banks identify as strategic to increase their relational and reputational capital with the expectations of stakeholders, through MM
Ortar (2018)	Survey (questionnaires)	39 participants with experience in corporate social responsibility (consultants, administrators, students)	Critically explore the concept of materiality in sustainability reporting
Calabrese et al. (2017)	Case Study (Observation and comparative analysis)	A small and medium-sized Italian entity operating in the water technology industry	Materiality analysis by comparing the GRI MM with a new "adequacy matrix"
Puroila &; Mäkelä (2019)	Archival research (content analysis)	44 sustainability reports from 2013 to 2014, which follow the GRI G4 Sustainability Reporting Guidelines (listed in the Global 100 Index)	Discussion on materiality in sustainability reporting, based on the literature on the subject and discuss the potential of materiality assessment for the promotion of more inclusive reporting

continued on following page

Table 1. Continued

Study	Methods (research techniques)	Source and sample	Research objectives
Saenz (2019)	Archival research (content analysis)	27 entities that make up the International Council on Mining and Metals	Explain the material issues of the mining industry and identify the shared value-creation strategies that can be applied to address each societal problem according to a materiality analysis framework
Torelli et al. (2020)	Archival research (content analysis)	160 entities that are characterized as Italian public interest entities that have published an NFI report for the year 2017 that are not from the banking, financial and insurance industries	Explain the influence of stakeholders in the materiality analysis process and, consequently, for the production of an NFI report
Ferrero-Ferrero et al. (2021)	Archival research (content analysis)	53 entities belonging to the clothing industry	Explore the extent to which corporate environmental performance is consistent, from two distinct approaches (entity's perspective and independent experts' perspective)
Jørgensen et al. (2022)	Survey (questionnaires and interviews)	30 respondents and 6 respondents (financial analysts, portfolio managers, financial market regulators, managers in financial positions, banking and insurance professionals, auditors and financial journalists)	Highlight the tensions between the two uses of the concept of materiality (GRI and SASB) and their implications for users of sustainability reporting
Ngu & Amran (2021)	Archival research (content analysis)	Reports and accounts of the 113 largest publicly traded entities in Malaysia in 2016	Analyse the determinants of the reporting of relevant information on sustainability in the reports and accounts
Geldres-Weiss et al. (2021)	Archival research (content analysis)	A case study on an entity in the wine industry	Understand the role that the material issues identified in an entity's MM play not only in identifying its sustainable business model but also in the value-creation process
D'Adamo (2023)	Archival research (content analysis)	A single Italian entity in the food industry, more precisely in pasta production	Integration of MM with the analytical hierarchization process (AHP), in theoretical and practical terms
Costa (2022)	Archival research (content analysis)	49 reports from entities in the tourism industry, with a time frame between 2018 and 2020 (using the most recent version of the GRI)	Understand how entities report on their relevant sustainability initiatives, shaping the business's contribution to the sustainable development goals

continued on following page

Table 1. Continued

Study	Methods (research techniques)	Source and sample	Research objectives
De Cristofaro & Raucci (2022)	Archival research (content analysis)	60 entities from different industries and countries reported between 2014 and 2020	Investigate the scenario of the positions and arguments of the insiders of the NFI disclosure on MM that emerged before the GRI 3 change
Garst et al. (2022)	Archival research (content analysis); Survey (questionnaires and interviews)	477 reports (annual report/sustainability report/integrated report) published by the members of the World Business Council for Sustainable Development in a period between 2017 and 2019 and semi-structured interviews with 20 managers of the respective entities	Presentation of six main steps of materiality assessments, taking into account the complexity, uncertainty and evaluative nature of sustainability issues
Rashed et al. (2022)	Archival research (content analysis)	11 sustainability reports issued between 2016 and 2020 from three Bahraini industrial entities	To investigate the contributions that MM presents in the NFI report to assist in the identification and prioritization of sustainable issues
Santos et al. (2023)	Archival research (content analysis)	Sustainability report of five entities in the wind energy industry in southern Brazil for the year 2017	Analyze whether the priorities identified in the MM correspond to the performance of the environmental indicators present in the sustainability reports
Rodrigues (2023)	Literature review	Santander Responsible Report 2021	Identify the main ESG issues that impact entities through their MM analysis, and how the entity can optimize its strategic orientation and direct internal management in responding to material issues.

Considering Table 1, the studies are fundamentally exploratory, using archival research as a method and content analysis as a research technique, despite the existence of other methods, such as surveys or literature reviews (Calabrese et al., 2017; Ferrero-Ferrero et al., 2021; Formisano et al., 2018; Geldres-Weiss et al., 2021; Ortar, 2018; Rashed et al., 2022; Rodrigues, 2023; Saenz, 2019). However, few studies extend their samples to entities from multiple countries and industries (De Cristofaro & Raucci, 2022; Garst et al., 2022; Puroila & Mäkelä, 2019).

The studies that analyze the material topics in the MM by ESG dimensions used different methods to identify them, being carried out through surveys (Ortar, 2018), by defining the material topics according to which has been reported by entities (Formisano et al., 2018; Rashed et al., 2022; Rodrigues, 2023; Saenz, 2019), or even by using NFI reporting frameworks and guidelines (Calabrese et al., 2017) or from diverse data sources (Ferrero-Ferrero et al., 2021; Geldres-Weiss et al., 2021). In addition, considering the small sample usually used in most studies, the set of material topics studied is not sufficiently detailed, focusing on specific topics of disclosure.

Thus, following the literature review previously carried out, and considering the issues inherent to MM explored in this sub-subsection, the following questions and respective research subquestion (RQ) related to the analysis of material topics across ESG dimensions where they fit were proposed:

- RQ1: Are there differences **in the disclosure level of material topics across the ESG dimensions**?
    - o   RQ1.1 Are there differences in the analysis of RQ1 **considering the entities' specific characteristics**?
- RQ2: Are there differences **in the level of global disclosure across the ESG dimensions**?
    - o   RQ2.1 Are there differences in the analysis of RQ2 **considering the entities' specific characteristics**?

The next section is dedicated to the presentation of the materials and methods underlying the empirical study carried out.

MATERIALS AND METHODS

The purpose of this exploratory study is related to the assessment of the entities' MM whenever they disclose it in a way that may be comparable among them, identifying the relative importance of material issues across ESG dimensions from the perspective of both entities and their stakeholders. The criteria underlying the entities' and data selection, including the materiality issues previously mentioned, are later explained in this section. Then, differences regarding the data collected were assessed considering the entities' specific characteristics. To this end, it uses archival research as a method and content analysis as an investigation technique.

For the sample of this study, six of the seven countries that are part of the main global securities market of the European Union, Euronext, were selected, for which the entity created local stock indices identifying each country. As a result, the only market not selected was Milan, as it does not have an associated index. The entities from each country under review are included in an index composed of the entities from each local market. In this sense, the sampled countries and their indices correspond to the local markets of Amsterdam (AEX index), Brussels (BEL-20 index), Dublin (ISEQ-20 index), Lisbon (PSI-20 index), Oslo (OBX GR index) and Paris (CAC-40 index). The identification of the entities was carried out by consulting the Euronext website. Finally, for entities that belonged to two or more indexes, the criterion of headquarters was used. At the end of the process, 144 entities that were part of these indexes were previously selected.

After this first selection criterion, a second criterion was adopted based on the identification of minimum disclosures regarding materiality in the NFI report used as a source, considering the search for the terms "material" and/or "materiality" in the reference language of the report. After applying this criterion, 33 entities were identified that did not address the issue of materiality in the NFI report and were consequently excluded. Thus, after applying these criteria, the final research sample for this study corresponds to 111 entities from the six main Euronext indices.

In addition to identifying the entities that made references to materiality and provided the MM, and as a further criterion underlying the entities and data selection, this information should be comparable. To be comparable, the MM must have been presented following the 3x3 model, where the "x" presents the impact of the material issues on the entity and the "y" the impact of the material issues on the stakeholders. After the application of this last procedure, the final sample under assessment was comprised of 69 entities.

Table 2 summarizes the criteria applied for this research sample by country.

Table 2. Research sample by country

Country: Index	Initial sample: Entities in their Euronext indices	Report materiality in the disclosure of NFI	Disclose MM	Disclose comparable MM	Sample Final
Netherlands: Amsterdam Index (AEX)	25	6	5	1	13 (18.8%)
Belgium: Brussels Index (BEL-20)	20	2	6	4	8 (11.6%)
Ireland: Dublin Index (ISEQ-20)	20	6	3	0	11 (15.9%)
Portugal: Lisbon index (PSI-20)	15	4	4	1	6 (8.7%)

(Exclusions – entities that do not: Report materiality in the disclosure of NFI / Disclose MM / Disclose comparable MM)

continued on following page

Table 2. Continued

Country: Index	Initial sample: Entities in their Euronext indices	Exclusions – entities that do not: Report materiality in the disclosure of NFI	Disclose MM	Disclose comparable MM	Sample Final
Norway: Oslo Index (OBX GR)	25	6	9	4	6 (8.7%)
France: Paris Index (CAC-40)	39	9	5	0	25 (36.2%)
Total	**144**	**33**	**32**	**10**	**69 (100.0%)**

In addition, Appendix A presents the list of entities by country: Index.

In turn, the number of entities that constitute each industry is shown in Table 3.

Table 3. Research sample by industry

Industry (ICB Rating)	Number of Entities	% of entities
Telecommunications (10) and Technologies (15)	9	13.1%
Health (20)	1	1.5%
Finance (30) and Real Estate (35)	16	23.2%
Consumer Goods (40)	17	24.7%
Industry (50) and basic materials (55)	20	29.0%
Energy (60) and utilities (65)	6	8.7%
Total	**69**	**100%**

Appendix B presents the list of entities by industry.

In the definition of the material topics, the total number of disclosures made by the different entities was considered. Notwithstanding, material topics that were disclosed on three or fewer occasions were excluded from analysis, as they were specific to a certain industry and/or entity, with less relevance.

Table 4 summarises the material topics gathered by ESG dimensions.

Table 4. Material topics by ESG dimensions

Dimensions	Material topics
Environmental (E_Total)	E1: Climate
	E2: Biodiversity
	E3: Water
	E4: Waste
	E5: Carbon emissions
	E6: Energy
	E7: Circular economy
	E8: Impact on the environment
	E9: Animal welfare
	E10: Sustainable product
	E11: Sustainable packaging
	E12: Product Management
Social (S_Total)	S1: Well-being, health and safety at work
	S2: Diversity and inclusion
	S3: Employee attraction and development
	S4: Human rights
	S5: Community Engagement
	S6: Social dialogue
	S7: Employee Engagement
	S8: Attractive working conditions
Governance (G_Total)	G1: Cybersecurity and data privacy
	G2: Business ethics
	G3: Responsible supply chain
	G4: Governance
	G5: Customer intimacy
	G6: Product quality and/or safety
	G7: Artificial Intelligence
	G8: Tax
	G9: Performance
	G10: Anti-corruption
	G11: Stakeholder engagement
	G12: Responsible investment
	G13: Risk profile
	G14: Operational efficiency
	G15: Politics

Based on the disclosure of the material topics in the MM, the levels of attributed importance by the entities and their stakeholders were quantified, and the quadrants of the MM associated with the level of importance attributed by each of the aforementioned parties were subsequently identified. The quantification of the material topics by their levels of importance (entities and stakeholders) was carried out by assigning the value "1" when they are disclosed and the value "0" otherwise. Thus, the identification of material issues in MM across ESG dimensions allowed the creation of a DI, materialized in equation 1.

$$DI = \frac{\sum_{i=1}^{m} d}{\sum_{i=1}^{n} d} (1) \; Where:$$

d = 1 when the material topic is disclosed,
d = 0 when the material topic is not disclosed,
m = number of material topics disclosed, and
n = number of material topics susceptible to disclosure.

Table 5 presents, in turn, the variables used for the analysis by subgroups (subsamples), considering studies related to the disclosure of NFI matters used for this purpose.

Table 5. Entities' characteristics, variables, and benchmark studies

Entities' characteristics under assessment	Variables used as proxies	Benchmark studies
Size	Total assets (Assets)	Chiu & Wang (2015); Fasan & Mio (2017); Osifo & Fasua (2017); Duran & Rodrigo (2018); Sierra-Garcia et al. (2018); Iredele (2019); Guping et al. (2020); Torelli et al. (2020); Ferrero-Ferrero et al. (2021); Arif et al. (2021); Ngu & Amran (2021); Elshandidy et al. (2022); Albuquerque et al. (2023)
Profitability	Net income for the period / Assets (ROA)	Setyorini & Ishak, (2012); Fasan & Mio (2017); Osifo & Fasua (2017); Durán & Rodrigo, (2018); Iredele (2019); García-Sánchez et al. (2019); Torelli et al. (2020); Ferrero-Ferrero et al. (2021); Arif et al. (2021); Kalbuana et al. (2022); Senani et al. (2022); Albuquerque et al. (2023)
Indebtedness	Liabilities / Equity (Debt)	Setyorini & Ishak, (2012); Iredele (2019); García-Sánchez et al. (2019); Ngu & Amran (2021); Albuquerque et al. (2023)
Size of the board of directors	Total number of members of the board of directors (M_BD)	Fasan & Mio (2017); Iredele (2019); García-Sánchez et al. (2019); Ngu & Amran (2021); Elshandidy et al. (2022)
Gender diversity on the board of directors	Weight of women on the board of directors (gender)	Fasan & Mio (2017); Iredele (2019); García-Sánchez et al. (2019); Zumente & Lāce (2020); Dobija et al. (2022); Wu et al. (2022); Albuquerque et al. (2023)

The data on size, profitability and indebtedness were obtained by consulting the financial statements of the sources consulted or additionally extracted for the same period, while the information on the number of members of the board of directors, as well as gender diversity was obtained from other components of such sources, namely the management report. For the continuous variable size, since it does not correspond to a ratio, the values were collected in millions of euros and were then subject to logarithmation. As the study includes a varied set of countries, and in cases where the currency used was different from the euro, the conversion to that currency was carried out based on the exchange rate at the reporting date for the year 2021. To distinguish the subgroups according to the characteristics of the entities, the median of the distribution was used as a reference, since these were continuous variables.

The statistical analyses proposed for this study include descriptive statistics and non-parametric tests, namely the Chi-square, Mann-Whitney U and Wilcoxon tests, performed with the support of the IBM ® SPSS Statistics software.

The Chi-square and Mann-Whitney tests were used to assess significant differences in the disclosure of the individual material topics found within MM and the Dis, respectively, by the different entities in each of the subgroups of the sample based on the entities' specific characteristics as well as by ESG dimension. Finally, the Wilcoxon test compares the mean of two independent distributions. In this specific case, this test was used to verify any differences between the normalized averages of the ESG dimensions overall, comparing each one of them with the remaining.

The normalization process mentioned above, as an auxiliary resource to data analysis using the Mann-Whitney U test and the Wilcoxon test, consisted of the "minimum-maximum" method. The method consists of calculating the relative percentages of each dimension for each entity. After its calculation, the highest and lowest relative percentages are checked, becoming our extremes of the range, i.e. 0 and 1. Thus, the normalized percentage is nothing more than the relative percentage deducted from the minimum extreme to be divided by the difference between the maximum extreme and the minimum extreme (Domingos et al., 2023).

In summary, and to answer the sub-questions proposed in the previous section, the following procedures were defined:

- For RQ1.1, identify potential differences in the disclosure level of material topics by ESG dimensions, considering the entities' specific characteristics proposed, through the analysis of relative percentages and the use of the Chi-square test;
- For RQ2.1, identify potential differences in the global disclosure level by ESG dimensions, also considering the entities' specific characteristics and

through the DI analysis and the use of the Mann-Whitney U and the Wilcoxon tests.

Table 6 summarizes the previous information, through the presentation of the proposed RQ, as well as the statistical techniques that will be used for the analysis of the results obtained.

Table 6. Research questions and statistical techniques used

Research Questions	Research subquestions	Statistical Techniques Used
RQ1- Differences in the disclosure level of material topics across ESG dimensions	RQ1.1- analysis by the entities' specific characteristics	Relative percentages and Chi-square test
RQ2- Differences for the global disclosure level across ESG dimensions	RQ2.2- analysis by the entities' specific characteristics	DI, teste U de Mann-Whitney e Wilcoxon tests

The next section is dedicated to the presentation and discussion of the results obtained for the objective defined for the study carried out.

PRESENTATION AND DISCUSSION OF RESULTS

This section is subdivided into two subsections, the first being dedicated to the presentation and analysis of the findings, while the second addresses their discussion.

Presentation of results

The following three tables (Table 7 to Table 9) show the disclosure level of material topics by each ESG dimension and the entities' characteristics.

Table 7 shows the disclosure level of material topics found for the environmental dimension in the MM by entities' characteristics.

Based on Table 7, the material topics for the environmental dimension are mentioned 244 times, with a global disclosure level of 29%. The most disclosed environmental topics are E1 (20%) and E2 (14%), conversely to the topics E9 to E12 with the lowest disclosure level (equal to or less than 2%).

Significant differences are found between the average global ID for the environmental dimension for the subgroups within the variables asset and ROA. Specifically, smaller and higher profitability entities have higher disclosure levels. It is also identified that the disclosure level of entities that are below the median threshold is higher in the context of the variables asset, debt and gender, despite not significantly.

By material topics for the environmental dimension, significant differences are observed in the environmental topics E3 and E9 (regarding ROA), E4 (regarding assets and debt), E6 (regarding assets and gender), E7 (regarding M_BD). In addition, it can be stressed that higher disclosure levels are found for the entities that are below the median threshold for the debt variable in E1 (83%).

Table 7. Topics on the environmental dimension by entities' characteristics (in percentage)

Topics in matter	Assets 0	Assets 1	ROA 0	ROA 1	Debt 0	Debt 1	M_BD 0	M_BD 1	Gender 0	Gender 1	ID Global
E1	73	69	67	76	83	63	63	74	66	76	71
E2	43	51	39	58	52	45	42	50	47	49	48
E3	53	36	28***	61***	52	38	53	40	50	38	43
E4	53***	21***	25*	45*	48*	25*	42	32	31	38	35
E5	50	33	33	48	34	45	47	38	41	41	41
E6	60***	15***	28	42	41	30	37	34	53***	19***	35
E7	20	38	25	36	31	30	11**	38**	22	38	30
E8	23	28	31	21	17	33	32	24	22	30	26
E9	10	8	3*	15*	14	5	5	10	6	11	9
E10	15	3	3	9	10	3	11	4	6	5	6
E11	7	8	6	9	10	5	0	10	9	5	7
E12	0	5	3	3	0	5	0	4	3	3	3
Average ID	34*	26*	24***	35***	33	27	29	30	30	29	29

Note: assets – the median of the size variable; ROA - the median of the profitability variable; debt- the median of the indebtedness variable; M_BD- the median of the total number of members in the board of directors; Gender - the median of the gender diversity variable in the board of directors; Subgroup "0": Below the median; Subgroup "1": Above the median; E1- Climate; E2- Biodiversity; E3- Water; E4- Waste; E5- Carbon emissions; E6- Energy; E7- Circular economy; E8- Impact on the environment; E9- Animal welfare; E10 - Sustainable product; E11- Sustainable packaging; E12- Product management; *Significance level at 10%; **Significance level at 5%; Significance level at 1%

Table 8 shows the disclosure level of material topics found for the social dimension in the MM by entities' characteristics.

Table 8. Topics on the social dimension by entities' characteristics (in percentage)

Topics in matter	Assets 0	Assets 1	ROA 0	ROA 1	Debt 0	Debt 1	M_BD 0	M_BD 1	Gender 0	Gender 1	ID Global
S1	87*	67*	67**	85**	83	70	74	76	78	73	75
S2	80	74	69	85	83	73	79	76	72	81	77
S3	70	67	67	70	66	70	68	68	59	76	68
S4	80**	54**	53**	79**	72	60	84*	58*	63	68	65
S5	57	62	67	52	55	63	53	62	72*	49*	59
S6	3*	21*	11	15	10	15	5	16	6	19	13
S7	13	15	17	12	7	20	11	16	16	14	14
S8	10*	0*	0*	9*	3	5	11	2	9*	0*	4
Average ID	50	45	44	51	47	47	48	47	47	47	47

Note: assets – the median of the size variable; ROA - the median of the profitability variable; debt- the median of the indebtedness variable; M_BD- the median of the total number of members in the board of directors; Gender - median of the gender diversity variable in the board of directors; Subgroup "0": Below the median; Subgroup "1": Above the median; S1- Well-being, health and safety at work; S2- Diversity and inclusion; S3- Attraction and development of workers; S4- Human rights; S5- Community involvement; S6- Social dialogue; S7-Employee involvement; S8- Attractive working conditions; *Significance level at 10%; **Significance level at 5%; Significance level at 1%

Considering Table 8, it is identified that material topics in the social dimension are mentioned 260 times, with a global disclosure level of 47%. The most disclosed social issues are S1 and S2, with around 20% in both cases, conversely to S6 to S8, which are characterised by their low level of disclosure (between 1% and 4%).

There are no significant differences in the analysis of the material topics for the social dimension by the entities' characteristics under assessment, as corroborated by the Mann-Whitney U test. Overall, and despite being not significant, entities that are below the median threshold have higher disclosure levels in the context of assets and M_BD.

By social material topics, there are significant differences for S1 (regarding assets and ROA), S4 (regarding assets, ROA and M_BD), S5 (regarding gender), S6 (regarding assets) and S8 (regarding assets, ROA and gender). It can be also stressed the higher disclosure levels of entities that are below the median threshold for the asset variable in S1 and S4 (87% and 80%, respectively), as well as entities that are above the median threshold for the ROA variable in S1 (85%).

Table 9 shows the disclosure level of material topics found for the governance dimension in the MM by entities' characteristics.

Table 9. Topics on the governance dimension by entities' characteristics (in percentage)

Topics in matter	Assets 0	Assets 1	ROA 0	ROA 1	Debt 0	Debt 1	M_BD 0	M_BD 1	Gender 0	Gender 1	ID Global
G1	67	67	69	64	59	73	63	68	72	62	67
G2	73	69	69	73	69	73	74	70	72	70	71
G3	63	46	53	55	55	53	58	52	56	51	54
G4	40	56	58*	39**	38*	58**	42	52	41	57	49
G5	27	49	53**	24**	21**	53**	32	42	31	46	39
G6	30	46	39	39	31	45	26	44	50	30	39
G7	30	38	39	30	21**	45**	21	40	38	32	35
G8	20	26	22	24	17	28	37	18	19	27	23
G9	7	21	25**	3**	7	20	0*	20*	22	8	14
G10	13	18	19	12	10	20	16	16	13	19	16
G11	10	10	8	12	3	15	5	12	13	8	10
G12	7	13	11	9	10	10	5	12	13	8	10
G13	0*	13*	11	3	0*	13*	0	10	9	5	7
G14	3	13	8	9	10	8	0	12	9	8	9
G15	7	5	6	6	3	8	5	6	3	8	6
Average ID	26	33	33	27	24***	35***	26	32	31	29	30

Note: assets – the median of the size variable; ROA – the median of the profitability variable; debt - the median of the indebtedness variable; M_BD - the median of the total number of members in the board of directors; Gender – the median of the gender diversity variable in the board of directors; Subgroup "0": Below the median; Subgroup "1": Above the median; G1- Cybersecurity and data privacy; G2- Business ethics; G3- Responsible supply chain; G4- Corporate governance; G5- Intimacy with the client; G6- Product quality and/or safety; G7- Artificial intelligence; G8- Tax; G9- Financial performance; G10- Anti-corruption; G11- Engagement with stakeholders; G12- Responsible investment; G13- Risk profile; G14- Operational efficiency; G15- Politics; *Significance level at 10%; **Significance level at 5%; Significance level at 1%

Data in Table 9 shows that the material topics for the governance dimension are mentioned 310 times, with a global disclosure level of 30%. The governance topics with the highest disclosure levels are G1 and G2 (between 15% and 16%), while the G8 to G14 are characterised by low disclosure levels (below 5%).

By the entities' characteristics, significant differences between the average global ID for the subgroups within the debt variable can be found, with the most indebted entities presenting higher disclosure levels. Overall, entities that are below the median threshold have higher disclosure levels in terms of ROA and gender.

By material topics for the governance, there are significant differences for the topics G4 and G5 (regarding ROA and debt), G7 (regarding debt), G9 (regarding ROA and M_CA) and G13 (regarding assets and debt).

Table 10 presents, finally, the average of the normalized disclosure levels by the entities' characteristics and ESG dimensions, as well as the results for the Wilcoxon test.

Table 10. Normalized disclosure levels by ESG dimensions and entities' characteristics (in percentage), and bilateral significance level for the Wilcoxon test

	Assets 0	Assets 1	ROA 0	ROA 1	Debt 0	Debt 1	M_BD 0	M_BD 1	Gender 0	Gender 1	Total
Percentage-normalized indices (in percentage)											
E_Nor	50	39	36	53	49	41	43	45	45	44	**44**
S_Nor	57	51	50	58	54	54	55	53	54	54	**54**
G_Nor	31	38	38	31	27	40	30	36	35	34	**35**
Wilcoxon test (bilateral significance level)											
S Nor - E Nor	22	0	0	20	21	0	3	2	4	3	0
G Nor - E Nor	0	43	99	0	0	60	1	10	6	4	1
G Nor - S Nor	0	0	0	0	0	0	0	0	0	0	0

Note: assets – the median of the size variable; ROA - the median of the profitability variable; debt- median of the indebtedness variable; M_BD- median of the total number of members in the board of directors; Gender - median of the gender diversity variable in the board of directors; Subgroup "0": Below the median; Subgroup "1": Above the median; E_Nor – normalised average percentages of environmental topics; S_Nor – normalised average percentages of social topics; G_Nor – normalised average percentages of governance topics

Table 10 shows that, concerning the entities' characteristics under analysis, in eight out of fifteen possible cases for material topics by ESG dimensions the entities above the median threshold have higher disclosure levels, compared to those below the same threshold.

The Wilcoxon test found that material topics have a significantly higher DI for the social dimension, compared to the environmental dimension, for entities that are below the median threshold in the context of the variables ROA, M_BD and gender, as well as for entities that are above the median threshold for the variables asset, debt, M_BD and gender. On the other hand, the material topics have a significantly higher DI for the environmental dimension, compared to the governance ones, for the entities that are below the median threshold in the context of the variables asset, debt and M_BD, as well as for the entities that are above the average threshold for the variables ROA and gender. Finally, social topics have a significantly higher DI, compared to the governance ones, for all the entities' characteristics under assessment.

After the presentation and analysis of the results obtained, the discussion of these results will be carried out in the following subsection.

Discussion of Results

Based on the results obtained, the social dimension is the ESG dimension with the highest disclosure level, with a disclosure level close to 50%, while the environmental and governance dimensions have overall disclosure levels lower than or equal to 30%. The analysis of the normalised disclosure indices for each of these dimensions points to significant differences, by around 10 percentage points, with social dimension at 54%, environmental at 44% and, finally, governance topics, at 35%. This finding is not in line with the results of some previous studies, such as that by Helfaya et al. (2023) and Baldini et al. (2018), who found the governance dimension with the highest level of disclosure. However, the divergence can be explained by the different methodologies adopted, as they did not focus on identifying the number of topics underlying each ESG dimension.

The analysis of the material topics disclosed in the MM allows us to conclude, in summary, considering RQ1 and RQ2, that there are still relevant differences in the disclosure level of material topics and the level of global disclosure between the three ESG dimensions, with some of the characteristics of the entities being distinctive elements in this context. An exception is made in this context for the analysis of information disseminated in the social dimension. More specifically, it was identified that the size and profitability of the entities are potential entities' specific characteristics that allow distinguishing the entities in terms of disclosure of material issues in the MM in the environmental dimension, as well as the indebtedness in the governance dimension.

The analysis of sub-questions RQ1.1 and RQ2.1, in particular, identified the existence of significant differences in the level of disclosure of material topics in all ESG dimensions. However, only for the environmental and governance dimensions there were differences in the average disclosure of the remaining entities' specific characteristics. Through this analysis, it was confirmed that the entities' size and profitability are potential elements that distinguish the entities in terms of disclosure of material topics in the MM in the environmental dimension, as well as debt in the governance dimension.

Such results find some support in the literature, which identifies both the size and profitability as entities' specific characteristics that explain the disclosure level of ESG information since larger and more profitable entities are expected to have greater capacity to disclose ESG information, to satisfy the needs of its stakeholders (Alsayegh et al., 2020; Costa et al., 2022; Manita et al., 2018; Sharma et al., 2020). Additionally, Alsayegh et al. (2020) also identified a direct association between indebtedness and the environmental and governance dimensions in the disclosure of ESG information, justified by the fact that higher levels of disclosure of ESG information could act as a reward, helping the most indebted entities in obtaining more favourable financing conditions with its financiers.

The following section presents the conclusions, limitations, and suggestions for future research.

CONCLUSION

This section is dedicated to the presentation of the general conclusions, limitations of the study and contributions to future research related to the topic of the present study, whose objective is associated with the information related to materiality in the reporting of NFI, focusing on the analysis of content to MM.

The study identified that the most publicized ESG dimension is the social one, with disclosure levels closer to 50%, with the other dimensions generally below 30%. Also in this context, still relevant differences were identified in the disclosure level of material topics across ESG dimensions in the analysis by potentially distinguishing the entities' specific characteristics. In addition, differences in the level of global disclosure were also identified across ESG dimensions and these characteristics, except for the social dimension.

The study presents contributions to the academic and business environment, which include regulatory bodies, supervisors, auditors and different stakeholders of the NFI report, namely in terms of content analysis to the materiality matrix. It also makes it possible to verify any patterns according to different distinctive elements of the entities, as well as the importance attributed by them and their stakeholders to material issues across ESG dimensions.

Nevertheless, the study has some limitations. The first limitation concerns the sample size, as an element of restriction of using more robust statistical techniques. In addition, the subjectivity inherent to the data collection process, as this is an investigation based on content analysis, can be subject to some biases. This may derive, for instance, from designations given differently by the different entities to the material topics or different forms of presentation of MM, requiring judgments by the researcher.

To fill these gaps, future research can expand the sample size and propose methods that eventually mitigate the role of the researcher in this prOslo,s, namely using software based on artificial intelligence and machine learning. Future studies may also identify whether events with adverse impacts on the entities, namely the COVID-19 pandemic or the war in Ukraine, caused changes in the disclosure regarding materiality in the entities' NFI reporting, both in terms of content and in terms of the disclosure level. Finally, future research will be able to identify the impacts of the waiver of MM implementation on NFI reporting, based on the new

GRI (2021) approach, in terms of the stakeholders' perceptions of the transparency and usefulness of the disclosed NFI.

REFERENCES

Adams, C., Abdullah, A., Xinwu, H., & Jie, T. (2021). The Double-Materiality Concept. Application and Issues. Project Report. Global Reporting Initiative. Available online: https://dro.dur.ac.uk/33139/1/33139.pdf

Albuquerque, F., Monteiro, E., & Rodrigues, M. A. B. (2023). The Explanatory Factors of Risk Disclosure in the Integrated Reports of Listed Entities in Brazil. *Risks, 11*(6), 108. https://doi.org/11060108DOI: 10.3390/risksetor

Alsayegh, M. F., Abdul, R. R., & Homayoun, S. (2020). Corporate Economic, Environmental, and Social Sustainability Performance Transformation through ESG Disclosure. *Sustainability (Basel)*, 12(9), 3910. Advance online publication. DOI: 10.3390/su12093910

Arif, M., Gan, C., & Nadeem, M. (2021). Regulating non-financial reporting: Evidence from European firms' environmental, social and governance disclosures and earnings risk. *Meditari Accountancy Research*, 30(3), 495–523. DOI: 10.1108/MEDAR-11-2020-1086

Baldini, M., Maso, L. D., Liberatore, G., Mazzi, F., & Terzani, S. (2018). Role of Country- and Firm-Level Determinants in Environmental, Social, and Governance Disclosure. *Journal of Business Ethics*, 150(1), 79–98. DOI: 10.1007/s10551-016-3139-1

Baumuller, J., & Sopp, K. (2022). Double materiality and the shift from non-financial to European sustainability reporting: Review, outlook and implications. *Journal of Applied Accounting Research*, 23(1), 8–28. DOI: 10.1108/JAAR-04-2021-0114

Bellantuono, N., Pontrandolfo, P., & Scozzi, B. (2016). Capturing the Stakeholders' View in Sustainability Reporting: A Novel Approach. *Sustainability (Basel)*, 8(4), 379. Advance online publication. DOI: 10.3390/su8040379

Beske, F., Haustein, E., & Lorson, P. C. (2020). Materiality analysis in sustainability and integrated reports. *Sustainability Accounting Management and Policy Journal*, 11(1), 162–186. DOI: 10.1108/SAMPJ-12-2018-0343

Calabrese, A., Costa, R., Ghiron, N. & Menichini, T. (2017). Materiality Analysis In Sustainability Reporting: A Method For Making It Work In Practice. *European Journal of Sustainable Development, 6*(3), 439-447. http://dx.doi.org/ 439DOI: 10.14207/ejsd.2017.v6n3país

Carmo, C., & Simões, A. (2021). *A Diretiva 2014/95/UE: passado, presente e futuro*. Apotec. https://www.researchgate.net/profile/Cecilia-Carmo/publication/356834363_A_Diretiva_201495UE_passado_presente_e_futuro/links/61af51cdb3c26a1e5d8eebfd/A-Diretiva-2014-95-UE-passado-presente-e-futuro.pdf

Chiu, T. K. & Wang, Y. H. (2015). Determinants of Social Disclosure Quality in Taiwan: An Application of Stakeholder Theory. Journal of Business Ethics, 129, 379–398. https://doi.org/ 10551-014-2160-5DOI: 10.1007/setor

Chong, H. G. (2015). A review on the evolution of the definitions of materiality. *Int. J. Economics and Accounting*, 6(1), 15–32. DOI: 10.1504/IJEA.2015.068978

Costa, R., Menichini, T., & Salierno, G. (2022). Do SDGs Really Matter for Business? Using GRI Sustainability Reporting to Answer the Question. *European Journal of Sustainable Development*, 11(1), 113. DOI: 10.14207/ejsd.2022.v11n1p113

D'Adamo, I. (2023). The analytic hierarchy process as an innovative way to enable stakeholder engagement for sustainability reporting in the food industry. *Environment, Development and Sustainability 25*. https://doi.org/10668-022-02700-0DOI: 10.1007/setor

De Cristofaro, T., & Raucci, D. (2022). Rise and Fall of the Materiality Matrix: Lessons from a Missed Takeoff. *Administrative Sciences*, 12(4), 186. Advance online publication. DOI: 10.3390/admsci12040186

Delgado-Ceballos, J., Ortiz-De-Mandojana, N., Antolín-López, R., & Montiel, I. (2023). Connecting the Sustainable Development Goals to firm-level sustainability and ESG factors: The need for double materiality. *Business Research Quarterly*, 26(1), 2–10. DOI: 10.1177/23409444221140919

Dobija, D., Arena, C., Kozlowski, L., Krasodomska, J., & Godawska, J. (2022). Towards sustainable development: The role of directors' international orientation and their diversity for non-financial disclosure. *Corporate Social Responsibility and Environmental Management*, 30(1), 66–90. DOI: 10.1002/csr.2339

Duran, I., & Rodrigo, P. (2018). Why Do Firms in Emerging Markets Report? A Stakeholder Theory Approach to Study the Determinants of Non-Financial Disclosure in Latin America. *Sustainability (Basel)*, 10(9), 3111. DOI: 10.3390/su10093111

Edgley, C. (2014). A genealogy of accounting materiality. *Critical Perspectives on Accounting*, 25(3), 255–271. DOI: 10.1016/j.cpa.2013.06.001

Elshandidy, T., Elmassri, M., & Elsayed, M. (2022). Integrated reporting, textual risk disclosure and market value. *Corporate Governance (Bradford)*, 22(1), 173–193. DOI: 10.1108/CG-01-2021-0002

European Parliament. (2014). Directive 2014/95/eu of the European Parliament and Council.https://eur-lex.europa.eu/legal-content/PT/TXT/HTML/?uri=CELEX: 32014L0095&from=EN

European Parliament. (2021). European Parliament and Council Directive. https://eur-lex.europa.eu/legal-content/PT/TXT/HTML/?uri=CELEX:52021PC0189&from=EN

Fasan, M., & Mio, C. (2017). Fostering stakeholder engagement: The role of materiality disclosure in integrated reporting. *Business Strategy and the Environment*, 26(3), 288–305. DOI: 10.1002/bse.1917

Ferreira, P. C. P. (2022). Influência do lobbying no processo de constituição do international sustainability standards board (ISSB) (Dissertação pós-graduação). Universidade Federal de Pernambuco. Pernambuco. https://repositorio.ufpe.br/bitstream/123456789/46246/1/DISSERTA%c3%87%c3%83O%20Priscila%20Cristine%20Pacheco%20Ferreira.pdf

Ferrero-Ferrero, I., León, R., & Muñoz-Torres, M. J. (2021). Sustainability materiality matrices in doubt: May prioritizations of aspects overestimate environmental performance? *Journal of Environmental Planning and Management*, 64(3), 432–463. DOI: 10.1080/09640568.2020.1766427

Formisano, V., Fedele, M., & Calabrese, M. (2018). The strategic priorities in the materiality matrix of the banking enterprise. *The TQM Journal*, 30(5), 589–607. DOI: 10.1108/TQM-11-2017-0134

García-Sánchez, I. M., Suárez-Fernández, O., & Martínez-Ferrero, J. (2019). Female directors and impression management in sustainability reporting. *International Business Review*, 28(2), 359–374. DOI: 10.1016/j.ibusrev.2018.10.007

Garst, J., Maas, K., & Suijs, J. (2022). Materiality Assessment Is an Art, Not a Science: Selecting ESG Topics for Sustainability Reports. *California Management Review*, 65(1), 64–90. DOI: 10.1177/00081256221120692

Geldres-Weiss, V. V., Gambetta, N., Massa, N. P., & Geldres-Weiss, S. L. (2021). Materiality Matrix Use in Aligning and Determining a Firm's Sustainable Business Model Archetype and Triple Bottom Line Impact on Stakeholders. *Sustainability (Basel)*, 13(3), 1065. DOI: 10.3390/su13031065

Gibassier, D. (2019). *Materiality assessment: contribution to single or double materiality debate*. Working paper, Audencia Business School, Nantes, France. https://www.anc.gouv.fr/files/live/sites/anc/files/contributed/ANC/3_Recherche/D_Etats%20generaux/2020/Policy%20papers/TR4_VE-paper-Delphine-Gibassier.pdf

Green, W., & Cheng, M. (2019). Materiality judgments in an integrated reporting setting: The effect of strategic relevance and strategy map. *Accounting, Organizations and Society*, 73, 1–14. DOI: 10.1016/j.aos.2018.07.001

GRI. (2021). GRI 3: Material Topics 2021. https://globalreporting.org/pdf.ashx?id=12453

GRI. (2023). About GRI. https://www.globalreporting.org/Information/about-gri/Pages/default.aspx

Guix, M., Bonilla-Priego, M. J., & Font, X. (2018). The process of sustainability reporting in international hotel groups: An analysis of stakeholder inclusiveness, materiality and responsiveness. *Journal of Sustainable Tourism*, 26(7), 1063–1084. DOI: 10.1080/09669582.2017.1410164

Guping, C., Safdar Sial, M., Wan, P., Badulescu, A., Badulescu, D., & Vianna Brugni, T. (2020). Do Board Gender Diversity and Non-Executive Directors Affect CSR Reporting? Insight from Agency Theory Perspective. *Sustainability (Basel)*, 12(20), 8597. Advance online publication. DOI: 10.3390/su12208597

Heineken, N. V. Annual Report (2021). https://www.theheinekencompany.com/sites/theheinekencompany/files/Investors/financial-information/results-reports-presentations/heineken-nv-annual-report-2021-25-02-2022.pdf

Helfaya, A., Morris, R., & Aboud, A. (2023). Investigating the Factors That Determine the ESG Disclosure Practices in Europe. *Sustainability (Basel)*, 15(6), 5508. Advance online publication. DOI: 10.3390/su15065508

Iredele, O. O. (2019). Examining the association between quality of integrated reports and corporate characteristics. *Heliyon*, 5(7), e01932. Advance online publication. DOI: 10.1016/j.heliyon.2019.e01932 PMID: 31317079

Jones, P., Comfort, D., & Hillier, D. (2016). Managing materiality: A preliminary examination of the adoption of the new GRI G4 guidelines on materiality within the business community. *Journal of Public Affairs*, 16(3), 222–230. DOI: 10.1002/pa.1586

Jørgensen, S., Mjøs, A., & Pedersen, L. J. T. (2022). Sustainability reporting and approaches to materiality: Tensions and potential resolutions. *Sustainability Accounting. Management and Policy Journal*, 13(2), 341–361. DOI: 10.1108/SAMPJ-01-2021-0009

Kalbuana, N., Kusiyah, K., Supriatiningsih, S., Budiharjo, R., Budyastuti, T., & Rusdiyanto, R. (2022). Effect of profitability, audit committee, company size, activity, and board of directors on sustainability. *Cogent Business & Management*, 9(1), 2129354. Advance online publication. DOI: 10.1080/23311975.2022.2129354

Kolk, A., & Van Tulder, R. (2010). International business, corporate social responsibility and sustainable development. *International Business Review*, 19(2), 119–125. DOI: 10.1016/j.ibusrev.2009.12.003

Lai, A., Melloni, G., & Stacchezzini, R. (2017). What does materiality mean to integrated reporting preparers? An empirical exploration. *Meditari Accountancy Research*, 25(4), 533–552. DOI: 10.1108/MEDAR-02-2017-0113

León, R. & Salesa, A. (2023). Is sustainability reporting disclosing what is relevant? Assessing materiality accuracy in the Spanish telecommunication industry. *Environment, Development and Sustainability*. https://doi.org/10668-023-03537-xDOI: 10.1007/setor

Madison, N., & Schiehll, E. (2021). The Effect of Financial Materiality on ESG Performance Assessment. *Sustainability (Basel)*, 13(7), 3652. Advance online publication. DOI: 10.3390/su13073652

Manita, R., Bruna, M. G., Dang, R., & Houanti, L. (2018). Board gender diversity and ESG disclosure: Evidence from the USA. *Journal of Applied Accounting Research*, 19(2), 206–224. DOI: 10.1108/JAAR-01-2017-0024

Mio, C., & Fasan, M. (2013). *Materiality from financial towards non-financial*. Working Paper Series. Universitá Ca'Foscari Venezia, Venezia. http://dx.doi.org/ DOI: 10.2139/ssrn.2340192

Mio, C., Fasan, M., & Costantini, A. (2020). Materiality in integrated and sustainability reporting: A paradigm shift? *Business Strategy and the Environment*, 29(1), 306–320. DOI: 10.1002/bse.2390

Moroney, R., & Trotman, K. T. (2016). Differences in auditors' materiality assessments when auditing financial statements and sustainability reports. *Contemporary Accounting Research*, 33(2), 551–575. DOI: 10.1111/1911-3846.12162

Ngu, S. B., & Amran, A. (2021). Materiality Disclosure in Sustainability Reporting: Evidence from Malaysia. *Asian Journal of Business and Accounting*, 14(1), 225–252. DOI: 10.22452/ajba.vol14no1.9

Opferkuch, K., Caeiro, S., Salomone, R., & Ramos, T. (2021). Circular economy in corporate sustainability reporting: A review of organisational approaches. *Business Strategy and the Environment*, 30(8), 1–22. DOI: 10.1002/bse.2854

Ortar, L. (2018). Materiality Matrixes in Sustainability Reporting: An Empirical Examination. http://dx.doi.org/DOI: 10.2139/ssrn.3117749

Osifo, O. & Fasua, H. (2017). Social and Environmental Disclosures and Holistic Growth in the Positive Accounting Theory (PAT) View. *IOSR Journal of Business and Management, 19*(6), 1-8. DOI: 10.9790/487X-1906030108

Puroila, J., & Mäkelä, H. (2019). Matter of opinion: Exploring the socio-political nature of materiality disclosures in sustainability reporting. *Accounting, Auditing & Accountability Journal*, 32(4), 1043–1072. DOI: 10.1108/AAAJ-11-2016-2788

Rashed, A. H., Rashdan, S. A., & Ali-Mohamed, A. Y. (2022). Towards Effective Environmental Sustainability Reporting in the Large Industrial Sector of Bahrain. *Sustainability (Basel)*, 14(1), 219. DOI: 10.3390/su14010219

Rodrigues, A. A. B. (2023). Materiality Matrices in the Environmental, Social and Governance Context. *International Journal of Engineering Business Management*, 7(2), 17–22. DOI: 10.22161/ijebm.7.2.3

Saenz, C. (2019). Creating shared value using materiality analysis: Strategies from the mining industry. *Corporate Social Responsibility and Environmental Management*, 26(6), 1351–1360. DOI: 10.1002/csr.1751

Santos, F.T.S., Ladwig, N.I., Peixoto, M.G.M. & Guerra, J. B. S. O. A. (2023). Materiality of sustainability reports: an environmental performance analysis' proposal of wind farms in Southern Brazil using the Analytic Hierarchy Process (AHP). *Clean Techn Environ Policy, 25*, 1241–1258. https://doi.org/10098-022-02440-9DOI: 10.1007/setor

Sardianou, E., Stauropoulou, A., Evangelinos, K., & Nikolaou, I. (2021). A materiality analysis framework to assess sustainable development goals of banking sector through sustainability reports. *Sustainable Production and Consumption*, 27, 1775–1793. DOI: 10.1016/j.spc.2021.04.020

Senani, K.G.P., Ajward, R. & Kumari, J.S. (2022). Determinants and consequences of integrated reporting disclosures of non-financial listed firms in an emerging economy. *Journal of Financial Reporting and Accounting*. DOI: 10.1108/JFRA-03-2022-0083

Setyorini, C., & Isahk, Z. (2012). Corporate Social and Environmental Disclosure: A Positive Accounting Theory View Point. https://www.researchgate.net/publication/336713992_Corporate_Social_and_Environmental_Disclosure_A_Positive_Accounting_Theory_View_Point

Sharma, P., Panday, P., & Dangwal, R. C. (2020). Determinants of environmental, social and corporate governance (ESG) disclosure: A study of Indian companies. *International Journal of Disclosure and Governance*, 17(4), 208–217. DOI: 10.1057/s41310-020-00085-y

Sierra-Garcia, L., Garcia-Benau, M., & Bollas-Araya, H. (2018). Empirical Analysis of Non-Financial Reporting by Spanish Companies. *Administrative Sciences*, 8(3), 29. Advance online publication. DOI: 10.3390/admsci8030029

Sousa, A. (2017). Investigação sobre materialidade: análise crítica e desenvolvimentos recentes. https://aeca.es/wp-content/uploads/2014/05/143a.pdf

Torelli, R., Balluchi, F., & Furlotti, K. (2020). The materiality assessment and stakeholder engagement: A content analysis of sustainability reports. *Corporate Social Responsibility and Environmental Management*, 27(2), 470–484. DOI: 10.1002/csr.1813

Wee, M., Tarca, A., Krug, L., Aerts, W., Pink, P., & Tilling, M. (2016). *Factors Affecting Preparers' and Auditors' Judgements about Materiality and Conciseness in Integrated Reporting*. ACCA. https://www.integratedreporting.org/wp-content/uploads/2016/08/pi-materiality-conciseness-ir-FINAL.pdf

Wu, Q., Furuoka, F., & Lau, S. C. (2022). Corporate social responsibility and board gender diversity: A meta-analysis. *Management Research Review*, 45(7), 956–983. DOI: 10.1108/MRR-03-2021-0236

Zumente, I., & Lāce, N. (2020). Does Diversity Drive Non-Financial Reporting: Evidence from the Baltic States. *Intellectual Economics*, 14(2), 50–66. DOI: 10.13165/IE-20-14-2-04

ADDITIONAL READING

Albuquerque, F., Gomes, M., & Barreiro Rodrigues, M. A. (2024). What material topics by ESG dimensions can be found within the materiality matrix from the European entities' sustainability reports? *Cogent Business & Management*, 11(1), 2369212. DOI: 10.1080/23311975.2024.2369212

Canning, M., O'Dwyer, B., & Georgakopoulos, G. (2019). Processes of auditability in sustainability assurance–the case of materiality construction. *Accounting and Business Research*, 49(1), 1–27. DOI: 10.1080/00014788.2018.1442208

Fiandrino, S., Tonelli, A., & Devalle, A. (2022). Sustainability materiality research: A systematic literature review of methods, theories and academic themes. *Qualitative Research in Accounting & Management*, 19(5), 665–695. DOI: 10.1108/QRAM-07-2021-0141

Khan, M., Serafeim, G., & Yoon, A. (2016). Corporate sustainability: First evidence on materiality. *The Accounting Review*, 91(6), 1697–1724. DOI: 10.2308/accr-51383

Whitehead, J. (2017). Prioritizing sustainability indicators: Using materiality analysis to guide sustainability assessment and strategy. *Business Strategy and the Environment*, 26(3), 399–412. DOI: 10.1002/bse.1928

APPENDIX I

The terms and definitions below are selected from IFRS Sustainability Disclosure Standard (IFRS S) 1 on General Requirements for Disclosure of Sustainability-related Financial Information issued by the International Sustainability Standards Board (ISSB), an entity under the aegis of the IFRS Foundation: • **Materiality** is an entity-specific aspect of relevance based on the nature or magnitude, or both, of the items to which the information relates, in the context of the entity's sustainability-related financial disclosures (paragraph 14). • An entity **shall disclose material information about the sustainability-related risks and opportunities** that could reasonably be expected to affect the entity's prospects (paragraph 16). • In the context of sustainability-related financial disclosures, **information is material if** omitting, misstating or obscuring that information could reasonably be expected to influence decisions that primary users of general purpose financial reports make on the basis of those reports, which include financial statements and sustainability-related financial disclosures and which provide information about a specific reporting entity (paragraph 17).

The terms and definitions below are selected from the European Financial Reporting Advisory Group (EFRAG) Implementation Guidance (IG) 1 on Materiality Assessment issued by the EFRAG as a non-authoritative document that accompanies the European Sustainability Reporting Standards (ESRS): • **The ESRS sustainability statement shall include relevant and faithful information about all impacts, risks and opportunities (also referred to as IROs) across environmental, social and governance matters determined to be material from the impact materiality perspective, the financial materiality perspective or both**. The materiality assessment is the process by which the undertaking determines material information on sustainability IROs. This is achieved by the determination of material matters and material information to be reported. The performance of a materiality assessment based on objective criteria is pivotal to sustainability reporting. The undertaking will use judgement when applying the criteria, and the related explanations are expected to provide transparency from the undertaking to the users of the sustainability statement (point 1).

• **The assessment considers the undertaking's entire value chain**, i.e., it includes the undertaking's upstream and downstream value chain in addition to its own operations (point 2). • Once the undertaking has identified an impact, risk or opportunity related to a sustainability matter as material, it firstly refers to the related Disclosure Requirements to identify the relevant information to be considered on the matter. Secondly, if the impact, risk or opportunity is not covered or insufficiently covered by the ESRS, the undertaking shall provide entity-specific disclosure on the matter. **Relevance is the criterion to identify the information to be disclosed and is based on** (point 3) o (a) the significance of the information in relation to the matter it depicts; or o (b) its decision-usefulness.

• **The ESRS do not mandate a specific process or sequence of steps to follow when performing the materiality assessment, and so this is left to the judgement of the undertaking**. Whichever process is used, it should reflect the undertaking's facts and circumstances (point 5).

• **As an illustration, a materiality assessment that would meet the requirements of the ESRS could include the following steps** (point 6):

o (a) understanding of the context;

o (b) identification of actual and potential IROs related to sustainability matters;

o (c) assessment and determination of the material IROs related to sustainability matters; and o (d) reporting.

Table 11. Sampled entities by Euronext market indices

Netherlands:	Amsterdam Index (AEX)	Belgium:	Brussels Index (BEL-20)	Ireland:	Dublin Index (ISEQ-20)
ABN Amro Bank N.V. Akzo Nobel Asm International Asml Holding Dsm Firmenich Ag Heineken Ing Groep N.V. Kpn Kon Nn Group Philips Kon Prosus Randstad Nv Wolters Kluwer	From Inbev Aedifica Ageas Ship Elia Group Kbc Proximus Umicore	Ab Group Blink Bank Of Ireland Gp Crh Plc Ord Flutter Entertain Glanbia Plc Glenveagh Prop.Plc Irish Res. Prop Kerry Group Plc Perm. Tsb Gp. Hold Ryanair Hold. Plc Smurfit Kappa GP	Other Sgps Bcp Corticeira Amorim Ctt Edp Our	Mpc Container Ship Nordic Semiconductor Pgs Storebrand Subsea 7 Tomra Systems	Airbus Alstom BNP Paribas Act. Bouygues Crossroads Crédit Agricole Danone Engie Hermes Intl Dry Legrand Recommended Orange Publicis Groupe Sa Renault Saffron Saint Gobain Schneider Electric Societe Generale Stellantis Nv Teleperformance Thales Unibail-Rodamco We Veolia approximately. Worldline

Table 12. Sampled entities by industry

Telecommunications (10) and Technologies (15)	Health (20)	Finance (30) and Real Estate (35)	Consumer Goods (40)	Industry (50) and basic materials (55)	Energy (60) and utilities (65)
Asm International Asml Holding Kpn Kon Prosus Ship Proximus Our Nordic Semiconductor Orange	Philips Kon	ABN Amro Bank N.V. Ing Groep N.V. Nn Group Aedifica Ageas Kbc Ab Group Blink Bank Of Ireland Gp Irish Res. Prop. Perm. Tsb Gp. Hold Bcp Storebrand BNP Paribas Act. Crédit Agricole Societe Generale Unibail-Rotamco-V	Dsm Firmenich Ag Heineken Wolters Kluwer From Inbev Flutter Entertain Glanbia Plc Glenveagh Prop.Plc Kerry Group Plc Ryanair Hold. Plc Crossroads Danone Hermes Intl Dry Recommended Publicis Groupe Sa Renault Stellantis Nv	Akzo Nobel Randstad Nv Umicore Crh Plc Ord Smurfit Kappa GP Other Sgps Corticeira Amorim Ctt Mpc Container Ship Tomra Systems Airbus Alstom Bouygues Legrand Saffron Saint Gobain Schneider Electric Teleperformance Thales Worldline	Elia Group Edp Pgs Subsea 7 Engie Veolia approximately.

Chapter 9
Application of Governance, Risk Management, and Compliance Practices in the Public Service, in Light of the Tam Model:
A Study at the Federal Institute of Bahia

Rômulo Brito Oliveira
Universidade de Pernambuco, Brazil

Luiz Carlos Miranda
Universidade de Pernambuco, Brazil

Carlos Pinho
 https://orcid.org/0000-0002-5509-2921
Universidade Aberta, Portugal

ABSTRACT

This work's main objective was to study the application of governance, risk management and compliance (GRC) practices at Federal Institute of Bahia (IFBA), based on COSO-ERM, ISO 31000, and PMBOK. The application was carried out from the perspective of the technology acceptance model (TAM) to investigate users' perception of using a GRC system. The study is based on a questionnaire graded

DOI: 10.4018/979-8-3693-5923-5.ch009

on a seven-point Likert scale. This model, originating in studies by Davis in 1986, located a fundamental conceptual framework for understanding how people perceive and adopt new technologies. The results demonstrate the applicability of the TAM model to measure perceived usefulness and ease of use in relation to the use of new technologies. It is also concluded that managers perceive greater usefulness and ease of use than subordinates, in relation to the proposed system. Thus, this study contributes to the development of studies on the GRC theme by systematizing practical implementation guided by international models, evaluating the perception of servers using the system in light of the TAM model.

1. INTRODUCTION

1.1 Endorsing the Investigation

The continuous evolution in management strategies has highlighted the importance of Governance, Risk Management and Compliance (GRC), driving debates on the integration of these elements to ensure better organizational performance. When integrated, GRC management encompasses the identification, control, definition, execution and monitoring, allowing the coordination and integration of these activities jointly (Hoeflich et al., 2016). Directing efforts to GRC activities is necessary, considering not only the constantly evolving regulatory demands, such as the fiscal responsibility law and the anti-corruption law, but also the intrinsic need to monitor practices to avoid crises and protect internal and external threats.

The convergence between GRC elements has been explored as a unified and broad approach to ensure compliance with standards and regulations, contributing to the promotion of transparency, ethics and responsibility. According to Winter (2008) GRC is a management model that fosters unification, communication and collaboration among various stakeholders in management, while controlling the organization's operations. GRC's contributions, therefore, are relevant to any organizational environment, whether in the private or public sector. Brazilian government organizations face increasing risks, including corruption, fraud, and embezzlement. Thus, its implementation in public agencies should be treated as a key element in the management strategy, adopting an internal control approach based on risk management. This robust recommendation leads the organization to achieve its objectives, even in an environment of uncertainty related to organizational activities. (OECD, 2011).

The adoption of GRC often requires information systems, since such technological tools must be used as an integral part of government modernization strategies, generating public value (Ministry of Planning, Development and Management,

2016). The evolution of technology and the era of digital transformation open new doors and challenges for leaders, seeking to improve the way entities conduct and deliver public services, becoming an essential factor to be explored by modern organizations. In this sense, the use of technological tools has become a necessity to face contemporary challenges.

This demand for the systematization of public activities drives the investigation of the perception of users in the use of these systems, encouraging the understanding of factors related to their effective use. The Technology Acceptance Model (TAM), originating from Davis' studies in 1989, provides a fundamental basis for understanding how people perceive and adopt new technologies, and is applicable in the analysis of the perception of GRC systems, as proposed in this study.

Previous studies using TAM demonstrate the importance of evaluating the perceived usefulness and ease of use of new technologies. In the study conducted by Da Silva, et al. (2023) entitled The technology acceptance model (TAM) is used as a theoretical framework and a survey is carried out with 110 students of the bachelor's degree course in Physical Education, with the objective of identifying the intention to use technology, based on the influence of the perception of use, perceived usefulness, perception of ease of use and the influence of subjective norms on the intention to use technology. The study points out that the constructs referring to perceived ease of use and perceived usefulness showed positive effects on the intention to use technology, contrary to subjective norms.

Also considering the possible different perceptions between managers and subordinates when evaluating the impact of both on the overall outcome of the evaluation. The study conducted by Melo (2020) compared the perceptions of managers and subordinates in relation to managerial roles and competencies. The study revealed significant differences between managers' and subordinates' perceptions, suggesting that different groups in an organization may have different views on governance.

Aiming to apply GRC in a public agency, the present research aims to evaluate the level of perceived usefulness and ease of use of a system created specifically for the agency under study. We did not find in the literature an empirical study carried out, which applied, developed a web system and evaluated the perception of use, in the combined context between the public service and GRC practices.

To achieve these goals, this investigation, following a quantitative approach, was conducted using a questionnaire answered using a seven-point *Likert* scale. Using graphical analysis, it evaluated the participants' perception of the GRC software developed, now used in the first study. This evaluation was made considering the perceived usefulness and perceived ease of use, parameters that make up the TAM model.

Guided by the aforementioned context, regarding the importance of GRC practices and the existence of norms, models and methods that help in this process, it is verified that there is a need for studies and improvement in relation to the establishment of a standard, especially in the public service.

In view of the most used GRC structures, it is unlikely that a single methodology would be able to encompass all the specificities of each organization and, therefore, each unit needs to develop its own way of applying GRC standards, specifically in managing its risks. According to the studies by Hill and Dinsdale (2003), these obstacles include the absence of an explicit process for decision-making in relation to risks, inadequate management of uncertainty and lack of attention to relevant controls that can result in serious consequences for the institution and society. The ineffectiveness of institutional management structures and systems can hinder this risk management and control process.

1.2 Objectives

The IFBA is a Federal autarchy, linked to the Ministry of Education, whose purpose is to provide educational services. The IFBA consists of 22 campuses covering throughout Bahia, with the campus in the city of Eunápolis being the unit chosen for this study. According to the management report for the 2020 fiscal year, the campus's institutional mission is "to promote the formation of the critical historical citizen, offering teaching, research and extension with socially referenced quality, aiming at the sustainable development of the country". Its academic community is made up of about 90 effective professors, 14 substitute professors, 49 administrative technicians and 1365 enrolled students.

The IFBA Campus Eunápolis unit, so far, has few actions related to GRC activities. This fact is a problem, since the TCU (Tribunal de Contas da União), through Ruling No. 821/2014 – Plenary, highlighted the importance of risk management, emphasizing the need to intensify actions to promote the improvement of risk management and controls in the Public Administration (TCU). Improvements are still needed on how GRC practices are carried out with a focus on risk management in Federal educational institutions in Brazil. Therefore, it is necessary to research the current condition in these institutions and what are the main challenges faced by risk managers in putting GRC activities into practice. Thus, based on the problem discussed above, the present research will be oriented to perceive the levels of perceived usefulness and perceived ease of use in the use of GRC systems, and their hierarchical influences.

The general objective is to evaluate the perception of usefulness and perceived ease of use, and the influence between managers and subordinates in the evaluation of the use of a developed GRC system, using the Technology Acceptance Model

- TAM as a basis. Specifically, it is intended to evaluate the perceived usefulness and perceived ease of use in relation to the use of the GRC system.

1.3 Relevance

In the managerial context of the public service, the issue of risks has recently been incorporated as an internal control procedure, as established by Joint Normative Instruction MP/CGU No. 1/2016. The rule provides information that guides a policy for the implementation, maintenance, monitoring and review of risk management for the agencies of the Federal Executive Branch.

The control bodies have been monitoring this process and issuing regulations that establish procedures to be adopted by federal public institutions. The CGU itself instituted through CGU Ordinance No. 915, of April 12, 2017, a risk management methodology. The structure aims to guide the units to implement it in accordance with their Risk Management Policy (PGR/CGU) and also serves as a reference for the other bodies of the Federal Executive Branch.

The search for the improvement of GRC mechanisms has led to an increase in the number of empirical studies on public governance. In this context, we highlight research conducted by Oliveira and Vieira (2019). The study aimed to analyse the public governance practices adopted by the Brazilian Federal Public Administration. Descriptive and multivariate analyses of secondary data were used for this purpose. It is noteworthy that most bodies created a board of directors. However, the evaluative variables, which reflect the evolution of the management of these councils, are not integrated or have not yet reached a level of maturity that allows effective management, especially in relation to risk management. In addition, some agencies have not yet recognized the need to adopt more advanced governance practices in the public sector. The authors came to the conclusion that, although the agencies have taken the first steps towards the adoption of better corporate governance practices, there is still much to be done.

Another factor to be considered is the growth of public universities, which bring with them more complex operations and, consequently, a potential for exposure to greater risks. The expansion of Federal Universities in Brazil has been a relevant theme in recent governments, with the creation of new units, the internalization of teaching, the increase in staff, and the availability of more vacancies, among other factors (Carvalho et al., 2018). Federal institutions of higher education in Brazil face a dynamic and uncertain environment, resulting from the expansion process, budgetary and financial constraints, and difficulties arising from the COVID-19 crisis, which increases and diversifies the uncertainties and doubts present. Risk management emerges as a primary approach to the management and control of these institutions (Sedrez and Fernandes, 2011). In this context, this expansion process can bring with it challenges for the governance of these higher education institutions.

Considering the current context in the public service, in which, in an environment of uncertainty, organizations have a certain difficulty in making decisions precisely because of the unpredictability of events (Gordon, Loeb and Tseng, 2009), Gazoulit and Oubal (2022) also highlight the complexity of the scenario in universities. This is especially relevant in the public sector, due to challenges that make it difficult to measure performance, establishing barriers to goal setting, planning, and strategy execution. The plurality of fields of activity, the difficulty in predicting performance and capabilities, as well as the diversity of stakeholders in Higher Education Institutions (HEIs), are factors that intensify these difficulties. This study is justified because it sought to deepen the process of application of GRC practices, focusing on risk management in the public sector, in the midst of the organizational dynamics of a Federal educational institution, aiming to analyse the impact of risks on the strategic, tactical and operational objectives of the organization, evaluating the different hierarchical perceptions in the use of systems, enabling the generation of useful information in the decision-making process, in response to possible negative impacts on the organizational context.

The present study contributes to the development of methodologies, promoting improvements and specific adaptations to the context of the academic public service, systematizing a structure proposal; contributes to the training and awareness of participating actors on the importance of governance, risk management and compliance; the analysis of the results reveals paths for good practices to be implemented by the participants, becoming a valuable resource for sharing and adoption in other academic institutions; based on the SWOT matrix, the survey offers insights to improve strategic decision-making in academic institutions, considering both strengths and challenges; based on the results of the Risk matrix, the survey provides recommendations to respond to the identified risks, promoting a safer and more efficient environment; The results support the formulation or review of institutional policies, promoting alignment with the best governance and compliance practices; improvement of the quality of academic services, reflecting positively on the academic community and society in general.

Since this is a topic that lacks studies that reflect the practical articulation of application techniques, based on international standards and their inherent complexity, the scarcity in the literature highlights the need to investigate this process taking into account particularities of the Brazilian context. Thus, it is interesting to assess the risks that may arise at each stage of the process, such as the lack of an explicit process for decision-making, in addition to the difficulty in dealing with uncertainty or simple ignorance of the risks.

2. GOVERNANCE MODELS ADOPTED IN THE PUBLIC SECTOR

Corporate governance has its roots in the concept of the separation of ownership and control, which became evident in the late nineteenth century with the proliferation of publicly traded companies (Aguilera, et al., 2018). It first emerged in the 1970s and 1980s, as a result of the need to address the issue of separation between ownership and control in organizations. This separation generates the so-called agency costs (Jensen; Meckling, 1976). These factors are associated with the need to monitor agents due to the differences in interest that may arise from the delegation of decision-making authority.

The discussion around governance in the public sector arises in a context marked by the need to deal with the challenges arising from corruption. Public governance integrates the procedures in which social actors interact for the guidelines of social coordination, which are fundamental for cooperation structures to allow the resolution of complex public problems of the State. They are the interactive processes through which society and the economy are directed in favour of common collective goals (Torfing et al., 2012; Torfing, 2016). This encompasses the mechanisms of evaluation, direction and monitoring, aiming to ensure the efficiency and effectiveness of the actions of government practices. This resulted in the establishment of the basic principles that guide good governance practices in public organizations: transparency, integrity and accountability (IFAC, 2001, Brazil, 2014).

In Brazil, the growing need for governance was driven by the process of redemocratization, due to the expansion of public services resulting from the promulgation of the Federal Constitution in 1988. It was institutionalized in 1995 with the creation of the IBGC, and encouraged by Constitutional Amendment (EC) No. 19, of June 4, 1998, which included in article 37 of the Federal Constitution the principle of efficiency, in order to mitigate the patrimonial and bureaucratic remnants existing in the Brazilian public administration (Brasil, 1988).

The publication of the Fiscal Responsibility Law (LRF) and the implementation of the State reform have encouraged public authorities to adopt practices that are already established in the private sector. This adaptation of methods emphasizes the importance of mechanisms that ensure accountability and responsibility in the management of public resources. However, governance in the public sector presents unique challenges due to the diversity of actors involved. According to Marcelli (2013), the movement of the new Public Management influenced the way public management was carried out, adapting and transferring managerial concepts inherent to the private sector to the public sector. Unlike the private sector, multiple interests and accountability to society pose additional challenges.

Good public governance plays an essential role in risk management and the implementation of internal controls. It seeks to strategically guide, supervise, engage stakeholders, and manage strategic risks. It is important to emphasize that governance initiatives must be guided by the objective of the common good and supported by ethical conduct. Ethical performance, together with principles and best practices, inhibit corruption and lead to good governance, increasing the organization's chances of success (IBGC, 2015).

Travaglia and Sá (2017) emphasize that the implementation of good governance practices can be an effective tool to enable managers to optimize the use of existing resources, resulting in improved quality of public services offered. From their analyses, they concluded that several actions, such as the selection of competent leaders and the evaluation of their performance, the adoption of strategies to combat deviations, the establishment of goals, risk management, the implementation of internal control mechanisms, transparency, the structuring of accountability systems and accountability, contribute significantly to strengthening governance in public organizations. These findings converge with the governance mechanisms of the TCU governance framework as shown in Figure 1.

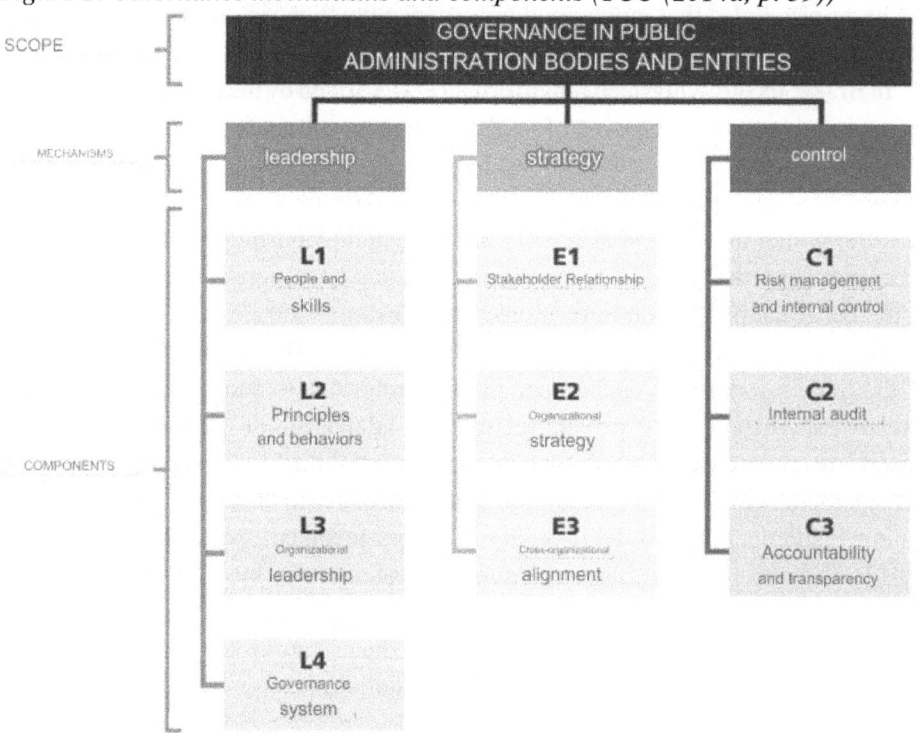

Figure 1. Governance mechanisms and components (TCU (2014a, p. 39))

Governance has gained worldwide prominence as a means of improving efficiency, reducing risk, and increasing the credibility of companies. However, there is still no consensus regarding the best practices and effectiveness of government regulations. The Covid-19 pandemic has exposed additional challenges. Vassileva (2021) argues that the crisis has increased the importance of corporate governance and the need for companies to respond quickly and effectively to ensure their survival. Governance has advanced significantly in recent years, with the adoption of transparency and accountability practices by public and private companies, but there are still challenges to be faced.

Based on the above, governance is a dynamic topic that evolves with time and circumstances. Its foundations have historical roots in the need to control the separation between ownership and control, but they are also influenced by more recent events, such as the Enron affair. Governance is essential to ensure the sustainability and success of organizations, whether public or private, as it allows them to establish and acquire ethical and legal standards, while protecting the interests of their *stakeholders*. In a broader context, governance is the system by which companies are directed and controlled, with responsibility attributed to senior management, whose actions are regulated by laws and regulations (Cadbury Committee, 1992). In this sense, it is essential to implement efficient governance in the public sector, indicating a high level of maturity in public management, as observed by Santos (2022).

3. RISK MANAGEMENT

3.1 Definition of Organizational Practices

Risk management is a practice that has been gaining prominence in organizations, it manifests itself as the second arm of the GRC structure. It is based on the identification, evaluation, and control of uncertain events that may affect the achievement of the organization's objectives. Lam (2003) describes that the function of risk management would be to generate a reduction in losses, the management of uncertainties and the optimization of the performance of companies. Risk in an organizational context is commonly described as any factor that can impact the achievement of corporate objectives (Hopkin, 2017).

The activities carried out by human beings, since ancient times, are closely linked to potential risks. In the corporate world, the study of risk emerged with the aim of minimizing losses in investments. For many years, the concept of risk was linked to activities in the financial sector (financial risk) and those related to extractivism (environmental risk). However, from the 1990s onwards, when the world economy expanded and provided an accelerated increase in competitiveness and accessibility to markets, companies began to be more concerned with risk and to seek guidance that incorporated a new vision combined with business management (Galvão et al., 2008).

In organizations, risk management has become a strategic tool that influences the decision-making process. When integrated into routines, it can improve performance, control, quality, reduce waste and rework, in addition to providing better conditions to face uncertainties and achieve results (Dhlamini, 2022). Modern risk management should focus on using data and information analysis tools to make predictions, which implies, according to Hill and Dinsdale (2003), predicting future risks and knowing how to deal proactively with them, thus achieving proactive management instead of reactive management. In this sense, modern risk management must be future-oriented, with the aim of ensuring the organization's strategic objectives. Research indicates that national and international studies on risk management applied to higher education institutions indicate that the more improved the risk management of organizations, the more viable its continuity is (Christopher and Sarens, 2015). Thus, a question arises: are there models that help the development and continuous improvement of a system for risk management?

As previously mentioned, risk management within the scope of the Brazilian Federal Executive Branch was regulated through Joint Normative Instruction MP/CGU No. 1/2016. In its scope, the influence of international risk management models is noticeable, especially the COSO ERM model and the ISO 31000:2009 Standard - Risk Management - principles and guidelines, which have become models of best practices (Sax & Andersen, 2019; Souza et al., 2020). Currently, some risk management models are used as good practices, which are conceptual frameworks that provide guidelines for identifying, assessing, monitoring, and mitigating risks in an organization. They help establish systematic and coherent processes to manage risks and make controlled decisions about how to deal with them. COSO ERM, ISO 31000:2018 - Risk Management - principles and guidelines, in addition to the PM-BOK (*Project Management Body of Knowledge*), are used as best practice models.

Created in 1985 in the United States, COSO (*Committee of Sponsoring Organizations of the Treadway Commission*) is a private non-profit organization whose objective is to prevent and avoid fraud in internal procedures and processes. It is composed of the American bodies AAA (*American Accounting Association*), AICPA (*American Institute of Certified Public Accountants*), FEI (*Financial Executives International*), IIA (*Institute of Internal Auditors*) and IMA (*Institute of Management Accountants*). The COSO model is the most used model for certification of compliance with Section 404 of SOX (a US law created in 2002 motivated by financial scandals, mainly the Enron case). This model provides the evaluation criteria through a cube, which exemplifies the evaluation of the control environment and its effectiveness as shown in Figure 2.

Figure 2. Internal control environment (Coso 1992)

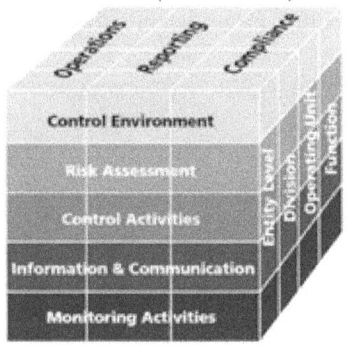

COSO ERM defines risk as everything that is outside the company's plan. Risk is an option in the actions taken, which depend on the degree of freedom of choice of the COSO manager (2004). Its dimensions are represented by figure 3 below.

Figure 3. COSO - IC and Coso ERM (COSO - IC 1992 and Coso ERM 2004) adapted to Portuguese

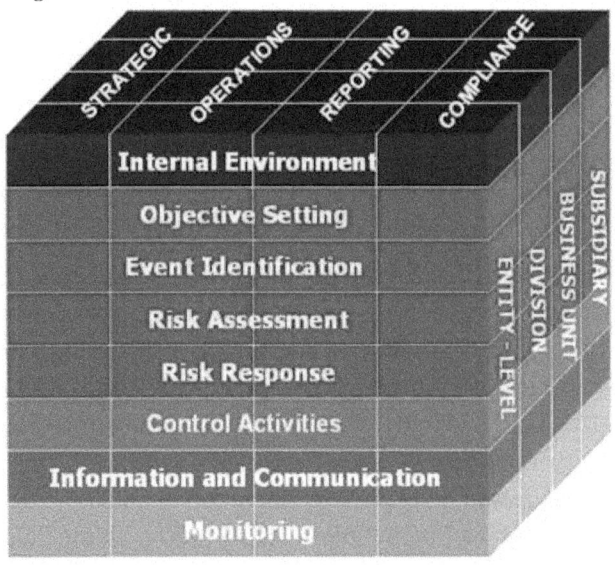

COSO (2004) warns of the need for managers to observe the interrelationship between the company's objectives, its elements (control environments) and its scope. In 2017, the scope of the framework was updated to include strategy and performance.

Figure 4. COSO enterprise risk management framework (Coso 2017 adapted to Portuguese)

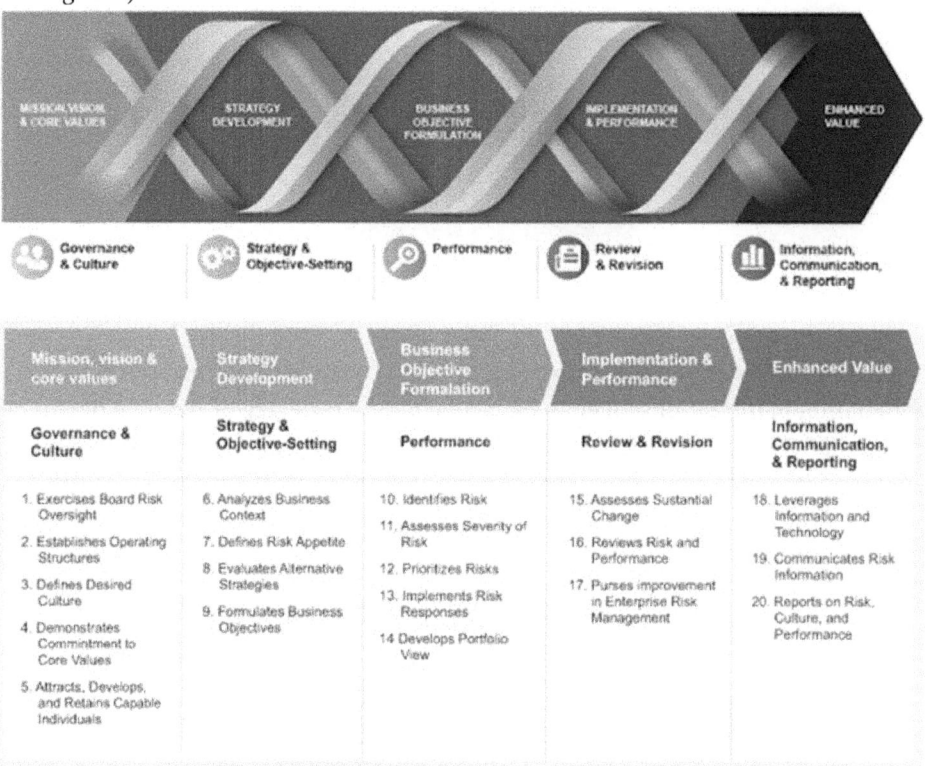

According to Souza et al. (2020), adopting COSO ERM can provide organizations with a comprehensive conceptual framework for managing their risks, promoting a better understanding of the risks they are exposed to and helping to identify opportunities for improvement in risk management processes. Additionally, using COSO ERM can provide a more integrated view of risks, allowing organizations to assess and manage risks more efficiently and effectively.

The ISO 31000 standard, published in 2009 (and updated in 2018), establishes a more simplified model than COSO ERM. ISO 31000 is an international standard that establishes the principles and guidelines for risk management in organizations. It is designed to be applicable to any type of organization, regardless of size, industry, or nature of the business (ABNT, 2018). The standard is not certifiable, but it can be used as a reference for the creation of internal risk management systems. If we use the ISO 31000:2018 guidelines, we will have the definition of risk as the "effect of uncertainty on objectives". Regarding the management of these risks, ISO defines it as the "coordinated process of activities to direct and control an organization with respect to risk" (ABNT, 2018, p. 6). The standard emphasizes that risk management must be integrated into all aspects of the organization and be a continuous and interactive process, with a focus on continuous improvement and increasing organizational resilience (ISO, 2018).

The risk management process, according to ISO, involves a scope of activities that, when carried out together, lead to good practices and, consequently, good results. However, the effectiveness of risk management will depend on its integration into governance and all the organization's activities, including decision-making. This requires the support of stakeholders, in particular the Senior Management (ABNT, 2018, p. 4). This risk management process is commonly carried out based on the generalities that the standard defines, as shown in figure 5 below.

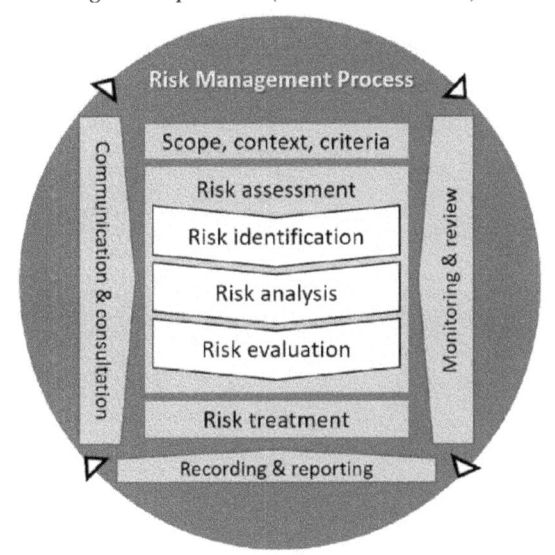

Figure 5. ISO risk management process (ISO 31000:2018)

According to several scientific articles, ISO 31000 is widely used around the world as a reference in risk management, regardless of different applications, disciplines or countries. For example, Purdy (2010) points out that, among the main risk management standards, ISO 31000 occupies a prominent role, due to the international recognition of the ISO body. This model is used by organizations around the world to manage their risks. In short, ISO 31000 provides a comprehensive and flexible framework for risk management in organizations of all types and sizes and is widely used as a benchmark for best practices in risk management around the world. Its systematic and structured approach helps organizations identify and manage risks effectively, bringing confidence to decision-making and sustainable value creation.

As a third tool, we have the Project Management Body of Knowledge (PMBOK), which is a collection of processes and areas of knowledge accepted as best practices for professional project management (Ramlaoui, S. Semma, A, 2014). It is a more comprehensive framework than the previous ones, as it provides a framework of good practices for project management, developed by the Project Management Institute (PMI) in the United States. Considering that the implementation of a GRC framework becomes a complete project management, we can draw several inspirations from this methodology. The PMBOK was initially launched in 1987 as a document containing basic information for project management and was updated in 1996, 2000, 2004, 2008, 2013, 2017 and 2021.

The conceptual framework of the PMBOK 7th edition is composed of twelve principles for value delivery, namely: Integrity, Team, Stakeholders, Value, Systemic Vision, Leadership, Adaptation, Quality, Complexity, Risk, Adaptability and Resilience, Change. Each of these principles includes a set of concepts that form a project management standard. In addition, the scope is composed of eight performance domains, which are groups of activities that relate the results of the project, as shown in Figure 6.

Figure 6. PMBOK project management principles (PMBOK 2021 7th edition)

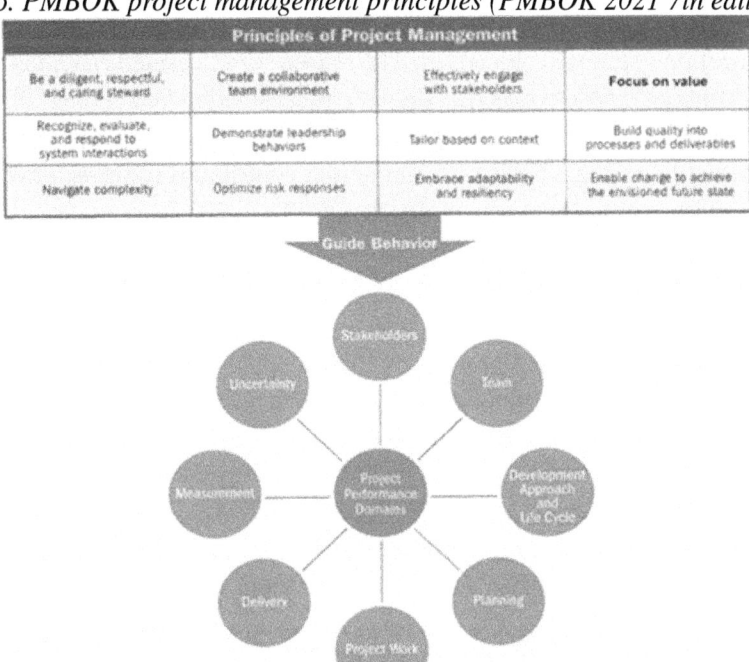

Principles of Project Management			
Be a diligent, respectful, and caring steward	Create a collaborative team environment	Effectively engage with stakeholders	Focus on value
Recognize, evaluate, and respond to system interactions	Demonstrate leadership behaviors	Tailor based on context	Build quality into processes and deliverables
Navigate complexity	Optimize risk responses	Embrace adaptability and resiliency	Enable change to achieve the envisioned future state

Guide Behavior

Project Performance Domains: Stakeholders, Team, Development Approach and Life Cycle, Planning, Project Work, Delivery, Measurement, Uncertainty

We realize that risk is constantly present in the processes and, therefore, deserves adequate attention. According to the PMBOK 7th edition, risk is "an uncertain event or condition, which, if it occurs, will cause a positive or negative effect on one or more of the project's objectives". In addition, it brings risk management as the process of identifying, analyzing, and responding to project risks. Its goal is to increase the likelihood and impact of positive events and reduce the likelihood and impact of adverse events on the project. Then, strategies are developed to deal with these risks, such as avoiding, transferring or mitigating them.

According to the arguments of (Ramlaoui, S. Semma, A, 2014), the tool provides project managers with fundamental practices necessary to achieve organizational results and excellence in the practice of project management. The use of the PMBOK to control risk management brings several benefits, such as: standardization, which helps to ensure that all risks are identified; improving communication between project stakeholders; mitigating project risks, which can help avoid delays, additional costs, and other issues; in addition to an improvement in decision-making.

In view of the arguments exposed, we note the importance of risk management for organizations, especially for public agencies, which are the objects of this study. The establishment of a continuous and intelligent risk management system tends to stimulate innovations. To this end, it is necessary to adopt control structures and techniques aimed at reducing risks and increasing confidence in the achievement of the organization's strategic objectives. The reason for integrated risk management is the "continuous, proactive, and systematic process of understanding, managing, and communicating risks from the perspective of the organization as a whole. Its goal is to enable strategic decision-making that contributes to the achievement of the organization's overall corporate objectives" (TBS, 2001).

3.2 Compliance

Compliance, also referred to as compliance, appears as the third pillar of the GRC framework. The term expresses a concept that acts within organizations with the objective of guiding management on rules and regulations, being considered a critical topic for business management. For the Brazilian Federation of Banks (Febraban), the term transcends the idea of "being in compliance" with laws, regulations, covering aspects of governance, conduct, transparency, and topics such as ethics and integrity (Febraban, 2018). Thus, although there is no equivalent translation into Portuguese, it is understood that the expression represents strict compliance with the rules and agreement with what is legal.

For Manzi (2008) The meaning of norms is linked to the fact that they are concretions and materializations of ethical, legal and democratic principles. The rule of law is a set of rules that give meaning to fundamental values, set limits on power, and provide guarantees to individual rights. In this sense, it is perceived as a consequence and even a demand of the democratic rule of law (Manzi, 2008; Singh and Bussen, 2015).

In the Brazilian system, after the Federal Constitution of 1988, there was a promotion of a series of laws to combat corruption and promote integrity in public and private organizations.

- the Bidding and Administrative Contracts Law (Law No. 8,666/1992);
- the Administrative Improbity Law (Law No. 8,429/1992);
- the Competition Law (Law No. 12,529/2011);
- the Money Laundering Law (Law No. 9,613/1998 and Law No. 12,683/2012);
- the Conflict of Interest Law (Law No. 12,813/2013);
- the Anti-Corruption Law (Law No. 12,846/2013).

With the implementation of these laws, a clear evolution is observed in line with the New Public Management (NPM). Public sector organizations underwent a managerial reform that introduced concepts such as efficiency, efficacy and effectiveness, along with the logic of results, relating them to the search for improvements in the performance of public entities, as occurs in the private sector (Cavalcante, 2018; Palermo, 2014). In addition, there was an improvement in corporate and government practices to prevent and combat corruption, aiming to promote the integrity of the State.

Good governance practices indicate that organizations must implement an integrity program, aiming to establish the promotion of transparency, participation, accountability, and integrity itself. In the case of public agencies, this will bring more credibility to the organization, being able to attract investors and, consequently, adding value. There are numerous reasons that justify the adoption of an integrity program in public agencies, linked to compliance with different rules and regulations, the prevention of corruption and other illicit acts (conflict of interest, money laundering and other frauds), in addition to the strengthening of corporate governance, which acts as a way to reinforce the image and reputation of organizations (Veríssimo, 2017).

The integrity program seeks to ensure the articulation of auditing, compliance, internal controls, business ethics, crisis management, risk management, corporate security and sustainability activities. This ecosystem collaborates with management by providing indicators and points of attention, acting as red flags in relation to all activities integrated by the system, through the provision of reports and guidelines that support the indicators. Coimbra and Manzi (2010) corroborate this system, arguing that the integrity system monitors key indicators and prudential limits, activating devices that interrupt and mitigate crises, whenever activities to prevent deviations fail.

The integrity plan should be seen as a tool for sustainability and organizational competitiveness, as the market and society increasingly demand that public and business decisions be guided by values such as transparency, ethics, and responsibility. According to the OECD, integrity is a cornerstone of good governance, being a condition for all other government activities not only to have trust and legitimacy, but also to be effective (OECD, 2018).

Therefore, in addition to the requirements of the legislation, compliance must ensure that the organization is operating in line with the standards established by governance. Due to the alignment of risks with strategic, tactical, and operational objectives, the risk prioritization developed by ERM helps to achieve the objectives set. It is important to note that the effectiveness of compliance and its effectiveness as a pillar of GRC depend not only on the adoption of clear policies and procedures with goals, but also on the commitment of senior management and the engagement of all organizational levels in promoting an ethical culture and compliance with applicable rules and regulations.

3.3 Techniques Applicable to GRC Practices

3.3.1 SWOT Analysis

To identify risks and overcome threats or prepare for them, management can create strategic actions in response to risks by understanding their conjuncture in relation to their weaknesses. To achieve this goal, SWOT analysis is particularly suitable because, when used correctly, it can provide insights and help the organization identify significant opportunities to explore. In short, it is an evaluation model that measures an organization's capabilities and limitations, as well as its potential risk areas. This tool is essential for assessing the organization's competitive position and identifying its strengths, weaknesses, opportunities, and threats. The SWOT analysis, according to Appio et al. (2009), is a tool that, by identifying the positive and negative aspects of the institution and correlating them, allows a holistic, complete and real knowledge of the context of action and of the institution itself, collaborating in decision-making to improve the company's performance.

The tool studies the competitiveness of an organization from the perspective of four variables: Strengths, Weaknesses, Opportunities and Threats. The fundamental objective of the SWOT analysis is to facilitate the choice of a specific strategy to achieve specific objectives through a critical evaluation of the internal and external environments. It is worth noting that, at the time of collecting information related to the factors of analysis, Chiavenato & Sapiro (2009) explain that they must be based on the strategic intention of the organization, taking into account the mission, vision, values and organizational objectives.

In relation to the internal environment, according to Rezende (2008), organizational strengths or strengths are internal and controllable variables that provide the organization with advantages in relation to its environment. These are attributes or characteristics of the organization that can positively impact its performance. Therefore, strengths should be widely exploited by the organization. Weaknesses, on the other hand, are considered deficiencies that inhibit the organization's ability to perform and must be overcome to avoid bankruptcy (Matos et al., 2007).

As for the external environment, opportunities are the external and non-controllable variables that can create favourable conditions for the organization, as long as it has the conditions or interest in using them, as exposed by Rezende (2008). According to Oliveira (2010), threats are external conditions that have an influence on the institution and can bring certain difficulties. Next, we have the visual arrangement of the SWOT Analysis through Figure 7.

Figure 7. SWOT analysis (Adapted from Silva (2009))

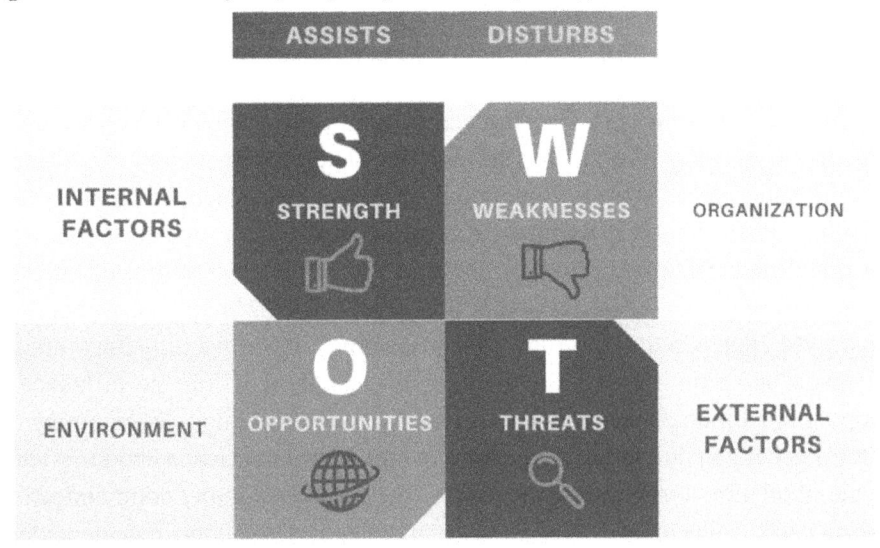

Studies point to the benefits of the tool. In an exploratory case study, published in 2018 in the Strategy & Development Magazine and entitled "SWOT Analysis: Case Study in a Higher Education Institution", the authors conclude that the impact of SWOT analysis on the company's strategy is like a kind of rudder, which guides to the best path to be followed. However, it is necessary to have the ability to understand what really needs to be done to obtain positive results.

A second study, entitled "Institutional Diagnosis of the Federal University of Paraíba from SWOT Analysis", published in the journal Meta: Evaluation in 2019, aimed to carry out an institutional diagnosis of the Federal University of Paraíba (UFPB) using SWOT analysis as a strategic management tool. The study highlights that the tool was useful for the composition of UFPB's institutional diagnosis, allowing the identification of relevant aspects for the university's strategic management. It is recommended to continue using this tool to improve the management of the institution and ensure its long-term sustainability.

In summary, studies indicate that SWOT analysis can be a useful tool for Brazilian educational institutions in identifying their internal strengths and weaknesses, as well as external opportunities and threats. However, it is necessary to adapt the tool to the specific context of the institution and integrate it with other management and planning processes to obtain better results.

3.3.2 Brainstorming

Brainstorming is an idea generation technique. The technique is composed of four basic rules: (1) Criticism should be banned - the evaluation of ideas should be saved for later moments; (2) The free generation of ideas should be encouraged; (3) Focus on quantity, the greater the number of ideas, the greater the chances of having valid ideas; (4) Combining and refining ideas generated by the group (PMBOK - PMI, 2004). Electronic "Brainstorming" aims to generate ideas via the web, where participants will have faster access to the ideas generated and will be able to develop new ideas (Aiken et al., 1994). This technique corresponds to an improved approach to traditional "Brainstorming", ensuring anonymity among participants and a similarity to the work team, since there will be no influence or monopoly of a participant in relation to the group, contributing to overcoming the problems generated due to the differences in hierarchy, experience and knowledge of some in relation to other team members. This enables parallel communication, allowing participants to enter comments simultaneously and contribute new ideas. The greater the number of information generated, the larger the participating group can be. There is also the automation of records, allowing all comments and ideas generated by the participating team to be stored (Morano, 2003).

According to ISO 31010:2012, which deals with risk management identification and assessment techniques, Brainstorming is classified as strongly applicable in this risk identification process, it is very useful where there is no data or where innovative solutions to problems are needed (ISO 31010, 2012).

After the information gathering stage, the ideas that emerged must be documented and organized, performing a critical analysis and weighing the advantages and disadvantages of each one. Therefore, online brainstorming can be highly effective, generate radical ideas, and include the shyest team members in the discussion, as well as automatically record all ideas in one place. However, care must be taken to overcome the aforementioned weaknesses.

3.3.3 Cause and Effect Analysis

Cause and effect analysis has the function of helping to detect the roots of a problem, and what effects or consequences these events may cause if they occur. For Werkema (1995), the cause and effect diagram is configured in using information to demonstrate the relationship between a result of a process, referring to the effect and the factors that may have changed the result of the process.

This technique is also known as the Ishikawa diagram or fishbone. Created in 1943 by Kaoru Ishikawa, a chemical engineer at the University of Tokyo, the Ishikawa diagram helps to identify the root cause of a problem and analyze all the factors involved in executing a process. One of the strengths of this tool is its ability to employ systems thinking, as the diagram takes into account all the data and aspects that may have caused the problem. In this way, using a cause and effect diagram, the chance of any influencing factor being forgotten or neglected is greatly reduced.

ISO 31010, 2012 treats the technique as an analysis that provides a structured graphical visualization of a list of causes for a specific effect. The effect can be positive (a goal) or negative (a problem), depending on the context.

3.3.4 Risk Matrix

The Risk Matrix is a visual arrangement, which establishes an individual comparison of risks based on impacts and probabilities of occurrence, in order to prioritize and manage them (ISO 31010, 2012). With the emergence of emerging risk events, the risk matrix must be promptly updated. In addition, it is essential to update it at least once a year, during the review of the organization's strategic planning, being a document in constant evolution. It is a 5 by 5 Matrix, calculated from the product of two scales ranging from 1 to 5, in a qualitative-quantitative way, in which the perceptions of those involved are essential for the evaluation. For the scope of this study, a five-point scale was chosen, according to the methodology of the Ministry of Planning, which has its scope based on the guidelines of COSO. For the impact, 5 analysis factors are used, each with its respective weight, as shown in Figure 8.

Figure 8. Strategic-operational and economic-financial aspects (Risk Matrix - Management of Integrity, Risks, and Internal Controls of Management - Ministry of Planning)

Impact - Factors for Analysis							
	Strategic-Operational					Economic-Financial	Weight
	Management Effort	Regulation	Reputation	Business/Services to Society	Hierarchical Intervention	Budgetary	
	15%	17%	12%	18%	13%	25%	100%
Guidelines for assigning weights	Event with the potential to cause the business or service to collapse	Determines interruption of activities	Featured in national and international media, being able to achieve strategic objectives and mission	It undermines the scope of the MP's mission	It would require the intervention [illegible]	> = 25%	5-Catastrophic
	Critical event, but with proper management it can be supported	Determines actions of a pecuniary nature (fines)	With some prominence in the national media, causing significant exposure	It undermines the scope of the Unit's mission	Would require the intervention of the Secretary	> = 10% < 25%	4-Large
	Significant event that can be managed under normal circumstances	Determines corrective actions	It may reach the media causing exposure for a short period of time.	It hinders the achievement of strategic objectives	Would require the Director's intervention	> = 3% < 10%	3-Moderate
	Event whose consequences can be absorbed, but lack management effort to minimize the impact	Determines actions of an advisory nature	Tends to be limited to the parties involved	It hinders the achievement of process goals	Would require the intervention of the Coordinator	> = 1% < 3%	2-Small
	Event whose impact can be absorbed through normal activities	Little or no impact	Internal impact only / no impact	Little or no impact on goals	It would be achieved in operation normal of activity	< 1%	1-Insignificant

Regarding probability, each point indicates a chance of occurrence, and a relative description is assigned to its score.

Figure 9. Observed/expected frequencies and their respective orientations (Risk Matrix - Management of Integrity, Risks, and Internal Controls of Management - Ministry of Planning)

Scale	Observed/Expected Frequency	Scale Description
5 - Very high	>= 90%	Event expected to occur under most circumstances
4 - High	>= 50% < 90%	Event likely to occur under most circumstances
3 - Possible	>= 30% < 50%	Event must occur at some point
2 - Low	>= 10% < 30%	Event may occur at some point
1 - Very low	< 10%	Event may only occur in exceptional circumstances

This process is carried out in order to calculate the inherent risk, which is a score obtained by multiplying the probability and impact of a risk event, without taking into account any control mechanisms. This multiplication results in a numerical value ranging from 1 to 25, representing the level of the risk event. The inherent risk can be classified as follows.

Figure 10. Levels of risks and respective cutoff points (Risk Matrix - Management of Integrity, Risks and Internal Controls of Management - Ministry of Planning)

Risk Level Scale	
Levels	Scoring
RC - Critical Risk	>=15<=25
RA - High Risk	>=8<=12
RM - Moderate Risk	>=4<=6
RP - Small Risk	>=1<=3

The matrix is able to provide 14 values that indicate the level of risk, calculated by the inherent risk. For example, if an event is classified as having a small impact with a score of 2, and the probability of occurrence is assessed with a score of 4, then the risk level will be considered High, as the product of these two factors will be equal to 8, as shown in Figure 11 as follows:

Figure 11. 5x5 risk matrix – Risk levels (Risk Matrix - Management of Integrity, Risks and Internal Controls of Management - Ministry of Planning)

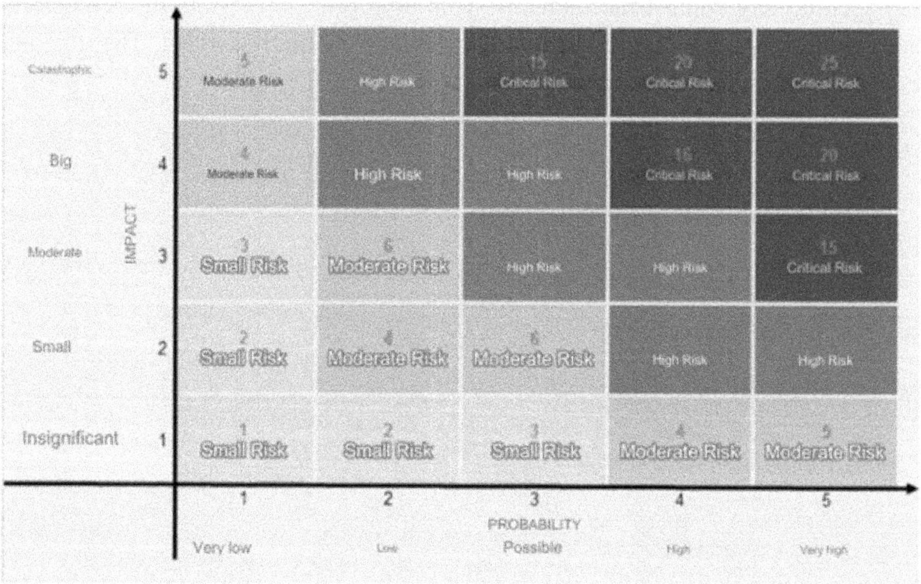

According to COSO ERM, the risk management process allows for a detailed analysis of the risks faced by the organization, identifying both operational risks and strategic and compliance risks. This helps to prioritize the areas of greatest impact and likelihood, allowing the organization to focus its resources and efforts on the most critical areas. Based on risk assessments, the organization can adopt appropriate preventive or corrective measures, making managers and other stakeholders aware of the existing risks and the measures adopted to mitigate them. Villanueva, Nuñez, and Martins (2022) highlight the importance of a risk management framework integrated into the business culture. This integration allows you to manage risk-related activities, assign responsibilities, and strengthen the integration and commitment of employees in the development of the process. Therefore, the preparation of the Risk Matrix provides benefits related to governance, risk management, decision-making, and regulatory compliance.

4. ANALYSIS OF THE PERCEPTION OF A GOVERNANCE, RISK MANAGEMENT AND COMPLIANCE SYSTEM USING THE TECHNOLOGY ACCEPTANCE MODEL (TAM)

4.1 Origin and Evolution of the TAM Model and Its Dimensions

The growing need for improvement in Governance, Risk Management and Compliance (GRC) is becoming one of the main requirements for organizations, driven by several factors. This includes the need to adhere to new regulations, such as fiscal responsibility, anti-corruption law, the ability to monitor these practices to reduce financial scandals, as well as the analysis of internal and external threats. As noted by Menzies (2006), the number, complexity, and importance of GRC requirements are constantly growing as organizations seek to meet international standards and expectations. This requires additional efforts to address risks and ensure compliance with laws, provisions, and voluntary obligations in order to improve its market position by promoting efficiency and effectiveness. When it comes to governance, Smet and Mayer (2016) state that information technology is no longer just a technical issue and, currently, its complexity and relevance in companies require essential attention. This drives modern organizations to equip themselves with technological tools that contribute to this process.

The demand for GRC from the business market in the private sector and from control and inspection agencies in the public sector has boosted the understanding of individuals' perception of these systems. This research aims to evaluate the use of a specific GRC system, investigating the influence of perception between managers and subordinates on the overall result, using the Technology Acceptance

Model (TAM) as a basis. This model, originated in Davis' studies in 1989, located a fundamental conceptual framework for understanding how people perceive and adopt new technologies. Its dimensions, perceived utility (PU) and perceived ease of use (FUP), have been extensively applied to understand the ease of information systems and technology in various contexts.

The general perception of the application of governance practices is a crucial element for the performance of organizations. Understanding the relationships between individuals' perceptions of the usability and ease of use of GRC systems and their management is essential for improving organizational performance.

Previous studies have explored the application of the TAM Model in different contexts, providing important data on the adoption of technological systems. However, there is a gap to be filled in the specific understanding of the hierarchical perception of systems in the public service intended for the application of GRC practices. In this study, a specific GRC software was used as an object of investigation, in the administrative area of the Federal Institute of Bahia (IFBA), Campus Eunápolis-BA.

The research is expected to evaluate the perceived usefulness and perceived ease of use, and from this verify if there are differences in perception between managers and subordinates in relation to the system. From this introduction, the literature review in section two, containing previous studies, presentation of the software; in section three, the methodology applied in the research, data collection; in section four, the presentation and discussion of the results, and finally in the fifth section, the final considerations. This framework aims to provide a comprehensive analysis of users' perceptions of the GRC system, exploring its dimensions, application contexts, and implications of governance strategies in the organization.

The Technology Acceptance Model (TAM), proposed by Davis in 1989, is a model derived from the Theory of Rational Action (ART) that seeks to explain the behaviour of technology use (Davis, 1989). ART is a general theory, which seeks to explain possibly any human behaviour. However, Davis realized the need for a more specific model for technology adoption and thus developed TAM, which is a methodology based on the idea that there are two key factors that influence how an innovation is accepted and how it is acted upon: Perceived Utility and Perceived Ease of Use (Davis, 1989). Perceived utility (PU) is defined as the user's perception that using a specific system will increase its performance. On the other hand, perceived ease of use (FUP) refers to the user's perception that using a system will not require effort. These two dimensions are considered the main determinants of a user's intention to adopt and use a technology. By considering these dimensions, researchers can gain interesting findings on how to improve the uptake and use of specific technologies. See Figure 12:

Figure 12. TAM model (Adapted from Davis, Bagozzi, and Wrshaw (1989) and Davis (1989))

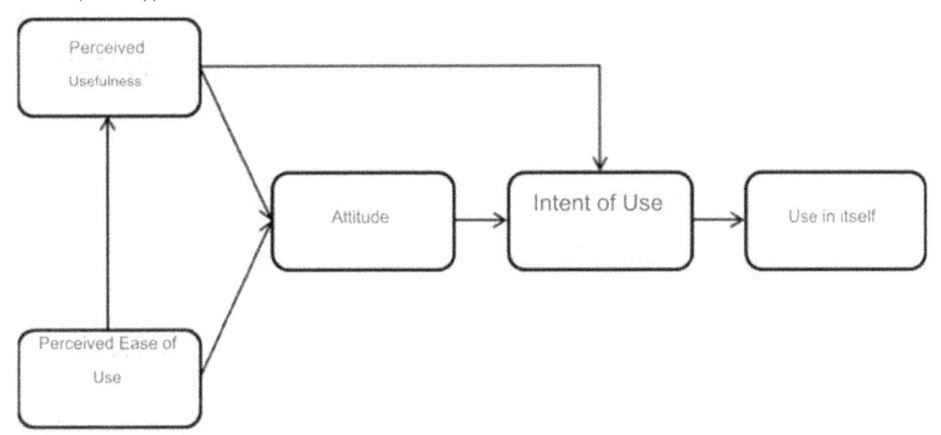

Over time, TAM has evolved and adapted, maintaining its relevance in predicting and explaining technological acceptance. Its applicability in various contexts and its ability to explain variations in the intent or actual use of technology have contributed to its prominence. It has been an influential model in technology acceptance research, with many subsequent studies expanding or modifying the original model to suit different contexts or to incorporate new variables. For example, TAM II, proposed by Venkatesh and Davis, added additional variables to explain the acceptance of technology in an organizational context. Similarly, TAM III, also proposed by Venkatesh and other scholars, incorporated even more variables to explain the technology's acceptance, including peer influence and previous experience with the technology.

By considering the external variables that affect technology adoption, TAM proposes a comprehensive understanding, including users' behavioural, and contextual characteristics (Davis, 1989). This is reflected in the representation of the model, seeking to capture the causal relationship between external factors and the acceptance of the technology by users, according to the flow of the TAM model, Figure 13.

Figure 13. List of constructs of the TAM model (Adapted from Davis; Bagozzi; Warshaw (1989))

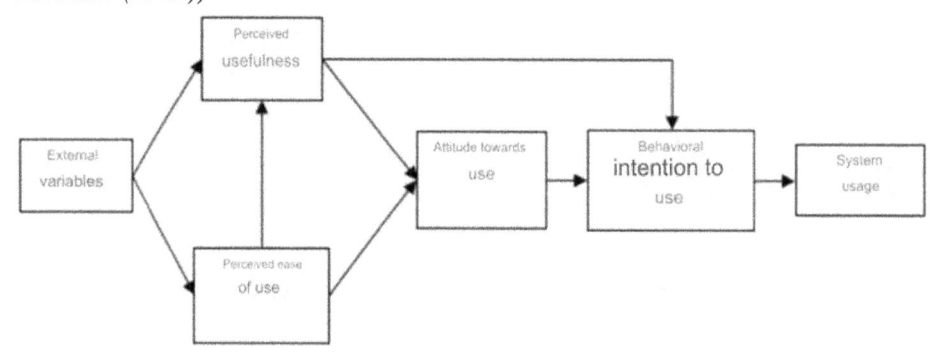

In summary, the TAM and its dimensions provide a good framework for understanding and predicting the acceptance and use of technology. Through the relationship between PU and FUP, the model provides a fundamental basis for tracking the impact of external variables on the behavioural intention to use (or not use) technology. The main result is that its structure provides a basis for the investigation of the behaviour of external variables. According to Davis (1989, p. 21), "external variables encompass all variables not explicitly represented in the model" (i.e., perceived ease of use, perceived utility, and use variables), including "demographic or personality characteristics of the actor, the nature of the particular behaviour under consideration, and the characteristics of the referents."

In this study, the TAM was applied to understand the acceptance of a governance, risk management and compliance system, based on the mediating role of PU and FUP in the relationship between system characteristics, with the application of the influence of perceptions in different groups of users.

4.2 Perception of Governance, Management, and Performance

Governance and management are two fundamental concepts in public and private administration. Governance, as defined by the World Bank, refers to organizational structures, functions, processes, and traditions that aim to ensure that planned actions are executed in such a way that they achieve goals and results in a transparent manner (World Bank, 2013).

Governance functions include setting the strategic direction, overseeing management, engaging stakeholders, managing strategic risks, managing internal conflicts, auditing and evaluating the management and control system, and promoting accountability and transparency. On the other hand, management refers to the day-to-day functioning of programs and organizations in the context of strategies, policies, processes and procedures that have been defined by the agency (World Bank, 2013). Management functions include implementing programs, ensuring compliance with regulations, reviewing and reporting on the progress of actions, ensuring administrative efficiency, maintaining communication with stakeholders, and evaluating performance and learning.

The relationship between governance and management is a two-way street. Governance provides the strategic direction and oversees management, while management implements the strategies and policies set by governance. Both concepts are essential for the effective functioning of any organization.

Figure 14. Relationship between governance and management (TCU Basic Governance Framework, 2014)

The basic framework of the TCU (2014) integrates governance practices related to organizational leadership, through evaluation, direction, and monitoring, especially regarding the achievement of organizational goals. This implies that the management defines guidelines for the fulfilment of such actions. In addition, senior management is presumed to evaluate, guide and monitor the performance of the organization's management, as well as its compliance with external standards and internal guidelines.

The search for organizational performance is a key element in the evaluation and success of organizations, this constant pursuit of good results is typified as a management attribution, which occupies a significant role in this evaluation. According to Otley (1999), performance is intrinsically linked to the achievement of organizational objectives and is a direct result of the interconnection between planning, decision, action and results obtained. This broader understanding of performance, as argued by Micheli and Mari (2014), transcends the merely economic aspect. Measurement should provide relevant information for decision-making and can be viewed through different lenses, as Oyadomari (2008) points out.

The use of systems for performance improvement, as defended by Otley (1999), is not limited only to the managerial aspect, but also has social, behaviour al and economic implications, considering the organizational context. Speklé and Verbeeten (2014) highlight the use of these systems to influence and facilitate managerial decisions in various operational and exploratory aspects. In this context, the experience in the use of integrated systems such as Kaplan and Norton's Balanced Scorecard (BSC), Simons' control levers, and Ferreira & Otley's performance control and management framework, as reported by Berry et al. (2009), provide models for organizational performance improvement and are frequently used by managers.

Improved performance, according to Abernethy; Bouwens and Van Lent (2013) involve attributing value to elements considered crucial by the organization, aligned with its strategic objectives. Thus, understanding and promoting organizational performance is a characteristic management activity, in addition, it is vital to guide objectives, strategies, and decisions, sustain competitiveness, and ensure the survival and growth of organizations.

Therefore, it is important to assess whether there are differences when assessing the perception of governance systems between different hierarchical groups in an organization. Understanding whether these perceptions influence the evaluation of GRC systems is an important challenge for researchers and practitioners in the field. Thus, this methodology provides a useful framework for understanding how (UP) and (FUP) influence a user's intention to adopt and use a technology (Davis, 1989), this time, including governance systems.

4.3. Review of Previous Studies Related to the Application of TAM

The model applied in this research has been the subject of several studies since it was proposed by Davis in 1989. Initially, the TAM was subjected to testing and validation in two different groups of users. One group was made up of 112 IBM users from Canada and the other was made up of 40 MBA students from Boston University, USA. Each group used two different systems, with acceptance tests applied to these groups. The results of these tests revealed different nuances regarding the perception and intention of use of these collaborators (Davis, Bagozzi and Warshaw, 1989).

Adam et al. (1992) replicated the TAM construct, demonstrating its internal consistency and reliability at two scales. These studies provided theoretical and empirical support for TAM, reinforcing its relevance and applicability in various contexts. Silva and Dias (2006) reinforced the need for empirical support for the model, both by researchers and professionals. They indicated that TAM's value proposition is based on the predictability of whether or not the new system is acceptable to users. In addition, TAM can help diagnose reasons for users' dissatisfaction with a system and suggest corrections to reverse this situation, thus increasing the acceptance of the adopted information system.

In Brazil, there are some studies that demonstrate how it can be explored in the most diverse sectors and market situations. The study by Farias and Borges (2012), investigated the acceptance of technology in the perception of restaurant managers and waiters, categorizing stimulus or resistance factors. The main factors of resistance to technology adoption by the waiters interviewed were the lack of adequate training, the complexity of the system, and the perception that technology could replace their jobs. The managers interviewed evaluated the impact of technology on the service efficiency of their restaurants as positive but emphasized the need for billing and control mechanisms to ensure proper use by employees. The study suggests that technology adoption in restaurants can be improved through proper training, clear communication, and incentives for employees.

The study conducted by Souza and Medeiros (2020), addresses the intention of managers of tourist enterprises to use cryptocurrencies as a form of payment. To better understand this intention, the authors use TAM, a model that seeks to explain how people adopt new technologies. The results indicate that managers consider it easy and have a positive attitude towards the use of cryptocurrencies, but the perception of usefulness does not directly interfere in the decision to use them. The TAM can serve to identify the factors that influence the adoption of cryptocurrencies in the tourism sector.

Finally, the study by Vasconcelos et al. (2023), presents an evaluation of the usability and acceptance of the Project Management Information System (SIGProj) in a Brazilian university. The study used an empirical approach, including usability tests, questionnaires, and interviews with SIGProj users. The results indicated that the current SIGProj presents usability problems and that users have a low perception of acceptance and intention to use. In addition, the study proposes a new system to improve the usability and design of SIGProj, which was positively evaluated by users. However, the sample size and other limitations of the survey may affect the validity of the results. As future studies, the authors suggest conducting a comparative study between the two versions of the SIGProj and evaluating engagement attributes. The theoretical model has been applied in several tourism and technology studies, including the use of cryptocurrencies by tourism development managers (Silva and Marques, 2022). These studies relate the implementation of the use of technology to managers, but there is still a gap for more research in the public service. Thus, the research proposes to study these perceptions in a Brazilian federal educational institution in the context of public service.

4.4 Governance, Risk Management, and Compliance Software Used in the Study

The GRC software is a project developed from the model proposed in the study by Oliveira and Miranda, (2024). The study sought to implement the practices of Governance, Risk Management and Compliance, materialized through the application of techniques directed by the international methodologies, COSO, ISO31000 and PMBOK, aimed at mapping existing risks and controls, identifying potential risks that may harm the strategic, tactical and operational objectives of the IFBA. The software developed on a web platform, with JavaScript programming language, contemplated with the following functionalities, as shown in Figure 15.

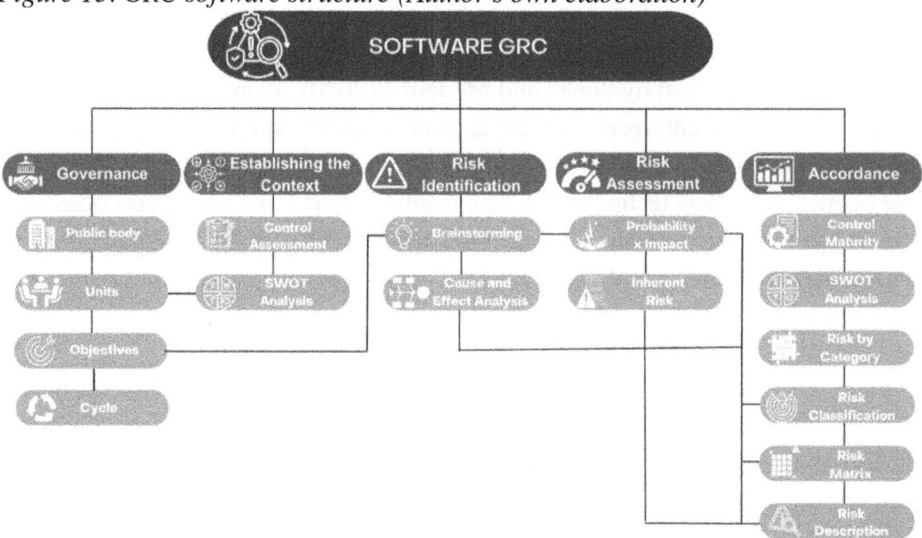

Figure 15. GRC software structure (Author's own elaboration)

The system has the first Governance section, where information about the participating agency, units, objectives and process cycle is recorded. The next sections are designated the governance strategy, and the second section is intended to establish the context: in this phase, the institution answers a questionnaire to assess the organization's level of maturity in relation to internal control. Soon after, it evaluates the internal and external environment with the application of SWOT analysis, to obtain internal knowledge of the organization.

The third section is the identification of risks: in this stage, the organization's risk events are identified, through the online *Brainstorming* technique. The starting point is to discover and define the risks in detail, investigating their causes and effects. The fourth section is the risk assessment: risks are evaluated through the dimension of their Impacts and their probabilities of occurrence, where the inherent risk is calculated, and through their classification, a Risk Matrix is prepared. In the fifth section, the software provides compliance reports for managerial analysis and decision-making. The model aims to systematize the application of GRC practices, using information technology as a strategy, contributing to the efficiency and optimization of management in the public service.

5. METHODOLOGY

For the evaluation of the (PU) and (FUP) in the perception of managers and subordinates about the proposed GRC system, it is indicated to achieve the main objective of the research, to adopt an exploratory and descriptive approach with the application of questionnaires. This type of research, as highlighted by Gil (2002), aims to explain the characteristics of observed phenomena, providing a new view of the problem.

Data collection was carried out in a virtual environment, with questions based on the study by Davies (1989) "user acceptance of information systems: the technology acceptance model (TAM)", with objective answers considering the *Likert scale*, to evaluate the questions between extremes, varying, for example, from "Strongly Agree" to "Strongly Disagree", with seven levels of agreement, twenty of which were questions aimed at analysing the TAM variables. The actors who responded to the survey were 8 administrative technicians, from the sectors linked to the administrative board of the IFBA, 1 Master's, 1 Master's student, 3 Postgraduates, 3 Graduates, in different areas of training, namely: Accounting Sciences, Administration, Law, Economics, Systems Analyst and Letters. The participants were chosen because they are active civil servants and allocated in that area, in addition to all of them obtaining more than 5 years of experience in public service. It is worth mentioning that those mentioned participated in the study that implemented a process of application of GRC practices at the IFBA, and had interaction with software, being divided into two hierarchical groups of managers and subordinates.

After data collection, the analysis was used to evaluate possible influences of a certain group among managers and subordinates regarding PU and FUP on the overall result of the evaluation, the information was analysed through the percentage analysis of the answers obtained.

6. RESULTS AND DISCUSSION

In this section, the results of the research are presented, discussed based on the data collected. Initially, the study aimed to evaluate the level of acceptance of the system in relation to the TAM parameters of UP and FUP. Graphical analysis suggests a positive evaluation between TAM variables in relation to the GRC system. The percentages of (PU) can be analyzed through Figure 16.

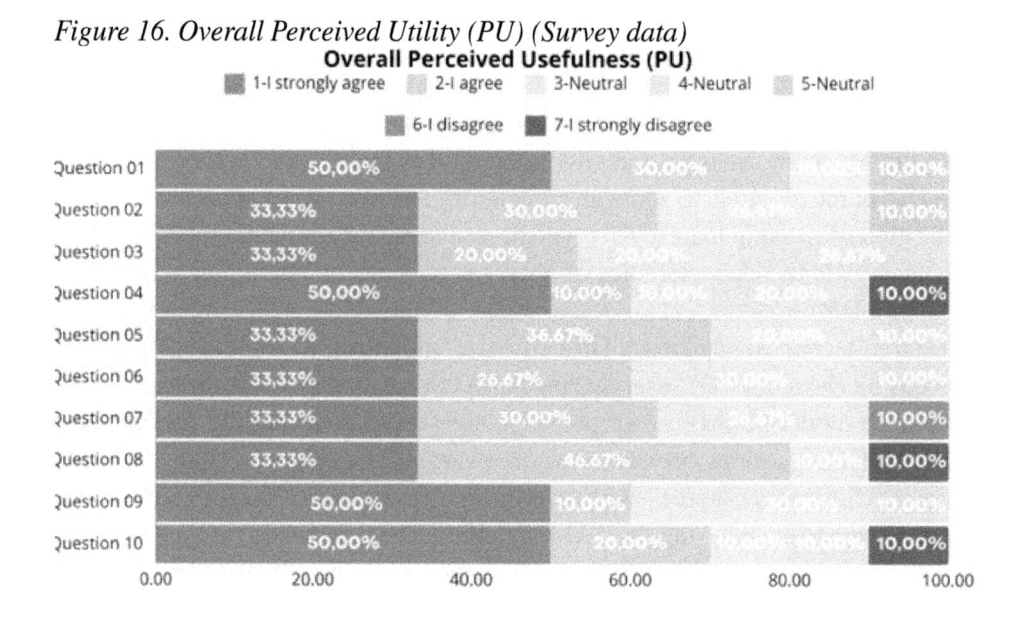

Figure 16. Overall Perceived Utility (PU) (Survey data)

Overall Perceived Usefulness (PU)

	1-I strongly agree	2-I agree	3-Neutral	4-Neutral	5-Neutral	6-I disagree	7-I strongly disagree
Question 01	50,00%	30,00%			10,00%		
Question 02	33,33%	30,00%			10,00%		
Question 03	33,33%	20,00%			26,67%		
Question 04	50,00%	10,00%					10,00%
Question 05	33,33%	36,67%			10,00%		
Question 06	33,33%	26,67%		30,00%			
Question 07	33,33%	30,00%					10,00%
Question 08	33,33%	46,67%					10,00%
Question 09	50,00%	10,00%					
Question 10	50,00%	20,00%					10,00%

The questions that had the highest percentages of strong agreement and UP agreement were: 1, 5, 8 and 10, with more than (70.00%) of agreement each. This suggests that users place a higher value on the quality, productivity, effectiveness, and overall usefulness aspects of the system for their work. These issues are related to the benefit that the GRC system brings to the performance of users and to the performance of their tasks.

The question that had the lowest PU agreement evaluation was question 3, with (46.67%) neutrality. This suggests that some users do not have a definite opinion or do not perceive the GRC system as a factor that increases their speed or their performance at work. These issues are related to the efficiency that the GRC system provides for users and for the execution of their tasks. Figure 17 shows the overall mean PU per level of agreement.

Figure 17. Overall average Perceived Utility (PU) (Survey data)

Perceived Usefulness (PU) overall average

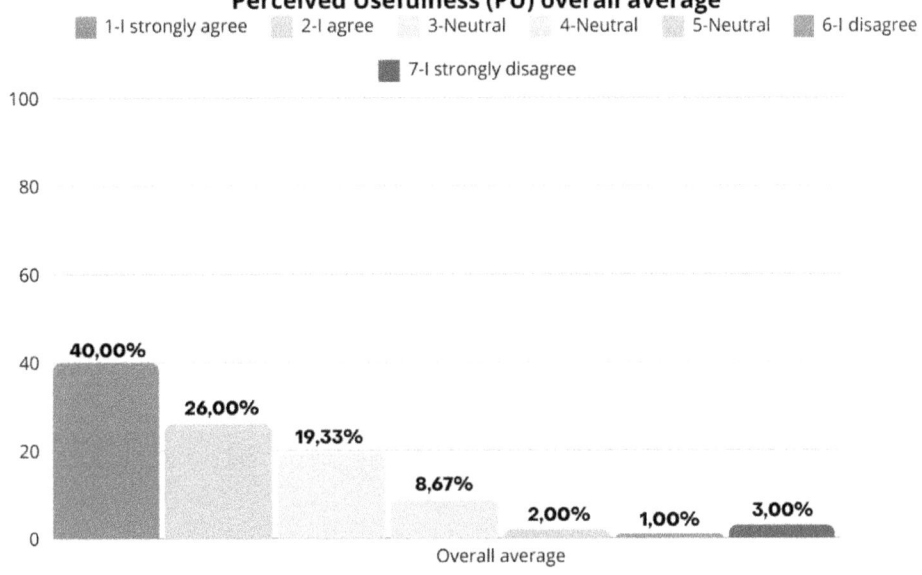

Legend: 1-I strongly agree, 2-I agree, 3-Neutral, 4-Neutral, 5-Neutral, 6-I disagree, 7-I strongly disagree

Category	Overall average
1-I strongly agree	40.00%
2-I agree	26.00%
3-Neutral	19.33%
4-Neutral	8.67%
5-Neutral	2.00%
6-I disagree	1.00%
7-I strongly disagree	3.00%

The overall mean PU was (66.00%) agreement, (30.00%) neutrality, and (4.00%) disagreement. This indicates that most users perceive the GRC system as useful for their work, but there is a significant portion of users who do not have a defined opinion and only (4.00%) disagree with this perception. Therefore, the percentages of FUP can be analyzed through Figure 18.

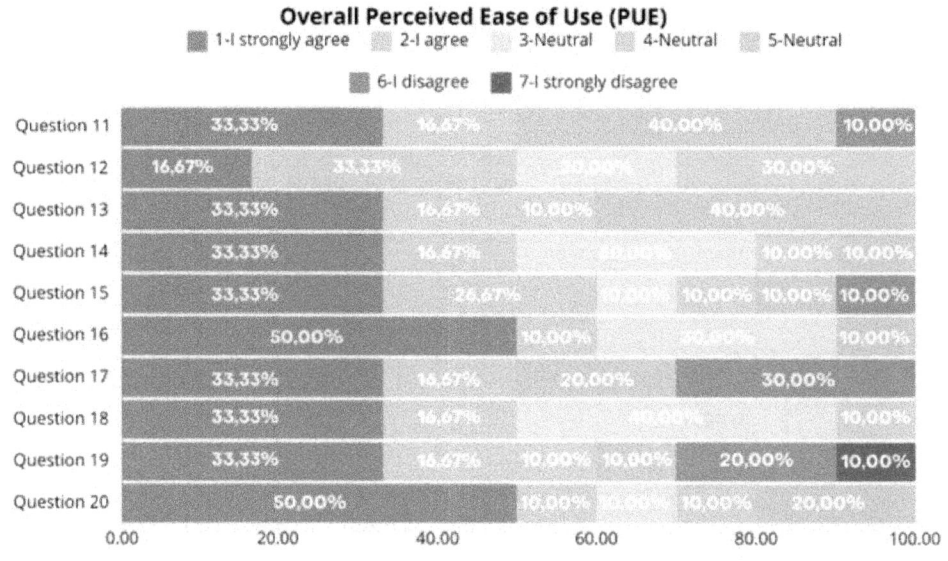

Figure 18. Overall Perceived Ease of Use (FUP) (Survey data)

Overall Perceived Ease of Use (PUE)

Question	1-I strongly agree	2-I agree	3-Neutral	4-Neutral	5-Neutral	6-I disagree	7-I strongly disagree
Question 11	33.33%	16.67%		40.00%			10.00%
Question 12	16.67%	33.33%	20.00%		30.00%		
Question 13	33.33%	16.67%	10.00%	40.00%			
Question 14	33.33%	16.67%	30.00%		10.00%	10.00%	
Question 15	33.33%	26.67%	10.00%	10.00%	10.00%	10.00%	
Question 16	50.00%		10.00%	30.00%		10.00%	
Question 17	33.33%	16.67%	20.00%		30.00%		
Question 18	33.33%	16.67%	40.00%			10.00%	
Question 19	33.33%	16.67%	10.00%	10.00%	20.00%	10.00%	
Question 20	50.00%		10.00%		10.00%	20.00%	

The questions that had the highest FUP averages were: 15, 16 and 20, with (60.00%) of agreement each. This suggests that most users consider the GRC system to be not rigid and inflexible and understand it as a facilitator of their work. These issues are related to the ease of learning and memorization of the system, and to its clarity and comprehensibility. On the other hand, the questions that had the highest disagreements of FUP were: 17 and 19, with (30.00%) of disagreement each. This suggests that some users understand that to use the system requires a certain skillful and mental effort. These issues are related to the complexity of the system. Figure 19 shows the overall mean FUP per level of agreement.

Figure 19. Overall average Perceived Ease of Use (FUP) (Survey data)

Perceived Ease of Use (PEU) overall average

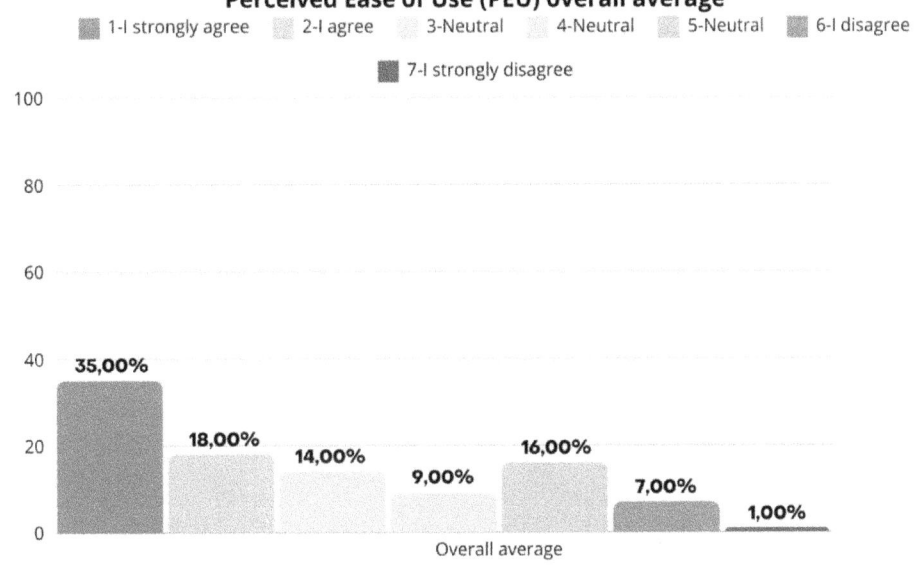

- 1-I strongly agree: 35,00%
- 2-I agree: 18,00%
- 3-Neutral: 14,00%
- 4-Neutral: 9,00%
- 5-Neutral: 16,00%
- 6-I disagree: 7,00%
- 7-I strongly disagree: 1,00%

The overall mean FUP shows an overall agreement of (53.00%), a neutrality of (39.00%), and (8.00%) of disagreement. This indicates that users have a more diverse opinion on the ease of use of the system, with most users rating it as easy, others indifferent, and few finding it difficult. In view of the data, it is possible to affirm that the proposed GRC system obtained good levels of perception of PU and FUP (65.00%) and (53.00%) respectively, considering that public governance is a complex activity that involves the 'government' of complex social networks in the political sectors (Kickert, 1997).

To verify possible influences on the overall result, segregated analysis by hierarchical groups was performed. The graphic analysis indicates that there is a positive influence of strong agreement on the part of managers and divided between agreement and neutral on the perception of subordinates, on the perception of perceived usefulness in relation to the system. The result points out that perceptions differ between the two groups. This can be understood through Figure 20.

Figure 20. Comparison of Perceived Utility (PU) between managers and subordinates (Survey Data)

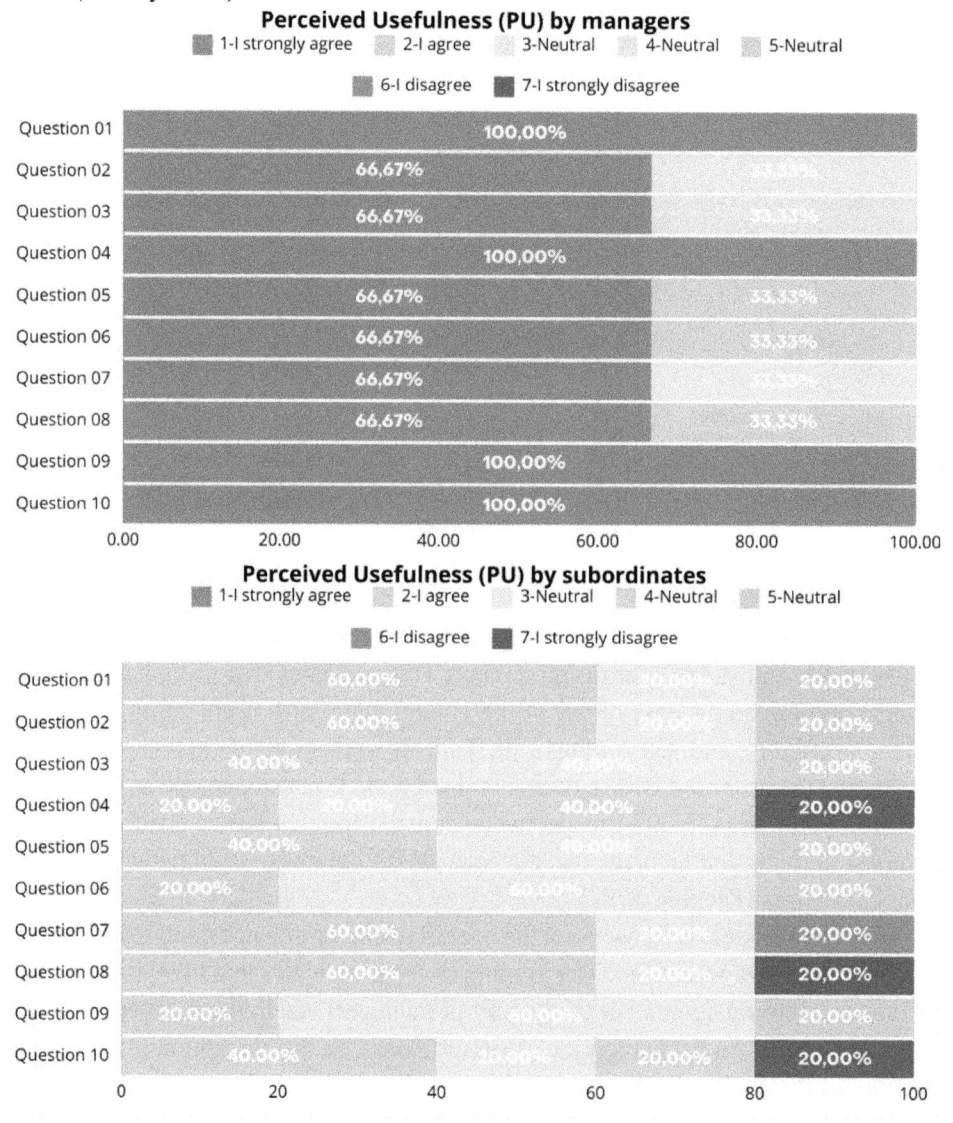

Perceived Usefulness (PU) by managers

Question	1-I strongly agree	2-I agree	3-Neutral	4-Neutral	5-Neutral	6-I disagree	7-I strongly disagree
Question 01	100,00%						
Question 02	66,67%			33,33%			
Question 03	66,67%			33,33%			
Question 04	100,00%						
Question 05	66,67%			33,33%			
Question 06	66,67%			33,33%			
Question 07	66,67%			33,33%			
Question 08	66,67%			33,33%			
Question 09	100,00%						
Question 10	100,00%						

Perceived Usefulness (PU) by subordinates

Question	1-I strongly agree	2-I agree	3-Neutral	4-Neutral	5-Neutral	6-I disagree	7-I strongly disagree
Question 01		60,00%		20,00%			20,00%
Question 02		60,00%		20,00%			20,00%
Question 03		40,00%		40,00%			20,00%
Question 04	20,00%	20,00%		40,00%			20,00%
Question 05		40,00%		40,00%			20,00%
Question 06	20,00%			60,00%			20,00%
Question 07		60,00%		20,00%			20,00%
Question 08		60,00%		20,00%			20,00%
Question 09	20,00%			60,00%			20,00%
Question 10		40,00%	20,00%	20,00%			20,00%

The results of the analysis of the perception of usefulness show, as shown in Figure 20, that managers express a higher acceptance of the proposed GRC system. The average percentages of agreement across all statements are higher among managers, indicating a more positive perception of how the system contributes to improving work quality, increasing productivity, and supporting critical aspects of job performance compared to subordinates. The highlights are that (100.00%) managers strongly agree that using the system improves the quality of work, supports critical aspects, can facilitate work and indicates great usefulness. However, the subordinates (60.00%) understand that the system improves quality, gives greater control, improves productivity and increases efficiency. However, due to the high degree of neutrality and strong disagreement (80.00%) believe that the system does not improve critical aspects, does not improve performance and does not facilitate work.

In the second case, it again points to a relevant difference in the perception of ease of use perceived between managers and subordinates in relation to the GRC system. The managers present agreement and strong unanimous agreement. However, subordinates have a high level of neutrality and some perceptions of disagreement. This indicates differences in these perceptions between the groups. It can also be demonstrated by analyzing Figure 21.

Figure 21. Comparison of Perceived Ease of Use (FUP) between managers and subordinates (Survey data)

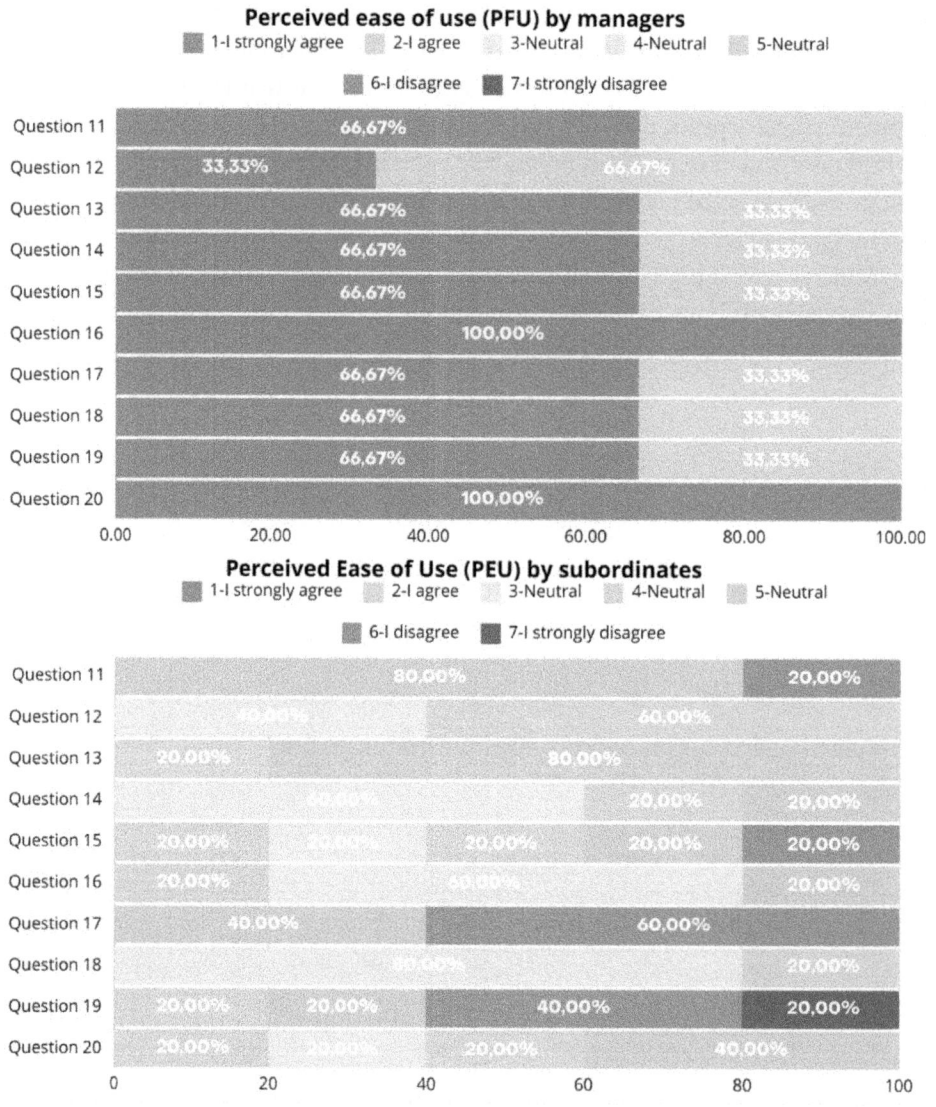

Perceived ease of use (PFU) by managers

	1-I strongly agree	2-I agree	3-Neutral	4-Neutral	5-Neutral	6-I disagree	7-I strongly disagree
Question 11		66,67%					
Question 12	33,33%			66,67%			
Question 13		66,67%				33,33%	
Question 14		66,67%				33,33%	
Question 15		66,67%				33,33%	
Question 16			100,00%				
Question 17		66,67%				33,33%	
Question 18		66,67%				33,33%	
Question 19		66,67%				33,33%	
Question 20			100,00%				

Perceived Ease of Use (PEU) by subordinates

	1-I strongly agree	2-I agree	3-Neutral	4-Neutral	5-Neutral	6-I disagree	7-I strongly disagree
Question 11			80,00%				20,00%
Question 12		40,00%		60,00%			
Question 13	20,00%		80,00%				
Question 14		60,00%			20,00%		20,00%
Question 15	20,00%	20,00%	20,00%		20,00%		20,00%
Question 16	20,00%		60,00%				20,00%
Question 17		40,00%		60,00%			
Question 18		80,00%					20,00%
Question 19	20,00%	20,00%		40,00%			20,00%
Question 20	20,00%		20,00%		40,00%		

The results of the analysis of the perception of ease of use indicate, as shown in figure 21, that, as in the first factor, managers also express a higher acceptance of the proposed GRC system. It is interesting to note that subordinates have a tendency to disagree more with the ease of use of the GRC system than managers. This is especially evident in statements related to ease of learning, non-frustrating interaction, and clear interaction with the system, where subordinates have higher rates of disagreement or neutrality. The most relevant facts are that (100.00%) managers strongly agree that it is easy to remember the tasks they perform in the system, they generally consider the system easy to use. Furthermore, they strongly agree and agree with all the other issues investigated. However, the subordinates (60.00%) understand that to use the system requires a lot of mental effort and that it takes a lot of effort to become skilled. It is noted that there is a very strong neutrality in most of the questions answered by subordinates.

There are several reasons to investigate why managers perceive more usefulness and ease in the GRC system than subordinates. Managers often take a broader view of the organization and understand how different parts fit together. Managers are often responsible for ensuring that the organization is compliant with various regulations, the GRC system can be a tool to help them fulfill these responsibilities, thereby increasing their perception of usefulness. In addition, managers face pressures to improve organizational performance, which makes tools such as the one in this study more useful for achieving these goals. As for perceived ease, managers generally have more experience and training, this can make them more comfortable with the technology and therefore realize that it is easier to use. Also, they are often involved in the process of selecting and implementing the systems, this can give them a better understanding of how the system works and how it can be used to benefit the organization.

These results corroborate aspects studied in the TAM model by demonstrating the positive relationship between the perception of usefulness and perceived ease of use with the general perception of the GRC system. This strengthens the theoretical understanding of how individual perceptions can influence the intentions of using technological systems in an organizational environment. The results also show the relevance of management in the promotion of organizational governance, with the vision of improving organizational performance being a crucial mechanism for the idea of action to achieve objectives, measurable in terms of adequacy, efficiency and effectiveness (Abbad, 1999). Callahan and Soileau (2017) noted that the level of maturity of enterprise risk management can positively influence the company's performance, influencing its comparative position with others in the same sector that have lower ERM levels.

These indications also reinforce the use of managerial competencies, studied by Ferreira Amorim (2016), who emphasizes that such competencies are determinant, since the attitudes and actions of managers are guiding elements of organizational competitiveness and sustainability. Cardoso (2009) emphasizes the importance of managerial competencies within the set of competencies of an organization, highlighting the fundamental role of managers in the implementation of organizational strategies. These ideas reinforce the report of the TCU's basic governance framework, which states that "management is inherent and integrated into organizational processes, being responsible for planning, execution, control, action, in short, for the management of resources and powers made available to bodies and entities to achieve their objectives" (TCU, 2014, p. 32).

7. CONCLUSION

The study verified the level of acceptance of a system by measuring the perceived usefulness and perceived ease of use, in the general and hierarchical evaluation between managers and subordinates in relation to a Governance, Risk Management and Compliance system, using the TAM model as an evaluation parameter. The results highlighted differences in this perception, managers showed greater perceived utility and perceived ease of use in favor of the GRC system, compared to subordinates. This result suggests an influence of hierarchical position, search for organizational performance and management responsibility in promoting governance, influencing the perception of the system and its potential contributions to the organization.

Thus, one of the contributions of this study is the finding that the model conceived by Davis (1986) is still efficient for evaluation in relation to the usefulness and ease of use of new technologies. It broadens the understanding of the TAM model by applying the specific context of public service, using information technology through the use of a GRC system, highlighting the importance of the perception of usefulness and ease of use in the accessibility and adoption of governance systems in organizations, in addition to the relevance of management in promoting organizational governance.

Managers, potentially due to their broad view of the organization, responsibilities, can perceive greater usefulness and ease of use of the GRC system, which influences its ease and effective use. These results reinforce the relationship between individual perceptions and as an objective of using technological systems in organizational environments, they provided important information to improve the implementation and adoption of GRC systems improving organizational performance. However, the identification of differences in the perception of usefulness and ease of use between managers and subordinates indicates the importance of specific training programs. These programs aim not only at familiarization with the systems but can also explain how such systems can be more useful and simple to use for each group, improving their ease and overall adoption. Considering that the use of information systems is useful to boost managerial processes. This perspective, according to Bracci et al. (2021), facilitates the risk control process through the use of specialized software.

Among the limitations of this study, we can mention the sample size, which was restricted to a specific context of an institution, with eight participating civil servants, which may limit the generalization of the results. In addition, the survey focused on the perception of usefulness and ease of use, without considering other possible factors influencing the adoption of the GRC system. This study demonstrates that the results are promising for future research in this area.

It is recommended to carry out longitudinal studies in different organizational contexts, using statistical tests to validate and expand the results obtained. In addition, explore other external variables, such as cultural influences and organizational aspects, considering the influence of implementation and training strategies on users' perception of the usefulness and ease of use of the systems inherent to the GRC area, which can enrich the understanding of the adoption of these technologies.

Finally, in terms of managerial implications in the implementation, the study may support the management strategy aimed at changing the presented framework, with the objective of obtaining general adherence to the GRC system, allowing the advancement of knowledge in the field of acceptance of Governance, Risk Management and Compliance practices.

REFERENCES

Abbad, G. (1999). An integrated model for evaluating the impact of on-the-job training – IMPACT. Thesis (Doctorate in Psychology). Institute of Psychology of the University of Brasilia, Brasília, Federal District, Brazil.

Abernethy, M. A., Bouwens, J., & Van Lent, L. (2013). The role of performance measures in the intertemporal decisions of business unit managers. Contemporary accounting research, 30(3), 925-961.

Aguilera, R. V., Judge, W. Q., & Terjesen, S. A. (2018). Corporate governance deviance. *Academy of Management Review*, 43(1), 87–109. DOI: 10.5465/amr.2014.0394

Ansell, C., & Torfing, J. (2016). Introduction: theories of governance. In Handbook on theories of governance (pp. 1-18). Edward Elgar Publishing. DOI: 10.4337/9781782548508.00008

Appio, J. (2009). Swot analysis as a competitive differential: An exploratory study at Cooperativa Muza Brasil. *Interdisciplinary Journal of Applied Science*, 3(3), 1–18.

Araújo, A., & Gomes, A. M. (2021). Risk management in the public sector: challenges in its adoption by Brazilian federal universities. Revista Contabilidade & Finanças, 32(86), 241-254. https://doi.org/DOI: 10.1590/1982-7849rac2018170391

Barbosa, A. F., Gemente, G. B., Sanches, M. N., Rodrigues, F. M., & Sabaa-Srur, A. U. (2016). *Importance of Quality Management in the Processors of Fruit and Vegetable Industries*.

Bracci, E., Tallaki, M., Gobbo, G., & Papi, L. (2021). Risk management in the public sector: a structured literature review. International Journal of Public Sector Management, 34(2), 205-223.

Brazilian Federation Of Banks (FEBRABAN). (2018). Guide: good compliance practices. Revised and updated edition.

Callahan, C., & Soileau, J. (2017). Does enterprise risk management enhance operating performance?. Advances in accounting, 37, 122-139.

Chiavenato, I. (2008). People management: the new role of human resources in organizations.

Chiavenato, I., & Sapiro, A. (2009). *Strategic Planning* (2nd ed.). Elsevier.

Christopher, J., & Sarens, G. (2015). Risk management: its adoption in Australian public universities within an environment of change management–A management perspective. Australian Accounting Review, 25(1), 2-12.

Committee of Sponsoring Organizations of the Treadway Commission. (2004). *Enterprise risk management-integrated framework*. No Title.

Committee Of Sponsoring Organizations Of The Treadway Commission. (2017). Enterprise risk management: Integrating with strategy and performance.

da Silva, A. C., Curth, M., Kerber, L. E., & Morouço, P. (2022). A intenção de uso de tecnologia por acadêmicos de Educação Física de uma universidade do Rio Grande do Sul-Brasil. *Caderno de Educação Física e Esporte*, 21(1), 59.

Davis, F. D. (1989). Perceived usefulness, perceived ease of use, and user acceptance of information technology. *Management Information Systems Quarterly*, 13(3), 319–340. DOI: 10.2307/249008

Davis, F. D., Bagozzi, R. P., & Warshaw, P. R. (1989). User acceptance of computer technology: A comparison of two theoretical models. *Management Science*, 35(8), 984. DOI: 10.1287/mnsc.35.8.982

De Smet, D., & Mayer, N. (2016, October). Integration of IT governance and security risk management: A systematic literature review. In 2016 International Conference on Information Society (i-Society) (pp. 143-148). IEEE. DOI: 10.1109/i-Society.2016.7854200

Dhlamini, J. (2022). Strategic risk management: A systematic review from 2001 to 2020. *Journal of Contemporary Management*, 19(2), 212–237. DOI: 10.35683/jcm22008.165

Farias, J. S., & Borges, D. M. (2012). Factors that influence the acceptance of technology: The perception of managers and employees in a restaurant chain. *Management & Technology Journal*, 12(2), 141–167.

Ferreira, G. R. (2016), Social competencies: a study with managers of the Attorney General's Office of the state of Pernambuco. Congress of Management and Controllership of UnoChapecó, Chapecó, Anais. CGC..

Galvão, A. (2008). *Corporate Finance: Business Theory and Practice in Brazil*. Elsevier.

Gazoulit, S.; Oubal, K. (2022), Risk Management in Public Universities In Search of Performance: A Synthesis of the Literature.

Gil, A. C. (2022). *How to Develop Research Projects* (Vol. 4). Atlas São Paulo.

Gonçalves, M., Magalhães, V., Marques, D. (2019), International financial cases and crises: a literature review. Ethics and Social Responsibility, 6-8.

Gordon, L. A., Loeb, M. P., & Tseng, C. Y. (2009). Enterprise risk management and firm performance: A contingency perspective. Journal of Accounting and Public Policy, 28(4), 301-327.

Hill, S., & Dinsdale, G. (2003). *A basis for the development of learning strategies for risk management in the public service. Translation: Luís Marcos de Vasconcelos.* ENAP.

Hoeflich, S. (2016). Risk management applied to organizations: integrating the silos of grc. 2016, Rio de Janeiro.

Hopkin, P. (2018). *Fundamentals of risk management: understanding, evaluating and implementing effective risk management.* Kogan Page Publishers.

ISO 31010 (2019) Risk Management. Techniques for the Risk Assessment Process.

ISO 31000 (2018) Risk Management – Guidelines. International Organization for Standardization.

Jensen, M. C., & Meckling, W. H. (2019). Theory of the firm: Managerial behaviour, agency costs and ownership structure. In *Corporate governance* (pp. 77–132). Gower.

Kickert, W. J. (1997). Public governance in The Netherlands: An alternative to Anglo-American 'managerialism'. *Public Administration*, 75(4), 731–752. DOI: 10.1111/1467-9299.00084

Lam, J. (2014). *Enterprise risk management: from incentives to controls.* John Wiley & Sons. DOI: 10.1002/9781118836477

Manso, A. (2021). Market Concentration before and after the European Audit Reform. Master's thesis, Instituto Superior de Contabilidade e Administração de Lisboa, Lisbon, Portugal.

Manzi, V. (2008). Compliance in Brazil - consolidation and prospects. São Paulo.

Marcelli, S. (2013). Governance in the public sector: diagnosis of the management practices of the Federal Police in the light of study 13 of the PSC/IFAC. Dissertation (Master's Degree) - Executive Master's Degree in Business Management, Center for Academic Training and Research, Brazilian School of Public and Business Administration, Rio de Janeiro.

Matos, J., Matos, R., & Almeida, J. (2007). *Analysis of the Corporate Environment: from organized chaos to planning.* E-papers.

Menon, K., & Williams, D. (2004). The use of management control mechanisms to manage trust and uncertainty in the virtual organization. *Frontiers of Information Systems*, 6(2), 175–193.

Menzies, C. (2006). *Sarbanes-Oxley und Corporate Compliance: Nachhaltigkeit, Optimierung, Integration.* No Title.

Micheli, P., & Mari, L. (2014). The theory and practice of performance measurement. *Management Accounting Research*, 25(2), 147–156. DOI: 10.1016/j.mar.2013.07.005

Ministry Of Planning, *Budget And Management*. (2016). Digital Governance Strategy of the Federal Public Administration 2016-2019, Brasilia.

Morano, C. (2003), Application of Risk Analysis Techniques in Construction Projects. 2003. 206 f. Dissertation (Master's Degree in Civil Engineering) – Fluminense Federal University – UFF, Niterói.

Oliveira, D. (2010), Strategic planning: concepts, methodologies and practice (28th ed.), São Paulo: Atlas.

Oliveira P., & Vieira O. (2019). Public Governance Practices Adopted by the Brazilian Federal Public Administration. Public Administration and Social Management.

Open Compliance & Ethics Group. (2015). *GRC capability model – version 3.0 (Red Book)*. OCEG.

Organisation for Economic Co-operation and Development. (2011). *OECD Assessments on Public Governance: OECD Assessment on the Integrity System of the Brazilian Federal Public Administration – Managing risks for a more honest public administration*. OECD Publishing.

Otley, D. (1999). Performance management: A framework for management control systems research. *Management Accounting Research*, 10(4), 363–382. DOI: 10.1006/mare.1999.0115

Oyadomari, J. (2008), Use of the management control system and performance: a study in Brazilian companies from the perspective of VBR (Resource-Based View). Doctoral Thesis in Accounting, University of São Paulo, São Paulo, SP, Brazil.

Palermo, T. (2014). Accountability and expertise in public sector risk management: A case study. *Financial Accountability & Management*, 30(3), 322–341. DOI: 10.1111/faam.12039

Purdy, G. (2010). ISO 31000: 2009—setting a new standard for risk management. Risk Analysis. *International Journal (Toronto, Ont.)*, 30(6), 881–886. PMID: 20636915

Ramlaoui, S., & Semma, A. (2014). Comparative study oComparative of COBIT with other IT Governance Frameworks. *International Journal of Computer Science Issues*, 11(6), 95.

Rezende, D. (2008). *Strategic planning for organizations: public and private*. Brasport.

Santos, R. (2021). *Formal Agenda and Substantive Agenda in Brazil's Adherence to OECD Budget Governance Recommendations*. IPEA Preliminary Publication.

Sax, J., & Andersen, T. J. (2019). Making risk management strategic: Integrating enterprise risk management with strategic planning. *European Management Review*, 16(3), 719–740. DOI: 10.1111/emre.12185

Sedrez, C., & Fernandes, F. (2011). Risk management in universities and university centers in the state of Santa Catarina. *University Management of Latin America*, (special issue), 70–93.

Shleifer, A., & Vishny, R. W. (1997). A survey of corporate governance. *The Journal of Finance*, 52(2), 737–783. DOI: 10.1111/j.1540-6261.1997.tb04820.x

Silva, G., Mendes Filho, L., & Marques, S. (2022). Intenção de usar criptomoedas por gestores de empreendimentos turísticos: uma abordagem utilizando o Technology Acceptance Model (TAM). Revista Brasileira de Pesquisa em Turismo, 16, e-2556.

Souza, A., & Medeiros, R. (2020). Intention to use cryptocurrencies by managers of tourism enterprises: An analysis with the Technology Acceptance Model. *Brazilian Journal of Tourism Research*, 14(3).

Spekle, R. F., & Verbeeten, F. H. (2014). The use of performance measurement systems in the public sector: Effects on performance. *Management Accounting Research*, 25(2), 131–146. DOI: 10.1016/j.mar.2013.07.004

Sundaram, A. K., & Inkpen, A. C. (2004). The corporate objective revisited. *Organization Science*, 15(3), 350–363. DOI: 10.1287/orsc.1040.0068

Torfing, J. (2012). *Interactive governance: Advancing the paradigm*. Oxford University Press. DOI: 10.1093/acprof:oso/9780199596751.001.0001

Travaglia, K. R., & de Sá, L. F. V. N. (2017). Fortalecimento da governança: uma agenda contemporânea para o setor público brasileiro. Revista Controle: Doutrinas e artigos, 15(1), 22-53.

Vasconcelos, L., Sampaio, I., Viterbo, J., & Trevisan, D. (2023), Evaluation of the usability and acceptance of an Information System and Project Management (SIG-Proj) in the context of university extension. In *Proceedings of the XIV Computer on the Beach Conference* (pp. 8-279). Florianópolis, SC, Brazil.

Vassileva, R. (2021). COVID-19 in Autocratic Bulgaria: How the Anti-Corruption Protests Temporarily Limited the Abuse of Questionable Legislation.VERÍSSIMO, Carla. Compliance: incentive to adopt anti-corruption measures. São Paulo: Saraiva.

Villanueva, E., Nuñez, M. A., & Martins, I. (2022). Impact of risk governance and associated practices and tools on enterprise risk management: Some evidence from Colombia. *Revista Finanzas y Política Económica*, 14(1), 187–206. DOI: 10.14718/revfinanzpolitecon.v14.n1.2022.8

Werkema, M. (1995). *Basic statistical tools for process management*. Cristiano Ottoni Foundation.

Winter, R., & Schelp, J. (2008, March). Enterprise architecture governance: the need for a business-to-IT approach. In *Proceedings of the 2008 ACM symposium on Applied computing* (pp. 548-552). DOI: 10.1145/1363686.1363820

World Bank. (2013). *The International Bank for Reconstruction and Development. Worldwide Governance Indicators*. WGI.

APPENDIX I

Questionnaire of Usefulness and Perceived Ease in the Use of Electronic Space Technologies GRC System

Please answer the questions by assigning each of the twenty questions scores ranging from 01 to 07 following the concepts as shown in the table below.

Table 1.-

Perceived usefulness of the risk management system	I strongly agree	Agree	Neutral		Disagree	I strongly disagree
	1	2	3	4 5	6	7
1. Using the GRC system improves the quality of the work I do.						
2. Using the GRC system gives me greater control over my work.						
3. The GRC risk management system allows me to get things done faster.						
4. The GRC system supports critical aspects of my work.						
5. Using GRC system increases my productivity.						
6. Using the GRC system improves my performance at work.						
7. Using GRC system allows me to accomplish more work than would otherwise be possible.						
8. The use of the GRC system increases my effectiveness at work.						
9. The use of the GRC system makes my job easier.						
10. Overall, I find the GRC system useful in my work.						
Perceived ease of risk management system						

continued on following page

Table 1. Continued

Perceived usefulness of the risk management system	I strongly agree	Agree	Neutral			Disagree	I strongly disagree
	1	2	3	4	5	6	7
11. I don't find the GRC system complicated to use.							
12. Learning how to operate the GRC system is easy for me.							
13. Interacting with the GRC system is not usually frustrating.							
14. I find it easy to get the GRC system to do what I want it to do.							
15. The GRC system is not rigid and inflexible to interact.							
16. It's easy for me to remember how to accomplish tasks using the GRC system.							
17. Interacting with the GRC system does not require much mental effort.							
18. My interaction with the GRC system is clear and understandable.							
19. I think it doesn't take much effort to become skilled in using electronics.							
20. Overall, I find the GRC system easy to use.							

Chapter 10
Gender Diversity and Audit Fees Across Diverse Institutional Settings

Kurt Desender
https://orcid.org/0000-0002-6528-8004
Universidad Carlos III de Madrid, Spain

Mónica López Puertas-Lamy
Universidad Carlos III de Madrid, Spain

ABSTRACT

This Study examines whether and how gender diversity at the board and top management team (TMT) level, as well as commitment to the UN's Sustainable Development Goal on Gender Equality (SDG5), influences financial reporting quality by studying the independent auditors' assessment of the risk of material misstatement. Employing a large global dataset, they find a positive relationship between board gender diversity and audit fees, which is consistent with an active monitoring role by the board. In contrast, we do not find a significant effect of TMT gender diversity, nor for the firm's commitment to the SDG Goal on Gender Equality. In addition, we find that the relationship between board gender diversity and audit fees is mainly driven by firms in countries without mandatory board gender quotas, and that the results are especially strong in settings where there is a lower perception of corruption and a greater representation of females in parliament.

DOI: 10.4018/979-8-3693-5923-5.ch010

INTRODUCTION

The lack of gender diversity on corporate boards and in leadership roles has emerged as a significant issue in corporate governance in recent years (Gow, Larcker, and Watts, 2023). Regulators, politicians, and investors are increasingly urging companies to address this imbalance at the board and executive levels (Zattoni et al., 2023). For example, the 'Women on Boards' law, approved by the European Parliament in November 2022, mandates that women must comprise at least 40% of non-executive board members at large companies in the European Union by mid-2026. Additionally, major institutional investors launched a campaign in 2017 to increase board gender diversity, resulting in U.S. corporations appointing 2.5 times more female directors in 2019 compared to 2016 (Gormley et al., 2023).

These regulatory and investor pressures underscore the perceived advantages of gender diversity on corporate boards, a topic that has received increasing attention in the literature. Numerous studies examine these advantages, indicating that increased gender diversity can stimulate creative thinking and introduce novel perspectives into board discussions (e.g., Benton, 2021; Perryman, Fernando, and Tripathy, 2016). Supporting this, a 2022 survey of U.S. corporate directors revealed that gender diversity was highly valued for introducing new ways of thinking to the boardroom (PwC Report, 2022). Prior research also indicates that women, compared to men, have less tolerance for engaging in opportunism (Bernardi and Arnold, 1997; Krishnan and Parsons, 2008; Thorne, Massey, and Magnan, 2003) and place less importance on self-interest (Arlow, 1991). These characteristics enhance strategic decision-making (Perryman et al., 2016) and reduce financial misconduct (Adams and Ferreira, 2009; Chen, Crossland, and Huang, 2016; Cumming, Leung, and Rui, 2015; Post and Byron, 2015).[1]

Financial reporting quality is a cornerstone of corporate governance, serving as the foundation for transparency, accountability, and oversight (Aguilera, Desender, and LópezPuertas-Lamy, 2021). Accurate and reliable financial information enables investors and other stakeholders to hold company management and boards accountable. In the contemporary business landscape, the audit function plays a critical role in ensuring the reliability and integrity of financial reporting (Aguilera et al., 2021). This study focuses on the growing importance of diversity at all organizational levels and its impact on financial reporting quality, adopting the perspective of external auditors, who are professionally trained to assess this quality. The research question we seek to address is: "How does gender diversity at various levels influence auditors' perceived risk of material misstatements?" Additionally, we explore how institutional factors shape this relationship."

To this end, we analyze auditors' proprietary evaluations of the reporting quality of firms with varying levels of gender diversity, inferred from audit engagement pricing. The purpose of the external audit is to obtain reasonable assurance that financial statements are free from material misstatements. The auditor's cost of gathering and verifying evidence, and rendering an opinion, depends on the audit effort, which is a function of the risk threshold for issuing an incorrect opinion on the financial statements (i.e., audit risk) that the auditor is willing to accept (Hay, Knechel, and Wong, 2006; Simunic, 1980; Simunic and Stein, 1996). According to the audit risk model, auditors aim to maintain overall audit risk at an acceptably low level. This involves choosing an acceptable level of audit risk and then assessing inherent and control risks to determine the desirable level of detection risk (Houston, Peters, and Pratt, 1999). Evaluating inherent risk involves examining the entity's operational nature, strategic objectives, and governance strategies, including management integrity and competence, transaction complexity, and accounting practices. Control risk evaluation reviews the effectiveness of internal control mechanisms, information systems robustness, and risk mitigation and oversight by management and the board (Ghosh and Tang, 2015; Johnstone, Grambling, and Rittenberg, 2014).

If auditors perceive that a client's financial reporting quality is low due to high inherent or control risk, they must set a lower detection risk to maintain acceptable audit risk levels. This adjustment requires modifications in audit procedures, impacting audit planning and procedures (Bedard and Johnstone, 2004; Bell, Landsman, and Shackelford, 2001). Perceived poor financial reporting quality and increased risk of financial statement manipulation typically lead auditors to allocate more resources to scrutinize high-risk accounts, resulting in higher audit fees (Simunic, 1980; Simunic and Stein, 1996). Moreover, auditors may employ more specialized personnel to reduce detection risk, further increasing audit fees (Bell et al., 2001).

Previous research has examined the link between board gender diversity and (post-audit) financial reporting quality[2], but findings are mixed and limited to single-country studies (e.g., Huang, Huang, and Lee, 2014; Lai et al., 2017; Nekhili et al., 2020; Sultana, Cahan, and Rahman, 2020). Compared to studies that rely on reporting quality models, which is mostly confined to analyzing one dimension of reporting quality (e.g., discretionary accruals), analyzing audit fees has several distinct advantages (Ghosh and Tang, 2015). First, audit fee models are typically well-specified with large R-squared values, which reduces the concerns on correlated omitted variables (DeFond and Zhang, 2014). Second, measures of accounting quality based on realized earnings may capture other firm characteristics, such as performance, in addition to reporting quality (Liu and Wysocki, 2007). Third, audit fees is a comprehensive measure, as it incorporates information from the financial statements and its footnotes, while financial reporting quality models tend to focus mainly on accruals (LópezPuertas-Lamy, Desender, and Epure, 2017). In addition, the audit fees contain the auditors' proprietary information about reporting quality, while accounting quality models are limited to public information (Ghosh and Tang, 2015).

Drawing on global data from Refinitiv Eikon for the period 2018-2022 and controlling for firm- and year-fixed effects, we find a robust positive relationship between board gender diversity and audit fees, suggesting that female directors play an active monitoring role. In contrast, we find no significant effect linked to TMT gender diversity or the firm's commitment to SDG 5. We also examine under which conditions the positive link between board gender diversity and audit fees is more pronounced. Specifically, we examine the importance of board gender quotas, perception of corruption in society, and the proportion of females in parliament. Consistent with the idea that board gender quotas may induce tokenism, we find that the relationship between board gender diversity and audit fees is stronger in countries without mandatory board gender quotas, i.e., where board gender diversity is voluntary. We also show that the relationship between board gender diversity and audit fees is stronger in countries with lower corruption perception and higher female parliamentary representation.

This paper makes several contributes to the literature. By examining the relationship between gender diversity and the auditor's assessment of the risk that the financial report contains material misstatements, our analysis helps to provide a better understanding of whether gender diversity is linked to more transparent and reliable financial information provided by the firm (i.e., the pre-audit financial reporting quality). Our results points to audit effort as a mechanism through which board gender diversity may influence the firm's financial reporting quality. In particular, our findings suggest that audit fees may be an important omitted variable for prior studies that examine the relationship between gender diversity and (post-audit) financial reporting quality. Additionally, our study responds to the call by Zattoni et al. (2023) who suggest that "future studies should theorize and investigate how different legal, regulatory, social and cultural contexts may affect the relationship between board diversity, processes, and outcomes." Specifically, our study is the first to investigate whether the relationship between gender diversity and financial reporting quality varies across institutional dimensions. Finally, we are the first to examine the influence of a firm's commitment to SDG 5 on audit fees, addressing evolving dynamics in corporate governance and audit practices.

In the next section, we review the relevant literature. Following that, we develop our hypotheses and describe our research design, including data collection and variable measurement. Subsequently, we present our empirical results, discuss our findings, their implications, and the limitations of our study, and suggest avenues for future research. We finish with a short conclusion.

PRIOR LITERATURE

Prior research shows important differences between women and men, on dimensions such as opportunism and accountability. Specifically, when compared to men, women have less tolerance for engaging in opportunism (Bernardi and Arnold 1997; Krishnan and Parsons 2008) and place less importance on self-interest (Arlow 1991). Interestingly, Thorne et al. (2003) indicate that female auditors resolve moral issues in auditing by applying more prescriptive reasoning than male auditors. These studies highlight individual attributes of female directors and indirectly suggest that boards with female directors are likely to demand greater accountability from managers and assurance of the financial reporting quality.

Focusing on group-level interactions, several studies suggest that gender diverse boards are more likely to avoid group thinking and have a more diverse perspective and creative thinking (Benton, 2021) and are less inhibited in discussing difficult and sensitive issues (Huse and Solberg 2006; McInerney-Lacombe, Billimoria, and Salipante 2008). Moreover, Post and Byron (2015) conduct a meta-analysis of the effects of women on boards on financial performance and conclude that female board representation is positively associated with board monitoring. In this line, McInerney-Lacombe et al. (2008) suggest that female directors are more likely to challenge the opinions of other directors and seek objective evidence to justify their position on the board, while Adams and Ferreira (2009) and Srinidhi, Sun, and Zhang (2015) provide evidence that female directors self-select into monitoring roles. In contrast, Reddy and Jadhav (2019) review the empirical evidence from both developed and emerging markets and find that the impact of board gender diversity on firm performance present inconclusive results. They argue that some studies find positive impacts, while others report negligible or even negative effects.

Several studies have focused on examining the link between board gender diversity and (post-audit) financial reporting quality. Krishnan and Parsons (2008) examine the effect of board gender diversity on earnings quality and find that firms with gender-diverse boards exhibit higher earnings quality, indicating more accurate and reliable financial reporting. Similarly, Srinidhi, Gul, and Tsui (2011), who find that gender-diverse boards are associated with higher quality earnings, suggest that female directors contribute to more diligent financial oversight and improved financial reporting standards. In the same line, Bravo and Alcaide-Ruiz (2019) find that firms with gender-diverse boards were less likely to engage in earnings management, while Garcia-Sanchez, Martinez-Ferrero, and Garcia-Meca (2017), who analyzed European firms, reveal that gender diversity positively influences the quality of financial reporting by reducing earnings manipulation and enhancing the informativeness of earnings.

The findings from the link between board gender diversity and audit fees are however mixed and often limited to single-country studies. For example, Lai et al. (2017) find that firms with gender-diverse boards in the U.S. incur in higher audit fees, suggesting that diverse boards may engage in more rigorous oversight, leading to increased audit efforts and costs. This finding aligns with the idea that gender-diverse boards enhance monitoring effectiveness, thereby demanding more thorough audits. Similarly, Ittonen, Miettinen, and Vähämaa (2010) explore the association between female board representation and audit fees in Finland. They find that the presence of female directors is linked to higher audit fees. The authors suggest that the result indicates more thorough auditing processes in response to enhanced board oversight.

In contrast, Nekhili et al. (2020) observe a negative effect in French firms, where gender diversity on boards is linked with lower audit fees. The authors contend that female independent directors and female audit committee members, by improving board monitoring effectiveness, affect the auditor's assessment of audit risk, resulting in lower audit fees.

Interestingly, Sultana, Cahan, and Rahman (2020) note that the positive association between audit committee gender diversity and audit quality becomes weaker after the introduction of diversity guidelines in Australia. This suggests that mandatory diversity guidelines could lead to tokenism, where the presence of female directors becomes more about compliance rather than enhancing board effectiveness.

The evidence on TMT is much more limited. Huang, Huang, and Lee (2014) find that firms with female CEOs are associated with higher audit fees for a sample of U.S firms. Harjoto, Laksmana, and Lee (2015) find that U.S. firms with female and ethnic minority CEOs pay significantly higher audit fees than those with male Caucasian CEOs, and that firms with female CEOs have shorter audit delay than firms with male CEOs.

HYPOTHESIS DEVELOPMENT

To the extent that gender diverse board adopt a stronger monitoring role, board gender diversity can affect audit fees in two opposite directions.

A negative relationship is expected if a gender-diverse board takes an active role in improving the design of internal controls and corporate governance in general. Gender-diverse boards may be more diligent in their oversight functions, leading to more effective internal control systems. Empirical evidence supports this argument. For instance, Krishnan and Parsons (2008) found that firms with gender-diverse boards exhibited higher earnings quality, suggesting that these boards are more effective in overseeing financial reporting processes. Effective internal controls reduce the perceived risk for auditors, as they can rely more on these controls to ensure the accuracy of financial reporting. When auditors perceive that a firm has strong internal controls, they can place greater reliance on these controls, thereby reducing the extent of required substantive testing (Cohen, Krishnamoorthy, and Wright, 2007; Collier and Gregory, 1996).

Conversely, a positive relationship between board gender diversity and audit fees may emerge if a gender-diverse board, instead of actively improving internal controls and overall reliability of financial reporting, shares information and concerns with the external auditor about internal control weaknesses and other accounting issues. This disclosure may prompt the auditor to increase the audit procedures to gather sufficient evidence to address these issues. This increased audit effort, aimed at mitigating audit risk, leads to higher audit fees (Hay, Knechel, and Ling, 2008). This scenario is supported by the idea that a more vigilant and questioning board will identify and communicate potential risks and weaknesses more openly with auditors. Empirical studies provide support for this perspective. Carcello et al. (2002) and Knechel and Willekens (2006) found that greater board independence, which can be analogous to the diversity of perspectives brought by gender-diverse boards, is associated with higher audit fees due to increased audit efforts to address identified risks.

Given the opposing arguments, we propose two competing hypotheses for board gender diversity:

H1a. Board gender diversity is positively associated with higher audit fees

H1b. Board gender diversity is negatively associated with higher audit fees

A diverse TMT could either raise or reduce the auditors' concerns about material misstatements. On one hand, a diverse TMT may lead to innovative thinking and enhanced decision-making capabilities, which can foster foresight capacity and a heightened sense of accountability among the team. Specifically, diverse leadership teams bring a variety of perspectives and problem-solving approaches, which can enhance the quality of strategic decisions and internal controls (Carter, Simkins, and Simpson, 2003). Enhanced decision-making capabilities can lead to better management of financial reporting risks, thus lowering the perceived risk for auditors. If auditors perceive that the TMT is effectively managing financial reporting risks, they are likely to reduce the extent of their substantive testing, resulting in lower audit fees.

Conversely, diversity within the TMT could also introduce concerns that might increase audit fees. If the diversity within the TMT results in unclear or inconsistent strategic direction due to conflicting viewpoints, or if it leads to delays in decision-making (Krause, Priem, and Love, 2015), auditors might perceive increased risks. In addition, TMT diversity initiatives, though designed to promote inclusivity, can inadvertently lead to perceived tokenism within an organization (Knippen, Shen, and Zhu, 2019). Tokenism, where individuals are seen as being selected based on their minority status rather than their qualifications, can have detrimental effects on group dynamics and overall talent retention. When diversity efforts are perceived as tokenistic, it can alienate talented individuals who feel that their contributions are undervalued or overshadowed by assumptions that they were promoted for diversity reasons (Jones et al., 2016). If auditors perceive that the TMT gender diversity is tokenistic, auditors might perceive increased risks. This increased audit effort, driven by the need to gather more evidence, would result in higher audit fees.

Additionally, the relationship between TMT diversity and audit outcomes might not be significant if the diversity does not lead to observable changes in strategic or accounting decisions. Given these arguments, the direction of the relationship between TMT gender diversity and audit fees is ex-ante unclear. We therefore propose two competing hypotheses:

H2a. TMT gender diversity is positively associated with higher audit fees

H2b. TMT gender diversity is negatively associated with higher audit fees

On 25 September 2015, the United Nations (UN) General Assembly adopted the 2030 Agenda for Sustainable Development, a pledge to "transform our world" and ensure no one is left behind in the economic, social, and environmental aspects of development (UN, 2015). This agenda is centered on 17 Sustainable Development Goals (SDGs), defining the sustainable development aspirations of UN Member countries and their stakeholders (Fukuda-Parr, 2014). Given that the SDGs are voluntary, lack sanctions, and have limited enforcement mechanisms, the 2030 Agenda constitutes a form of "soft" international law (Van Zanten and Van Tulder, 2018). While a large stream of research has developed around understanding the consequences of increased gender diversity, much less is known about the impact of a firm's commitment towards the Sustainable Development Goal (SDG) on gender diversity (Beloskar, Haldar, and Gupta, 2024).[3]

SDG 5, which aims to achieve gender equality and empower women, reflects a firm's broader commitment to ethical standards and social responsibility. This commitment may influence auditors' perception of the risk of material misstatements in two opposing ways. A firm's genuine commitment to SDG 5 may signal robust corporate governance and a proactive approach to compliance with evolving societal norms. Firms that authentically integrate gender diversity into their operational and strategic frameworks might exhibit stronger ethical behavior and better risk management practices. These firms are likely to implement comprehensive internal controls and transparent reporting practices, thereby reducing the perceived risk of material misstatement. This enhanced trust could potentially result in a lower perceived risk of material misstatements, thus reducing the need for extensive substantive testing and, consequently, lowering audit fees (Cohen et al., 2007; Collier and Gregory, 1996).

Conversely, if a firm's commitment to SDG 5 is perceived as superficial and symbolic, auditors may remain skeptical of the firm's true dedication to ethical practices and effective governance. This skepticism could arise if the firm's initiatives lack depth or tangible outcomes, leading auditors to question the reliability of the financial reporting process. In such cases, auditors may increase their audit procedures to mitigate the perceived higher risk of material misstatements, which would result in higher audit fees (Simunic, 1980; Hay et al., 2008).

Given these opposing possibilities, the relationship between a firm's commitment to SDG 5 and audit fees could manifest in two distinct ways. Therefore, we propose two competing hypotheses:

H3a: There is a negative relationship between a firm's commitment to SDG 5 on gender diversity and audit fees.

H3b: There is a positive relationship between a firm's commitment to SDG 5 on gender diversity and audit fees.

RESEARCH DESIGN

An extensive body of literature has examined the level and nature of audit fees in organizations. Most existing research on audit fees is based on the seminal work by Simunic (1980), who was the first to develop a positive model on the determinants of audit fees. Building on his initial model, the audit pricing literature has further developed (e.g., Ghosh and Lustgarten, 2006; Hay et al. 2006; Hogan and Wilkins, 2008; LópezPuertas-Lamy et al., 2017; Liu, Lobo and Yu, 2021; enhancing the list of relevant control variables. Building on the extensive audit fee literature, we specify the following enhanced audit fee pricing model:

$$\begin{aligned}
\text{Audit-Fees}_{it} = {} & \alpha + \beta_1 \text{Board-Gender-Diversity}_{it} + \beta_2 \text{TMT-Gender-Diversity}_{it} \\
& + \beta_3 \text{SDG5-Gender-Equality}_{it} + \beta_4 \text{Firm Size}_{it} + \beta_5 \text{Leverage}_{it} + \beta_6 \text{Return-on-Assets}_{it} \\
& + \beta_7 \text{RSales-Growth}_{it} + \beta_8 \text{Loss-in-current-year}_{it} + \beta_9 \beta_{12} \text{Current-Assets-to-Total-Assets}_{it} \\
& + \beta_{10} \text{ESG-Score}_{it} + \beta_{10} \text{Board-Independence}_{it} + \beta_{10} \text{CEO-Duality}_{it} \\
& + \beta_{10} \text{Auditor-Change}_{it} + \beta_{10} \text{Auditor-Tenure}_{it} + \text{Firm- Dummies} + \text{Year-Dummies} + \varepsilon_{it}
\end{aligned} \quad (1)$$

Consistent with the audit literature, we define our dependent variable (Audit-fees) as the natural logarithm of the total fees charged by the auditor for the financial statement audit work. Our three main variables of interest are *Board-Gender-Diversity* which is calculated as the percentage of female board members over the total number of board members. *TMT-Gender-Diversity,* which is calculated as the percentage of female TMT members over the total number of TMT members. Finally, *SDG5-*

Gender-Equality is an indicator variable equal to one when the firm has committed itself to the UN's SDG Goal 5 on Gender Equality.

The control variables related to client characteristics are defined as follows. *Size* is the natural logarithm of total assets. Size is one of the most important determinants of audit fees, as larger firms tend to have more accounts and more complex transactions, and thus larger audit fees (Hay et al., 2006). *Leverage* is the ratio of the sum of the long-term and short-term debt to total assets. We expect a positive effect of leverage on audit risk since leverage is linked to the risk of a client failing, which potentially exposes the auditor to loss (Hay et al., 2006). *Return-on-assets* is the ratio of net income to total assets. Higher return-on-assets ratios are expected to reflect lower financial risk and therefore a negative association with audit fees is expected (LópezPuertas-Lamy et al., 2017). *Sales-growth* is the percentage growth in sales. Positive signs are expected for both of these variables' coefficients since firms with large amounts of current assets and high growth ratios may require additional audit attention (LópezPuertas-Lamy et al., 2017). *Loss-in-current-year* is an indicator variable equal to one when the current year's net income is negative, and zero otherwise (Desender et al., 2016). Reporting a loss in the current year indicates higher financial risk and is expected to be positively related to audit fees (Desender et al., 2016). *Current-Assets-to-Total-Assets* is the ratio of current assets to total assets. We expect a positive relation between this variable and audit fees since large amounts of current assets may require additional audit attention (LópezPuertas-Lamy et al., 2017).

The control variables related to the firm's corporate governance characteristics are as follows. *ESG-Score* is the ESG score produced by Refinitiv Eikon. We expect a positive sign as ESG has been linked with stronger stakeholder ties and ethical standards (similar to Kim, Park, and Wier, 2012). We also control for *Board-Independence* which is the ratio of independent board members to the total number of board members. We expect a positive sign for board independence, as an active monitoring board is likely to share information and concerns with the external auditor about internal control weaknesses and other accounting issues (Carcello et al., 2002; Hay, Knechel and Ling, 2008; Desender et al., 2016). *CEO-duality* is an indicator variable equal to one when the CEO also holds the chair position, and zero otherwise. CEO duality is often viewed as an impediment to the board's monitoring of top executives (Aguilera and Jackson, 2003) and can serve to entrench a CEO within an organization by compromising the board's ability to monitor and discipline management. We expect a negative sign for CEO-duality (similar to Desender et al., 2013).

The control variables related to auditor characteristics are auditor-tenure and auditor-specialization. *Auditor-tenure* is defined as the number of years of the audit engagement. Following the mixed evidence in previous studies (Hay et al., 2006), we have no clear prediction on the direction of this variable. We expect a positive sign for the coefficient of auditor specialization, as specialized personnel may be more costly (Bell et al., 2001). *Auditor-Change* is an indicator variable equal to one when the client engages a new auditor in a given year and zero otherwise. Changing auditors is usually related to lower audit fees (Hay et al., 2006), which may be the result of discounts being offered to attract new business (a practice known as low-balling). In addition, due to the particular characteristics of our international sample, and to reduce omitted variable concerns, we add firm and year dummies.

In additional analyses, we consider the impact of board gender quotas and two relevant institutional dimensions. For each year, we identify whether a firm is subject to mandatory board gender quotas or not, using the latest report by Deloitte (2024) which summarizes the gender quota initiatives for each country and year. To examine the impact of gender quotas, we estimate equation (1) for two subsamples, i.e., the sample with firms that are subject to mandatory gender quotas and the sample that is not. At the institutional level, we draw on data from the World Bank Database to obtain two relevant institutional dimensions: Control of Corruption and Women in Parliament. *Control of Corruption* is an index variable that measures the extent to which public power is exercised for private gain; lower corruption levels are linked to transparent and merit-based business practices, potentially enhancing gender diversity. *Women in Parliament* measures the proportion of seats held by women in national parliaments. This metric represents the percentage of parliamentary seats in a single or lower chamber that are occupied by women, and reflect broader societal attitudes towards gender roles and equality. Societies that elect more women to legislative positions often have more progressive views on gender diversity and support for women in leadership roles. Conversely, low representation may indicate persistent gender biases and barriers. To examine the impact of the institutional context, we add the interaction between board gender diversity and the institutional dimension to equation (1). All variables are defined in the Appendix.

DATA AND SAMPLE DESCRIPTION

For our empirical investigation, we start from all the firms for which there is detailed audit fee data and corporate governance information available in the Refinitiv Eikon database over the period 2018-2022. As the gender diversity debate has become an important topic in the last years (Gormley et al., 2023), it is important to focus on recent data. We start our time period in 2018, as this is the first year for which data on the firms' commitment to SDG 5 is available for a large sample. Firm-level financial data are obtained from Refinitiv Eikon. We restrict our sample to firms that have a Big-4 auditor for consistency (only about ten percent of the initial observations had a non-Big-4 auditor). Finally, we winsorize our main variables at the one percent top and bottom levels to avoid outlier-related problems. Our final sample comprises 26,965 firm-year observations from 33 countries.

Table 1. Descriptive statistics

Variable	Observations	Mean	St.dev	Min	Max
Ln(Audit Fees)	26,965	13.824	1.398	10.003	18.201
Board Gender Diversity	26,965	0.223	0.144	0.000	1.000
TMT Gender Diversity	26,965	0.155	0.158	0.000	1.000
SDG Goal 5 - Gender equality	26,965	0.297	0.457	0.000	1.000
Ln(Total Assets)	26,965	21.586	1.770	14.758	27.780
Leverage	26,965	0.526	0.223	0.033	1.467
ROA	26,965	0.020	0.130	-1.075	0.300
Sales Growth	26,965	0.115	0.349	-0.937	3.290
Loss in past year	26,965	0.225	0.418	0.000	1.000
Current to Total Assets	26,965	0.425	0.238	0.000	1.000
ESG score	26,965	45.431	20.556	0.900	95.640
Board Independence	26,965	0.605	0.240	0.000	1.000
CEO duality	26,965	0.319	0.466	0.000	1.000
Auditor Change	26,965	0.084	0.278	0.000	1.000
Auditor Tenure	26,965	8.340	6.470	1.000	36.000
Control of Corruption	26,965	1.099	0.746	-1.323	2.403
Women in Parliament	26,965	0.277	0.094	0.012	0.504

This table describes the main variables used for the analysis. All variables span the 2018-2022 period and correspond to 26,965 firm-year observations from 33 countries. Variable definitions are provided in the Appendix.

Table 1 presents the summary statistics of the main variables used in the audit fee regressions. The mean audit fees are $2.9 million. The mean level of board gender diversity is 23.3 percent, while the mean TMT gender diversity is 15.5 percent. Close to 30 percent of all firms have made a commitment to SDG 5 on Gender Equality. Regarding the client firms' control variables, the mean total assets are $11.1 billion, while the mean leverage is 52.6 percent. The average return on assets is 2.0 percent, while 22.5 percent of firms report a negative net income in our sample. The mean growth in sales is 11.5 percent, while the ratio of current assets to total assets is 42.5 percent. The average board independence is 60.1 percent, while in only 32 percent of firm does the CEO hold the chair position. The average auditor tenure in our sample is around 8.3 years.

Table 2. Correlations

	Variable	1	2	3	4	5	6	7	8	9	10	11	12	13	14	15	16
1	Ln(Audit Fees)	1.00															
2	Board Gender Diversity	**0.17**	1.00														
3	TMT Gender Diversity	0.01	**0.36**	1.00													
4	SDG Goal 5 - Gender equality	**0.18**	**0.15**	**0.05**	1.00												
5	Ln(Total Assets)	**0.66**	**0.05**	-0.02	**0.27**	1.00											
6	Leverage	**0.35**	**0.12**	**0.03**	**0.07**	**0.28**	1.00										
7	ROA	-0.01	0.02	-0.01	**0.11**	**0.23**	**-0.13**	1.00									
8	Sales Growth	-0.03	0.00	0.00	-0.03	-0.04	-0.03	**0.07**	1.00								
9	Loss in past year	0.00	-0.01	0.01	**-0.11**	**-0.21**	**0.11**	**-0.66**	**-0.05**	1.00							
10	Current to Total Assets	**-0.15**	**-0.13**	**-0.10**	**-0.08**	**-0.27**	**-0.11**	**-0.10**	0.03	0.04	1.00						
11	ESG score	**0.48**	**0.32**	**0.12**	**0.44**	**0.54**	**0.18**	**0.18**	-0.09	**-0.17**	**-0.16**	1.00					
12	Board Independence	**0.27**	**0.31**	**0.16**	-0.03	0.00	**0.09**	-0.09	0.04	**0.10**	**-0.16**	**0.19**	1.00				
13	CEO duality	**0.14**	-0.04	-0.02	-0.05	**0.07**	0.04	0.00	0.03	0.01	0.03	-0.06	**0.08**	1.00			
14	Auditor Change	**-0.09**	-0.02	0.00	0.00	-0.03	-0.01	-0.01	0.00	0.01	0.01	-0.01	-0.06	-0.04	1.00		
15	Auditor Tenure	**0.29**	**0.06**	**0.04**	-0.01	**0.17**	**0.09**	**0.07**	-0.02	-0.05	**-0.11**	**0.09**	**0.27**	**0.16**	**-0.35**	1.00	
16	Control of Corruption	**0.27**	**0.24**	**0.05**	**0.07**	-0.06	**0.08**	-0.08	-0.04	**0.08**	**-0.17**	**0.13**	**0.23**	**-0.10**	-0.08	**0.12**	1.00
17	Women in Parliament	0.02	**0.44**	**0.23**	**0.04**	**-0.16**	**0.10**	-0.05	0.03	0.06	**-0.13**	0.06	**0.21**	-0.08	0.03	-0.07	**0.43**

This table presents the correlations of the main variables used for the analysis. All variables span the 2018-2022 period and correspond to 26,965 firm-year observations from 33 countries. Correlation coefficients that are significant at the 5% level are marked in bold. All variables are defined in the Appendix.

Table 2 presents the correlation matrix. The correlation between the Board gender diversity and audit fees is positive with a level of 0.17, which is indicative of a significant overall positive effect in the absence of relevant controls. TMT gender diversity shows a much weaker correlation of only 0.01, while commitment to the SDG Goal 5 on Gender equality shows a positive correlation of 0.18. Furthermore, audit-fees show relatively high correlation coefficients with firm size, leverage, current to total assets, ESG score, board independence, CEO duality and auditor tenure.

Table 3. Sample breakdown

Country	Obs	Board Gender Diversity	TMT Gender Diversity	SDG Goal 5 - Gender equality	Women in Parliament	ΔBoard Gender Diversity (2018-2022)	ΔTMT Gender Diversity (2018-2022)	ΔSDG Goal 5 - Gender equality (2019-2022)
Australia	1384	0.271	0.214	0.270	0.320	0.082	0.050	0.289
Austria	137	0.252	0.064	0.496	0.389	0.105	0.060	0.350
Belgium	189	0.357	0.178	0.361	0.412	0.050	-0.028	0.337
Brazil	29	0.093	0.050	0.630	0.155	-0.018	0.056	0.583
Canada	1261	0.253	0.165	0.283	0.292	0.059	0.041	0.224
China	3429	0.143	0.159	0.198	0.249	0.034	0.012	0.233
Cyprus	31	0.168	0.198	0.214	0.161	0.076	-0.006	0.000
Denmark	212	0.281	0.159	0.561	0.402	0.075	0.038	0.394
Finland	266	0.317	0.232	0.321	0.456	-0.020	0.034	0.221
France	627	0.443	0.190	0.531	0.392	0.018	0.072	0.246
Germany	987	0.253	0.091	0.330	0.329	0.013	0.045	0.241
Greece	63	0.118	0.173	0.623	0.209	0.097	-0.018	0.143
India	1223	0.181	0.085	0.313	0.144	0.046	0.031	0.017
Ireland	184	0.257	0.171	0.344	0.224	0.136	0.041	0.438
Israel	88	0.201	0.174	0.173	0.262	0.069	0.029	0.044
Italy	313	0.369	0.118	0.527	0.350	0.042	-0.013	0.347
Japan	2070	0.094	0.028	0.521	0.099	0.063	0.013	0.329
Korea	625	0.058	0.038	0.407	0.181	0.078	0.037	0.233
Luxembourg	123	0.208	0.133	0.472	0.295	0.074	-0.027	0.236
Malaysia	526	0.231	0.303	0.396	0.145	0.019	0.047	0.183
Netherlands	268	0.301	0.154	0.326	0.362	0.129	0.046	0.292
New Zealand	243	0.318	0.258	0.260	0.454	0.085	0.066	0.187
Norway	250	0.415	0.225	0.459	0.429	0.046	0.044	0.343
Poland	100	0.188	0.120	0.293	0.284	-0.030	-0.015	0.226
Portugal	48	0.277	0.180	0.725	0.382	0.130	0.116	0.364
Singapore	314	0.180	0.299	0.297	0.275	0.056	0.072	0.264
South Africa	396	0.308	0.249	0.411	0.457	0.072	0.051	0.277
Spain	251	0.272	0.165	0.607	0.427	0.132	0.081	0.382
Sweden	950	0.338	0.236	0.514	0.468	0.003	0.041	0.315
Switzerland	582	0.186	0.084	0.275	0.403	0.060	0.043	0.336
Turkey	69	0.187	0.109	0.739	0.173	0.202	0.121	0.583
United Kingdom	1984	0.282	0.184	0.327	0.335	0.075	0.048	0.247
United States	7743	0.224	0.162	0.136	0.258	0.080	0.035	0.072

This table presents an overview of the diversity dimensions per country. All variables span the 2018-2022 period and correspond to 26,965 firm-year observations from 33 countries. All variables are defined in the Appendix.

Table 3 presents a sample breakdown by country and present the mean values of board gender diversity and TMT gender diversity, the proportion of firms with a commitment to SDG 5 on Gender Equality. We have included the proportion of women in parliament to allow a comparison between corporate and political leadership. We also show for each country the 5-year change in board and TMT gender diversity and the 4-year change in the commitment to SDG 5 on Gender Equality by country. The country with the highest level of board gender diversity is France, standing at 44.3 percent, followed by Norway at 41.5 percent. In stark contrast, Korea records the lowest at only 5.8 percent, followed by Brazil (at 9.3 percent). Similarly, Malaysia stands out for its high TMT gender diversity, at 30.3 percent, followed by New Zealand (at 25.8 percent). On the other hand, Japan has the lowest TMT gender diversity with a mere 2.8 percent, followed by Korea (at 3.8 percent). When examining commitments to Sustainable Development Goal 5, which focuses on gender equality, Turkish firms score highest with 73.9 percent of Turkish firms showing this commitment. Finland has the second highest proportion of firms committed to the SDG 5. Conversely, the United States lags significantly behind with the lowest score, at 13.6 percent. Looking at the representation of women in parliament as a measure of comparison, Sweden features the highest percentage of women in parliament at 46.8 percent, whereas Japan shows a much lower female involvement in parliament with a score of 9.9 percent.

In terms of changes over time from 2018 to 2022 in board gender diversity, Turkey and Spain witnessed the most substantial increase, improving by 20.2 percent and 13.2 percent, respectively. Poland and Japan, however, experienced a decline in board gender diversity, reducing by 3 percent. For TMT gender diversity over the same period, Portugal saw the most significant improvement, with an increase of 11.6 percent, while Belgium saw a decline, each dropping by about 2.7 percent. Additionally, concerning changes in commitment to SDG 5 from 2019 to 2022, Brazil and Turkey both experienced notable increases, whereas India showed the smallest change at just 0.017.

EMPIRICAL RESULTS

In Table 4, model (1) estimates the baseline audit fee model with firm and year fixed effects (equation 1). In model (2), we include Board Gender Diversity, while in model (3) we include TMT Gender Diversity. In model (4) we include the firm's commitment to the SDG 5 as our main variable of interest. Finally, model (5) includes all three dimensions of gender diversity.

The results for model (1) shows the expected signs for the control variables. Specifically, larger, and less profitable firms tend to incur higher audit fees. Leverage also significantly impacts audit fees, with higher leverage leading to increased audit costs. This indicates that firms with greater financial risk are subject to more rigorous audit procedures, as auditors need to address the heightened risk of financial misstatements. Sales growth is another significant factor, with higher growth rates associated with increased audit fees. Lastly, the ratio of current assets to total assets is significantly negatively related to audit fees. Firms with a higher proportion of current assets tend to have lower audit fees, possibly because current assets are generally simpler to audit compared to non-current assets, reducing the overall audit effort required.

Table 4. Regression results: Gender diversity and audit fees

DV: Ln(Audit Fees)	(1)	(2)	(3)	(4)	(5)
Board Gender Diversity		0.099***			0.101***
		(0.036)			(0.038)
TMT Gender Diversity			0.01		-0.002
			(0.030)	0.00	(0.030)
SDG Goal 5 - Gender equality				-0.002	-0.001
				(0.007)	(0.007)
Ln(Total Assets)	0.342***	0.341***	0.342***	0.338***	0.337***
	(0.015)	(0.015)	(0.016)	(0.017)	(0.017)
Leverage	0.089**	0.086**	0.090**	0.080*	0.078*
	(0.040)	(0.040)	(0.040)	(0.045)	(0.045)
ROA	-0.308***	-0.307***	-0.306***	-0.310***	-0.307***
	(0.039)	(0.039)	(0.039)	(0.043)	(0.043)
Sales Growth	0.044***	0.044***	0.044***	0.041***	0.042***
	(0.007)	(0.007)	(0.007)	(0.008)	(0.008)
Loss in past year	-0.001	-0.001	-0.001	0.000	0.000
	(0.007)	(0.007)	(0.007)	(0.008)	(0.008)
Current to Total Assets	-0.120***	-0.120***	-0.120***	-0.132***	-0.133***
	(0.043)	(0.043)	(0.043)	(0.047)	(0.047)
ESG score	0.000	0.000	0.000	0.000	0.000
	(0.000)	(0.000)	(0.000)	(0.000)	(0.000)

continued on following page

Table 4. Continued

DV: Ln(Audit Fees)	(1)	(2)	(3)	(4)	(5)
Board Independence	0.038	0.032	0.040	0.037	0.033
	(0.029)	(0.029)	(0.029)	(0.031)	(0.031)
CEO duality	-0.015	-0.015	-0.014	-0.019*	-0.019*
	(0.010)	(0.010)	(0.010)	(0.011)	(0.011)
Auditor Change	-0.019**	-0.019**	-0.019**	-0.019**	-0.019**
	(0.008)	(0.008)	(0.008)	(0.009)	(0.009)
Auditor Tenure	-0.002*	-0.002*	-0.002*	-0.002*	-0.002*
	(0.001)	(0.001)	(0.001)	(0.001)	(0.001)
Constant	6.388***	6.402***	6.389***	6.446***	6.463***
	(0.338)	(0.337)	(0.338)	(0.371)	(0.370)
Firm-Fixed Effects	Y	Y	Y	Y	Y
Year-Fixed Effects	Y	Y	Y	Y	Y
R-squared	0.17	0.17	0.169	0.153	0.153
N	26965	26965	26965	23913	23856

* $p<0.10$, ** $p<0.05$, *** $p<0.01$. The dependent variable for all models is the natural logarithm of Audit fees. Specifications (1) to (4) report the regression results from the audit fee model (equation 1). All variables are defined in the Appendix. Standard errors are reported in parentheses.

In model (2), the coefficient of Board Gender Diversity is positive and significant at the one percent level. This result suggests that after controlling for other factors, a 10 percent increase in Board Gender Diversity is associated with an increase in the audit fees by 1 percent. This result is in line with the idea that gender-diverse boards, shares information and concerns with the external auditor about internal control weaknesses and other accounting issues, leading to more extensive audit procedures.

In Model (3), we shift our focus to TMT Gender Diversity. Diverse TMTs may introduce innovative thinking and varied approaches to problem-solving, which could affect the firm's operations and, subsequently, its audit fees. Alternatively, TMT Gender Diversity could introduce added complexities that require additional audit scrutiny. The coefficient is close to zero, and the result do not lend support to either H2a or H2b.

Model (4) introduces the firm's commitment to Sustainable Development Goal (SDG) 5. A firm's commitment to SDG 5 reflects its adherence to broader ethical standards and social responsibility. From an auditor's perspective, this commitment can influence the perceived risk of material misstatements. If a firm genuinely integrates gender equality into its operations, it may signal robust governance and ethical behavior, potentially reducing audit fees. Conversely, if auditors perceive this commitment as superficial or as greenwashing, it could lead to increased audit procedures and higher fees to mitigate the perceived risks. The coefficient is close to zero, and the result do not lend support to either H3a or H3b.

Finally, Model (5) incorporates all three dimensions of gender diversity: Board Gender Diversity, TMT Gender Diversity, and the firm's commitment to SDG 5. When we consider all gender diversity dimensions in the same regression, the result for board gender diversity remains significant with a slightly larger magnitude. These results highlight the importance of board diversity for the external audit process, in line with our hypothesis 1a. The positive effect is in line with the idea that a gender diverse board, instead of actively improving internal controls and overall reliability of financial reporting, share information and concerns with the external auditor about internal control weaknesses and other accounting issues. This information then leads the auditor to increase the amount of audit evidence and, hence, the audit fees. The coefficients for TMT gender diversity and the firm's commitment to SDG 5 are not significant.

ADDITIONAL ANALYSES: THE ROLE OF BOARD GENDER QUOTAS

To better understand the positive effect of board gender diversity on audit fees, we next examine whether these results are weaker or stronger in countries that enforce gender quotas.

While gender quotas may induce a critical mass of female directors on the one hand, thereby strengthening the monitoring ability of female directors, it could also lead to tokenism and symbolic compliance, which could weaken their monitoring ability (Solal and Snellman, 2019). The concept of a critical mass suggests that once a certain threshold of female representation on boards is reached, female directors are more likely to exert significant influence on board decisions and governance practices (Torchia, Calabrò, & Huse, 2011). On the other hand, the implementation of gender quotas may also lead to tokenism, where female directors are appointed to meet regulatory requirements rather than based on their qualifications and potential contributions. Tokenism can undermine the effectiveness of female directors by isolating them and subjecting them to increased scrutiny and pressure (Knippen et al., 2019). To the extent that board gender quotas would induce symbolic compliance, it may weakening the monitoring role of female directors.

To examine the relevance of board gender quotas, in Table 5 we split our sample between countries with (model 7) and without board gender quotas (model 6). The results show a strong significant sign for board gender diversity for our subsample of firms in countries without board gender quotas. For countries with board gender quotas, the coefficient is also positive, but not significant. These results are in line with the idea that board quotas may induce a greater level of tokenism, which could limit the ability of female directors to influence board monitoring, and financial reporting quality.

Table 5. Regression results: The role of quotas and institutions

DV: Ln(Audit Fees)	(6)	(7)	(8)	(9)
Sample	No Quotas	Quotas	Full Sample	Full Sample
Board Gender Diversity	0.107***	0.036	-0.139**	-0.317***
	(0.040)	(0.080)	(0.061)	(0.109)
Control of Corruption			-0.060**	
			(0.025)	
Control of Corruption*Board Gender Diversity			0.189***	
			(0.043)	
Women in Parliament				-0.365**
				(0.162)
Women in Parliament *Board Gender Diversity				1.404***
				(0.355)
Ln(Total Assets)	0.346***	0.304***	0.340***	0.340***
	(0.016)	(0.047)	(0.015)	(0.015)
Leverage	0.06	0.274**	0.085**	0.086**
	(0.041)	(0.119)	(0.040)	(0.040)
ROA	-0.344***	-0.02	-0.306***	-0.305***
	(0.042)	(0.113)	(0.039)	(0.039)
Sales Growth	0.049***	-0.001	0.043***	0.044***
	(0.008)	(0.020)	(0.007)	(0.007)
Loss in past year	-0.002	0.009	0.000	-0.001
	(0.008)	(0.018)	(0.007)	(0.007)
Current to Total Assets	-0.098**	-0.217*	-0.121***	-0.118***
	(0.044)	(0.118)	(0.043)	(0.043)
ESG score	0.000	0.001	0.000	0.000
	(0.000)	(0.001)	(0.000)	(0.000)
Board Independence	0.039	0.004	0.027	0.033
	(0.036)	(0.050)	(0.029)	(0.029)
CEO duality	-0.018*	0.008	-0.015	-0.014
	(0.011)	(0.030)	(0.010)	(0.010)

continued on following page

Table 5. Continued

DV: Ln(Audit Fees)	(6)	(7)	(8)	(9)
Auditor Change	-0.017*	-0.025	-0.020**	-0.018**
	(0.009)	(0.019)	(0.008)	(0.008)
Auditor Tenure	-0.002*	-0.001	-0.002*	-0.002
	(0.001)	(0.003)	(0.001)	(0.001)
Constant	6.364***	6.767***	6.499***	6.508***
	(0.338)	(1.014)	(0.336)	(0.337)
Firm-Fixed Effects	Y	Y	Y	Y
Year-Fixed Effects	Y	Y	Y	Y
R-squared	0.18	0.134	0.171	0.171
N	22265	4938	26965	26965

* $p<0.10$, ** $p<0.05$, *** $p<0.01$. The dependent variable for all models is the natural logarithm of Audit fees. Specifications (6) and (7) report the regression results from the audit fee model (1), when we split our sample between firms that are subject to mandatory board gender quotas, and those that are not. We obtain data on board gender quotas from the latest report by Deloitte (2024) which summarizes the gender quota initiatives for each country and year. Specification (8) reports the regression results from the audit fee model (equation 1), when adding the interaction between board gender diversity and control of corruption, while specification (9) reports the regression results from the audit fee model (1), when adding the interaction between board gender diversity and Women in Parliament. All variables are defined in the Appendix. Standard errors are reported in parentheses.

ADDITIONAL ANALYSES: THE IMPORTANCE OF INSTITUTIONS

Scholars working in the fields of comparative capitalism and cross-national governance have long acknowledged that institutions matter for explaining firms' adoption of certain structures and practices, and that substantial variation exists across countries in terms of the institutions that matter most (Aguilera and Jackson, 2003; Bell, Filatotchev and Aguilera, 2014; Desender et al., 2020; Hall and Soskice, 2001). Different countries feature different institutional configurations, reflecting the "rules of the game" with respect to social relations as well as economic activity (Matten and Moon, 2008). To better understand the positive link between board gender diversity and audit fees, we next explore whether board gender diversity plays a stronger role in societies that facilitate trust, transparency and gender equality.

Whitley et al. (1996) argue that when there is a lack of generalized trust in society, managers tend to rely on informal networks and trust, often based on family or clan relationships (Kong, 2016). Conversely, societies characterized by trust and social capital tend to foster altruistic behavior and discourage self-serving conduct (Onyx and Bullen, 2000). In the context of corporate boards, McDonald and Westphal (2013) suggest that women's exclusion from elite social networks limits their access to social capital, mentoring, and patronage resources, which are important for influential board appointments. Additionally, Allemand et al. (2022) propose that recruitment practices based on networks may impact board gender diversity, as different genders tend to belong to different networks, and directors' and CEOs' networks influence their appointments. Promoting equality and civil liberties is also linked to higher representation of women in top government positions, such as parliament (Inglehart et al., 2002), implying that talented women may aspire to similar positions in other organizations, including corporations. In this line, Carrasco et al. (2015) find that a nation's tolerance for equality is associated with greater representation of women on corporate boards. We therefore expect that countries characterized by higher social capital and trust may provide a supportive environment for women to pursue leadership roles, thereby leading to a greater influence on board monitoring.

To capture a society's orientation toward trust and equality, we focus on two measures. Our first measure is "Control of Corruption" an index developed by the World Bank. This measure reflects perceptions of the extent to which public power is exercised for private gain, including both petty and grand forms of corruption, as well as "capture" of the state by elites and private interests, taking into account various dimensions such as the frequency of extra-legal payments to obtain favorable judicial decisions and the prevalence of nepotism in the civil service . Our second measure "Women in Parliament", provided by the World Bank, measures the proportion of parliamentary seats held by women in a country's national legislature. This indicator measures the role of women in political decision-making at the highest levels.

Table 5 shows the regression results when we consider the two interaction terms, in models (8) and (9). In model (8), we interact board gender diversity with control of corruption, and find that the effect of board gender diversity on audit fees critically depend on the institutional context. In settings where corruption is perceived to be high, board gender diversity is negatively related to audit fees, while the relationship becomes positive as control of corruption improves. This result provide support to the idea that female directors have a greater influence in settings that emphasize transparency and fairness. Model (9) find a similar result, when we consider the proportion of women in parliament. For countries with low female political representation, the relationship between board impendence and audit fees is negative, but this relationship becomes positive as female political representation increases.

DISCUSSION

The lack of gender diversity of corporate boards and leadership has been one of the most significant issues in corporate governance in recent years (Gow et al., 2023). Previous literature (e.g., (Adams and Ferreira, 2009; Chen et al., 2016; Cumming et al., 2015; Post and Byron, 2015) presented a two-sided debate on how gender diversity at the board or TMT level may affect financial reporting quality. While one side of the debate argues that enhanced gender diversity is linked to enhanced creative thinking and decision-making and a lower likelihood to engage and accept opportunistic behaviors, the other side explains the pressure on gender diversity could lead to tokenism, where the presence of female directors becomes more about compliance than enhancing board and TMT effectiveness. The prior research that has examined the link between board gender diversity and financial reporting quality has mostly focused on a single dimension of gender diversity in a single country, and presents mixed evidence.

In this study, we provide a comprehensive examination of whether and how gender diversity at the board and TMT level, as well as the firm's commitment to the UN's Sustainable Development Goal on Gender equality (SDG5) influences financial reporting quality, by studying the independent auditors' assessment of the risk of material misstatements. To the extent that gender diverse boards adopt a stronger monitoring role, board gender diversity can affect financial reporting quality, and in particular, audit fees in two opposite directions. First, a negative relationship is expected if a gender diverse board takes an active role in improving the design of internal controls and internal governance in general. A greater reliance on internal controls would therefore result in less substantive audit testing and a lower audit fee (Cohen et al., 2007; Collier and Gregory, 1996). Second, a positive relation is expected if a gender diverse board, instead of actively improving internal controls, shares information and concerns with the external auditor about internal control weaknesses and other accounting issues. This information obtained from a more engaged board may lead the auditor to increase the amount of audit evidence and hence the audit fees. When considering diversity at the TMT level or the firm's commitment to the UN's Sustainable Development Goal on Gender equality, the same set of arguments does not necessarily apply, as the role of the board and the TMT is fundamentally different. A diverse Top Management Team (TMT) can lead to both increased and decreased audit concerns about material misstatements. On one hand, diversity can enhance decision-making and strategic oversight, thereby reducing the perceived risk of material misstatements and potentially lowering audit fees. On the other hand, tokenism could potentially increasing audit risks and resulting in higher audit fees. Finally, while a firm's genuine commitment to SDG 5 may signal ethical practices, potentially lowering the perceived risk of material misstatements and audit fees, superficial compliance might lead to skepticism and higher audit fees due to increased audit procedures.

Employing a large global dataset, we find a positive relationship between board gender diversity and audit fees, which is consistent with an active monitoring role by the board. These results are in line with the findings of Lai et al. (2017) for a U.S. sample and Ittonen et al. (2010) for Finnish firms, and go against the findings of Nekhili et al. (2020) who find a negative effect in French firms. In contrast, we do not find a significant effect of TMT gender diversity, nor for the firm's commitment to the SDG 5 on Gender Equality. Compared to our findings at the TMT level, Huang, Huang, and Lee (2014) find that firms with female CEOs are associated with higher audit fees for a sample of U.S. firms over the period 2003-2010.

In addition, we find that the relationship between board gender diversity and audit fees is mainly driven by firms in countries without mandatory board gender quotas. This result is in line with the findings of Sultana, Cahan, and Rahman (2020), who note that the positive association between audit committee gender diversity and audit quality becomes weaker after the introduction of diversity guidelines in Australia. We also show that the relationship between board gender diversity and audit fees is especially strong in settings where there is a lower perception of corruption and a greater representation of females in parliament.

Our results reinforce the importance of board gender diversity for effective corporate governance, but also highlight the need to consider local institutional factors when implementing diversity policies. This nuanced understanding aids in reconciling the mixed results from previous studies and provides a richer perspective on how gender diversity influences financial reporting and audit practices globally. This study also opens an avenue for future research that re-examines the importance of institutional factors to better understand international differences in audit pricing. Comparative studies across countries with different regulatory environments, cultural norms, and levels of gender equality could provide valuable insights into how these factors interact with organizational gender diversity to influence corporate governance and audit practices. Further research could also explore the interaction between gender diversity and other dimensions of diversity, such as racial and ethnic diversity, to examine their combined effects on corporate governance and audit outcomes. Investigating these interactions could reveal whether different types of diversity complement or substitute for each other in enhancing governance and reducing audit risk. Additionally, incorporating qualitative data through case studies or interviews could offer richer insights into the roles and influence of female directors and executives within organizations, thereby providing a more nuanced understanding of gender diversity's impact.

One important limitation of our study relates to the measurement of gender diversity, which focuses on gender diversity at the board and TMT level. However, this approach may not fully capture the complexity and nuances of gender diversity within organizations. For instance, merely having female directors and executives does not necessarily mean they have significant influence or roles within the organization. Another limitation of our study is the inability to rule out endogeneity. While the models in this study include a comprehensive set of controls, and audit fees reflect an independent and expert perspective, unobserved variables may still influence both the independent and dependent variables, potentially biasing our results.

CONCLUSION

Our study investigates the influence of gender diversity at the board and Top Management Team (TMT) levels, as well as firms' commitment to the UN's Sustainable Development Goal on Gender Equality (SDG5), on audit fees. Through a comprehensive analysis of a large global dataset from 2018-2022, we find a significant positive relationship between board gender diversity and audit fees, indicating that gender-diverse boards engage in more active monitoring, thereby increasing the perceived audit risk and associated fees. In contrast, we do not find a significant effect for TMT gender diversity and commitment to SDG5. Additionally, we show that the effect of board gender diversity on audit fees is more pronounced in countries without mandatory gender quotas and in environments with lower corruption and higher female parliamentary representation. These findings underscore the complex role of gender diversity in corporate governance and its varying implications across different institutional settings, enriching the current understanding of how gender dynamics influence audit practices and financial reporting quality.

ACKNOWLEDGEMENT

The authors acknowledge financial support from the Spanish Agencia Estatal de Investigación (PID2022-140026NB-I00 & PID2019-111143GB-C32/AEI/10.13039/501100011033).

REFERENCES

Adams, R. B., & Ferreira, D. (2009). Women in the boardroom and their impact on governance and performance. *Journal of Financial Economics*, 94(2), 291–309. DOI: 10.1016/j.jfineco.2008.10.007

Aguilera, R. V., Desender, K., & López-Puertas Lamy, M. (2021). Bridging accounting and Corporate Governance: New avenues of research. *The International Journal of Accounting*, 56(01), 2180001. DOI: 10.1142/S1094406021800019

Aguilera, R. V., & Jackson, G. (2003). The cross-national diversity of corporate governance: Dimensions and determinants. *Academy of Management Review*, 28(3), 447–465. DOI: 10.2307/30040732

Allemand, I., Bédard, J., Brullebaut, B., & Deschênes, J. (2022). Role of old boys' networks and regulatory approaches in selection processes for female directors. *British Journal of Management*, 33(2), 784–805. DOI: 10.1111/1467-8551.12485

Arlow, P. (1991). Personal characteristics in college students' evaluations of business ethics and corporate social responsibility. *Journal of Business Ethics*, 10(1), 63–69. DOI: 10.1007/BF00383694

Bedard, J., & Johnstone, K. (2004). Earnings manipulation risk, corporate governance risk, and auditors' planning decisions. *The Accounting Review*, 79(2), 277–304. DOI: 10.2308/accr.2004.79.2.277

Bell, T. B., Landsman, W. R., & Shackelford, D. A. (2001). Auditors' perceived business risk and audit fees: Analysis and evidence. *Journal of Accounting Research*, 39(1), 35–43. DOI: 10.1111/1475-679X.00002

Beloskar, V. D., Haldar, A., & Gupta, A. (2024). Gender equality and women's empowerment: A bibliometric review of the literature on SDG 5 through the management lens. *Journal of Business Research*, 172(114442). DOI: 10.1016/j.jbusres.2023.114442

Benton, R. A. (2021). Women in the inner circle: Gender and director networks after the fracturing of the corporate elite. *Organization Science*, 32(6), 1492–1522. DOI: 10.1287/orsc.2021.1433

Bernardi, R. A., & Arnold, D. F.Sr. (1997). An examination of moral development within public accounting by gender, staff level, and firm. *Contemporary Accounting Research*, 14(4), 653–668. DOI: 10.1111/j.1911-3846.1997.tb00545.x

Bravo, F., & Alcaide-Ruiz, M. D. (2019). The impact of board gender diversity on earnings management: Evidence from Spain. *Sustainability*, 11(3), 658.

Carcello, J. V., Hermanson, D. R., Neal, T. L., & Riley, R. R.Jr. (2002). Board characteristics and audit fees. *Contemporary Accounting Research*, 19(3), 365–384.

Carrasco, A., Francoeur, C., Labelle, R., Laffarga, J., & Ruiz-Barbadillo, E. (2015). Appointing women to boards: Is there a cultural bias? *Journal of Business Ethics*, 129(2), 429–444. DOI: 10.1007/s10551-014-2166-z

Chen, G., Crossland, C., & Huang, S. (2016). Female board representation and corporate acquisition intensity. *Strategic Management Journal*, 37(2), 303–313. DOI: 10.1002/smj.2323

Cohen, J. R., Krishnamoorthy, G., & Wright, A. M. (2007). The impact of roles of the board on auditors' risk assessments and program planning decisions. *Auditing*, 26(1), 91–112. DOI: 10.2308/aud.2007.26.1.91

Cumming, D., Leung, T. Y., & Rui, O. (2015). Gender diversity and securities fraud. *Academy of Management Journal*, 58(5), 1571–1593. DOI: 10.5465/amj.2013.0750

DeFond, M., & Zhang, J. (2014). A review of archival auditing research. A review of archival auditing research. *Journal of Accounting and Economics*, 58(2), 275–326. DOI: 10.1016/j.jacceco.2014.09.002

Deloitte. (2024). *Women in the boardroom: a global perspective*. Deloitte Global Boardroom Program, Eight Edition.

Desender, K., Aguilera, R. V., Crespi-Cladera, R., & Garcia Cestona, M. A. (2013). When does ownership matter? Board characteristics and behavior. *Strategic Management Journal*, 34(7), 823–842. DOI: 10.1002/smj.2046

Desender, K. A. & LópezPuertas-Lamy, M. (2024). What drives corporate gender diversity in Latin America? Working Paper.

Desender, K. A., Aguilera, R. V., Lópezpuertas-Lamy, M., & Crespi, R. (2016). A clash of governance logics: Foreign ownership and board monitoring: Foreign Ownership and Board Monitoring. *Strategic Management Journal*, 37(2), 349–369. DOI: 10.1002/smj.2344

Desender, K. A., LópezPuertas-Lamy, M., Pattitoni, P., & Petracci, B. (2020). Corporate social responsibility and cost of financing—The importance of the international corporate governance system. *Corporate Governance*, 28(3), 207–234. DOI: 10.1111/corg.12312

European Parliament and Council of the European Union. Directive (EU) 2022/2381 of 23 November 2022 on improving the gender balance among directors of listed companies and related measures. *Official Journal of the European Union*, L 315, 44-56.

Fukuda-Parr, S. (2014). Global goals as a policy tool: Intended and unintended consequences. *Journal of Human Development and Capabilities*, 15(2–3), 118–131. DOI: 10.1080/19452829.2014.910180

Garcia-Sanchez, I. M., Martinez-Ferrero, J., & Garcia-Meca, E. (2017). Gender diversity, financial expertise and its effects on accounting quality. *Management Decision*, 55(2), 347–382. DOI: 10.1108/MD-02-2016-0090

Ghosh, A., & Lustgarten, S. (2006). Pricing of initial audit engagements by large and small audit firms. *Contemporary Accounting Research*, 23(2), 333–368. DOI: 10.1506/927U-JGJY-35TA-7NT1

Ghosh, A., & Tang, C. Y. (2015). Assessing financial reporting quality of family firms: The auditors perspective. *Journal of Accounting and Economics*, 60(1), 95–116. DOI: 10.1016/j.jacceco.2015.03.002

Gormley, T. A., Gupta, V. K., Matsa, D. A., Mortal, S. C., & Yang, L. (2023). The Big Three and board gender diversity: The effectiveness of shareholder voice. *Journal of Financial Economics*, 149(2), 323–348. DOI: 10.1016/j.jfineco.2023.04.001

Gow, I. D., Larcker, D. F., & Watts, E. M. (2023). Board diversity and shareholder voting. *Journal of Corporate Finance*, 83(102487), 102487. DOI: 10.1016/j.jcorpfin.2023.102487

Gregory, A., & Collier, P. (1996). Audit fees and auditor change: An investigation of the persistence of fee reduction by type of change. *Journal of Business Finance & Accounting*, 23(1), 13–28. DOI: 10.1111/j.1468-5957.1996.tb00399.x

Hall, P. A., & Soskice, D. (Eds.). (2001). *Varieties of capitalism: The institutional foundations of comparative advantage.* Oxford University Press. DOI: 10.1093/0199247757.001.0001

Harjoto, M. A., Laksmana, I., & Lee, R. (2015). The impact of demographic characteristics of CEOs and directors on audit fees and audit delay. *Managerial Auditing Journal*, 30(8/9), 963–997. DOI: 10.1108/MAJ-01-2015-1147

Hay, D., Knechel, W. R., & Ling, H. (2008). Evidence on the impact of internal control and corporate governance on audit fees. *International Journal of Auditing*, 12(1), 9–24. DOI: 10.1111/j.1099-1123.2008.00367.x

Hay, D., Knechel, W. R., & Wong, N. (2006). Audit fees: A meta-analysis of the effect of supply and demand attributes. *Contemporary Accounting Research*, 23(1), 141–191. DOI: 10.1506/4XR4-KT5V-E8CN-91GX

Hogan, C. E., & Wilkins, M. S. (2008). Evidence on the audit risk model: Do auditors increase audit fees in the presence of internal control deficiencies? *Contemporary Accounting Research*, 25(1), 219–242. DOI: 10.1506/car.25.1.9

Houston, R. W., Peters, M. F., & Pratt, J. H. (1999). The audit risk model, business risk and audit planning decisions. *The Accounting Review*, 74(3), 281–298. DOI: 10.2308/accr.1999.74.3.281

Huang, T.-C., Huang, H.-W., & Lee, C.-C. (2014). Corporate executive's gender and audit fees. *Managerial Auditing Journal*, 29(6), 527–547. DOI: 10.1108/MAJ-03-2013-0837

Huse, M., & Solberg, A. (2006). Gender related boardroom dynamics: How women make and can make contributions on corporate boards. *Women in Management Review*, 21(2), 113–130. DOI: 10.1108/09649420610650693

Inglehart, R., Norris, P., & Welzel, C. (2002). Gender equality and democracy. *Comparative Sociology*, 1(3–4), 321–345.

Ittonen, K., Miettinen, J., & Vähämaa, S. (2010). Does female representation on audit committees affect audit fees? *Quarterly Journal of Finance and Accounting*, 49(3), 113–139.

Johnstone, K., Grambling, A., & Rittenberg, L. E. (2014). *Auditing: A risk-based approach to conducting a quality audit* (10th ed.). Cengage Learning.

Jones, K. P., Peddie, C. I., Gilrane, V. L., King, E. B., & Gray, A. L. (2016). Not So Subtle: A Meta-Analytic Investigation of the Correlates of Subtle and Overt Discrimination. *Journal of Management*, 42(6), 1588–1613. DOI: 10.1177/0149206313506466

Kim, Y., Park, M. S., & Wier, B. (2012). Is earnings quality associated with corporate social responsibility? *The Accounting Review*, 87(3), 761–796. DOI: 10.2308/accr-10209

Knechel, W. R., & Willekens, M. (2006). The role of risk management and governance in determining audit demand. *Journal of Business Finance & Accounting*, 33(9-10), 1344–1367. DOI: 10.1111/j.1468-5957.2006.01238.x

Knippen, J. M., Shen, W., & Zhu, Q. (2019). Limited progress? The effect of external pressure for board gender diversity on the increase of female directors. *Strategic Management Journal*, 40(7), 1123–1150. DOI: 10.1002/smj.3014

Kong, D. T. (2016). A gene-dependent climatoeconomic model of generalized trust. *Journal of World Business*, 51(2), 226–236. DOI: 10.1016/j.jwb.2015.08.018

Krause, R., Priem, R., & Love, L. (2015). Who's in charge here? Co-CEOs, power gaps, and firm performance: Co-CEOs, Power Gaps, and Firm Performance. *Strategic Management Journal*, 36(13), 2099–2110. DOI: 10.1002/smj.2325

Krishnan, G. V., & Parsons, L. M. (2008). Getting to the bottom line: An exploration of gender and earnings quality. *Journal of Business Ethics*, 78(1–2), 65–76. DOI: 10.1007/s10551-006-9314-z

Lai, K. M. Y., Srinidhi, B., Gul, F. A., & Tsui, J. S. L. (2017). Board gender diversity, auditor fees, and auditor choice. *Contemporary Accounting Research*, 34(3), 1681–1714. DOI: 10.1111/1911-3846.12313

Liu, M., & Wysocki, P. (2007). Cross-sectional determinants of information quality proxies and cost of capital measures. *The Quarterly Journal of Finance*, 7(2), 1650016. DOI: 10.1142/S2010139216500166

Liu, X., Lobo, G. J., & Yu, H.-C. (2021). Is audit committee equity compensation related to audit fees? *Contemporary Accounting Research*, 38(1), 740–769. DOI: 10.1111/1911-3846.12632

LópezPuertas-Lamy, M., Desender, K., & Epure, M. (2017). Corporate social responsibility and the assessment by auditors of the risk of material misstatement. *Journal of Business Finance & Accounting*, 44(9-10), 1276–1314. DOI: 10.1111/jbfa.12268

Matten, D., & Moon, J. (2008). "Implicit" and "Explicit" CSR: A conceptual framework for a comparative understanding of corporate social responsibility. *Academy of Management Review*, 33(2), 404–424. DOI: 10.5465/amr.2008.31193458

McDonald, M. L., & Westphal, J. D. (2013). Access denied: Low mentoring of women and minority first-time directors and its negative effect on appointments to additional boards. *Academy of Management Journal*, 56(4), 1169–1198. DOI: 10.5465/amj.2011.0230

McInerney-Lacombe, N., Billimoria, D., & Salipante, P. (2008). Championing the discussion of tough issues: How women corporate directors contribute to board deliberations. In Vinnicombe, S., Singh, V., Burke, R. J., Billimoria, D., & Huse, M. (Eds.), *Women on corporate boards of directors* (pp. 123–129). Edward Elgar. DOI: 10.4337/9781848445192.00021

Nekhili, M., Gull, A. A., Chtioui, T., & Radhouane, I. (2020). Gender-diverse boards and audit fees: What difference does gender quota legislation make? *Journal of Business Finance & Accounting*, 47(1–2), 52–99. DOI: 10.1111/jbfa.12409

Perryman, A. A., Fernando, G. D., & Tripathy, A. (2016). Do gender differences persist? An examination of gender diversity on firm performance, risk, and executive compensation. *Journal of Business Research*, 69(2), 579–586. DOI: 10.1016/j.jbusres.2015.05.013

Post, C., & Byron, K. (2015). Women on boards and firm financial performance: A meta-analysis. *Academy of Management Journal*, 58(5), 1546–1571. DOI: 10.5465/amj.2013.0319

PwC Report. (2022). ESG-focused institutional investment seen soaring 84% to US$33.9 trillion in 2026, making up 21.5% of assets under management.

Reddy, S., & Jadhav, A. M. (2019). Gender diversity in boardrooms – A literature review. *Cogent Economics & Finance*, 7(1), 1644703. DOI: 10.1080/23322039.2019.1644703

Simunic, D. (1980). The pricing of audit services: Theory and evidence. *Journal of Accounting Research*, 18(1), 161–190. DOI: 10.2307/2490397

Simunic, D., & Stein, M. (1996). The impact of litigation risk on audit pricing: A review of the economics and the evidence. *Auditing*, 15(Supplement), 119–134.

Solal, I., & Snellman, K. (2019). Women don't mean business? Gender penalty in board composition. *Organization Science*, 30(6), 1270–1288. DOI: 10.1287/orsc.2019.1301

Srinidhi, B., Gul, F. A., & Tsui, J. S. L. (2011). Female directors and earnings quality. *Contemporary Accounting Research*, 28(5), 1610–1644. DOI: 10.1111/j.1911-3846.2011.01071.x

Srinidhi, B., Sun, Y., & Zhang, H. (2015). Why are female board directors more effective norm-change agents than male directors? Working paper, University of Texas at Arlington.

Sultana, N., Cahan, S. F., & Rahman, A. (2020). Do gender diversity recommendations in corporate governance codes matter? Evidence from audit committees. *Auditing*, 39(1), 173–197. DOI: 10.2308/ajpt-52560

Thorne, L., Massey, D. W., & Magnan, M. (2003). Institutional context and auditors' moral reasoning: A Canada-U.S. comparison. *Journal of Business Ethics*, 43(4), 305–321. DOI: 10.1023/A:1023005311277

Torchia, M., Calabrò, A., & Huse, M. (2011). Women directors on corporate boards: From tokenism to critical mass. *Journal of Business Ethics*, 102(2), 299–317. DOI: 10.1007/s10551-011-0815-z

United Nations. (2015). Transforming our world: The 2030 Agenda for Sustainable Development. Resolution adopted by the General Assembly on 25 September 2015. A/RES/70/1. UN General Assembly, Seventieth Session. Agenda items 15 and 116. New York: United Nations.

United Nations Women. (2018). Turning promises into action: Gender equality in the 2030 Agenda. https://www.unwomen.org/en/digital-library/publications/2018/2/gender-equality-in-the-2030-agenda-for-sustainable-development-2018

Van Zanten, J. A., & Van Tulder, R. (2018). Multinational enterprises and the sustainable development goals: An institutional approach to corporate engagement. *Journal of International Business Policy*, 1(3-4), 208–233. DOI: 10.1057/s42214-018-0008-x

Whitley, R., Henderson, J., Czaban, L., & Lengvel, G. (1996). Trust and contractual relations in an emerging capitalist economy: The changing trading relationships of ten large Hungarian enterprises. *Organization Studies*, 17(3), 397–420. DOI: 10.1177/017084069601700303

Zattoni, A., Leventis, S., Van Ees, H., & De Masi, S. (2023). Board diversity's antecedents and consequences: A review and research agenda. *The Leadership Quarterly*, 34(1), 101659. DOI: 10.1016/j.leaqua.2022.101659

ENDNOTES

[1] In line with these benefits, the United Nations (UN)' Sustainable Development Goal 5 (SDG 5) aims to achieve gender equality and empower all women and girls by 2030. Achieving gender equality is seen as integral to the success of other SDGs, as it contributes to economic growth, poverty reduction, and improved health outcomes (UN Women, 2018).

[2] The existing literature on the link between gender diversity and financial reporting quality focuses on earning quality constructs that are computed based on financial reports that are issued after the completion of the audit. We therefore refer to this stream of literature as linking gender diversity to (post-audit) financial reporting quality.

[3] Only a few studies have used firm's commitment towards the Sustainable Development Goal (SDG) on gender diversity (SDG 5), either as dependent or independent variable. For example, Desender and LópezPuertas-Lamy (2024) show that ESG performance is an important driver of SDG 5 for a sample of Latin-American companies.

APPENDIX I

Table 6. Variable definitions

Variable	Definition	Source
Ln(Audit Fees)	The natural log of the fees paid to auditor for the financial statement audit work	Refinitiv Eikon
Board Gender Diversity	The percentage of female board members over the total number of board members	Refinitiv Eikon
TMT Gender Diversity	The percentage of female TMT members over the total number of TMT members	Refinitiv Eikon
SDG Goal 5 - Gender equality	An indicator variable equal to one when the firm has committed itself to the UN's SDG Goal 5 on Gender Equality	Refinitiv Eikon
Ln(Total Assets)	The natural log of the total assets' value of the firm	Refinitiv Eikon
Leverage	The ratio of the sum of the long-term and short-term debt to total assets	Refinitiv Eikon
ROA	Return on assets defined as net income divided by total assets	Refinitiv Eikon
Sales Growth	The percentage of sales growth defined as: $(sales_t - sales_{t-1}) / sales_{t-1}$	Refinitiv Eikon
Loss in past year	A dummy that takes the value of one if the firm reports a loss during the current year, and zero otherwise	Refinitiv Eikon
Current to Total Assets	The ratio of current assets to total assets	Refinitiv Eikon
ESG score	Refinitiv Eikon benchmarked ESG score	Refinitiv Eikon
Board Independence	ratio of independent board members to the total number of board members	Refinitiv Eikon
CEO duality	An indicator variable equal to one when the CEO also holds the Chair position and zero otherwise	Refinitiv Eikon
Auditor Change	A dummy that takes the value of one when the client contracts a new auditor and zero otherwise	Refinitiv Eikon
Auditor Tenure	The number of years an auditor has been in the firm	Refinitiv Eikon
Control of Corruption	An indicator that reflects perceptions of the extent to which public power is exercised for private gain	WorldBank
Women in Parliament	The proportion of parliamentary seats held by women in a country's national legislature	WorldBank

Compilation of References

Aamer, A., Sahara, C. R., & Al-Awlaqi, M. A. (2023). Digitalization of the supply chain: Transformation factors. *Journal of Science and Technology Policy Management*, 14(4), 713–733. DOI: 10.1108/JSTPM-01-2021-0001

Abbad, G. (1999). An integrated model for evaluating the impact of on-the-job training – IMPACT. Thesis (Doctorate in Psychology). Institute of Psychology of the University of Brasilia, Brasília, Federal District, Brazil.

Abdul-Azeez, O., Ihechere, A. O., & Idemudia, C. (2024). Enhancing business performance: The role of data-driven analytics in strategic decision-making. *International Journal of Management & Entrepreneurship Research*, 6(7), 2066–2081. DOI: 10.51594/ijmer.v6i7.1257

Abernethy, M. A., Bouwens, J., & Van Lent, L. (2013). The role of performance measures in the intertemporal decisions of business unit managers. Contemporary accounting research, 30(3), 925-961.

Abhishek, N., Suraj, N., Rahiman, H. U., Nawaz, N., Kodikal, R., Kulal, A., & Raj, K. (2024). Digital transformation in accounting: elevating effectiveness across accounting, auditing, reporting and regulatory compliance. *Journal of Accounting & Organizational Change*, (ahead-of-print). DOI: 10.1108/JAOC-01-2024-0039

Aboagye-Otchere, F., & Agbeibor, J. (2012). The International Financial Reporting Standard for Small and Medium-sized Entities (IFRS for SMES): Suitability for small businesses in Ghana. *Journal of Financial Reporting and Accounting*, 10(2), 190–214. DOI: 10.1108/19852511211273723

Achibane, M., & Elhamma, A. (2016). Balanced Scorecard Et Incertitude Environnementale: Cas Des Entreprises Au Maroc. *European Scientific Journal*, 12(7), 459–469. DOI: 10.19044/esj.2016.v12n7p459

Adaga, E. M., Egieya, Z. E., Ewuga, S. K., Abdul, A. A., & Abrahams, T. O. (2024). A comprehensive review of ethical practices in banking and finance. *Finance & Accounting Research Journal*, 6(1), 1–20. DOI: 10.51594/farj.v6i1.705

Adams, C., Abdullah, A., Xinwu, H., & Jie, T. (2021). The Double-Materiality Concept. Application and Issues. Project Report. Global Reporting Initiative. Available online: https://dro.dur.ac.uk/33139/1/33139.pdf

Adams, R. B., & Ferreira, D. (2009). Women in the boardroom and their impact on governance and performance. *Journal of Financial Economics*, 94(2), 291–309. DOI: 10.1016/j.jfineco.2008.10.007

Adebiyi, O. O., Olabanji, S. O., & Olaniyi, O. O. (2023). Promoting inclusive accounting education through the integration of STEM principles for a diverse classroom. *Asian Journal of Education and Social Studies*, 49(4), 152–171. DOI: 10.9734/ajess/2023/v49i41196

Adelakun, B. O. (2022). Ethical Considerations in the Use of AI for Auditing: Balancing Innovation and Integrity. *European Journal of Accounting. Auditing and Finance Research*, 10(12), 91–108. DOI: 10.37745/ejaafr.2013/vol10n1291108

Adelakun, B. O. (2023). AI-Driven Financial Forecasting: Innovations and Implications for Accounting Practices. *International Journal of Advanced Economics*, 5(9), 323–338. DOI: 10.51594/ijae.v5i9.1231

Adelberg, A. H. (1979). Narrative disclosures contained in financial reports: Means of communication or manipulation? *Accounting and Business Research*, 9(35), 179–190. DOI: 10.1080/00014788.1979.9729157

Adeyelu, O. O., Ugochukwu, C. E., & Shonibare, M. A. (2024). The impact of artificial intelligence on accounting practices: Advancements, challenges, and opportunities. *International Journal of Management & Entrepreneurship Research*, 6(4), 1200–1210. DOI: 10.51594/ijmer.v6i4.1031

Ageeva, O., Karp, M., & Sidorov, A. (2020). The application of digital technologies in financial reporting and auditing. In Popkova, E. G., & Sergi, B. S. (Eds.), *Smart Technologies" for Society, State and Economy* (pp. 1526–1534). Springer International Publishing. DOI: 10.1007/978-3-030-59126-7_167__

Agibalova, E. N. (2020). Blockchain Technology in Smart Contracts: Is It a Constitutive Attribute or a Technological Neutrality? In Popkova, E., & Sergi, B. (Eds.), *Scientific and Technical Revolution: Yesterday, Today and Tomorrow. ISC 2019. Lecture Notes in Networks and Systems* (Vol. 129). Springer. DOI: 10.1007/978-3-030-47945-9_19

Agostino, D., Saliterer, I., & Steccolini, I. (2022). Digitalization, accounting and accountability: A literature review and reflections on future research in public services. *Financial Accountability & Management*, 38(2), 152–176. DOI: 10.1111/faam.12301

Aguilera, R. V., Desender, K., & López-Puertas Lamy, M. (2021). Bridging accounting and Corporate Governance: New avenues of research. *The International Journal of Accounting*, 56(01), 2180001. DOI: 10.1142/S1094406021800019

Aguilera, R. V., & Jackson, G. (2003). The cross-national diversity of corporate governance: Dimensions and determinants. *Academy of Management Review*, 28(3), 447–465. DOI: 10.2307/30040732

Aguilera, R. V., Judge, W. Q., & Terjesen, S. A. (2018). Corporate governance deviance. *Academy of Management Review*, 43(1), 87–109. DOI: 10.5465/amr.2014.0394

Ahamed, S. F., Vijayasankar, A., Thenmozhi, M., Rajendar, S., Bindu, P., & Rao, T. S. M. (2023). Machine learning models for forecasting and estimation of business operations. *The Journal of High Technology Management Research*, 34(1), 100455. Advance online publication. DOI: 10.1016/j.hitech.2023.100455

Ahmed, R., Shaheen, S., & Philbin, S. P. (2022). The role of big data analytics and decision-making in achieving project success. *Journal of Engineering and Technology Management*, 65, 101697. DOI: 10.1016/j.jengtecman.2022.101697

Ajayi-Nifise, A. O., Odeyemi, O., Mhlongo, N. Z., Ibeh, C. V., Elufioye, O. A., & Awonuga, K. F. (2024). The future of accounting: Predictions on automation and AI integration. *World Journal of Advanced Research and Reviews*, 21(2), 399–407. DOI: 10.30574/wjarr.2024.21.2.0466

Ajibade, A. T., Okutu, N., Akande, F., Kwarbai, J. D., Olayinka, I. M., & Olotu, A. (2022). IFRS adoption, corporate governance and faithful representation of financial reporting quality in Nigeria's development banks. *Cogent Business and Management*, 9(1), 2139213. Advance online publication. DOI: 10.1080/23311975.2022.2139213

Akisik, O., Gal, G., & Mangaliso, M. P. (2020). IFRS, FDI, economic growth and human development: The experience of Anglophone and Francophone African countries. *Emerging Markets Review*, 45, 45. DOI: 10.1016/j.ememar.2020.100725

Akisik, O., & Mangaliso, M. P. (2020). How IFRS influence the relationship between the types of FDI and economic growth: An empirical analysis on African countries. *Journal of Applied Accounting Research*, 21(1), 60–76. DOI: 10.1108/JAAR-02-2018-0025

Akkio. (2024). Google Sheets Data Visualization: Comprehensive Guide. Retrieved from: https://www.akkio.com/post/google-sheets-data-visualization#:~:text= Google%20Sheets%20allows%20users%20to%20create%20bar%20charts%2C%20 histograms%20pie,many%20more%20for%20data%20visualization

Al Najjar, M., Gaber Ghanem, M., Mahboub, R., & Nakhal, B. (2024). The Role of Artificial Intelligence in Eliminating Accounting Errors. *Journal of Risk and Financial Management*, 17(8), 353. DOI: 10.3390/jrfm17080353

Albuquerque, F., & Rodrigues, N. M. B. (2015). As características qualitativas da informação financeira: Uma análise ao relato das entidades cotadas nas principais bolsas europeias. *Congresso Dos TOC*. https://www.occ.pt/news/trabalhoscongv/ pdf/73.pdf

Albuquerque, F., Monteiro, E., & Rodrigues, M. A. B. (2023). The Explanatory Factors of Risk Disclosure in the Integrated Reports of Listed Entities in Brazil. *Risks, 11*(6), 108. https://doi.org/11060108DOI: 10.3390/risksetor

Aldoseri, A., Al-Khalifa, K. N., & Hamouda, A. M. (2023). Re-thinking data strategy and integration for artificial intelligence: Concepts, opportunities, and challenges. *Applied Sciences (Basel, Switzerland)*, 13(12), 7082. DOI: 10.3390/app13127082

Aljohani, A. (2023). Predictive analytics and machine learning for real-time supply chain risk mitigation and agility. *Sustainability (Basel)*, 15(20), 15088. DOI: 10.3390/su152015088

Alkan, B. Ş. (2021). Real-time Blockchain accounting system as a new paradigm. *Muhasebe ve Finansman Dergisi*, 41-58. DOI: 10.25095/mufad.950162

Allemand, I., Bédard, J., Brullebaut, B., & Deschênes, J. (2022). Role of old boys' networks and regulatory approaches in selection processes for female directors. *British Journal of Management*, 33(2), 784–805. DOI: 10.1111/1467-8551.12485

Almeida, F. L. (2017). Benefits, challenges and tools of big data management. *Journal of Systems Integration*, 8(4). http://dx.doi.org/DOI: 10.20470/jsi.v8i4.311

AlMuhayfith, S., & Shaiti, H. (2020). The impact of enterprise resource planning on business performance: With the discussion on its relationship with open innovation. *Journal of Open Innovation*, 6(3), 87. DOI: 10.3390/joitmc6030087

Alnaas, A., & Rashid, A. (2019). Firm characteristics and compliance with IAS/ IFRS: Evidence from North African companies. *Journal of Financial Reporting and Accounting*, 17(3), 383–410. DOI: 10.1108/JFRA-06-2018-0052

Alqodsi, E. M., & Gura, D. (2023). High tech and legal challenges: Artificial intelligence-caused damage regulation. *Cogent Social Sciences*, 9(2), 2270751. DOI: 10.1080/23311886.2023.2270751

ALSaqa, Z. H., Hussein, A. I., & Mahmood, S. M. (2019). The impact of blockchain on accounting information systems. *Journal of Information Technology Management*, 11(3), 62–80. DOI: 10.22059/jitm.2019.74301

Alsayegh, M. F., Abdul, R. R., & Homayoun, S. (2020). Corporate Economic, Environmental, and Social Sustainability Performance Transformation through ESG Disclosure. *Sustainability (Basel)*, 12(9), 3910. Advance online publication. DOI: 10.3390/su12093910

Alsoufi, M. A., Razak, S., Siraj, M. M., Nafea, I., Ghaleb, F. A., Saeed, F., & Nasser, M. (2021). Anomaly-based intrusion detection systems in IoT using deep learning: A systematic literature review. *Applied Sciences (Basel, Switzerland)*, 11(18), 8383. DOI: 10.3390/app11188383

Amaresan, S. (2024, May 30). How to Let Customers Know About a Price Increase (Without Losing Them), According to Pros Who've Done It. Retrieved from: https://blog.hubspot.com/service/price-increase

Ameyaw, M. N., Idemudia, C., & Iyelolu, T. V. (2024). Financial compliance as a pillar of corporate integrity: A thorough analysis of fraud prevention. *Finance & Accounting Research Journal*, 6(7), 1157–1177. DOI: 10.51594/farj.v6i7.1271

Anagnoste, S. 2017. Robotic automation process: The next major revolution in terms of back office operations improvement. *Proceedings of the International Conference on Business Excellence, 11*(1), 676–86. DOI: 10.1515/picbe-2017-0072

Ansell, C., & Torfing, J. (2016). Introduction: theories of governance. In Handbook on theories of governance (pp. 1-18). Edward Elgar Publishing. DOI: 10.4337/9781782548508.00008

Antunes, L. (2019). *Tecnologia blockchain e criptomoedas: o que é isto?* (1ª edição). Plátano Editora.

Antwi, B. O., Adelakun, B. O., & Eziefule, A. O. (2024). Transforming Financial Reporting with AI: Enhancing Accuracy and Timeliness. *International Journal of Advanced Economics*, 6(6), 205-223. DOI: 10.51594/ijae.v6i6.1229

Anyanwu, A., Olorunsogo, T., Abrahams, T. O., Akindote, O. J., & Reis, O. (2024). Data confidentiality and integrity: A review of accounting and cybersecurity controls in superannuation organizations. *Computer Science & IT Research Journal*, 5(1), 237–253. DOI: 10.51594/csitrj.v5i1.735

Appiah, K., Awunyo-Vitor, D., Mireku, K., & Ahiagbah, C. (2016). Compliance with international financial reporting standards: The case of listed firms in Ghana. *Journal of Financial Reporting and Accounting*, 14(1), 131–156. DOI: 10.1108/JFRA-01-2015-0003

Appio, J. (2009). Swot analysis as a competitive differential: An exploratory study at Cooperativa Muza Brasil. *Interdisciplinary Journal of Applied Science*, 3(3), 1–18.

Araújo, A., & Gomes, A. M. (2021). Risk management in the public sector: challenges in its adoption by Brazilian federal universities. Revista Contabilidade & Finanças, 32(86), 241-254. https://doi.org/DOI: 10.1590/1982-7849rac2018170391

Arbelo, A., Arbelo-Pérez, M., & Pérez-Gómez, P. (2021). Profit efficiency as a measure of performance and frontier models: A resource-based view. *Business Research Quarterly*, 24(2), 143–159. DOI: 10.1177/2340944420924336

Arif, M., Gan, C., & Nadeem, M. (2021). Regulating non-financial reporting: Evidence from European firms' environmental, social and governance disclosures and earnings risk. *Meditari Accountancy Research*, 30(3), 495–523. DOI: 10.1108/MEDAR-11-2020-1086

Arlow, P. (1991). Personal characteristics in college students' evaluations of business ethics and corporate social responsibility. *Journal of Business Ethics*, 10(1), 63–69. DOI: 10.1007/BF00383694

Armstrong, S. C., Barth, M. E., Jagolinzer, A. D., & Riedl, E. J. (2010). Market Reaction to the Adoption of IFRS in Europe. *The Accounting Review*, 85(1), 31–61. DOI: 10.2308/accr.2010.85.1.31

Arnold, A. (2018, August 28). Blockchain is not a threat to accounting, it's an opportunity. *Forbes*. https://www.forbes.com/sites/andrewarnold/2018/08/28/blockchain-is-not-a-threat-to-accounting-its-an-opportunity/

Ashtiani, M. N., & Raahemi, B. (2021). Intelligent fraud detection in financial statements using machine learning and data mining: A systematic literature review. *IEEE Access : Practical Innovations, Open Solutions*, 10, 72504–72525. DOI: 10.1109/ACCESS.2021.3096799

Attaran, M., Attaran, S., & Kirkland, D. (2020). Technology and organizational change: Harnessing the power of digital workplace. In Idemudia, E. C. (Ed.), *Handbook of Research on Social and Organizational Dynamics in the Digital Era* (pp. 383–408). IGI Global., DOI: 10.4018/978-1-5225-8933-4.ch018

Aunoa. (2024, March 5). Everything you need to know about Anthropic. Retrieved from: https://aunoa.ai/blog/todo-lo-que-debes-saber-sobre-anthropic/#:~:text=Comprensi%C3%B3n%20contextual%3A%20Anthropic%20puede%20entender,la%20tristeza%20y%20el%20miedo

Avira, S., Setyaningsih, E., & Utami, S. S. (2023). Digital transformation in financial management: Harnessing technology for business success. *Influence: International Journal of Science Review*, 5(2), 336–345. DOI: 10.54783/influencejournal.v5i2.161

Ayinla, B. S., Atadoga, A., Ike, C. U., Ndubuisi, N. L., Asuzu, O. F., & Adeleye, R. A. (2024). The Role of Robotic Process Automation (RPA) in Modern Accounting: A Review-Investigating how Automation Tools are Transforming Traditional Accounting Practices. *Engineering Science & Technology Journal*, 5(2), 427–447. DOI: 10.51594/estj.v5i2.804

Azambuja, R., Baudot, L., & Malsch, B. (2023). Navigating multiple accountabilities through managers' boundary work in professional service firms. *Accounting, Auditing & Accountability Journal*, 36(7/8), 1734–1762. DOI: 10.1108/AAAJ-08-2021-5407

Baba, A. I., Neupane, S., Wu, F., & Yaroh, F. F. (2021). Blockchain in accounting: Challenges and future prospects. *International Journal of Blockchains and Cryptocurrencies*, 2(1), 44. DOI: 10.1504/IJBC.2021.117810

Bachinskiy, A. (2019, February 21). Follow The Growing Impact of AI in Financial Services: Six Examples. Towards Data Science. Retrieved from: https://towardsdatascience.com/the-growing-impact-of-ai-in-financial-services-six-examples-da386c0301b2

Bahoo, S., Cucculelli, M., Goga, X., & Mondolo, J. (2024). Artificial intelligence in Finance: A comprehensive review through bibliometric and content analysis. *SN Business & Economics*, 4(2), 23. DOI: 10.1007/s43546-023-00618-x

Bai, X., Nunez, M., & Kalagnanam, J. R. (2012). Managing data quality risk in accounting information systems. *Information Systems Research*, 23(2), 453–473. DOI: 10.1287/isre.1110.0371

Bakhshi, T., & Ghita, B. (2021). Perspectives on Auditing and Regulatory Compliance in Blockchain Transactions. In Rehman, M. H., Svetinovic, D., Salah, K., & Damiani, E. (Eds.), *Trust Models for Next-Generation Blockchain Ecosystems* (pp. 37–65). Springer International Publishing. DOI: 10.1007/978-3-030-75107-4_2

Bakhtiyari, K., Salehi, H., Embi, M. A., Shakiba, M., Isfandyari-Moghaddam, A., Dadkhah, M., & Farhadi, M. (2014). Ethical challenges in academic research. *International Journal of High-Rise Buildings*, 3(4), 285–298.

Balamurugan, A., Krishna, M. V., Bhattacharya, R., Mohammed, S., Haralayya, B., & Kaushik, P. (2022). Robotic Process Automation (RPA) in Accounting and Auditing of Business and Financial Information. *British Journal of Administrative Management*, 58(157), 127–142.

Baldini, M., Maso, L. D., Liberatore, G., Mazzi, F., & Terzani, S. (2018). Role of Country- and Firm-Level Determinants in Environmental, Social, and Governance Disclosure. *Journal of Business Ethics*, 150(1), 79–98. DOI: 10.1007/s10551-016-3139-1

Ballamudi, K. R. (2016). Blockchain as a Type of Distributed Ledger Technology. *Asian Journal of Humanity. Art and Literature*, 3(2), 127–136. DOI: 10.18034/ajhal.v3i2.528

Barac, K., Plant, K., Kunz, R., & Kirstein, M. (2021). Audit practice: A straightforward trade or a complex system? *International Journal of Auditing*, 25(3), 797–812. DOI: 10.1111/ijau.12249

Barbosa, A. F., Gemente, G. B., Sanches, M. N., Rodrigues, F. M., & Sabaa-Srur, A. U. (2016). *Importance of Quality Management in the Processors of Fruit and Vegetable Industries.*

Barchard, K. A., & Pace, L. A. (2011). Preventing human error: The impact of data entry methods on data accuracy and statistical results. *Computers in Human Behavior*, 27(5), 1834–1839. DOI: 10.1016/j.chb.2011.04.004

Barros, V. D. M. (2005). O novo velho enfoque da informação contábil. *Revista Contabilidade & Finanças*, 16(38), 102–112. DOI: 10.1590/S1519-70772005000200009

Barr-Pulliam, D., Joe, J., Mason, S., & Sanderson, K. A. (2020). The auditor-valuation specialist coopetitive alliance in the fair value audit of complex financial instruments.

Barth, M. E., Landsman, W. R., & Lang, M. H. (2008). International accounting standards and accounting quality. *Journal of Accounting Research*, 46(3), 467–498. DOI: 10.1111/j.1475-679X.2008.00287.x

Barth, M. E., & Schipper, K. (2008). Financial reporting transparency. *Journal of Accounting, Auditing & Finance*, 23(2), 173–190. DOI: 10.1177/0148558X0802300203

Bartov, E., Goldberg, S. R., & Kim, M. (2005). Comparative value relevance among German, US and International Accounting Standards: A German stock market perspective. *Journal of Accounting, Auditing & Finance*, 20(2), 95–119. DOI: 10.1177/0148558X0502000201

Baumuller, J., & Sopp, K. (2022). Double materiality and the shift from non-financial to European sustainability reporting: Review, outlook and implications. *Journal of Applied Accounting Research*, 23(1), 8–28. DOI: 10.1108/JAAR-04-2021-0114

Bebbington, J., & Rubin, A. (2022). Accounting in the Anthropocene: A roadmap for stewardship. *Accounting and Business Research*, 52(5), 582–596. DOI: 10.1080/00014788.2022.2079780

Bedard, J., & Johnstone, K. (2004). Earnings manipulation risk, corporate governance risk, and auditors' planning decisions. *The Accounting Review*, 79(2), 277–304. DOI: 10.2308/accr.2004.79.2.277

Bellantuono, N., Pontrandolfo, P., & Scozzi, B. (2016). Capturing the Stakeholders' View in Sustainability Reporting: A Novel Approach. *Sustainability (Basel)*, 8(4), 379. Advance online publication. DOI: 10.3390/su8040379

Bell, T. B., Landsman, W. R., & Shackelford, D. A. (2001). Auditors' perceived business risk and audit fees: Analysis and evidence. *Journal of Accounting Research*, 39(1), 35–43. DOI: 10.1111/1475-679X.00002

Beloskar, V. D., Haldar, A., & Gupta, A. (2024). Gender equality and women's empowerment: A bibliometric review of the literature on SDG 5 through the management lens. *Journal of Business Research*, 172(114442). DOI: 10.1016/j.jbusres.2023.114442

Bennani, S., & Elhamma, A. (2015). *La comptabilité en finance islamique selon les normes AAOIFI*. Editions Universitaires Européennes.

Benton, R. A. (2021). Women in the inner circle: Gender and director networks after the fracturing of the corporate elite. *Organization Science*, 32(6), 1492–1522. DOI: 10.1287/orsc.2021.1433

Berdiyeva, O., Umar Islam, M., & Saeedi, M. (2021). Artificial Intelligence in Accounting and Finance: Meta-Analysis. Nust Business Review, 3(1), 56-79. Retrieved from: https://www.researchgate.net/profile/Oguljan-Berdiyeva/publication/353641654_Artificial_Intelligence_in_Accounting_and_Finance_Meta-Analysis/links/6107fe971e95fe241aa349ba/Artificial-Intelligence-in-Accounting-and-Finance-Meta-Analysis.pdf

Berikol, B. Z., & Killi, M. (2021). The effects of digital transformation process on accounting profession and accounting education. In Caliyurt, K. T. (Ed.), *Ethics and Sustainability in Accounting and Finance* (Vol. II, pp. 219–231). Springer Nature. DOI: 10.1007/978-981-15-1928-4_13

Bernardi, R. A., & Arnold, D. F. Sr. (1997). An examination of moral development within public accounting by gender, staff level, and firm. *Contemporary Accounting Research*, 14(4), 653–668. DOI: 10.1111/j.1911-3846.1997.tb00545.x

Beske, F., Haustein, E., & Lorson, P. C. (2020). Materiality analysis in sustainability and integrated reports. *Sustainability Accounting Management and Policy Journal*, 11(1), 162–186. DOI: 10.1108/SAMPJ-12-2018-0343

Bhattacharya, I., & Mickovic, A. (2024). Accounting fraud detection using contextual language learning. *International Journal of Accounting Information Systems*, 53, 100682. DOI: 10.1016/j.accinf.2024.100682

Bhimani, A. (2020). Digital data and management accounting: Why we need to rethink research methods. *Journal of Management Control*, 31(1), 9–23. DOI: 10.1007/s00187-020-00295-z

Bhimani, A., & Willcocks, L. (2014). Digitisation, 'Big Data' and the transformation of accounting information. *Accounting and Business Research*, 44(4), 469–490. DOI: 10.1080/00014788.2014.910051

Bochkay, K., Brown, S. V., Leone, A. J., & Tucker, J. W. (2023). Textual Analysis in Accounting: What's Next? *Contemporary Accounting Research*, 40(2), 765–805. DOI: 10.1111/1911-3846.12825

Bodle, K. A., Cybinski, P. J., & Monem, R. (2016). Effect of IFRS adoption on financial reporting quality: Evidence from bankruptcy prediction. *Accounting Research Journal*, 29(3), 292–312. DOI: 10.1108/ARJ-03-2014-0029

Bomfim, V. C. (2020). Os avanços tecnológicos e o perfil do contador frente à era digital. *Revista Trevisan*, 18(173), 60.

Bonfim, M. P. (2023). A Contabilidade nas instituições Católicas nos Séculos XVII e XVIII. *Revista de Contabilidade da UFBA*, 17(1), e2319–e2319. DOI: 10.9771/rcufba.v17i1.49372

Bonsón, E., & Bednárová, M. (2018). Blockchain y los registros contables consensuados compartidos (RC3). XVIII Encuentro Internacional AECA, 20-21 de setembro. Lisboa, Portugal.

Boolaky, P. K., Omoteso, K., Ibrahim, M. U., & Adelopo, I. (2018). The development of accounting practices and the adoption of IFRS in selected MENA countries. *Journal of Accounting in Emerging Economies*, 8(3), 327–351. DOI: 10.1108/JAEE-07-2015-0052

Boolaky, P. K., Tawiah, V., & Soobaroyen, T. (2020). Why do African countries adopt IFRS? An institutional perspective. *The International Journal of Accounting*, 55(1), 1–40. DOI: 10.1142/S1094406020500055

Bordo, M. D., & Siklos, P. L. (2017). *Central Banks: Evolution and Innovation in Historical Perspective* (Economics Working Papers, Issue April).

Borhani, S., Babajani, J., Vanani, I., Anaqiz, S., & Jamaliyanpour, M. (2021). Adopting Blockchain Technology to Improve Financial Reporting by Using the Technology Acceptance Model (TAM). *International Journal of Finance & Managerial Accounting*, 6(22), 155–171. http://www.ijfma.ir/article_17481.html

Borker, D. R. (2013). Accounting and Cultural Values: IFRS in 3G Economies. *The International Business & Economics Research Journal*, 12(6), 671. DOI: 10.19030/iber.v12i6.7872

Bose, S., Dey, S. K., & Bhattacharjee, S. (2023). Big data, data analytics and artificial intelligence in accounting: An overview. In Akter, S., & Wamba, S. F. (Eds.), *Handbook of Big Data Research Methods* (pp. 32–51). Edward Elgar Publishing. DOI: 10.4337/9781800888555.00007

Bova, F., & Pereira, R. (2012). The determinants and consequences of heterogeneous IFRS compliance levels following mandatory IFRS adoption: Evidence from a developing country. *Journal of International Accounting Research*, 11(1), 83–111. DOI: 10.2308/jiar-10211

Bracci, E., Tallaki, M., Gobbo, G., & Papi, L. (2021). Risk management in the public sector: a structured literature review. International Journal of Public Sector Management, 34(2), 205-223.

Braga, N. C. L.; Colares, A. C. V.(2020) Contabilidade digital: os desafios do profissional

Bravo, F., & Alcaide-Ruiz, M. D. (2019). The impact of board gender diversity on earnings management: Evidence from Spain. *Sustainability*, 11(3), 658.

Brazilian Federation Of Banks (FEBRABAN). (2018). Guide: good compliance practices. Revised and updated edition.

Broccardo, L., Zicari, A., Jabeen, F., & Bhatti, Z. A. (2023). How digitalization supports a sustainable business model: A literature review. *Technological Forecasting and Social Change*, 187(6-7), 122146. DOI: 10.1016/j.techfore.2022.122146

Brunetti, F., Matt, D. T., Bonfanti, A., De Longhi, A., Pedrini, G., & Orzes, G. (2020). Digital transformation challenges: Strategies emerging from a multi-stakeholder approach. *The TQM Journal*, 32(4), 697–724. DOI: 10.1108/TQM-12-2019-0309

Brunnermeier, M. K., James, H., & Landau, J.-P. (2019). The Digitization of Money. *NBER Working Paper Series*.

Cagle, M. N. (2020). Reflections of digitalization on accounting: the effects of industry 4.0 on financial statements and financial ratios. In Hacioglu, U. (Ed.), *Digital Business Strategies in Blockchain Ecosystems: Transformational Design and Future of Global Business* (pp. 473–501). Springer International Publishing. DOI: 10.1007/978-3-030-29739-8_23

Calabrese, A., Costa, R., Ghiron, N. & Menichini, T. (2017). Materiality Analysis In Sustainability Reporting: A Method For Making It Work In Practice. *European Journal of Sustainable Development,* 6(3), 439-447. http://dx.doi.org/ 439DOI: 10.14207/ejsd.2017.v6n3país

Calderon-Monge, E., & Ribeiro-Soriano, D. (2024). The role of digitalization in business and management: A systematic literature review. *Review of Managerial Science*, 18(2), 449–491. DOI: 10.1007/s11846-023-00647-8

Callahan, C., & Soileau, J. (2017). Does enterprise risk management enhance operating performance?. Advances in accounting, 37, 122-139.

Calm. (2024). How to overcome fear of change: 8 ways to navigate the unknown. Retrieved from: https://www.calm.com/blog/fear-of-change#:~:text=An%20intense %20fear%20of%20change,becoming%20a%20more%20debilitating%20fear

Capital, C. (2023, November 20). *DIY Financial Planning: How to Get Started* [Video]. YouTube. Retrieved from: https://www.youtube.com/watch?v=JObYz6u-_JU

Carcello, J. V., Hermanson, D. R., Neal, T. L., & Riley, R. R.Jr. (2002). Board characteristics and audit fees. *Contemporary Accounting Research*, 19(3), 365–384.

Cardoso, J. A. A., & Pinto, J. de S. (2018). Blockchain e Smart Contracts: Um Estudo Sobre Soluções para Seguradoras. *2o. CONGENTI, October 2018*, 1–17.

Carmo, C., & Simões, A. (2021). *A Diretiva 2014/95/UE: passado, presente e futuro*. Apotec. https://www.researchgate.net/profile/Cecilia-Carmo/publication/356834363 _A_Diretiva_201495UE_passado_presente_e_futuro/links/61af51cdb3c26a1 e5d8eebfd/A-Diretiva-2014-95-UE-passado-presente-e-futuro.pdf

Carrasco, A., Francoeur, C., Labelle, R., Laffarga, J., & Ruiz-Barbadillo, E. (2015). Appointing women to boards: Is there a cultural bias? *Journal of Business Ethics*, 129(2), 429–444. DOI: 10.1007/s10551-014-2166-z

Carter, D. (2020). Regulation and ethics in artificial intelligence and machine learning technologies: Where are we now? Who is responsible? Can the information professional play a role? *Business Information Review*, 37(2), 60–68. DOI: 10.1177/0266382120923962

Caruso, J. (2024, April 29). Drink the Kool-Aid all you want, but don't call AI an existential threat. *Bulletin of the Atomic Scientists*. Retrieved from: https://thebulletin.org/2024/04/drink-the-kool-aid-all-you-want-but-dont-call-ai-an-existential-threat/?utm_source=Newsletter&utm_medium=Email&utm_campaign=MondayNewsletter04292024&utm_content=DisruptiveTechnologies_AIExistentialThreat_04292024

Cascio, W. F., & Montealegre, R. (2016). How technology is changing work and organizations. *Annual Review of Organizational Psychology and Organizational Behavior*, 3(1), 349–375. DOI: 10.1146/annurev-orgpsych-041015-062352

Cerchiello, P., & Giudici, P. (2016). Big data analysis for financial risk management. *Journal of Big Data*, 3(1), 1–12. DOI: 10.1186/s40537-016-0053-4

Chai, H., Tang, Q., Jiang, Y., & Lin, Z. (2010). The Role of International Financial Reporting Standards in Accounting Quality, Evidence from the European Union. *Journal of International Financial Management & Accounting*, 21(3), 220–278. DOI: 10.1111/j.1467-646X.2010.01041.x

Chamisa, E. (2000). The relevance and observance of the IASC standards in developing countries and the particular case of Zimbabwe. *The International Journal of Accounting*, 35(2), 267–286. DOI: 10.1016/S0020-7063(00)00049-2

Chen, G., Crossland, C., & Huang, S. (2016). Female board representation and corporate acquisition intensity. *Strategic Management Journal*, 37(2), 303–313. DOI: 10.1002/smj.2323

Chiavenato, I. (2008). People management: the new role of human resources in organizations.

Chiavenato, I., & Sapiro, A. (2009). *Strategic Planning* (2nd ed.). Elsevier.

Chiu, T. K. & Wang, Y. H. (2015). Determinants of Social Disclosure Quality in Taiwan: An Application of Stakeholder Theory. Journal of Business Ethics, 129, 379–398. https://doi.org/ 10551-014-2160-5DOI: 10.1007/setor

Chohan, U. (2022). Cryptocurrencies: A Brief Thematic Review. In *Discussion Paper Series: Notes on the 21st Century*. https://doi.org/DOI: 10.2139/ssrn.3024330

Chong, H. G. (2015). A review on the evolution of the definitions of materiality. *Int. J. Economics and Accounting*, 6(1), 15–32. DOI: 10.1504/IJEA.2015.068978

Cho, O. H. (2024). Analysis of the Impact of Artificial Intelligence Applications on the Development of Accounting Industry. *Nanotechnology Perceptions*, 20(S1), 74–83. DOI: 10.62441/nano-ntp.v20iS1.7

Cho, S., Vasarhelyi, M. A., Sun, T., & Zhang, C. (2020). Learning from machine learning in accounting and assurance. *Journal of Emerging Technologies in Accounting*, 17(1), 1–10. DOI: 10.2308/jeta-10718

Chowdhury, E. K. (2023). Integration of Artificial Intelligence Technology in Management Accounting Information System: An Empirical Study. In Abedin, M. Z., & Hajek, P. (Eds.), *Novel financial applications of machine learning and deep learning: algorithms, product modeling, and applications* (pp. 35–46). Springer International Publishing. DOI: 10.1007/978-3-031-18552-6_3

Christopher, J., & Sarens, G. (2015). Risk management: its adoption in Australian public universities within an environment of change management–A management perspective. Australian Accounting Review, 25(1), 2-12.

Chui, M., & Yee, L. (2023, July 7). AI could increase corporate profits by $4.4 trillion a year, according to new research, *McKinsey Global Institute*. Retrieved from: https://www.mckinsey.com/mgi/overview/in-the-news/ai-could-increase-corporate-profits-by-4-trillion-a-year-according-to-new-research

Chyzhevska, L., Voloschuk, L., Shatskova, L., & Sokolenko, L. (2021). Digitalization as a vector of information systems development and accounting system modernization. *Studia Universitatis Vasile Goldi Arad. Seria tiin e Economice*, 31(4), 18–39. DOI: 10.2478/sues-2021-0017

Coelho, M., & Menezes, I. (2021). University social responsibility, service learning, and students' personal, professional, and civic education. *Frontiers in Psychology*, 12, 617300. DOI: 10.3389/fpsyg.2021.617300 PMID: 33716883

Coetzee, S., & Schmulian, A. (2013). The Effect of IFRS Adoption on Financial Reporting Pedagogy in South Africa. *Issues in Accounting Education*, 28(2), 243–251. DOI: 10.2308/iace-50386

Coffie, W., & Bedi, I. (2019). The effects of IFRS adoption and firm size on audit fees in financial institutions in Ghana. *Accounting Research Journal*, 32(3), 436–453. DOI: 10.1108/ARJ-07-2017-0114

Cohen, J. R., Krishnamoorthy, G., & Wright, A. M. (2007). The impact of roles of the board on auditors' risk assessments and program planning decisions. *Auditing*, 26(1), 91–112. DOI: 10.2308/aud.2007.26.1.91

Cohen, M., Rozario, A., & Zhang, C. (2019). Exploring the use of robotic process automation (RPA) in substantive audit procedures: Certified public accountant. *The CPA Journal*, 89(7), 49–53.

Coman, D. M., Ionescu, C. A., Duică, A., Coman, M. D., Uzlau, M. C., Stanescu, S. G., & State, V. (2022). Digitization of accounting: The premise of the paradigm shift of role of the professional accountant. *Applied Sciences (Basel, Switzerland)*, 12(7), 3359. DOI: 10.3390/app12073359

Committee of Sponsoring Organizations of the Treadway Commission. (2004). *Enterprise risk management-integrated framework*. No Title.

Committee Of Sponsoring Organizations Of The Treadway Commission. (2017). Enterprise risk management: Integrating with strategy and performance.

Connect, F. (2024a). Artificial intelligence has arrived in financial services. Retrieved from: https://blog.finerioconnect.com/la-inteligencia-artificial-ha-llegado-a-los-servicios-financieros/

Connect, F. (2024b). Leading Open Finance Solutions for Latin America. Retrieved from: https://finerioconnect.com/

Cook, B. (2024). Navigating AI's Impact on Accounting: Uses, Trends and Tools, *Tipalti Accounting Hub*. Retrieved from: https://tipalti.com/accounting-hub/ai-accounting/

Coombs, C., Hislop, D., Taneva, S. K., & Barnard, S. (2020). The strategic impacts of Intelligent Automation for knowledge and service work: An interdisciplinary review. *The Journal of Strategic Information Systems*, 29(4), 101600. DOI: 10.1016/j.jsis.2020.101600

Cooper, L. A., Holderness, D. K.Jr, Sorensen, T. L., & Wood, D. A. (2019). Robotic process automation in public accounting. *Accounting Horizons*, 33(4), 15–35. DOI: 10.2308/acch-52466

Coram, P. J., & Wang, L. (2021). The effect of disclosing key audit matters and accounting standard precision on the audit expectation gap. *International Journal of Auditing*, 25(2), 270–282. DOI: 10.1111/ijau.12203

Corkern, S. M., Kimmel, S. B., & Morehead, B. (2015). Accountants need to be prepared for the big question: Should I move to the cloud? *International Journal of Management & Information Systems*, 19(1), 13. DOI: 10.19030/ijmis.v19i1.9085

Costa, R., Menichini, T., & Salierno, G. (2022). Do SDGs Really Matter for Business? Using GRI Sustainability Reporting to Answer the Question. *European Journal of Sustainable Development*, 11(1), 113. DOI: 10.14207/ejsd.2022.v11n1p113

Cualain, O. (2023). Review of IFRS consequences in Europe: An enforcement perspective. *Cogent Business & Management*, 10(1), 1–19. DOI: 10.1080/23311975.2022.2148869

Cumming, D., Leung, T. Y., & Rui, O. (2015). Gender diversity and securities fraud. *Academy of Management Journal*, 58(5), 1571–1593. DOI: 10.5465/amj.2013.0750

da Silva, C. G., Eyerkaufer, M. L., & Rengel, R. (2019). Inovação tecnológica e os desafios para uma contabilidade interativa: estudo dos escritórios de contabilidade do estado de santa Catarina. Revista Destaques Acadêmicos, 11(1).

da Silva, A. C., Curth, M., Kerber, L. E., & Morouço, P. (2022). A intenção de uso de tecnologia por acadêmicos de Educação Física de uma universidade do Rio Grande do Sul-Brasil. *Caderno de Educação Física e Esporte*, 21(1), 59.

Danach, K., Hejase, H. J., Faroukh, A., Fayyad-Kazan, H., & Moukadem, I. (2024). Assessing the Impact of Blockchain Technology on Financial Reporting and Audit Practices. *Asian Business Research*, 9(1), 30. DOI: 10.20849/abr.v9i1.1427

Datacamp. (2023, July). What is Data Analysis? An Expert Guide With Examples. Retrieved from: https://www.datacamp.com/blog/what-is-data-analysis-expert-guide

Datrics. (2024). AI Credit Scoring: The Future of Credit Risk Assessment. Retrieved from:_https://www.datrics.ai/articles/the-essentials-of-ai-based-credit-scoring#:~:text=A%20credit%20AI%20score%20is,likelihood%20of%20repaying%20a%20loan

Davenport, T. H., & Ronanki, R. (2018). Artificial intelligence for the real world. *Harvard Business Review*, 96(1), 108–116. https://hbr.org/2018/01/artificial-intelligence-for-the-real-world

Davis, F. D. (1989). Perceived usefulness, perceived ease of use, and user acceptance of information technology. *Management Information Systems Quarterly*, 13(3), 319–340. DOI: 10.2307/249008

Davis, F. D., Bagozzi, R. P., & Warshaw, P. R. (1989). User acceptance of computer technology: A comparison of two theoretical models. *Management Science*, 35(8), 984. DOI: 10.1287/mnsc.35.8.982

De Cristofaro, T., & Raucci, D. (2022). Rise and Fall of the Materiality Matrix: Lessons from a Missed Takeoff. *Administrative Sciences*, 12(4), 186. Advance online publication. DOI: 10.3390/admsci12040186

De Long, D. W., & Fahey, L. (2000). Diagnosing cultural barriers to knowledge management. *The Academy of Management Perspectives*, 14(4), 113–127. DOI: 10.5465/ame.2000.3979820

De Smet, D., & Mayer, N. (2016, October). Integration of IT governance and security risk management: A systematic literature review. In 2016 International Conference on Information Society (i-Society) (pp. 143-148). IEEE. DOI: 10.1109/i-Society.2016.7854200

De Villiers, R. (2021). Seven principles to ensure future-ready accounting graduates–a model for future research and practice. *Meditari Accountancy Research*, 29(6), 1354–1380. DOI: 10.1108/MEDAR-04-2020-0867

DeFond, M., & Zhang, J. (2014). A review of archival auditing research. A review of archival auditing research. *Journal of Accounting and Economics*, 58(2), 275–326. DOI: 10.1016/j.jacceco.2014.09.002

Degos, J.-G., Levant, Y., & Touron, P. (2019). The history of accounting standards in French-speaking African countries since independence: The uneasy path toward IFRS. *Accounting, Auditing & Accountability Journal*, 32(1), 75–100. DOI: 10.1108/AAAJ-03-2016-2459

Delgado-Ceballos, J., Ortiz-De-Mandojana, N., Antolín-López, R., & Montiel, I. (2023). Connecting the Sustainable Development Goals to firm-level sustainability and ESG factors: The need for double materiality. *Business Research Quarterly*, 26(1), 2–10. DOI: 10.1177/23409444221140919

Deloitte. (2024). *Women in the boardroom: a global perspective*. Deloitte Global Boardroom Program, Eight Edition.

Dempsey, K., & van Dyk, V. (2023). The Role of Data Analytics in Enhancing External Audit Quality. In Moloi, T., & George, B. (Eds.), *Towards Digitally Transforming Accounting and Business Processes* (pp. 399–423). Springer Nature Switzerland. DOI: 10.1007/978-3-031-46177-4_22

Desender, K. A. & LópezPuertas-Lamy, M. (2024). What drives corporate gender diversity in Latin America? Working Paper.

Desender, K. A., Aguilera, R. V., Lópezpuertas-Lamy, M., & Crespi, R. (2016). A clash of governance logics: Foreign ownership and board monitoring: Foreign Ownership and Board Monitoring. *Strategic Management Journal*, 37(2), 349–369. DOI: 10.1002/smj.2344

Desender, K. A., LópezPuertas-Lamy, M., Pattitoni, P., & Petracci, B. (2020). Corporate social responsibility and cost of financing—The importance of the international corporate governance system. *Corporate Governance*, 28(3), 207–234. DOI: 10.1111/corg.12312

Desender, K., Aguilera, R. V., Crespi-Cladera, R., & Garcia Cestona, M. A. (2013). When does ownership matter? Board characteristics and behavior. *Strategic Management Journal*, 34(7), 823–842. DOI: 10.1002/smj.2046

Desplebin, O., Lux, G., & Petit, N. (2021). To be or not to be: Blockchain and the future of accounting and auditing. *Accounting Perspectives*, 20(4), 743–769. DOI: 10.1111/1911-3838.12265

Dhlamini, J. (2022). Strategic risk management: A systematic review from 2001 to 2020. *Journal of Contemporary Management*, 19(2), 212–237. DOI: 10.35683/jcm22008.165

Dicko, S., & Fortin, A. (2014). IFRS adoption and the opinion of OHADA Accountants. *Afro-Asian J. Finance and Accounting*, 4(2), 141–162. DOI: 10.1504/AAJFA.2014.063746

Dilla, W., Janvrin, D. J., & Raschke, R. (2010). Interactive data visualization: New directions for accounting information systems research. *Journal of Information Systems*, 24(2), 1–37. DOI: 10.2308/jis.2010.24.2.1

Dobija, D., Arena, C., Kozlowski, L., Krasodomska, J., & Godawska, J. (2022). Towards sustainable development: The role of directors' international orientation and their diversity for non-financial disclosure. *Corporate Social Responsibility and Environmental Management*, 30(1), 66–90. DOI: 10.1002/csr.2339

Dobija, D., & Klimczak, K. M. (2008). Development of accounting in Poland: Market efficiency and the value relevance of reported earnings. *The International Journal of Accounting*, 45(3), 356–374. DOI: 10.1016/j.intacc.2010.06.010

Dong, S., Abbas, K., Li, M., & Kamruzzaman, J. (2023). Blockchain technology and application: An overview. *PeerJ. Computer Science*, 9, e1705. DOI: 10.7717/peerj-cs.1705 PMID: 38077532

Drollette, D., Jr. (2023, November 8). Charging ahead: Steven Chu, Nobel Prize-winner and former Energy Secretary, on today's battery research—and more. *Bulletin of the Atomic Scientists*. Retrieved from: https://thebulletin.org/premium/2023-11/charging-ahead-steven-chu-nobel-prize-winner-and-former-energy-secretary-on-todays-battery-research-and-more/#post-heading

Drollette, D., Jr. (2024, January 15). Interview with Sneha Revanur, "the Greta Thunberg of AI". *Bulletin of the Atomic Scientists*. Retrieved from: https://thebulletin.org/premium/2024-01/interview-with-sneha-revanur-the-greta-thunberg-of-ai/#post-heading

Du, H., Vasarhelyi, M. A., & Zheng, X. (2013). XBRL mandate: Thousands of filing errors and so what? *Journal of Information Systems*, 27(1), 61–78. DOI: 10.2308/isys-50399

Duran, I., & Rodrigo, P. (2018). Why Do Firms in Emerging Markets Report? A Stakeholder Theory Approach to Study the Determinants of Non-Financial Disclosure in Latin America. *Sustainability (Basel)*, 10(9), 3111. DOI: 10.3390/su10093111

Ebirim, G. U., Unigwe, I. F., Oshioste, E. E., Ndubuisi, N. L., Odonkor, B., & Asuzu, O. F. (2024). Innovations in accounting and auditing: A comprehensive review of current trends and their impact on US businesses. *International Journal of Science and Research Archive*, 11(1), 965–974. DOI: 10.30574/ijsra.2024.11.1.0134

Edgley, C. (2014). A genealogy of accounting materiality. *Critical Perspectives on Accounting*, 25(3), 255–271. DOI: 10.1016/j.cpa.2013.06.001

Effah, N. A. A. (2024). A bibliometric review of IFRS adoption and compliance research in Africa. *Journal of Business and Socio-economic Development*, 4(3), 193–209. DOI: 10.1108/JBSED-01-2023-0001

Elgendy, N., & Elragal, A. (2016). Big data analytics in support of the decision making process. *Procedia Computer Science*, 100, 1071–1084. DOI: 10.1016/j.procs.2016.09.251

Elhamma, A. (2023), Cinquante ans des normes comptables internationales IAS/IFRS: adoption, conséquences et où en est-on au Maroc? Ouvrage Collectif: « 50 ans de Management: regards croisés d'un demi-siècle du management », sous la direction de M'Rabet R. et Issami M.A., édition EDISCA, pp. 121-136.

Elhamma, A. (2023). Impact of mandatory IFRS adoption on foreign direct investment: the moderating role of conflict of interest regulation. *Journal of Financial Reporting and Accounting*, Vol. ahead-of-print No. ahead-of-print. DOI: 10.1108/JFRA-04-2022-0145

Elhamma, A. (2012). The activity based costing in morocco: Adoption and diffusion. *Arabian Journal of Business and Management Review*, 1(6), 33–45. DOI: 10.12816/0002111

Elhamma, A. (2014). Performance du Balanced Scorecard: Perception des responsables d'entreprises. *Revue Internationale de Management et de Stratégie*, 5(2), 1–9.

Elhamma, A. (2023). Impact of mandatory IFRS adoption on economic growth: The moderating role of Covid-19 crisis in developing countries. *Journal of Accounting and Management Information Systems*, 22(3), 554–568. DOI: 10.24818/jamis.2023.03007

Elhamma, A. (2024). Determinants of national IFRS adoption: Evidence from the Middle East and North Africa region. International Journal of Accounting. *Auditing and Performance Evaluation*, 20(1/2), 69–90. DOI: 10.1504/IJAAPE.2024.135535

Elhamma, A., & Moalla, H. (2015). Impact of uncertainty and decentralization on activity-based costing use. *International Journal of Accounting and Economics Studies*, 3(2), 148–155. DOI: 10.14419/ijaes.v3i2.4817

Elhamma, A., & Zhang, Yi. (2013). The relationship between activity-based costing, business strategy and performance in Moroccan enterprises. *Journal of Accounting and Management Information Systems*, 12(1), 22–38.

Ellili, N., Nobanee, H., Haddad, A., Alodat, A. Y., & AlShalloudi, M. (2024). Emerging trends in forensic accounting research: Bridging research gaps and prioritizing new frontiers. *Journal of Economic Criminology*, 100065.

Elshandidy, T., Elmassri, M., & Elsayed, M. (2022). Integrated reporting, textual risk disclosure and market value. *Corporate Governance (Bradford)*, 22(1), 173–193. DOI: 10.1108/CG-01-2021-0002

Enholm, I. M., Papagiannidis, E., Mikalef, P., & Krogstie, J. (2022). Artificial Intelligence and Business Value: A Literature Review. *Information Systems Frontiers*, 24(5), 1709–1734. DOI: 10.1007/s10796-021-10186-w

ERICA Working Group. (2023). *XBRL in European CBSO*. Brussels: European Committee of Central Balance Sheet Data Offices. https://www.bde.es/wbe/en/areas-actuacion/central-balances/colaboracion-con-otras-instiuciones/comite-europeo-centrales-balances

European Investment Bank. (2021). *Artificial intelligence, blockchain and the future of Europe: How disruptive technologies create opportunities for a green and digital economy*. Brussels: European Commission. https://www.eib.org/en/publications/artifical-intelligence-blockchain-and-the-future-of-europe-report

European Parliament and Council of the European Union. Directive (EU) 2022/2381 of 23 November 2022 on improving the gender balance among directors of listed companies and related measures. *Official Journal of the European Union*, L 315, 44-56.

European Parliament. (2014). Directive 2014/95/eu of the European Parliament and Council. https://eur-lex.europa.eu/legal-content/PT/TXT/HTML/?uri=CELEX: 32014L0095&from=EN

European Parliament. (2021). European Parliament and Council Directive. https://eur-lex.europa.eu/legal-content/PT/TXT/HTML/?uri=CELEX:52021PC0189& from=EN

European Parliamentary Research Service. (2020). *The impact of the General Data Protection Regulation (GDPR) on artificial intelligence*. Brussels: European Parliament. https://www.europarl.europa.eu/RegData/etudes/STUD/2020/641530/EPRS_STU(2020)641530_EN.pdf

Faccia, A., McDonald, J., & George, B. (2024). NLP Sentiment Analysis and Accounting Transparency: A New Era of Financial Record Keeping. *Computers*, 13(1), 5. DOI: 10.3390/computers13010005

Faccia, A., & Petratos, P. (2021). Blockchain, enterprise resource planning (ERP) and accounting information systems (AIS): Research on e-procurement and system integration. *Applied Sciences (Basel, Switzerland)*, 11(15), 6792. DOI: 10.3390/app11156792

Fakalou, C. (2024). The Sociolinguistics of Asylum Decision-Writing in the Context of the Greek Appeals Authority. *International Journal for the Semiotics of Law*, 37(2), 305–328. DOI: 10.1007/s11196-023-10039-6

Farayola, O. A., Adaga, E. M., Egieya, Z. E., Ewuga, S. K., Abdul, A. A., & Abrahams, T. O. (2024). Advancements in predictive analytics: A philosophical and practical overview. *World Journal of Advanced Research and Reviews*, 21(3), 240–252. DOI: 10.30574/wjarr.2024.21.3.2706

Farias, J. S., & Borges, D. M. (2012). Factors that influence the acceptance of technology: The perception of managers and employees in a restaurant chain. *Management & Technology Journal*, 12(2), 141–167.

Fasan, M., & Mio, C. (2017). Fostering stakeholder engagement: The role of materiality disclosure in integrated reporting. *Business Strategy and the Environment*, 26(3), 288–305. DOI: 10.1002/bse.1917

Feng, J. (2015). Cloud Accounting: The Transition of Accounting Information Model in the Big Data Background. *2015 International Conference on Intelligent Transportation, Big Data & Smart City (ICITBS)*, 207-211. DOI: 10.1109/ICITBS.2015.58

Fernandez-Vidal, J., Perotti, F. A., Gonzalez, R., & Gasco, J. (2022). Managing digital transformation: The view from the top. *Journal of Business Research*, 152, 29–41. DOI: 10.1016/j.jbusres.2022.07.020

Ferreira, G. R. (2016), Social competencies: a study with managers of the Attorney General's Office of the state of Pernambuco. Congress of Management and Controllership of UnoChapecó, Chapecó, Anais. CGC..

Ferreira, P. C. P. (2022). Influência do lobbying no processo de constituição do international sustainability standards board (ISSB) (Dissertação pós-graduação). Universidade Federal de Pernambuco. Pernambuco. https://repositorio.ufpe.br/bitstream/123456789/46246/1/DISSERTA%c3%87%c3%83O%20Priscila%20Cristine%20Pacheco%20Ferreira.pdf

Ferreira, T. T. (2022). Evolução da contabilidade digital e seus desafios.

Ferrero-Ferrero, I., León, R., & Muñoz-Torres, M. J. (2021). Sustainability materiality matrices in doubt: May prioritizations of aspects overestimate environmental performance? *Journal of Environmental Planning and Management*, 64(3), 432–463. DOI: 10.1080/09640568.2020.1766427

Fetzer, T. H., Gibson, Y. S., & Kuhn, J. R. (2023). Technological Transformation of Accounting–Need for Firms to add Technology Training Employee Skill Sets. *International Journal of Professional Business Review*, 8(12), e03858–e03858. DOI: 10.26668/businessreview/2023.v8i12.3858

Financial Executives Research Foundation Inc. [FERF] (2018). *Blockchain for Financial Leaders: Opportunity Vs. Reality*. https://www2.deloitte.com/content/dam/Deloitte/us/Documents/financial-services/us-fsi-fei-blockchain-report-future-hr.pdf

Fisher, I. E., Garnsey, M. R., Goel, S., & Tam, K. (2010). The Role of Text Analytics and Information Retrieval in the Accounting Domain. *Journal of Emerging Technologies in Accounting*, 7(1), 1–24. DOI: 10.2308/jeta.2010.7.1.1

Fisher, I. E., Garnsey, M. R., & Hughes, M. E. (2016). Natural Language Processing in accounting, auditing, and finance: A synthesis of the literature with a roadmap for future research. *International Journal of Intelligent Systems in Accounting Finance & Management*, 23(3), 157–214. DOI: 10.1002/isaf.1386

Fitz-Gibbon, C. (1990). *Performance indicators, BERA Dialogues (2)*. Taylor & Francis.

Formisano, V., Fedele, M., & Calabrese, M. (2018). The strategic priorities in the materiality matrix of the banking enterprise. *The TQM Journal*, 30(5), 589–607. DOI: 10.1108/TQM-11-2017-0134

Fortin, A., & Dicko, S. (2009). The impact of the new OHADA accounting system on the judgments and decisions of Cameroonian bankers. *Advances in Accounting, Incorporating. Advances in Accounting*, 25(1), 89–105. DOI: 10.1016/j.adiac.2009.02.006

Fritz-Morgenthal, S., Hein, B., & Papenbrock, J. (2022). Financial risk management and explainable, trustworthy, responsible AI. *Frontiers in Artificial Intelligence*, 5, 779799. DOI: 10.3389/frai.2022.779799 PMID: 35295866

Fukuda-Parr, S. (2014). Global goals as a policy tool: Intended and unintended consequences. *Journal of Human Development and Capabilities*, 15(2–3), 118–131. DOI: 10.1080/19452829.2014.910180

Fullana, O., & Ruiz, J. (2021). Accounting information systems in the blockchain era. *International Journal of Intellectual Property Management*, 11(1), 63–80. DOI: 10.1504/IJIPM.2021.113357

Furnell, S., Fischer, P., & Finch, A. (2017). Can't get the staff? The growing need for cyber-security skills. *Computer Fraud & Security*, 2017(2), 5–10. DOI: 10.1016/S1361-3723(17)30013-1

Galindo-Martín, M. A., Castaño-Martínez, M. S., & Méndez-Picazo, M. T. (2023). Digitalization, entrepreneurship and competitiveness: An analysis from 19 European countries. *Review of Managerial Science*, 17(5), 1809–1826. DOI: 10.1007/s11846-023-00640-1

Galvão, A. (2008). *Corporate Finance: Business Theory and Practice in Brazil*. Elsevier.

Gandía, J. L., & Huguet, D. (2021). Textual analysis and sentiment analysis in accounting. *Revista de Contabilidad-Spanish Accounting Review*, 24(2). DOI: 10.6018/rcsar.386541

Gao, X. (2023). Digital transformation in finance and its role in promoting financial transparency. *Global Finance Journal*, 58, 100903. DOI: 10.1016/j.gfj.2023.100903

Garanina, T., Ranta, M., & Dumay, J. (2022). Blockchain in accounting research: Current trends and emerging topics. *Accounting, Auditing & Accountability Journal*, 35(7), 1507–1533. DOI: 10.1108/AAAJ-10-2020-4991

Garcia-Sanchez, I. M., Martinez-Ferrero, J., & Garcia-Meca, E. (2017). Gender diversity, financial expertise and its effects on accounting quality. *Management Decision*, 55(2), 347–382. DOI: 10.1108/MD-02-2016-0090

García-Sánchez, I. M., Suárez-Fernández, O., & Martínez-Ferrero, J. (2019). Female directors and impression management in sustainability reporting. *International Business Review*, 28(2), 359–374. DOI: 10.1016/j.ibusrev.2018.10.007

Garst, J., Maas, K., & Suijs, J. (2022). Materiality Assessment Is an Art, Not a Science: Selecting ESG Topics for Sustainability Reports. *California Management Review*, 65(1), 64–90. DOI: 10.1177/00081256221120692

Gartner Research. (2018, August 20). Understanding Gartner's Hype Cycles. Retrieved from: https://www.gartner.com/en/documents/3887767

Gartner Research. (2024, July 31). Hype Cycle for Generative AI, 2024. Retrieved from https://www.gartner.com/en/documents/5636791

Gateway, B. (2024). Increase your profitability. Retrieved from: https://www.bgateway.com/resources/increase-your-profitability

Gazoulit, S.; Oubal, K. (2022), Risk Management in Public Universities In Search of Performance: A Synthesis of the Literature.

Gebremeskel, B. K., Jonathan, G. M., & Yalew, S. D. (2023). Information security challenges during digital transformation. *Procedia Computer Science*, 219, 44–51. DOI: 10.1016/j.procs.2023.01.262

Geldres-Weiss, V. V., Gambetta, N., Massa, N. P., & Geldres-Weiss, S. L. (2021). Materiality Matrix Use in Aligning and Determining a Firm's Sustainable Business Model Archetype and Triple Bottom Line Impact on Stakeholders. *Sustainability (Basel)*, 13(3), 1065. DOI: 10.3390/su13031065

Ghani, E., Laswad, F., & Tooley, S. (2009). Digital reporting formats: Users' perceptions, preferences and performances. *The International Journal of Digital Accounting Research*, 9(1), 45–98. DOI: 10.4192/1577-8517-v9_3

Ghosh, A., & Lustgarten, S. (2006). Pricing of initial audit engagements by large and small audit firms. *Contemporary Accounting Research*, 23(2), 333–368. DOI: 10.1506/927U-JGJY-35TA-7NT1

Ghosh, A., & Tang, C. Y. (2015). Assessing financial reporting quality of family firms: The auditors perspective. *Journal of Accounting and Economics*, 60(1), 95–116. DOI: 10.1016/j.jacceco.2015.03.002

Gibassier, D. (2019). *Materiality assessment: contribution to single or double materiality debate*. Working paper, Audencia Business School, Nantes, France. https://www.anc.gouv.fr/files/live/sites/anc/files/contributed/ANC/3_Recherche/D_Etats%20generaux/2020/Policy%20papers/TR4_VE-paper-Delphine-Gibassier.pdf

Gierusz, J., Kolesnik, K., Silska-Gembka, S., & Zamojska, A. (2022). The influence of culture on accounting judgment – Evidence from Poland and the United Kingdom. *Cogent Business & Management*, 9(1), 1993556. Advance online publication. DOI: 10.1080/23311975.2021.1993556

Gil, A. C. (2022). *How to Develop Research Projects* (Vol. 4). Atlas São Paulo.

Goldman, S. (2024, August 6). Generative AI is getting kicked off its pedestal — it will be painful but it's not a bad thing. *Fortune*. Retrieved from: https://fortune.com/2024/08/06/generative-ai-reality-check-tech-selloff-new-phase-less-hype-more-roi/

Goldston, J. (2020). The evolution of ERP systems: A literature review. *International Journal of Research Publications*, 50(1), 21–37.

Gonçalves, M., Magalhães, V., Marques, D. (2019), International financial cases and crises: a literature review. Ethics and Social Responsibility, 6-8.

Gonçalves, M. J. A., da Silva, A. C. F., & Ferreira, C. G. (2022). The future of accounting: How will digital transformation impact the sector? *Informatics (MDPI)*, 9(1), 1–17. DOI: 10.3390/informatics9010019

González Páramo, J. M. (2017). Financial innovation in the digital age: Challenges for regulation and supervision. *Revista de Estabilidad Financiera/Banco de España*, 32, 9-37. https://repositorio.bde.es/handle/123456789/11293

Google Workspace Learning Center. (2024). Switch from Excel to Sheets: What you'll learn. Retrieved from: https://support.google.com/a/users/answer/13189180?hl=en&visit_id=638585167896129518-2721732101&ref_topic=9296611&rd=1

Google. (2024). Use Analytics with your site. Retrieved from: https://support.google.com/sites/answer/97459?hl=en

Gordon, E. A. (2008). Sustainability in global financial reporting and innovation in institutions. *Accounting Research Journal*, 21(3), 231–238. DOI: 10.1108/10309610810922486

Gordon, L. A., Loeb, M. P., & Sohail, T. (2010). Market value of voluntary disclosures concerning information security. *Management Information Systems Quarterly*, 34(3), 567–594. DOI: 10.2307/25750692

Gordon, L. A., Loeb, M. P., & Tseng, C. Y. (2009). Enterprise risk management and firm performance: A contingency perspective. Journal of Accounting and Public Policy, 28(4), 301-327.

Gormley, T. A., Gupta, V. K., Matsa, D. A., Mortal, S. C., & Yang, L. (2023). The Big Three and board gender diversity: The effectiveness of shareholder voice. *Journal of Financial Economics*, 149(2), 323–348. DOI: 10.1016/j.jfineco.2023.04.001

Gotthardt, M., Koivulaakso, D., Paksoy, O., Saramo, C., Martikainen, M., & Lehner, O. (2020). *Current state and challenges in the implementation of smart robotic process automation in accounting and auditing.* ACRN Journal of Finance and Risk Perspectives. DOI: 10.35944/jofrp.2020.9.1.007

Gouadain, D., & Wade, E. B. (2009). 'SYSCOA/OHADA'. In *Encyclopédie de Comptabilité, Contrôle de gestion et Audit*. Économica.

Gow, I. D., Larcker, D. F., & Watts, E. M. (2023). Board diversity and shareholder voting. *Journal of Corporate Finance*, 83(102487), 102487. DOI: 10.1016/j.jcorpfin.2023.102487

Gowry, Y., Subadar Agathee, U. & Soobaroyen, T. (2023). IFRS and the evolution of value relevance: evidence from an African developing country. *Journal of Financial Reporting and Accounting*, Vol. ahead-of-print No. ahead-of-print. DOI: 10.1108/JFRA-07-2022-0252

Grabski, S. V., Leech, S. A., & Schmidt, P. J. (2011). A review of ERP research: A future agenda for accounting information systems. *Journal of Information Systems*, 25(1), 37–78. DOI: 10.2308/jis.2011.25.1.37

Green, W., & Cheng, M. (2019). Materiality judgments in an integrated reporting setting: The effect of strategic relevance and strategy map. *Accounting, Organizations and Society*, 73, 1–14. DOI: 10.1016/j.aos.2018.07.001

Gregory, A., & Collier, P. (1996). Audit fees and auditor change: An investigation of the persistence of fee reduction by type of change. *Journal of Business Finance & Accounting*, 23(1), 13–28. DOI: 10.1111/j.1468-5957.1996.tb00399.x

GRI. (2021). GRI 3: Material Topics 2021. https://globalreporting.org/pdf.ashx?id=12453

GRI. (2023). About GRI. https://www.globalreporting.org/Information/about-gri/Pages/default.aspx

Guix, M., Bonilla-Priego, M. J., & Font, X. (2018). The process of sustainability reporting in international hotel groups: An analysis of stakeholder inclusiveness, materiality and responsiveness. *Journal of Sustainable Tourism*, 26(7), 1063–1084. DOI: 10.1080/09669582.2017.1410164

Guo, C., Ke, Y., & Zhang, J. (2023). Digital transformation along the supply chain. *Pacific-Basin Finance Journal*, 80, 102088. DOI: 10.1016/j.pacfin.2023.102088

Guping, C., Safdar Sial, M., Wan, P., Badulescu, A., Badulescu, D., & Vianna Brugni, T. (2020). Do Board Gender Diversity and Non-Executive Directors Affect CSR Reporting? Insight from Agency Theory Perspective. *Sustainability (Basel)*, 12(20), 8597. Advance online publication. DOI: 10.3390/su12208597

Gupta, S., Tuunanen, T., Kar, A. K., & Modgil, S. (2023). Managing digital knowledge for ensuring business efficiency and continuity. *Journal of Knowledge Management*, 27(2), 245–263. DOI: 10.1108/JKM-09-2021-0703

Guth, C. (2024, April 17). Google Sheets VS. Excel: Complete Overview. Retrieved from: https://sada.com/blog/google-sheets-vs-excel/

Haber, S., & Scott Stornetta, W. (1991). How to time-stamp a digital document. *Lecture Notes in Computer Science (Including Subseries Lecture Notes in Artificial Intelligence and Lecture Notes in Bioinformatics), 537 LNCS*, 437–455. DOI: 10.1007/3-540-38424-3_32

Hajek, P., & Munk, M. (2023). Speech emotion recognition and text sentiment analysis for financial distress prediction. *Neural Computing & Applications*, 35(29), 21463–21477. DOI: 10.1007/s00521-023-08470-8

Hall, P. A., & Soskice, D. (Eds.). (2001). *Varieties of capitalism: The institutional foundations of comparative advantage*. Oxford University Press. DOI: 10.1093/0199247757.001.0001

Hamed, S., Ezzat, M., & Hefny, H. (2020). A Review of Sentiment Analysis Techniques. *International Journal of Computer Applications*, 176(37), 20–24. DOI: 10.5120/ijca2020920480

Hamilton, M. (2019). Blockchain distributed ledger technology: An introduction and focus on smart contracts. *Journal of Corporate Accounting & Finance*, 31(2), 7–12. DOI: 10.1002/jcaf.22421

Handoyo, S. (2024). Evolving paradigms in accounting education: A bibliometric study on the impact of information technology. *International Journal of Management Education*, 22(3), 100998. DOI: 10.1016/j.ijme.2024.100998

Handoyo, S., Suharman, H., Ghani, E. K., & Soedarsono, S. (2023). A business strategy, operational efficiency, ownership structure, and manufacturing performance: The moderating role of market uncertainty and competition intensity and its implication on open innovation. *Journal of Open Innovation*, 9(2), 100039. DOI: 10.1016/j.joitmc.2023.100039

Han, H., Shiwakoti, R. K., Jarvis, R., Mordi, C., & Botchie, D. (2023). Accounting and auditing with blockchain technology and artificial Intelligence: A literature review. *International Journal of Accounting Information Systems*, 48, 100598. DOI: 10.1016/j.accinf.2022.100598

Harjoto, M. A., Laksmana, I., & Lee, R. (2015). The impact of demographic characteristics of CEOs and directors on audit fees and audit delay. *Managerial Auditing Journal*, 30(8/9), 963–997. DOI: 10.1108/MAJ-01-2015-1147

Harrast, S. A. (2020). Robotic process automation in accounting systems. *Journal of Corporate Accounting & Finance*, 31(4), 209–213. DOI: 10.1002/jcaf.22457

Harshitha, T. N., Sudha, M., Ramachandran, M., & Ramu, K. (2023). A Review on Regulations of Financial Reporting. *Recent trends in Management and Commerce*, 4(2), 144-156. http://dx.doi.org/DOI: 10.46632/rmc/4/2

Hartley, B. R., & Dammeyer, L. (2024, July 30). The Best Robo-Advisors Of April 2024. *Forbes*. Retrieved from: https://www.forbes.com/advisor/investing/best-robo-advisors/

Hasan, A. R. (2022). Artificial Intelligence (AI) in Accounting & Auditing: A Literature Review. *Open Journal of Business and Management*, 10(1), 440–465. DOI: 10.4236/ojbm.2022.101026

Hay, D., Knechel, W. R., & Ling, H. (2008). Evidence on the impact of internal control and corporate governance on audit fees. *International Journal of Auditing*, 12(1), 9–24. DOI: 10.1111/j.1099-1123.2008.00367.x

Hay, D., Knechel, W. R., & Wong, N. (2006). Audit fees: A meta-analysis of the effect of supply and demand attributes. *Contemporary Accounting Research*, 23(1), 141–191. DOI: 10.1506/4XR4-KT5V-E8CN-91GX

Hayes, A., & Smith, A. (2023, September 1). Are Robo-Advisors Worth It? *Investopedia*. Retrieved from: https://www.investopedia.com/are-robo-advisors-worth-it-7568057#:~:text=Key%20Takeaways,investors%20seeking%20competent%20portfolio%20management

Hazar, H. B., & Toplu, C. (2023). The use of robotic process automation in accounting. *Prizren Social Science Journal*, 7(3), 45–50. DOI: 10.32936/pssj.v7i3.481

Heineken, N. V. Annual Report (2021). https://www.theheinekencompany.com/sites/theheinekencompany/files/Investors/financial-information/results-reports-presentations/heineken-nv-annual-report-2021-25-02-2022.pdf

Helfaya, A., Morris, R., & Aboud, A. (2023). Investigating the Factors That Determine the ESG Disclosure Practices in Europe. *Sustainability (Basel)*, 15(6), 5508. Advance online publication. DOI: 10.3390/su15065508

Hellmann, A., & Patel, C. (2021). Translation of International Financial Reporting Standards and implications for judgments and decision-making. *Journal of Behavioral and Experimental Finance*, 30, 100479. DOI: 10.1016/j.jbef.2021.100479

Hellmann, A., Patel, C., & Tsunogaya, N. (2021). Foreign-language effect and professionals' judgments on fair value measurement: Evidence from Germany and the United Kingdom. *Journal of Behavioral and Experimental Finance*, 30, 100478. DOI: 10.1016/j.jbef.2021.100478

Hessayri, M., & Saihi, M. (2018). Ownership dynamics around IFRS adoption: Emerging markets context. *Journal of Accounting in Emerging Economies*, 8(1), 2–28. DOI: 10.1108/JAEE-01-2016-0002

He, W., & Zhang, Z. (2019). Enterprise cybersecurity training and awareness programs: Recommendations for success. *Journal of Organizational Computing and Electronic Commerce*, 29(4), 249–257. DOI: 10.1080/10919392.2019.1611528

Hilal, W., Gadsden, S. A., & Yawney, J. (2022). Financial fraud: A review of anomaly detection techniques and recent advances. *Expert Systems with Applications*, 193, 116429. DOI: 10.1016/j.eswa.2021.116429

Hill, S., & Dinsdale, G. (2003). *A basis for the development of learning strategies for risk management in the public service. Translation: Luís Marcos de Vasconcelos*. ENAP.

Hodge, F. D., Kennedy, J. J., & Maines, L. A. (2004). Does search-facilitating technology improve the transparency of financial reporting? *The Accounting Review*, 79(3), 687–703. DOI: 10.2308/accr.2004.79.3.687

Hoeflich, S. (2016). Risk management applied to organizations: integrating the silos of grc. 2016, Rio de Janeiro.

Hoe, S. L. (2019). Digitalization in practice: The fifth discipline advantage. *The Learning Organization*, 27(1), 54–64. DOI: 10.1108/TLO-09-2019-0137

Hofbauer, G., & Sangl, A. (2019). Blockchain technology and application possibilities in the digital transformation of transaction processes. *Forum Scientiae Oeconomia*, 7(4), 25–40. DOI: 10.23762/FSO_VOL7_NO4_2

Hoffmann, C. H., & Hahn, B. (2020). Decentered ethics in the machine era and guidance for AI regulation. *AI & Society*, 35(3), 635–644. DOI: 10.1007/s00146-019-00920-z

Hogan, C. E., & Wilkins, M. S. (2008). Evidence on the audit risk model: Do auditors increase audit fees in the presence of internal control deficiencies? *Contemporary Accounting Research*, 25(1), 219–242. DOI: 10.1506/car.25.1.9

Hoofnagle, C. J., Van Der Sloot, B., & Borgesius, F. Z. (2019). The European Union general data protection regulation: What it is and what it means. *Information & Communications Technology Law*, 28(1), 65–98. DOI: 10.1080/13600834.2019.1573501

Hopkin, P. (2018). *Fundamentals of risk management: understanding, evaluating and implementing effective risk management.* Kogan Page Publishers.

Houqe, N. (2018). A review of the current debate on the determinants and consequences of mandatory IFRS adoption. *International Journal of Accounting and Information Management*, 26(3), 413–442. DOI: 10.1108/IJAIM-03-2017-0034

Houston, R. W., Peters, M. F., & Pratt, J. H. (1999). The audit risk model, business risk and audit planning decisions. *The Accounting Review*, 74(3), 281–298. DOI: 10.2308/accr.1999.74.3.281

Huang, F., & Vasarhelyi, M. A. (2019). Applying robotic process automation (RPA) in auditing: A framework. *International Journal of Accounting Information Systems*, 35, 100433. DOI: 10.1016/j.accinf.2019.100433

Huang, T.-C., Huang, H.-W., & Lee, C.-C. (2014). Corporate executive's gender and audit fees. *Managerial Auditing Journal*, 29(6), 527–547. DOI: 10.1108/MAJ-03-2013-0837

Hund, A., Wagner, H. T., Beimborn, D., & Weitzel, T. (2021). Digital innovation: Review and novel perspective. *The Journal of Strategic Information Systems*, 30(4), 101695. DOI: 10.1016/j.jsis.2021.101695

Hung, M., & Subramanyam, K. (2007). Financial Statement Effects of Adopting International Accounting standards: The case of Germany. *Review of Accounting Studies*, 12(4), 623–657. DOI: 10.1007/s11142-007-9049-9

Huse, M., & Solberg, A. (2006). Gender related boardroom dynamics: How women make and can make contributions on corporate boards. *Women in Management Review*, 21(2), 113–130. DOI: 10.1108/09649420610650693

Hussin, N. A. K. M., Bukhari, N. A. N. M., Hashim, N. H. A. N., Bahari, S. N. A. S., & Ali, M. M. (2024). The Impact of Artificial Intelligence on the Accounting Profession: A Concept Paper. *Business Management and Strategy*, 15(1), 34–50. DOI: 10.5296/bms.v15i1.21620

Iatridis, G. (2010). International Financial Reporting Standards and the Quality of Financial Statement Information. *International Review of Financial Analysis*, 19(3), 193–204. DOI: 10.1016/j.irfa.2010.02.004

IBN Technologies Limited. (2024, January 2). Advantages of AI Accounting: Unlocking Efficiency and Accuracy. Retrieved from: https://www.ibntech.com/blog/ai-accounting-benefits-and-challenges/

Ibrahim, A. E. A., Elamer, A. A., & Ezat, A. N. (2021). The convergence of big data and accounting: Innovative research opportunities. *Technological Forecasting and Social Change*, 173, 121171. DOI: 10.1016/j.techfore.2021.121171

IFRS. (2024). *Digital Financial Reporting. Facilitating digital comparability and analysis of financial reports*. London: International Accounting Standards Board. https://www.ifrs.org/digital-financial-reporting/

Indeed Editorial Team. (2023, March 10). 17 Strategies for Increasing the Profitability of a Business. Retrieved from: https://www.indeed.com/career-advice/career-development/increase-profitability

Inglehart, R., Norris, P., & Welzel, C. (2002). Gender equality and democracy. *Comparative Sociology*, 1(3–4), 321–345.

Institute of Chartered Accountants in England and Wales [ICAEW] (2018). Blockchain And The Future Of Accountancy. *Icaew Thought Leadership*, 1–12. https://www.icaew.com/technical/technology/blockchain-and-cryptoassets/blockchain-articles/blockchain-and-the-accounting-perspective

Intezari, A., & Gressel, S. (2017). Information and reformation in KM systems: Big data and strategic decision-making. *Journal of Knowledge Management*, 21(1), 71–91. DOI: 10.1108/JKM-07-2015-0293

Ionaşcu, I., Ionaşcu, M., Nechita, E., Săcărin, M., & Minu, M. (2022). Digital transformation, financial performance and sustainability: Evidence for European Union listed companies. *Amfiteatru Economic*, 24(59), 94–109. DOI: 10.24818/EA/2022/59/94

Iredele, O. O. (2019). Examining the association between quality of integrated reports and corporate characteristics. *Heliyon*, 5(7), e01932. Advance online publication. DOI: 10.1016/j.heliyon.2019.e01932 PMID: 31317079

ISO 31000 (2018) Risk Management – Guidelines. International Organization for Standardization.

ISO 31010 (2019) Risk Management. Techniques for the Risk Assessment Process.

Issac, R., Muni, R., & Desai, K. (2018, February). Delineated analysis of robotic process automation tools. In *2018 Second International Conference on Advances in Electronics, Computers and Communications (ICAECC)* (pp. 1-5). IEEE. DOI: 10.1109/ICAECC.2018.8479511

Ittonen, K., Miettinen, J., & Vähämaa, S. (2010). Does female representation on audit committees affect audit fees? *Quarterly Journal of Finance and Accounting*, 49(3), 113–139.

Jain, A., & Ranjan, S. (2020). Implications of emerging technologies on the future of work. *IIMB Management Review*, 32(4), 448–454. DOI: 10.1016/j.iimb.2020.11.004

Jędrzejka, D. (2019). Robotic process automation and its impact on accounting. *Zeszyty Teoretyczne Rachunkowości*, 105(161), 137–166. DOI: 10.5604/01.3001.0013.6061

Jeffery, N. (2009). Stakeholder engagement: A road map to meaningful engagement. *Doughty Centre, Cranfield School of Management, 2*, 19-48. http://hdl.handle.net/1826/3801

Jejeniwa, T. O., Mhlongo, N. Z., & Jejeniwa, T. O. (2024). A comprehensive review of the impact of artificial intelligence on modern accounting practices and financial reporting. *Computer Science & IT Research Journal*, 5(4), 1031–1047. DOI: 10.51594/csitrj.v5i4.1086

Jensen, M. C., & Meckling, W. H. (2019). Theory of the firm: Managerial behaviour, agency costs and ownership structure. In *Corporate governance* (pp. 77–132). Gower.

JieWei, W., JianQiang, C., Li, L., YuZheng, L., Zhenhong, G. U., & Loang, O. K. (2023). The Impact of Digital Transformation on Financial Reporting and Analysis in the Accounting Industry. *The International Journal of Accounting*, 8(50), 290–309. DOI: 10.55573/IJAFB.085021

Johnstone, K., Grambling, A., & Rittenberg, L. E. (2014). *Auditing: A risk-based approach to conducting a quality audit* (10th ed.). Cengage Learning.

Jones, K. P., Peddie, C. I., Gilrane, V. L., King, E. B., & Gray, A. L. (2016). Not So Subtle: A Meta-Analytic Investigation of the Correlates of Subtle and Overt Discrimination. *Journal of Management*, 42(6), 1588–1613. DOI: 10.1177/0149206313506466

Jones, P., Comfort, D., & Hillier, D. (2016). Managing materiality: A preliminary examination of the adoption of the new GRI G4 guidelines on materiality within the business community. *Journal of Public Affairs*, 16(3), 222–230. DOI: 10.1002/pa.1586

Jørgensen, S., Mjøs, A., & Pedersen, L. J. T. (2022). Sustainability reporting and approaches to materiality: Tensions and potential resolutions. *Sustainability Accounting. Management and Policy Journal*, 13(2), 341–361. DOI: 10.1108/SAMPJ-01-2021-0009

Justice, E. (2024a). Encode Justice is mobilizing communities for AI aligned with human values. Retrieved from: https://encodejustice.org/what-we-do/

Justice, E. (2024b). We're reimagining our generation's collective AI future. Retrieved from: https://encodejustice.org/#:~:text=Encode%20Justice%20is%20the%20world%27s,movement%20for%20safe%2C%20equitable%20AI

Kabwe, M., Mwanaumo, E., & Chalu, H. (2021). Effect of corporate governance attributes on IFRS compliance: Evidence from a developing country. *Corporate Governance (Bradford)*, 21(1), 1–22. DOI: 10.1108/CG-03-2020-0103

Kalbuana, N., Kusiyah, K., Supriatiningsih, S., Budiharjo, R., Budyastuti, T., & Rusdiyanto, R. (2022). Effect of profitability, audit committee, company size, activity, and board of directors on sustainability. *Cogent Business & Management*, 9(1), 2129354. Advance online publication. DOI: 10.1080/23311975.2022.2129354

Kang, Y., Cai, Z., Tan, C. W., Huang, Q., & Liu, H. (2020). Natural language processing (NLP) in management research: A literature review. *Journal of Management Analytics*, 7(2), 139–172. DOI: 10.1080/23270012.2020.1756939

Karğin, S. (2013). The impact of IFRS on the value relevance of accounting information: Evidence from Turkish firms. *International Journal of Economics and Finance*, 5(4), 71–80. DOI: 10.5539/ijef.v5n4p71

Kaur, R., Gabrijelčič, D., & Klobučar, T. (2023). Artificial intelligence for cybersecurity: Literature review and future research directions. *Information Fusion*, 97, 101804. DOI: 10.1016/j.inffus.2023.101804

Kaya, C. T., Turkyilmaz, M., & Birol, B. (2019). Impact of RPA technologies on accounting systems. *Muhasebe ve Finansman Dergisi*, 82, 235–250. DOI: 10.25095/mufad.536083

Kearney, C., & Liu, S. (2014). Textual sentiment in finance: A survey of methods and models. *International Review of Financial Analysis*, 33, 171–185. DOI: 10.1016/j.irfa.2014.02.006

Kenneth, M., & Grazyina, M. (2013). The Adoption of International Financial reporting Standards for small and medium enterprises in Zimbabwe. *International Journal of Asian Social Science*, 3(11), 2315–2349.

Khaled AlKoheji, A., & Al-Sartawi, A. (2022). Artificial intelligence and its impact on accounting systems. In Al-Sartawi, A., Razzque, A., & Kamel, M. M. (Eds.), *From the Internet of Things to the Internet of Ideas: The role of Artificial Intelligence* (pp. 647–655). Springer International Publishing. DOI: 10.1007/978-3-031-17746-0_51

Khatri, A., & Gupta, N. (2022). Impact of Data Visualization on Management Decisions. *London Journal of Research in Management and Business*, 22, 53–62.

Khlif, H., Kamran, A., & Manzurul, A. (2020). Accounting Regulations and IFRS Adoption in Francophone North African Countries: The Experience of Algeria, Morocco, and Tunisia. *The International Journal of Accounting*, 55(1), 2050004. DOI: 10.1142/S1094406020500043

Kickert, W. J. (1997). Public governance in The Netherlands: An alternative to Anglo-American 'managerialism'. *Public Administration*, 75(4), 731–752. DOI: 10.1111/1467-9299.00084

Kim, Y., Park, M. S., & Wier, B. (2012). Is earnings quality associated with corporate social responsibility? *The Accounting Review*, 87(3), 761–796. DOI: 10.2308/accr-10209

Kinderman, D. (2020). The challenges of upward regulatory harmonization: The case of sustainability reporting in the European Union. *Regulation & Governance*, 14(4), 674–697. DOI: 10.1111/rego.12240

Klinger, B., & Szczeoanski, J. (2017). Blockchain - History, Features and Main Areas of Application. *Człowiek W Cyberprzestrzeni, 1*(810), 7–20.

Klish, A. A., Shubita, M. F. S., & Wu, J. (2022). IFRS adoption and financial reporting quality in the MENA region. *Journal of Applied Accounting Research*, 23(3), 570–603. DOI: 10.1108/JAAR-08-2020-0155

Knechel, W. R., & Willekens, M. (2006). The role of risk management and governance in determining audit demand. *Journal of Business Finance & Accounting*, 33(9-10), 1344–1367. DOI: 10.1111/j.1468-5957.2006.01238.x

Knippen, J. M., Shen, W., & Zhu, Q. (2019). Limited progress? The effect of external pressure for board gender diversity on the increase of female directors. *Strategic Management Journal*, 40(7), 1123–1150. DOI: 10.1002/smj.3014

Knudsen, E. S., Lien, L. B., Timmermans, B., Belik, I., & Pandey, S. (2021). Stability in turbulent times? The effect of digitalization on the sustainability of competitive advantage. *Journal of Business Research*, 128, 360–369. DOI: 10.1016/j.jbusres.2021.02.008

Kokina, J., & Blanchette, S. (2019). Early evidence of digital labor in accounting: Innovation with Robotic Process Automation. *International Journal of Accounting Information Systems*, 35, 100431. DOI: 10.1016/j.accinf.2019.100431

Kolk, A., & Van Tulder, R. (2010). International business, corporate social responsibility and sustainable development. *International Business Review*, 19(2), 119–125. DOI: 10.1016/j.ibusrev.2009.12.003

Kong, D. T. (2016). A gene-dependent climatoeconomic model of generalized trust. *Journal of World Business*, 51(2), 226–236. DOI: 10.1016/j.jwb.2015.08.018

Korhonen, T., Selos, E., Laine, T., & Suomala, P. (2021). Exploring the programmability of management accounting work for increasing automation: An interventionist case study. *Accounting, Auditing & Accountability Journal*, 34(2), 253–280. DOI: 10.1108/AAAJ-12-2016-2809

Korkut, E. H., & Surer, E. (2023). Visualization in virtual reality: A systematic review. *Virtual Reality (Waltham Cross)*, 27(2), 1447–1480. DOI: 10.1007/s10055-023-00753-8

Kothakota, M. G., & Kiss, D. E. (2020). Use of Visualization Tools to Improve Financial Knowledge: An Experimental Approach. *Financial Counseling and Planning*, 31(2), 193–208. DOI: 10.1891/JFCP-18-00070

KPMG. (2019). Automation of financial reporting and technical accounting. Amstelveen: KMPG International. https://assets.kpmg.com/content/dam/kpmg/uk/pdf/2019/09/automation-of-financial-reporting-and-technical-accounting.pdf

Krause, R., Priem, R., & Love, L. (2015). Who's in charge here? Co-CEOs, power gaps, and firm performance: Co-CEOs, Power Gaps, and Firm Performance. *Strategic Management Journal*, 36(13), 2099–2110. DOI: 10.1002/smj.2325

Kraus, S., Durst, S., Ferreira, J. J., Veiga, P., Kailer, N., & Weinmann, A. (2022). Digital transformation in business and management research: An overview of the current status quo. *International Journal of Information Management*, 63(4), 102466. DOI: 10.1016/j.ijinfomgt.2021.102466

Kraus, S., Jones, P., Kailer, N., Weinmann, A., Chaparro-Banegas, N., & Roig-Tierno, N. (2021). Digital transformation: An overview of the current state of the art of research. *SAGE Open*, 11(3), 1–15. DOI: 10.1177/21582440211047576

Krishnamoorthy, S. (2018). Sentiment analysis of financial news articles using performance indicators. *Knowledge and Information Systems*, 56(2), 373–394. DOI: 10.1007/s10115-017-1134-1

Krishnan, G. V., & Parsons, L. M. (2008). Getting to the bottom line: An exploration of gender and earnings quality. *Journal of Business Ethics*, 78(1–2), 65–76. DOI: 10.1007/s10551-006-9314-z

Kroon, N., do Céu Alves, M., & Martins, I. (2021). The impacts of emerging technologies on accountants' role and skills: Connecting to open innovation—a systematic literature review. *Journal of Open Innovation*, 7(3), 163. DOI: 10.3390/joitmc7030163

Kusumawardhani, F., Ratmono, D., Wibowo, S., Darsono, D., Widyatmoko, S., & Rokhman, N. (2024). The impact of digitalization in accounting systems on information quality, cost reduction and decision making: Evidence from SMEs. *International Journal of Data and Network Science*, 8(2), 1111–1116. DOI: 10.5267/j.ijdns.2023.11.023

L.M. & Alur. (2023). Mapping the Research Landscape of Chatbots, Conversational Agents, and Virtual Assistants in Business, Management, and Accounting: A Bibliometric Review. *Qubahan Academic Journal*, 3(4), 502–513. Retrieved from: https://journal.qubahan.com/index.php/qaj/article/view/252

Lai, A., Melloni, G., & Stacchezzini, R. (2017). What does materiality mean to integrated reporting preparers? An empirical exploration. *Meditari Accountancy Research*, 25(4), 533–552. DOI: 10.1108/MEDAR-02-2017-0113

Lai, K. M. Y., Srinidhi, B., Gul, F. A., & Tsui, J. S. L. (2017). Board gender diversity, auditor fees, and auditor choice. *Contemporary Accounting Research*, 34(3), 1681–1714. DOI: 10.1111/1911-3846.12313

Lam, J. (2014). *Enterprise risk management: from incentives to controls*. John Wiley & Sons. DOI: 10.1002/9781118836477

Langa, E., & Albuquerque, F. (2024). Conservatism as a cultural accounting value: An empirical study from the perspective of chartered accountants and auditors in Mozambique. *Contaduría y Administración*, 69(1), 1–22. DOI: 10.22201/fca.24488410e.2024.4682

Leão, P., & da Silva, M. M. (2021). Impacts of digital transformation on firms' competitive advantages: A systematic literature review. *Strategic Change*, 30(5), 421–441. DOI: 10.1002/jsc.2459

Leitner-Hanetseder, S., Lehner, O. M., Eisl, C., & Forstenlechner, C. (2021). A profession in transition: Actors, tasks and roles in AI-based accounting. *Journal of Applied Accounting Research*, 22(3), 539–556. DOI: 10.1108/JAAR-10-2020-0201

Lenormand, G. & Touchais, L. (2009). Les IFRS améliorent-elles la qualité de l'information financière ? Approche par la value relevance. *Comptabilité- Contrôle- Audit*, 15(2), 145 – 164.

Lin, J., Zeng, Y., Wu, S., & Luo, X. R. (2024). How does artificial intelligence affect the environmental performance of organizations? The role of green innovation and green culture. *Information & Management*, 61(2), 103924. DOI: 10.1016/j.im.2024.103924

Liu, J., Kauffman, R. J., & Ma, D. (2015). Competition, cooperation, and regulation: Understanding the evolution of the mobile payments technology ecosystem. *Electronic Commerce Research and Applications*, 14(5), 372–391. DOI: 10.1016/j.elerap.2015.03.003

Liu, J., & Liu, C. (2007). Value relevance of accounting information in different stock market segments: The case of Chinese A-, B-, and H-shares. *Journal of International Accounting Research*, 6(2), 55–81. DOI: 10.2308/jiar.2007.6.2.55

Liu, M., & Wysocki, P. (2007). Cross-sectional determinants of information quality proxies and cost of capital measures. *The Quarterly Journal of Finance*, 7(2), 1650016. DOI: 10.1142/S2010139216500166

Liu, X., & Ishak, N. N. B. M. (2023). Research on the application and development of RPA in accounting higher vocational education: A Chinese perspective. *International Journal of Education and Humanities*, 10(2), 178–182. DOI: 10.54097/ijeh.v10i2.11592

Liu, X., Lobo, G. J., & Yu, H.-C. (2021). Is audit committee equity compensation related to audit fees? *Contemporary Accounting Research*, 38(1), 740–769. DOI: 10.1111/1911-3846.12632

Liu, Y., Heinberg, M., Huang, X., & Eisingerich, A. B. (2023). Building a competitive advantage based on transparency: When and why does transparency matter for corporate social responsibility? *Business Horizons*, 66(4), 517–527. DOI: 10.1016/j.bushor.2022.10.004

Liu, Z., & Zhang, N. (2023). The productivity effect of digital financial reporting. *Review of Accounting Studies*, 29(3), 1–41. DOI: 10.1007/s11142-022-09737-6

Lobschat, L., Mueller, B., Eggers, F., Brandimarte, L., Diefenbach, S., Kroschke, M., & Wirtz, J. (2021). Corporate digital responsibility. *Journal of Business Research*, 122, 875–888. DOI: 10.1016/j.jbusres.2019.10.006

Lois, P., Drogalas, G., Karagiorgos, A., & Tsikalakis, K. (2020). Internal audits in the digital era: Opportunities risks and challenges. *EuroMed Journal of Business*, 15(2), 205–217. DOI: 10.1108/EMJB-07-2019-0097

Lombardi, R., & Secundo, G. (2021). The digital transformation of corporate reporting–a systematic literature review and avenues for future research. *Meditari Accountancy Research*, 29(5), 1179–1208. DOI: 10.1108/MEDAR-04-2020-0870

Lopes, C. A. R. (2020). Automatização robótica de processos financeiros-automatização de processos financeiros SAP pela introdução de RPA (Doctoral dissertation).

LópezPuertas-Lamy, M., Desender, K., & Epure, M. (2017). Corporate social responsibility and the assessment by auditors of the risk of material misstatement. *Journal of Business Finance & Accounting*, 44(9-10), 1276–1314. DOI: 10.1111/jbfa.12268

Loughran, T., & McDonald, B. (2016). Textual analysis in accounting and finance: A survey. *Journal of Accounting Research*, 54(4), 1187–1230. DOI: 10.1111/1475-679X.12123

Luo, X., Wang, T., Yang, L., Zhao, X., & Zhang, Y. (2023). Initial evidence on the market impact of the iXBRL adoption. *Accounting Horizons*, 37(1), 143–171. DOI: 10.2308/HORIZONS-2020-023

Luo, Y. (2022). A general framework of digitization risks in international business. *Journal of International Business Studies*, 53(3), 344–361. DOI: 10.1057/s41267-021-00448-9 PMID: 34075261

Madison, N., & Schiehll, E. (2021). The Effect of Financial Materiality on ESG Performance Assessment. *Sustainability (Basel)*, 13(7), 3652. Advance online publication. DOI: 10.3390/su13073652

Mähönen, J. (2020). Comprehensive approach to relevant and reliable reporting in Europe: A Dream impossible? *Sustainability (Basel)*, 12(13), 5277. DOI: 10.3390/su12135277

Manita, R., Bruna, M. G., Dang, R., & Houanti, L. (2018). Board gender diversity and ESG disclosure: Evidence from the USA. *Journal of Applied Accounting Research*, 19(2), 206–224. DOI: 10.1108/JAAR-01-2017-0024

Manita, R., Elommal, N., Baudier, P., & Hikkerova, L. (2020). The digital transformation of external audit and its impact on corporate governance. *Technological Forecasting and Social Change*, 150, 119751. DOI: 10.1016/j.techfore.2019.119751

Mannapova, R. (2023). Application of IFRS in the conditions of digital technologies. *Science and Innovation*, 2(A11), 301–307. DOI: 10.5281/zenodo.10113335

Manso, A. (2021). Market Concentration before and after the European Audit Reform. Master's thesis, Instituto Superior de Contabilidade e Administração de Lisboa, Lisbon, Portugal.

Manzi, V. (2008). Compliance in Brazil - consolidation and prospects. São Paulo.

Maradona, A. F., Chand, P., & Lodhia, S. (2024). Professional skills required by accountants for applying international financial reporting standards: Implications from Indonesia. *Meditari Accountancy Research*, 32(2), 269–293. DOI: 10.1108/MEDAR-02-2022-1591

Marcelino, M. M., Albuquerque, F., Justino, M. D. R., & Quirós, J. T. (2016). The influence of culture and professional judgment on Accounting: An analysis from the perspective of financial information preparers in Portugal. *Journal of Education and Research in Accounting*, 10(1), 63–87. DOI: 10.17524/repec.v10i1.1214

Marcelli, S. (2013). Governance in the public sector: diagnosis of the management practices of the Federal Police in the light of study 13 of the PSC/IFAC. Dissertation (Master's Degree) - Executive Master's Degree in Business Management, Center for Academic Training and Research, Brazilian School of Public and Business Administration, Rio de Janeiro.

Marotta, A., & Madnick, S. (2021). Convergence and divergence of regulatory compliance and cybersecurity. *Issues in Information Systems*, 22(1), 10–50. DOI: 10.48009/1_iis_2021_10-50

Martínez-Peláez, R., Ochoa-Brust, A., Rivera, S., Félix, V. G., Ostos, R., Brito, H., Félix, R. A., & Mena, L. J. (2023). Role of digital transformation for achieving sustainability: Mediated role of stakeholders, key capabilities, and technology. *Sustainability (Basel)*, 15(14), 11221. DOI: 10.3390/su151411221

Matos, J., Matos, R., & Almeida, J. (2007). *Analysis of the Corporate Environment: from organized chaos to planning*. E-papers.

Matoušková, D. (2022). Digitalization and Its Impact on Business. *Theory Methodology Practice*, 18(2), 51–67. DOI: 10.18096/TMP.2022.02.03

Matten, D., & Moon, J. (2008). "Implicit" and "Explicit" CSR: A conceptual framework for a comparative understanding of corporate social responsibility. *Academy of Management Review*, 33(2), 404–424. DOI: 10.5465/amr.2008.31193458

Matthies, B. (2020). Assessing the automation potentials of management reporting processes. *The International Journal of Digital Accounting Research*, 20, 75–101. DOI: 10.4192/1577-8517-v20_4

McCallig, J., Robb, A., & Rohde, F. (2019). Establishing the representational faithfulness of financial accounting information using multiparty security, network analysis and a blockchain. *International Journal of Accounting Information Systems*, 33, 47–58. DOI: 10.1016/j.accinf.2019.03.004

McComb, J. M.II, & Smalt, S. W. (2018). The rise of blockchain technology and its potential for improving the quality of accounting information. *Journal of Finance and Accountancy*, 23, 1–7. http://www.aabri.com/copyright.html

McDonald, M. L., & Westphal, J. D. (2013). Access denied: Low mentoring of women and minority first-time directors and its negative effect on appointments to additional boards. *Academy of Management Journal*, 56(4), 1169–1198. DOI: 10.5465/amj.2011.0230

McInerney-Lacombe, N., Billimoria, D., & Salipante, P. (2008). Championing the discussion of tough issues: How women corporate directors contribute to board deliberations. In Vinnicombe, S., Singh, V., Burke, R. J., Billimoria, D., & Huse, M. (Eds.), *Women on corporate boards of directors* (pp. 123–129). Edward Elgar. DOI: 10.4337/9781848445192.00021

Meier, K. J., & Krause, G. A. (2003). The scientific study of bureaucracy: An overview. *Politics, Policy, and Organizations: Frontiers in the Scientific Study of Bureaucracy*, 1-19.

Menon, K., & Williams, D. (2004). The use of management control mechanisms to manage trust and uncertainty in the virtual organization. *Frontiers of Information Systems*, 6(2), 175–193.

Menzies, C. (2006). *Sarbanes-Oxley und Corporate Compliance: Nachhaltigkeit, Optimierung, Integration*. No Title.

Meraghni, O., Bekkouche, L., & Demdoum, Z. (2021). Impact of digital transformation on accounting information systems–evidence from Algerian firms. *Economics and Business*, 35(1), 249–264. DOI: 10.2478/eb-2021-0017

Merkl-Davies, D. M., & Brennan, N. M. (2017). A theoretical framework of external accounting communication: Research perspectives, traditions, and theories. *Accounting, Auditing & Accountability Journal*, 30(2), 433–469. DOI: 10.1108/AAAJ-04-2015-2039

Micheler, E., & Whaley, A. (2020). Regulatory technology: Replacing law with computer code. *European Business Organization Law Review*, 21(2), 349–377. DOI: 10.1007/s40804-019-00151-1

Micheli, P., & Mari, L. (2014). The theory and practice of performance measurement. *Management Accounting Research*, 25(2), 147–156. DOI: 10.1016/j.mar.2013.07.005

Michelon, G. (2021). Accounting research boundaries, multiple centers and academic empathy. *Critical Perspectives on Accounting*, 76, 102204. DOI: 10.1016/j.cpa.2020.102204

Mihu, C., Pitic, A. G., & Bayraktar, D. (2023). Drivers of digital transformation and their impact on organizational management. *Studies in Business and Economics*, 18(1), 149–170. DOI: 10.2478/sbe-2023-0009

Mihus, I. (2022). Evolution of practical use of blockchain technologies by companies. *Economics. Finance and Management Review*, 1(1), 42–50. DOI: 10.36690/2674-5208-2022-1-42

Ministry Of Planning, *Budget And Management*. (2016). Digital Governance Strategy of the Federal Public Administration 2016-2019, Brasilia.

Mio, C., & Fasan, M. (2013). *Materiality from financial towards non-financial*. Working Paper Series. Universitá Ca'Foscari Venezia, Venezia. http://dx.doi.org/ DOI: 10.2139/ssrn.2340192

Mio, C., Fasan, M., & Costantini, A. (2020). Materiality in integrated and sustainability reporting: A paradigm shift? *Business Strategy and the Environment*, 29(1), 306–320. DOI: 10.1002/bse.2390

Mita, A. F., Utama, S., Fitriany, F., & Wulandari, E. R. (2018). The adoption of IFRS, comparability of financial statements and foreign investors' ownership. *Asian Review of Accounting*, 26(3), 391–411. DOI: 10.1108/ARA-04-2017-0064

Moffitt, K. C., Rozario, A. M., & Vasarhelyi, M. A. (2018). Robotic process automation for auditing. *Journal of Emerging Technologies in Accounting*, 15(1), 1–10. DOI: 10.2308/jeta-10589

Mok, A. (2023, September 14). EY has created its own large-language model — and says it will train all 400,000 employees to use it as part of a $1.4 billion investment. *Business Insider.* Retrieved from: https://www.businessinsider.com/ey-ernst-young-consulting-invests-ai-strategy-training-model-tools-2023-9?r=MX&IR=T#:~:text=EY%20has%20created%20its%20own,of%20a%20%241.4%20billion%20investment&text=Ernst%20%26%20Young%20has%20invested%20%241.4,its%20own%20large%20language%20model

Monica, M., & Stefan, B. (2019). Ifrs 9 benchmarking test: Too complicated to worth doing it? *Economic Computation and Economic Cybernetics Studies and Research*, 53(1), 217–230. DOI: 10.24818/18423264/53.1.19.14

Morais, A. I., & Curto, J. D. (2008). Accounting quality and the adoption of IASB standards: Portuguese evidence. *Revista Contabilidade & Finanças*, 19(48), 103–111. DOI: 10.1590/S1519-70772008000300009

Morano, C. (2003), Application of Risk Analysis Techniques in Construction Projects. 2003. 206 f. Dissertation (Master's Degree in Civil Engineering) – Fluminense Federal University – UFF, Niterói.

Moroney, R., & Trotman, K. T. (2016). Differences in auditors' materiality assessments when auditing financial statements and sustainability reports. *Contemporary Accounting Research*, 33(2), 551–575. DOI: 10.1111/1911-3846.12162

Mućko, P. (2021). Sentiment analysis of CSR disclosures in annual reports of EU companies. *Procedia Computer Science*, 192, 3351–3359. DOI: 10.1016/j.procs.2021.09.108

Muhamad, L., & Demeter, D. (2021). *Design and Implementation of a Signaling Approach for the Detection of Net Neutrality Breaches using Blockchain-based Smart Contracts*. University of Zurich.

Mujiono, M. N. (2021). The shifting role of accountants in the era of digital disruption. *International Journal of Multidisciplinary: Applied Business and Education Research*, 2(11), 1259–1274. DOI: 10.11594/10.11594/ijmaber.02.11.18

Mujtaba, B. G. (2024). Cybercrimes and safety policies to protect data and organizations. *Journal of Crime and Criminal Behavior*, 4(1), 91–112. DOI: 10.47509/JCCB.2024.v04i01.04

Mustikarini, A., & Adhariani, D. (2022). In auditor we trust: 44 years of research on the auditor-client relationship and future research directions. *Meditari Accountancy Research*, 30(2), 267–292. DOI: 10.1108/MEDAR-11-2020-1062

Nakamoto, S. (2022). Bitcoin: A Peer-to-Peer Electronic Cash System. SSRN *Electronic Journal*, 1–9. DOI: 10.2139/ssrn.3977007

Nassar, A., & Kamal, M. (2021). Ethical dilemmas in AI-powered decision-making: A deep dive into big data-driven ethical considerations. *International Journal of Responsible Artificial Intelligence*, 11(8), 1–11. https://neuralslate.com/index.php/Journal-of-Responsible-AI/article/view/43

Nassif, A. B., Talib, M. A., Nasir, Q., & Dakalbab, F. M. (2021). Machine learning for anomaly detection: A systematic review. *IEEE Access : Practical Innovations, Open Solutions*, 9, 78658–78700. DOI: 10.1109/ACCESS.2021.3083060

Nekhili, M., Gull, A. A., Chtioui, T., & Radhouane, I. (2020). Gender-diverse boards and audit fees: What difference does gender quota legislation make? *Journal of Business Finance & Accounting*, 47(1–2), 52–99. DOI: 10.1111/jbfa.12409

Ngu, S. B., & Amran, A. (2021). Materiality Disclosure in Sustainability Reporting: Evidence from Malaysia. *Asian Journal of Business and Accounting*, 14(1), 225–252. DOI: 10.22452/ajba.vol14no1.9

Nicolaou, A. I. (2010). Integrated information systems and transparency in business reporting. *International Journal of Disclosure and Governance*, 7(3), 216–226. DOI: 10.1057/jdg.2009.27

Nicolau, A. (2023). The impact of AI on internal audit and accounting practices. *Internal Auditing & Risk Management*, (Supplement), 38–56.

Nik Abdullah, N. H., Krishnan, S., Mohd Zakaria, A. A., & Morris, G. (2022). Strategic management accounting practices in business: A systematic review of the literature and future research directions. *Cogent Business & Management*, 9(1), 2093488. DOI: 10.1080/23311975.2022.2093488

Nnadi, M., & Soobaroyen, T. (2015). International financial reporting standards and foreign direct investment: The case of Africa. *Advances in Accounting*, 31(2), 228–238. DOI: 10.1016/j.adiac.2015.09.007

Nobes, C. W., & Stadler, C. (2015). The qualitative characteristics of financial information, and managers accounting decisions: Evidence from IFRS policy changes. *Accounting and Business Research*, 45(5), 572–601. DOI: 10.1080/00014788.2015.1044495

Noor, S. A. M., Isa, M. M., Anbarasan, D., & Kin, G. W. (2019). Blockchain-Enabled Task and Time Sheet Management for Accounting Services Provision. *E-Proceeding of the International Conference on Social Science Research 2019*, 10–20. https://www.academia.edu/download/62083682/Syafiq20200212-29057-2jmukg.pdf

Odeyemi, O., Awonuga, K. F., Mhlongo, N. Z., Ndubuisi, N. L., Olatoye, F. O., & Daraojimb, A. I. (2024). The role of AI in transforming auditing practices: A global perspective review. *World Journal of Advanced Research and Reviews*, 21(2), 359–370. DOI: 10.30574/wjarr.2024.21.2.0460

Odoemelam, N., Okafor, R. G., & Ofoegbu, N. G. (2019). Effect of international financial reporting standard (IFRS) adoption on earnings value relevance of quoted Nigerian firms. *Cogent Business and Management*, 6(1), 1–22. DOI: 10.1080/23311975.2019.1643520

Odonkor, B., Kaggwa, S., Uwaoma, P. U., Hassan, A. O., & Farayola, O. A. (2024). The impact of AI on accounting practices: A review: Exploring how artificial intelligence is transforming traditional accounting methods and financial reporting. *World Journal of Advanced Research and Reviews*, 21(1), 172–188. DOI: 10.30574/wjarr.2024.21.1.2721

Okafor, O. N., Anderson, M., & Warsame, H. (2016). IFRS and value relevance: Evidence based on Canadian adoption. *International Journal of Managerial Finance*, 12(2), 136–160. DOI: 10.1108/IJMF-02-2015-0033

Oladejo, M. T., & Jack, L. (2020). Fraud prevention and detection in a blockchain technology environment: Challenges posed to forensic accountants. *International Journal of Economics and Accounting*, 9(4), 315–335. DOI: 10.1504/IJEA.2020.110162

Olaniyi, O. O., Olabanji, S. O., & Adebiyi, O. O. (2023). Promoting inclusive accounting education through the integration of STEM principles for a diverse classroom.

Oliveira P., & Vieira O. (2019). Public Governance Practices Adopted by the Brazilian Federal Public Administration. Public Administration and Social Management.

Oliveira, D. (2010), Strategic planning: concepts, methodologies and practice (28th ed.), São Paulo: Atlas.

Oliveira, E. D. (2019). Impacto do uso da inteligência artificial em sistemas de gestão empresarial no exercício da profissão contábil.

Oluwagbemiga, O. E. (2021). The Influence of IFRS Adoption on the Quality of Financial Reporting in Nigerian Listed Companies. In Advances in Pacific Basin Business, Economics and Finance. Emerald Publishing Limited.

Olweny, F. (2024). Navigating the nexus of security and privacy in modern financial technologies. *GSC Advanced Research and Reviews*, 18(2), 167–197. DOI: 10.30574/gscarr.2024.18.2.0043

Onsight. (2024). What the heck is the Pareto Principle and how does it apply to sales? *Blog - Sales techniques and processes*. Retrieved from: https://www.onsightapp.com/blog/pareto-principle-how-it-applies-to-sales

Open Compliance & Ethics Group. (2015). *GRC capability model – version 3.0 (Red Book)*. OCEG.

Opferkuch, K., Caeiro, S., Salomone, R., & Ramos, T. (2021). Circular economy in corporate sustainability reporting: A review of organisational approaches. *Business Strategy and the Environment*, 30(8), 1–22. DOI: 10.1002/bse.2854

Organisation for Economic Co-operation and Development. (2011). *OECD Assessments on Public Governance: OECD Assessment on the Integrity System of the Brazilian Federal Public Administration – Managing risks for a more honest public administration*. OECD Publishing.

Ortar, L. (2018). Materiality Matrixes in Sustainability Reporting: An Empirical Examination. http://dx.doi.org/DOI: 10.2139/ssrn.3117749

Osasere A.O. & Ilaboya O.J. (2018). IFRS Adoption and Financial Reporting Quality: IASB Qualitative Characteristics Approach. *Accounting & Taxation Review*, 2(3).

Osifo, O. & Fasua, H. (2017). Social and Environmental Disclosures and Holistic Growth in the Positive Accounting Theory (PAT) View. *IOSR Journal of Business and Management*, 19(6), 1-8. DOI: 10.9790/487X-1906030108

Osinubi, I. S. (2020). The three pillars of institutional theory and IFRS implementation in Nigeria. *Journal of Accounting in Emerging Economies*, 10(4), 575–599. DOI: 10.1108/JAEE-07-2019-0139

Otley, D. (1999). Performance management: A framework for management control systems research. *Management Accounting Research*, 10(4), 363–382. DOI: 10.1006/mare.1999.0115

Oyadomari, J. (2008), Use of the management control system and performance: a study in Brazilian companies from the perspective of VBR (Resource-Based View). Doctoral Thesis in Accounting, University of São Paulo, São Paulo, SP, Brazil.

Oyewole, A. T., Oguejiofor, B. B., Eneh, N. E., Akpuokwe, C. U., & Bakare, S. S. (2024). Data privacy laws and their impact on financial technology companies: A review. *Computer Science & IT Research Journal*, 5(3), 628–650. DOI: 10.51594/csitrj.v5i3.911

Ozili, P. K. (2018). Impact of digital finance on financial inclusion and stability. *Borsa Istanbul Review*, 18(4), 329–340. DOI: 10.1016/j.bir.2017.12.003

Pagliarussi, M.S., Aguiar, M.O., & Galdi, F.C. (2016). Sentiment analysis in annual reports from Brazilian companies listed at the BM&FBOVESPA. *BASE - Revista de Administração e Contabilidade da Unisinos*, 13(1). DOI: 10.4013/base.2016.131.04

Palermo, T. (2014). Accountability and expertise in public sector risk management: A case study. *Financial Accountability & Management*, 30(3), 322–341. DOI: 10.1111/faam.12039

Panda, K. C., & Agrawal, S. (2021). Predictive Analytics: An Overview of Evolving Trends and Methodologies. *Journal of Scientific and Engineering Research*, 8(10), 175–180. DOI: 10.5281/zenodo.11232896

Pandey, S., Singh, R. K., Gunasekaran, A., & Kaushik, A. (2020). Cyber security risks in globalized supply chains: Conceptual framework. *Journal of Global Operations and Strategic Sourcing*, 13(1), 103–128. DOI: 10.1108/JGOSS-05-2019-0042

Pansara, R. R. (2022). Cybersecurity Measures in Master Data Management: Safeguarding Sensitive Information. *International Numeric Journal of Machine Learning and Robots*, 6(6), 1-12. https://injmr.com/index.php/fewfewf/article/view/35

Pasolo, F. (2024). Understanding the interplay between accounting practices and organizational structures for strategic management. *Advances: Jurnal Ekonomi & Bisnis*, 2(3), 136–150.

Patelli, L., & Pedrini, M. (2015). Is Tone at the Top Associated with Financial Reporting Aggressiveness? *Journal of Business Ethics*, 126(1), 3–19. DOI: 10.1007/s10551-013-1994-6

Pattnaik, D., Ray, S., & Raman, R. (2024). Applications of artificial intelligence and machine learning in the financial services industry: A bibliometric review. *Heliyon*, 10(1), e23492. DOI: 10.1016/j.heliyon.2023.e23492 PMID: 38187262

Pauleski, R. K. (2023). Impactos da inteligência artificial no trabalho do profissional que atua em escritório de contabilidade: um estudo de caso.

Paul, J., Ueno, A., Dennis, C., Alamanos, E., Curtis, L., Foroudi, P., Kacprzak, A., Kunz, W. H., Liu, J., Marvi, R., Nair, S. L. S., Ozdemir, O., Pantano, E., Papadopoulos, T., Petir, O., Tyagi, S., & Wirtz, J. (2024). Digital transformation: A multidisciplinary perspective and future research agenda. *International Journal of Consumer Studies*, 48(2), e13015. DOI: 10.1111/ijcs.13015

Pedras, S. R. G. (2020). Implementação do Robotic Process Automation em Pequenos Escritórios de Contabilidade: um Estudo Exploratório.

Pedreño, E. P., Gelashvili, V., & Nebreda, L. P. (2021). Blockchain and its application to accounting. *Intangible Capital*, 17(1), 1–16. DOI: 10.3926/ic.1522

Peng, Y., Ahmad, S. F., Ahmad, A. Y. B., Al Shaikh, M. S., Daoud, M. K., & Alhamdi, F. M. H. (2023). Riding the waves of artificial intelligence in advancing accounting and its implications for sustainable development goals. *Sustainability (Basel)*, 15(19), 14165. DOI: 10.3390/su151914165

Perez, J. R., & de Pablos, P. O. (2003). Knowledge management and organizational competitiveness: A framework for human capital analysis. *Journal of Knowledge Management*, 7(3), 82–91. DOI: 10.1108/13673270310485640

Perkhofer, L. M., Hofer, P., Walchshofer, C., Plank, T., & Jetter, H. C. (2019). Interactive visualization of big data in the field of accounting: A survey of current practice and potential barriers for adoption. *Journal of Applied Accounting Research*, 20(4), 497–525. DOI: 10.1108/JAAR-10-2017-0114

Perryman, A. A., Fernando, G. D., & Tripathy, A. (2016). Do gender differences persist? An examination of gender diversity on firm performance, risk, and executive compensation. *Journal of Business Research*, 69(2), 579–586. DOI: 10.1016/j.jbusres.2015.05.013

Pimentel, E., & Boulianne, E. (2020). Blockchain in Accounting Research and Practice: Current Trends and Future Opportunities. *Accounting Perspectives*, 19(4), 325–361. DOI: 10.1111/1911-3838.12239

Pimentel, E., Boulianne, E., Eskandari, S., & Clark, J. (2021). Systemizing the challenges of auditing blockchain-based assets. *Journal of Information Systems*, 35(2), 61–75. DOI: 10.2308/ISYS-19-007

Pizzi, S., Caputo, A., Venturelli, A., & Caputo, F. (2022). Embedding and managing blockchain in sustainability reporting: A practical framework. *Sustainability Accounting. Management and Policy Journal*, 13(3), 545–567. DOI: 10.1108/SAMPJ-07-2021-0288

Plekhanov, D., Franke, H., & Netland, T. H. (2023). Digital transformation: A review and research agenda. *European Management Journal*, 41(6), 821–844. DOI: 10.1016/j.emj.2022.09.007

Pontoppidan, C. A. (2024). Teaching the next generation of accountants: integrating financial, environmental, social and governance accounting and reporting practices. In *Business Education in the 21st Century* (pp. 371–385). Edward Elgar Publishing. DOI: 10.4337/9781802202694.00029

Post, C., & Byron, K. (2015). Women on boards and firm financial performance: A meta-analysis. *Academy of Management Journal*, 58(5), 1546–1571. DOI: 10.5465/amj.2013.0319

Potosky, D., & Azan, W. (2023). Leadership behaviors and human agency in the valley of despair: A meta-framework for organizational change implementation. *Human Resource Management Review*, 33(1), 100927. DOI: 10.1016/j.hrmr.2022.100927

Powell, L., & McGuigan, N. (2023). Responding to crises: Rewilding accounting education for the Anthropocene. *Meditari Accountancy Research*, 31(1), 101–120. DOI: 10.1108/MEDAR-06-2021-1333

Prasetianingrum, S., & Sonjaya, Y. (2024). The Evolution of Digital Accounting and Accounting Information Systems in the Modern Business Landscape. *Advances in Applied Accounting Research*, 2(1), 39–53. DOI: 10.60079/aaar.v2i1.165

Pratama, A. H., Dwita, S., & Sum, R. M. (2023). Digitalization Disclosure and Accounting Information Quality. *Wahana Riset Akuntansi*, 11(2), 109–123. DOI: 10.24036/wra.v11i2.124490

Prebanić, K. R., & Vukomanović, M. (2021). Realizing the need for digital transformation of stakeholder management: A systematic review in the construction industry. *Sustainability (Basel)*, 13(22), 12690. DOI: 10.3390/su132212690

Pugna, I. B., & Duțescu, A. (2020). Blockchain – the accounting perspective. *Proceedings of the International Conference on Business Excellence*, 14(1), 214–224. DOI: 10.2478/picbe-2020-0020

Purdy, G. (2010). ISO 31000: 2009—setting a new standard for risk management. Risk Analysis. *International Journal (Toronto, Ont.)*, 30(6), 881–886. PMID: 20636915

Puroila, J., & Mäkelä, H. (2019). Matter of opinion: Exploring the socio-political nature of materiality disclosures in sustainability reporting. *Accounting, Auditing & Accountability Journal*, 32(4), 1043–1072. DOI: 10.1108/AAAJ-11-2016-2788

PwC Report. (2022). ESG-focused institutional investment seen soaring 84% to US$33.9 trillion in 2026, making up 21.5% of assets under management.

Qasim, A., & Kharbat, F. F. (2020). Blockchain technology, business data analytics, and artificial intelligence: Use in the accounting profession and ideas for inclusion into the accounting curriculum. *Journal of Emerging Technologies in Accounting*, 17(1), 107–117. DOI: 10.2308/jeta-52649

Qatawneh, A. (2022). The influence of data mining on accounting information system performance: A mediating role of information technology infrastructure. *Journal of Governance and Regulation*, 11(1), 141–151. DOI: 10.22495/jgrv11i1art13

Quach, S., Thaichon, P., Martin, K. D., Weaven, S., & Palmatier, R. W. (2022). Digital technologies: Tensions in privacy and data. *Journal of the Academy of Marketing Science*, 50(6), 1299–1323. DOI: 10.1007/s11747-022-00845-y PMID: 35281634

Quinn, S., & Roberds, W. (2008). The Evolution of the Check as a Means of Payment: A Historical Survey. *Federal Reserve Bank of Atlanta Economic Review*, 93(4). Advance online publication. DOI: 10.1016/S1365-6937(04)00375-2

Ramírez, Y., & Tejada, Á. (2018). Corporate governance of universities: Improving transparency and accountability. *International Journal of Disclosure and Governance*, 15(1), 29–39. DOI: 10.1057/s41310-018-0034-2

Ramlaoui, S., & Semma, A. (2014). Comparative study oComparative of COBIT with other IT Governance Frameworks. *International Journal of Computer Science Issues*, 11(6), 95.

Rashed, A. H., Rashdan, S. A., & Ali-Mohamed, A. Y. (2022). Towards Effective Environmental Sustainability Reporting in the Large Industrial Sector of Bahrain. *Sustainability (Basel)*, 14(1), 219. DOI: 10.3390/su14010219

Reddy, S., & Jadhav, A. M. (2019). Gender diversity in boardrooms – A literature review. *Cogent Economics & Finance*, 7(1), 1644703. DOI: 10.1080/23322039.2019.1644703

Reier Forradellas, R. F., & Garay Gallastegui, L. M. (2021). Digital transformation and artificial intelligence applied to business: Legal regulations, economic impact and perspective. *Laws*, 10(3), 70. DOI: 10.3390/laws10030070

Reiff, N. (2022, July 23). What Was the First Cryptocurrency? There were cryptocurrencies before bitcoin. Investopedia. https://www.investopedia.com/tech/were-there-cryptocurrencies-bitcoin/

Rezende, D. (2008). *Strategic planning for organizations: public and private*. Brasport.

Rinaldi, L. (2023, July). Accounting and the COVID-19 pandemic two years on: Insights, gaps, and an agenda for future research. *Accounting Forum*, 47(3), 333–364. DOI: 10.1080/01559982.2022.2045418

Ritter, T., & Pedersen, C. L. (2020). Digitization capability and the digitalization of business models in business-to-business firms: Past, present, and future. *Industrial Marketing Management*, 86, 180–190. DOI: 10.1016/j.indmarman.2019.11.019

Rodrigues, A. A. B. (2023). Materiality Matrices in the Environmental, Social and Governance Context. *International Journal of Engineering Business Management*, 7(2), 17–22. DOI: 10.22161/ijebm.7.2.3

Rodríguez-Espíndola, O., Chowdhury, S., Dey, P. K., Albores, P., & Emrouznejad, A. (2022). Analysis of the adoption of emergent technologies for risk management in the era of digital manufacturing. *Technological Forecasting and Social Change*, 178, 121562. DOI: 10.1016/j.techfore.2022.121562

Roszkowska, P. (2020). Fintech in financial reporting and audit for fraud prevention and safeguarding equity investments. *Journal of Accounting & Organizational Change*, 17(2), 164–196. DOI: 10.1108/JAOC-09-2019-0098

Rowbottom, N., Locke, J., & Troshani, I. (2021). When the tail wags the dog? Digitalisation and corporate reporting. *Accounting, Organizations and Society*, 92, 101226. DOI: 10.1016/j.aos.2021.101226

Saarikko, T., Westergren, U. H., & Blomquist, T. (2020). Digital transformation: Five recommendations for the digitally conscious firm. *Business Horizons*, 63(6), 825–839. DOI: 10.1016/j.bushor.2020.07.005

Saboni, K., Bennis, L., & Anguer, N. E. (2024). A retrospective on the 2008 financial crisis: In-depth analysis. *International Journal of Accounting, Finance, Auditing. Management and Economics*, 5(5), 619–632. DOI: 10.5281/zenodo.11269142

Sadok, H., Sakka, F., & El Maknouzi, M. E. H. (2022). Artificial intelligence and bank credit analysis: A review. *Cogent Economics & Finance*, 10(1), 2023262. Advance online publication. DOI: 10.1080/23322039.2021.2023262

Saenz, C. (2019). Creating shared value using materiality analysis: Strategies from the mining industry. *Corporate Social Responsibility and Environmental Management*, 26(6), 1351–1360. DOI: 10.1002/csr.1751

Salim, R., & Ferran, C. (2008). From Ledgers to ERP. In Ferran, C., & Salim, R. (Eds.), *Enterprise Resource Planning for Global Economies: Managerial Issues and Challenges* (pp. 1–22). IGI Global. DOI: 10.4018/978-1-59904-531-3.ch001

Salleh, N. M. Z. N., Moorthy, K., & Jasmon, A. (2023). A review of scholarly discourses on accounting technical skills for IR 4.0. *Journal of Higher Education Theory and Practice*, 23(9).

SallyPort. (2021, November 10). 10 Strategies to Increase Profitability in Small Business. Retrieved from: https://sallyportcf.com/10-strategies-to-increase-profitability-in-small-business/

Salvi, A., Vitolla, F., Rubino, M., Giakoumelou, A., & Raimo, N. (2021). Online information on digitalisation processes and its impact on firm value. *Journal of Business Research*, 124, 437–444. DOI: 10.1016/j.jbusres.2020.10.025

Samuelsen, J., Chen, W., & Wasson, B. (2019). Integrating multiple data sources for learning analytics—Review of literature. *Research and Practice in Technology Enhanced Learning*, 14(1), 11. DOI: 10.1186/s41039-019-0105-4

Sander, F., Semeijn, J., & Mahr, D. (2018). The acceptance of blockchain technology in meat traceability and transparency. *British Food Journal*, 120(9), 2066–2079. DOI: 10.1108/BFJ-07-2017-0365

Santos, E. L. D. (2014). *Do escambo à inclusão financeira: a evolução dos meios de pagamento*. Linotipo Digital.

Santos, R. (2021). *Formal Agenda and Substantive Agenda in Brazil's Adherence to OECD Budget Governance Recommendations*. IPEA Preliminary Publication.

Sardianou, E., Stauropoulou, A., Evangelinos, K., & Nikolaou, I. (2021). A materiality analysis framework to assess sustainable development goals of banking sector through sustainability reports. *Sustainable Production and Consumption*, 27, 1775–1793. DOI: 10.1016/j.spc.2021.04.020

Sarkar, S., Boss, S. R., & Gray, J. (2021). Pedagogical practices of accounting departments addressing AACSB technology requirements. *Issues in Accounting Education*, 36(4), 59–85. DOI: 10.2308/ISSUES-19-082

Sarker, I. H. (2021). Machine learning: Algorithms, real-world applications and research directions. *SN Computer Science*, 2(3), 160. DOI: 10.1007/s42979-021-00592-x PMID: 33778771

Sax, J., & Andersen, T. J. (2019). Making risk management strategic: Integrating enterprise risk management with strategic planning. *European Management Review*, 16(3), 719–740. DOI: 10.1111/emre.12185

Schallmo, D., Williams, C. A., & Boardman, L. (2017). Digital transformation of business models—Best practice, enablers, and roadmap. *International Journal of Innovation Management*, 21(08), 1740014. DOI: 10.1142/S136391961740014X

Scheifler, T., Faiz, E. B., Ludwig, J. P., & Drege, A. A. (2016). Automação como meio para aumento de produtividade e competitividade–Estudo de caso. Revista ESPACIOS, 37(28).

Schiebel, A. (2006). Empirical value relevance of German GAAP and IFRS. *Journal of Economic and Financial Sciences*, 1(2), 141–170. DOI: 10.4102/jef.v1i2.365

Schiuma, G., Schettini, E., & Santarsiero, F. (2021). How wise companies drive digital transformation. *Journal of Open Innovation*, 7(2), 122. DOI: 10.3390/joitmc7020122

Schnackenberg, A. K., & Tomlinson, E. C. (2016). Organizational transparency: A new perspective on managing trust in organization-stakeholder relationships. *Journal of Management*, 42(7), 1784–1810. DOI: 10.1177/0149206314525202

Scholar, G. (2024). Retrieved from: https://scholar.google.com.mx/scholar?q=innovative+uses+and+applications+of+AI+in+accounting+and+financial+processes&hl=en&as_sdt=0&as_vis=1&oi=scholart

Scholkmann, A. B. (2021). Resistance to (digital) change: Individual, systemic and learning-related perspectives. In Ifenthaler, D., Hofhues, S., Egloffstein, M., & Helbig, C. (Eds.), *Digital Transformation of Learning Organizations* (pp. 219–236). Springer. DOI: 10.1007/978-3-030-55878-9_13

Schreckinger, B. (2023, May 1). Meet the Greta Thunberg of AI. *POLITICO Global Playbook*. Retrieved from: https://www.politico.com/newsletters/digital-future-daily/2023/05/01/meet-the-greta-thunberg-of-ai-00094709

Schwarzmüller, T., Brosi, P., Duman, D., & Welpe, I. M. (2018). How does the digital transformation affect organizations? Key themes of change in work design and leadership. *Management Review*, 29(2), 114–138. DOI: 10.5771/0935-9915-2018-2-114

Sebastian, I. M., Ross, J. W., Beath, C., Mocker, M., Moloney, K. G., & Fonstad, N. O. (2020). How big old companies navigate digital transformation. In Galliers, R. D., Leidner, D. E., & Simenova, B. (Eds.), *Strategic Information Management* (pp. 133–150). Routledge. DOI: 10.4324/9780429286797-6

Secinaro, S., Dal Mas, F., Brescia, V., & Calandra, D. (2021). Blockchain in the accounting, auditing and accountability fields: A bibliometric and coding analysis. *Accounting, Auditing & Accountability Journal*, 35(9), 168–203. DOI: 10.1108/AAAJ-10-2020-4987

Sedrez, C., & Fernandes, F. (2011). Risk management in universities and university centers in the state of Santa Catarina. *University Management of Latin America*, (special issue), 70–93.

Sellami, Y., & Fendri, H. (2017). The effect of audit committee characteristics on compliance with IFRS for related party disclosures: Evidence from South Africa. *Managerial Auditing Journal*, 32(6), 603–626. DOI: 10.1108/MAJ-06-2016-1395

Senani, K.G.P., Ajward, R. & Kumari, J.S. (2022). Determinants and consequences of integrated reporting disclosures of non-financial listed firms in an emerging economy. *Journal of Financial Reporting and Accounting*. DOI: 10.1108/JFRA-03-2022-0083

Serapicos. (2021). *Transformações digitais para financeiros - blockchain big data*. Lisboa: Ordem dos Contabilistas Certificados.

Setiawan, R., Cavaliere, L. P. L., Halder, S., Koti, K., Sarsengaliy, B., Ashok, K., Pallathadka, H., & Rajan, R. (2021). The concept of the cryptocurrency and the downfall of the banking sector in reflecting on the financial market. *Rentgenologiyai Radiologiya*, 60(S1), 17–33.

Setyorini, C., & Isahk, Z. (2012). Corporate Social and Environmental Disclosure: A Positive Accounting Theory View Point. https://www.researchgate.net/publication/336713992_Corporate_Social_and_Environmental_Disclosure_A_Positive_Accounting_Theory_View_Point

Shaleh, M. (2024). Advances in Management & Financial Reporting.

Shanmugam, G., Rajendran, D., Thanarajan, T., Murugaraj, S. S., & Rajendran, S. (2023). Artificial intelligence as a catalyst in digital marketing: Enhancing profitability and market potential. *Ingénierie des Systèmes d'Information*, 28(6), 1627–1636. DOI: 10.18280/isi.280620

Sharma, P., Panday, P., & Dangwal, R. C. (2020). Determinants of environmental, social and corporate governance (ESG) disclosure: A study of Indian companies. *International Journal of Disclosure and Governance*, 17(4), 208–217. DOI: 10.1057/s41310-020-00085-y

Sharma, R. (2021, October - December). A study of adoption & impact of robotic process automation in accounting and auditing. *International Journal of Innovations & Research Analysis*, 01(03), 31–36.

Sheela, S., Alsmady, A. A., Tanaraj, K., & Izani, I. (2023). Navigating the Future: Blockchain's Impact on Accounting and Auditing Practices. *Sustainability (Basel)*, 15(24), 16887. DOI: 10.3390/su152416887

Sherif, K., & Mohsin, H. (2021). The effect of emergent technologies on accountants ethical blindness. *The International Journal of Digital Accounting Research*, 21, 61–94. DOI: 10.4192/1577-8517-v21_3

Shields, K., Clacher, I., & Zhang, Q. (2019). Negative Tone in Lobbying the International Accounting Standards Board. *The International Journal of Accounting*, 54(03), 1950010. DOI: 10.1142/S1094406019500100

Shleifer, A., & Vishny, R. W. (1997). A survey of corporate governance. *The Journal of Finance*, 52(2), 737–783. DOI: 10.1111/j.1540-6261.1997.tb04820.x

Sierra-Garcia, L., Garcia-Benau, M., & Bollas-Araya, H. (2018). Empirical Analysis of Non-Financial Reporting by Spanish Companies. *Administrative Sciences*, 8(3), 29. Advance online publication. DOI: 10.3390/admsci8030029

Silva, G., Mendes Filho, L., & Marques, S. (2022). Intenção de usar criptomoedas por gestores de empreendimentos turísticos: uma abordagem utilizando o Technology Acceptance Model (TAM). Revista Brasileira de Pesquisa em Turismo, 16, e-2556.

Simplilearn. (2024a, July 31). What Is Data Analysis: A Comprehensive Guide. Retrieved from: https://www.simplilearn.com/data-analysis-methods-process-types-article

Simplilearn. (2024b, July 24). Top 24 Data Analysis Tools for 2024. Retrieved from: https://www.simplilearn.com/top-data-analysis-tools-article

Simunic, D. (1980). The pricing of audit services: Theory and evidence. *Journal of Accounting Research*, 18(1), 161–190. DOI: 10.2307/2490397

Simunic, D., & Stein, M. (1996). The impact of litigation risk on audit pricing: A review of the economics and the evidence. *Auditing*, 15(Supplement), 119–134.

Singh, A. (2022). Blockchain Technology: A Paradigm Shift in Accounting. *SMS Journal of Enterpreneurship & Innovation*, 8(1). Advance online publication. DOI: 10.21844/smsjei.v8i01.30006

Sivabalachandran, T., & Gooneratne, T. (2023). Roles at crossroads: Complexities and conflicts surrounding management accountants' roles based on evidence from the Sri Lankan context. *Asian Journal of Accounting Research*, 8(1), 80–93. DOI: 10.1108/AJAR-11-2021-0242

Sivarajah, U., Kamal, M. M., Irani, Z., & Weerakkody, V. (2017). Critical analysis of Big Data challenges and analytical methods. *Journal of Business Research*, 70, 263–286. DOI: 10.1016/j.jbusres.2016.08.001

Soderstrom, N. S., & Sun, K. J. (2007). IFRS adoption and accounting quality: A review. *European Accounting Review*, 16(4), 675–702. DOI: 10.1080/09638180701706732

Sokołowska, E. (2015). Innovations in the payment card market: The case of Poland. *Electronic Commerce Research and Applications*, 14(5), 292–304. DOI: 10.1016/j.elerap.2015.07.005

Solal, I., & Snellman, K. (2019). Women don't mean business? Gender penalty in board composition. *Organization Science*, 30(6), 1270–1288. DOI: 10.1287/orsc.2019.1301

Soori, M., Arezoo, B., & Dastres, R. (2023). Artificial intelligence, machine learning and deep learning in advanced robotics, a review. *Cognitive Robotics*, 3, 54–70. DOI: 10.1016/j.cogr.2023.04.001

Sousa, A. (2017). Investigação sobre materialidade: análise crítica e desenvolvimentos recentes. https://aeca.es/wp-content/uploads/2014/05/143a.pdf

Souza, A., & Medeiros, R. (2020). Intention to use cryptocurrencies by managers of tourism enterprises: An analysis with the Technology Acceptance Model. *Brazilian Journal of Tourism Research*, 14(3).

Spekle, R. F., & Verbeeten, F. H. (2014). The use of performance measurement systems in the public sector: Effects on performance. *Management Accounting Research*, 25(2), 131–146. DOI: 10.1016/j.mar.2013.07.004

Srinidhi, B., Sun, Y., & Zhang, H. (2015). Why are female board directors more effective norm-change agents than male directors? Working paper, University of Texas at Arlington.

Srinidhi, B., Gul, F. A., & Tsui, J. S. L. (2011). Female directors and earnings quality. *Contemporary Accounting Research*, 28(5), 1610–1644. DOI: 10.1111/j.1911-3846.2011.01071.x

Stach, C., Gritti, C., Bräcker, J., Behringer, M., & Mitschang, B. (2022). Protecting sensitive data in the information age: State of the art and future prospects. *Future Internet*, 14(11), 302. DOI: 10.3390/fi14110302

Suadiye, G. (2017). Does mandatory IFRS adoption improve financial reporting quality? Empirical evidence from an emerging economy. *European Journal of Business and Social Sciences*, 6(5), 63–80.

Suhaimi, N. S. A., Nawawi, A., & Salin, A. S. A. P. (2016). Impact of Enterprise Resource Planning on Management Control System and Accountants' Role. *International Journal of Economics & Management*, 10(1), 93–108.

Sujová, E., Čierna, H., & Żabińska, I. (2019). Application of digitization procedures of production in practice. *Management Systems in Production Engineering*, 27(1), 23–28. DOI: 10.1515/mspe-2019-0004

Sultana, N., Cahan, S. F., & Rahman, A. (2020). Do gender diversity recommendations in corporate governance codes matter? Evidence from audit committees. *Auditing*, 39(1), 173–197. DOI: 10.2308/ajpt-52560

Sundaram, A. K., & Inkpen, A. C. (2004). The corporate objective revisited. *Organization Science*, 15(3), 350–363. DOI: 10.1287/orsc.1040.0068

Supriadi, I., Harjanti, W., Suprihandari, M. D., Dwi Prasetyo, H., & Muslikhun, . (2020). Blockchain Innovation and Its Capacity to Enhance the Quality From Accounting Information Systems. *International Journal of Scientific Research and Management*, 8(02), 1590–1595. DOI: 10.18535/ijsrm/v8i02.em05

Suri, V. K., Elia, M., & van Hillegersberg, J. (2017). Software bots-the next frontier for shared services and functional excellence. In *Global Sourcing of Digital Services: Micro and Macro Perspectives*, 81-94. Cham: Springer International Publishing. DOI: 10.1007/978-3-319-70305-3_5

Surjadi, M. (2024, August 5). Colleges Race to Ready Students for the AI Workplace. *The Wall Street Journal*. Retrieved from: https://www.wsj.com/us-news/education/colleges-race-to-ready-students-for-the-ai-workplace-cc936e5b

Szmajser, R., Kędzior, M., Andrzejewski, M., & Świetla, K. (2022). Implementation of new technologies in accounting and financial processes: An effectiveness assessment. *International Entrepreneurship Review*, 8(3), 7–21. DOI: 10.15678/IER.2022.0803.01

Szymanek, A., & Wiśniewski, T. (2023). Digitalization of reporting standards on the capital markets. In Gasiorkiewicz, L., & Monkiewicz, J. (Eds.), *The Digital Revolution in Banking, Insurance and Capital Markets* (pp. 236–251). Routledge. DOI: 10.4324/9781003310082-20

Tagscherer, F., & Carbon, C. C. (2023). Leadership for successful digitalization: A literature review on companies' internal and external aspects of digitalization. *Sustainable Technology and Entrepreneurship*, 2(2), 100039. DOI: 10.1016/j.stae.2023.100039

Taib, A., Awang, Y., Shuhidan, S. M., Rashid, N., & Hasan, M. S. (2022). Digitalization in accounting: Technology knowledge and readiness of future accountants. *Universal Journal of Accounting and Finance*, 10(1), 348–357. DOI: 10.13189/ujaf.2022.100135

Tarca, A. (2020). The IASB and comparability of international financial reporting: Research evidence and implications. *Australian Accounting Review*, 30(4), 231–242. DOI: 10.1111/auar.12326

Tariq, M. U. (2024). Harnessing Persuasive Technologies for Enhanced Learner Engagement and Motivation. In M. Sanmugam, D. Lim, N. Mohd Barkhaya, W. Wan Yahaya, & Z. Khlaif (Eds.), *Power of Persuasive Educational Technologies in Enhancing Learning* (pp. 30-62). IGI Global. DOI: 10.4018/979-8-3693-6397-3.ch002

Tariq, M. U. (2024). Cybersecurity Risk Assessment Models and Theories in the Travel and Tourism Industry. In Thealla, P., Nadda, V., Dadwal, S., Oztosun, L., & Cantafio, G. (Eds.), *Corporate Cybersecurity in the Aviation, Tourism, and Hospitality Sector* (pp. 1–17). IGI Global. DOI: 10.4018/979-8-3693-2715-9.ch001

Tariq, M. U. (2024). Enhancing Students and Learning Achievement as 21st-Century Skills Through Transdisciplinary Approaches. In Kumar, R., Ong, E., Anggoro, S., & Toh, T. (Eds.), *Transdisciplinary Approaches to Learning Outcomes in Higher Education* (pp. 220–257). IGI Global. DOI: 10.4018/979-8-3693-3699-1.ch007

Tariq, M. U. (2024). Integration of IoMT for Enhanced Healthcare: Sleep Monitoring, Body Movement Detection, and Rehabilitation Evaluation. In Liu, H., Tripathy, R., & Bhattacharya, P. (Eds.), *Clinical Practice and Unmet Challenges in AI-Enhanced Healthcare Systems* (pp. 70–95). IGI Global. DOI: 10.4018/979-8-3693-2703-6.ch004

Tariq, M. U. (2024). Navigating the Personalization Pathway: Implementing Adaptive Learning Technologies in Higher Education. In Minh Tung, T. (Ed.), *Adaptive Learning Technologies for Higher Education* (pp. 265–291). IGI Global. DOI: 10.4018/979-8-3693-3641-0.ch012

Tariq, M. U. (2024). Smart Transportation Systems: Paving the Way for Sustainable Urban Mobility. In Munuhwa, S. (Ed.), *Contemporary Solutions for Sustainable Transportation Practices* (pp. 254–283). IGI Global. DOI: 10.4018/979-8-3693-3755-4.ch010

Taulli, T. (2020). The robotic process automation handbook. The Robotic Process Automation Handbook. https://doi. Org/10.1007/978-1-4842-5729-6

Tawiah, V. (2019). The state of IFRS in Africa. *Journal of Financial Reporting and Accounting*, 17(4), 635–649. DOI: 10.1108/JFRA-08-2018-0067

Tawiah, V., & Boolaky, P. (2020). A review of literature on IFRS in Africa. *Journal of Accounting & Organizational Change*, 16(1), 47–70. DOI: 10.1108/JAOC-09-2018-0090

Technologies, D. (2024, April 23). Human-AI Collaboration: The Key to Workplace Efficiency and Innovation. Retrieved from: https://www.businessinsider.com/events/human-ai-collaboration?r=MX&IR=T

Tekic, Z., & Koroteev, D. (2019). From disruptively digital to proudly analog: A holistic typology of digital transformation strategies. *Business Horizons*, 62(6), 683–693. DOI: 10.1016/j.bushor.2019.07.002

Tendeloo, B., & Vanstraelen, A. (2005). Earnings Management under German GAAP versus IFRS. *European Accounting Review*, 14(1), 155–180. DOI: 10.1080/0963818042000338988

The Sphere Group. (2024). 6 strategies for increasing the profitability of a business. Retrieved from: https://thespheregroup.com.au/6-strategies-for-increasing-the-profitability-of-a-business/

Thorne, L., Massey, D. W., & Magnan, M. (2003). Institutional context and auditors' moral reasoning: A Canada-U.S. comparison. *Journal of Business Ethics*, 43(4), 305–321. DOI: 10.1023/A:1023005311277

Tiron-Tudor, A., Deliu, D., Farcane, N., & Dontu, A. (2021). Managing change with and through blockchain in accountancy organizations: A systematic literature review. *Journal of Organizational Change Management*, 34(2), 477–506. DOI: 10.1108/JOCM-10-2020-0302

Tiron-Tudor, A., Lacurezeanu, R., Bresfelean, V. P., & Dontu, A. N. (2024). Perspectives on How Robotic Process Automation Is Transforming Accounting and Auditing Services. *Accounting Perspectives*, 23(1), 7–38. DOI: 10.1111/1911-3838.12351

Tiwari, K., & Khan, M. S. (2020). Sustainability accounting and reporting in the industry 4.0. *Journal of Cleaner Production*, 258, 120783. DOI: 10.1016/j.jclepro.2020.120783

Torchia, M., Calabrò, A., & Huse, M. (2011). Women directors on corporate boards: From tokenism to critical mass. *Journal of Business Ethics*, 102(2), 299–317. DOI: 10.1007/s10551-011-0815-z

Torelli, R., Balluchi, F., & Furlotti, K. (2020). The materiality assessment and stakeholder engagement: A content analysis of sustainability reports. *Corporate Social Responsibility and Environmental Management*, 27(2), 470–484. DOI: 10.1002/csr.1813

Torfing, J. (2012). *Interactive governance: Advancing the paradigm*. Oxford University Press. DOI: 10.1093/acprof:oso/9780199596751.001.0001

Transnational Auditors Committee. (2007). Tone at the Top and Audit Quality. Forum of firms. https://www.iasplus.com/en/binary/ifac/0712toneatthetop.pdf

Travaglia, K. R., & de Sá, L. F. V. N. (2017). Fortalecimento da governança: uma agenda contemporânea para o setor público brasileiro. *Revista Controle: Doutrinas e artigos*, 15(1), 22-53.

Tripathi, G., Ahad, M. A., & Casalino, G. (2023). A comprehensive review of blockchain technology: Underlying principles and historical background with future challenges. *Decision Analytics Journal*, 9(1), 100344. DOI: 10.1016/j.dajour.2023.100344

Troshani, I., & Rowbottom, N. (2021). Digital corporate reporting: Research developments and implications. *Australian Accounting Review*, 31(3), 213–232. DOI: 10.1111/auar.12334

Udeh, E. O., Amajuoyi, P., Adeusi, K. B., & Scott, A. O. (2024). The role of Blockchain technology in enhancing transparency and trust in green finance markets. *Finance & Accounting Research Journal*, 6(6), 825–850. DOI: 10.51594/farj.v6i6.1181

Ulas, D. (2019). Digital transformation process and SMEs. *Procedia Computer Science*, 158, 662–671. DOI: 10.1016/j.procs.2019.09.101

Ullrich, A., Reißig, M., Niehoff, S., & Beier, G. (2023). Employee involvement and participation in digital transformation: A combined analysis of literature and practitioners' expertise. *Journal of Organizational Change Management*, 36(8), 29–48. DOI: 10.1108/JOCM-10-2022-0302

United Nations Women. (2018). Turning promises into action: Gender equality in the 2030 Agenda. https://www.unwomen.org/en/digital-library/publications/2018/2/gender-equality-in-the-2030-agenda-for-sustainable-development-2018

United Nations. (2015). Transforming our world: The 2030 Agenda for Sustainable Development. Resolution adopted by the General Assembly on 25 September 2015. A/RES/70/1. UN General Assembly, Seventieth Session. Agenda items 15 and 116. New York: United Nations.

Universidad de la Costa. (2024). How will Public Accounting be transformed with the arrival of artificial intelligence? Retrieved from: https://virtual.cuc.edu.co/blog/inteligencia-artificial-contaduria-publica#:~:text=Contabilidad%20invisible&text=La%20IA%20puede%20realizar%20tareas,el%20riesgo%20de%20errores%20humanos

Urbach, N., Ahlemann, F., Böhmann, T., Drews, P., Brenner, W., Schaudel, F., & Schütte, R. (2019). The impact of digitalization on the IT department. *Business & Information Systems Engineering*, 61(1), 123–131. DOI: 10.1007/s12599-018-0570-0

Urefe, O., Odonkor, T. N., & Agu, E. E. (2024). Enhancing financial reporting accuracy and compliance efficiency in legal firms through technological innovations. *International Journal of Management & Entrepreneurship Research*, 6(8), 2549–2560. DOI: 10.51594/ijmer.v6i8.1386

Van den Berg, E., & Rothmann, S. (2024). Twenty-first-century competencies and capabilities for financial accounting students. *Suid-Afrikaanse Tydskrif vir Ekonomiese en Bestuurswetenskappe*, 27(1), 11. DOI: 10.4102/sajems.v27i1.5535

Van der Merwe, N. (2021). The future of accounting: Will we be replaced by robots? Nico van der Merwe.

Van Thanh Le, C. P., El Ioini, N., & D'Atri, G. (2019). Enabling financial reports transparency and trustworthiness using blockchain technology. *International Journal on Advances in Security*, 12(3-4), 236–247. https://hdl.handle.net/10863/12122

Van Zanten, J. A., & Van Tulder, R. (2018). Multinational enterprises and the sustainable development goals: An institutional approach to corporate engagement. *Journal of International Business Policy*, 1(3-4), 208–233. DOI: 10.1057/s42214-018-0008-x

Vasconcelos, L., Sampaio, I., Viterbo, J., & Trevisan, D. (2023), Evaluation of the usability and acceptance of an Information System and Project Management (SIG-Proj) in the context of university extension. In *Proceedings of the XIV Computer on the Beach Conference* (pp. 8-279). Florianópolis, SC, Brazil.

Vassileva, R. (2021). COVID-19 in Autocratic Bulgaria: How the Anti-Corruption Protests Temporarily Limited the Abuse of Questionable Legislation. VERÍSSIMO, Carla. Compliance: incentive to adopt anti-corruption measures. São Paulo: Saraiva.

Verhoef, P. C., Broekhuizen, T., Bart, Y., Bhattacharya, A., Dong, J. Q., Fabian, N., & Haenlein, M. (2021). Digital transformation: A multidisciplinary reflection and research agenda. *Journal of Business Research*, 122, 889–901. DOI: 10.1016/j.jbusres.2019.09.022

Vieira, J. P. (2017). *A história do dinheiro*. Academia das Ciências de Lisboa.

Villanueva, E., Nuñez, M. A., & Martins, I. (2022). Impact of risk governance and associated practices and tools on enterprise risk management: Some evidence from Colombia. *Revista Finanzas y Política Económica*, 14(1), 187–206. DOI: 10.14718/revfinanzpolitecon.v14.n1.2022.8

Vuchkovski, D., Zalaznik, M., Mitręga, M., & Pfajfar, G. (2023). A look at the future of work: The digital transformation of teams from conventional to virtual. *Journal of Business Research*, 163, 113912. DOI: 10.1016/j.jbusres.2023.113912

Wang, X., Lin, X., & Shao, B. (2022). How does artificial intelligence create business agility? Evidence from chatbots. *International Journal of Information Management*, 66, 102535. DOI: 10.1016/j.ijinfomgt.2022.102535

Wang, Y., & Kogan, A. (2018). Designing confidentiality-preserving Blockchain-based transaction processing systems. *International Journal of Accounting Information Systems*, 30(June), 1–18. DOI: 10.1016/j.accinf.2018.06.001

Wee, M., Tarca, A., Krug, L., Aerts, W., Pink, P., & Tilling, M. (2016). *Factors Affecting Preparers' and Auditors' Judgements about Materiality and Conciseness in Integrated Reporting.* ACCA. https://www.integratedreporting.org/wp-content/uploads/2016/08/pi-materiality-conciseness-ir-FINAL.pdf

Werkema, M. (1995). *Basic statistical tools for process management.* Cristiano Ottoni Foundation.

Whitehead, T. A. (2022). Training and Development: Investing in Employees Through Assessment. *Scholar Chatter*, 3(1), 1–6. DOI: 10.47036/SC.3.1.1-6.2022

Whitley, R., Henderson, J., Czaban, L., & Lengvel, G. (1996). Trust and contractual relations in an emerging capitalist economy: The changing trading relationships of ten large Hungarian enterprises. *Organization Studies*, 17(3), 397–420. DOI: 10.1177/017084069601700303

Wibowo, T., & Christian, Y. (2021). Usage of blockchain to ensure audit data integrity. *Equity*, 24(1), 47–58. DOI: 10.34209/equ.v24i1.2357

Wilson, R. A., & Sangster, A. (1992). The automation of accounting practice. *Journal of Information Technology*, 7(2), 65–75. DOI: 10.1177/026839629200700202

Winter, R., & Schelp, J. (2008, March). Enterprise architecture governance: the need for a business-to-IT approach. In *Proceedings of the 2008 ACM symposium on Applied computing* (pp. 548-552). DOI: 10.1145/1363686.1363820

World Bank. (2013). *The International Bank for Reconstruction and Development. Worldwide Governance Indicators.* WGI.

World Bank. (2020). World Bank's 2020 Doing Business Report.

Wu, Q., Furuoka, F., & Lau, S. C. (2022). Corporate social responsibility and board gender diversity: A meta-analysis. *Management Research Review*, 45(7), 956–983. DOI: 10.1108/MRR-03-2021-0236

Xiao, X., & Shailer, G. (2022). Stakeholders' perceptions of factors affecting the credibility of sustainability reports. *The British Accounting Review*, 54(1), 101002. DOI: 10.1016/j.bar.2021.101002

Yarmoliuk, O., Abramov, A., Mulyk, T., Smirnova, N., & Ponomarova, N. (2024). Digital technologies in accounting and reporting: Benefits, limitations, and possible risks. *Amazonia Investiga*, 13(74), 323–333. DOI: 10.34069/AI/2024.74.02.27

Yoon, S. (2020). A study on the transformation of accounting based on new technologies: Evidence from Korea. *Sustainability (Basel)*, 12(20), 8669. DOI: 10.3390/su12208669

Yurisandi, T., & Puspitasari, E. (2015). Financial reporting Quality – Before and After IFRS Adoption Using NiCE Qualitative Characteristics Measurement. *Procedia: Social and Behavioral Sciences*, 211, 644–652. DOI: 10.1016/j.sbspro.2015.11.091

Yu, T., Lin, Z., & Tang, Q. (2018). Blockchain: The Introduction and Its Application in Financial Accounting. *Journal of Corporate Accounting & Finance*, 29(4), 37–47. DOI: 10.1002/jcaf.22365

Zattoni, A., Leventis, S., Van Ees, H., & De Masi, S. (2023). Board diversity's antecedents and consequences: A review and research agenda. *The Leadership Quarterly*, 34(1), 101659. DOI: 10.1016/j.leaqua.2022.101659

Zhang, Y., De Zoysa, A., & Cortese, C. (2019). Uncertainty expressions in accounting: Critical issues and recommendations. *Australasian Accounting Business and Finance Journal*, 13(4), 4–22. DOI: 10.14453/aabfj.v13i4.2

Zhang, Y., De Zoysa, A., & Cortese, C. (2020). The directionality of uncertainty expressions and the foreign language effect: Context and accounting judgement. *Meditari Accountancy Research*, 28(3), 543–563. DOI: 10.1108/MEDAR-09-2018-0377

Zhao, J., & Wang, X. (2024). Unleashing efficiency and insights: Exploring the potential applications and challenges of ChatGPT in accounting. *Journal of Corporate Accounting & Finance*, 35(1), 269–276. DOI: 10.1002/jcaf.22663

Zhao, W. (2019). Blockchain technology: Development and prospects. *National Science Review*, 6(2), 369–373. DOI: 10.1093/nsr/nwy133 PMID: 34691875

Zheng, R. (2021). Applications Research of Blockchain Technology in Accounting System. *Journal of Physics: Conference Series*, 1955(1), 012068. Advance online publication. DOI: 10.1088/1742-6596/1955/1/012068

Zhong, N., & Ren, J. (2022). Using sentiment analysis to study the relationship between subjective expression in financial reports and company performance. *Frontiers in Psychology*, 13, 949881. DOI: 10.3389/fpsyg.2022.949881 PMID: 35936313

Zhyvko, Z., Nikolashyn, A., Semenets, I., Karpenko, Y., Zos-Kior, M., Hnatenko, I., Klymenchukova, N., & Krakhmalova, N. (2022). Secure aspects of digitalization in management accounting and finances of the subject of the national economy in the context of globalization. *Journal of Hygienic Engineering and Design*, 39, 259–269.

Zumente, I., & Lãce, N. (2020). Does Diversity Drive Non-Financial Reporting: Evidence from the Baltic States. *Intellectual Economics*, 14(2), 50–66. DOI: 10.13165/IE-20-14-2-04

About the Contributors

Fábio Albuquerque is the Coordinator Professor of accounting and auditing and Director of the master's in accounting at Lisbon Accounting and Business School (ISCAL) of the Politécnico de Lisboa, Portugal. He is a PhD in Financial Economics and Accounting and has a master's degree in Auditing and a bachelor's degree in accounting. Prof. Albuquerque worked for several entities in areas such as accounting, financial reporting, and statistics, in addition to providing business consulting and training on national and international accounting and financial reporting standards. His research has covered accounting, auditing, as well as other related scientific areas such as education and corporate social responsibility. He is a reviewer and member of the editorial boards of several journals in the accounting and reporting areas.

Paula Gomes dos Santos is a distinguished scholar with a Ph.D. in Management from the Universidade Lusíada de Lisboa. Her research focuses on Accounting, Audit, and Taxation, particularly in the context of public governance and financial sustainability. Dr. Santos has led several research projects funded by the Instituto Politécnico de Lisboa, investigating topics such as the financial sustainability of Portuguese subnational governments and the implementation of financial regulations. She has also been actively involved in organizing and participating in scientific events, serving on the scientific committees of international conferences and acting as a referee for conferences and journals. Dr. Santos has published extensively in international journals and conference proceedings, contributing significantly to the advancement of knowledge in her field.

***

João Borralho is an Assistant Professor at the Lusofona University, Lisbon Centre, in the School of Economic Sciences and Organisations (Portugal). He was previously a public auditor at the Inspeção-geral de Finanças (Inspectorate General of Finance). His main research interests include family businesses, earnings management and sustainability. His work has appeared in journals such as Journal of Cleaner Production, Revista de Contabilidad-Spanish Accounting Accounting Review, Spanish Journal of Finance and Accounting Accounting/Revista Española de Financiación y Contabilidad, y European Journal of Family Business (EJFB).

Kurt Desender is an Assistant Professor (with tenure) in the Department of Business Administration at the University Carlos III. His research interests lay in the areas of Corporate Governance, Corporate Social Responsibility, Strategic Management and Financial Accounting.

Flory Dieck-Assad, PhD in Finance from Tulane University, USA. Author of "Financial Institutions" by McGraw-Hill in 2003 and second edition in 2014. With over 400 publications in refereed journals and magazines of national and international scope, is member of the National System of Researchers since December 2005 to date; "Texas A & M University Press" published in 2005 her second book "Energy and Sustainable Development in Mexico", honored with the Romulo Garza Award 2007 with its second printing in 2008. Awarded with the Prize for Teaching & Research 2007, 2010, 2014, and 2022; the National Ethics Award 2013, the 2015 Distinguished Professor of the Institute of Chartered Accountants of the State of Nuevo Leon, Mexico, and the 2015 National Energy Prize for her contributions to the energy sector. Tenured professor at Tecnologico de Monterrey. fdieck@tec.mx (mailing author).

Ana Isabel Dias is a PhD in Economics and Business from the University of Extremadura, Master's in Management with a focus on Finance from the University of Évora, Bachelor's degree in Auditing, and Bachelor in Accounting and Administration from the Lisbon Institute of Accounting and Administration (ISCAL). Professor at ISCAL / Polytechnic of Lisbon, belonging to the scientific area of Accounting and Auditing. Teaches courses in the undergraduate program in Accounting and Administration, specializing in Accounting and Taxation, as well as in the master's program of Accounting. Currently, serves as the director of the undergraduate program in Accounting and Administration (Accounting branch) and as the deputy director of the Master's Program in Accounting. She is an integrated member of the Research Centre on Accounting and Taxation at IPCA (CICF) since february of 2024. Author of scientific articles published and/or presented at national and international conferences and journals, as well as technical books in the field of financial accounting.

Mónica LópezPuertas-Lamy is an Assistant Professor (with tenure) in the Department of Business Administration at the University Carlos III. Her research interests focus on determinants and consequences of accounting, corporate governance and corporate finance decisions on firms' access to credit and bank risk.

João Marcelo Macêdo is a PhD in Accounting Sciences (UnB/UFPB/UFRN - 2017), Master in Accounting Sciences (UFPE - 2010), Specialist in Public Management and Auditing (IESP - 2009), Degree in Accounting Sciences (UFPB - Campus I - 2006). Law degree in progress (UNIPê). Currently Associate Professor I - T40 - DE at the Federal University of Paraíba - Campus IV - North Coast, where he is Coordinator of the Undergraduate Course in Accounting (re-elected until March/2026) and Permanent Professor of the Postgraduate Program in Public Management and International Cooperation. He is also a CRCPB Board Member (2022/2026 term) and a Board Member of Sicredi CREDUNI. He has experience in Administration and Higher Education, with an emphasis on Accounting, Cooperativism, Public Management and University Teaching. Professionally, he has experience in public management positions, having worked at EMATER-PB/Gov. of the State of Paraíba, at IDEP/UFPB, at the University Prefecture and in the advisory department of the UFPB rector's office. He is a member of the following research groups: GESFIN-Grupo de Estudos em Finanças and GEPEC - Grupo de Educação e Pesquisa em Contabilidade and is a member of LIM/UFPB - Laboratório de Interação e Mídia.

María-Pilar Martín-Zamora holds a degree and is a doctor (PhD) in Business Administration from the University of Sevilla (Spain). At present, she is an Associate Professor at the University of Huelva, in the Department of Accounting and Finance. Since 1985, when she started her career in higher education, she has taught different subjects in the field of Financial Accounting. Her basic research is oriented towards Tax Accounting and Business Management. She is the author of some books and articles published in journals and she has presented papers in national and international conferences.

Maria Albertina Barreiro Rodrigues is a Member of the Board of Auditors of Bank of Portugal, since 2023. Integrated Member of CETRAD – Centre for Transdisciplinary Development Studies. Ambassador of the Sustainable Development Goals (SDG) Portugal Alliance, United Nations Global Compact Network. Professor at Universidade Europeia. Invited Professor at Lisbon Accounting and Business School; ISM - International School of Management, Germany and ISCAM, Mozambique. PhD in Management; specialist in Financial Audit; postgraduate studies in Digital Education; MBA in Management; Degree in Business

Management and a bachelor's degree in Accounting and Administration. Has published academic articles in journals in the research areas of corporate reporting, sustainability, integrated reporting, audit, assurance, corporate governance, ethics, and higher education. With a professional career of over 30 years, 5 as Chair of Audit Committees of public sector entities, 3 as Manager of the Advisory Department, and 10 as Financial Manager of an international company. Financial and statutory auditor, Member of committees from the Portuguese Institute of Statutory Auditors, Certified accountant since 1992.

Gelyel Santos is a Master's student in Federal University of Rio Grande do Norte, and Graduate in Accounting Federal University of Paraíba – UFPB.

Yanne Silva is a graduate in Accounting Federal University of Paraíba - UFPB.

Muhammad Usman Tariq has more than 16+ year's experience in industry and academia. He has authored more than 200+ research articles, 100+ case studies, 70+ book chapters and several books other than 4 patents. He is founder and CEO of The Case HQ, a unique repository for courses, narrative and video case studies. He has been working as a consultant and trainer for industries representing six sigma, quality, health and safety, environmental systems, project management, and information security standards. His work has encompassed sectors in aviation, manufacturing, food, hospitality, education, finance, research, software and transportation. He has diverse and significant experience working with accreditation agencies of ABET, ACBSP, AACSB, WASC, CAA, EFQM and NCEAC. Additionally, Dr. Tariq has operational experience in incubators, research labs, government research projects, private sector startups, program creation and management at various industrial and academic levels. He is Certified Higher Education Teacher from Harvard University, USA, Certified Online Educator from HMBSU, Certified Six Sigma Master Black Belt and has been awarded PFHEA, SMIEEE, and CMBE.

Index

A

Accounting 1, 2, 3, 4, 5, 6, 7, 8, 9, 10, 11, 12, 13, 14, 15, 16, 17, 18, 19, 20, 23, 24, 25, 26, 27, 28, 29, 30, 33, 34, 35, 36, 41, 44, 52, 53, 55, 56, 57, 59, 60, 61, 62, 63, 65, 66, 67, 68, 70, 71, 72, 73, 74, 75, 76, 77, 78, 79, 81, 82, 83, 85, 86, 87, 88, 89, 90, 92, 93, 95, 96, 97, 98, 100, 101, 102, 103, 104, 105, 106, 107, 109, 111, 112, 113, 114, 115, 116, 117, 118, 119, 120, 121, 124, 125, 126, 127, 129, 131, 135, 136, 138, 139, 140, 141, 142, 143, 144, 145, 146, 147, 148, 149, 150, 151, 152, 153, 154, 155, 156, 157, 158, 159, 160, 161, 162, 165, 166, 167, 168, 170, 177, 178, 179, 180, 181, 182, 183, 184, 185, 186, 188, 189, 190, 191, 192, 193, 194, 195, 196, 197, 198, 199, 200, 201, 202, 203, 204, 205, 206, 207, 208, 209, 211, 212, 234, 235, 237, 238, 239, 240, 241, 254, 277, 288, 289, 290, 291, 292, 299, 300, 303, 304, 306, 313, 314, 318, 321, 322, 323, 324, 325, 326

Accounting Education 2, 3, 4, 14, 15, 16, 23, 24, 25, 144, 204

Accounting Firms 95, 96, 97, 106, 111, 112, 113, 116, 118

AI 1, 2, 3, 5, 6, 7, 8, 11, 12, 24, 26, 27, 28, 29, 31, 33, 34, 35, 36, 37, 38, 39, 41, 42, 43, 44, 45, 46, 48, 49, 50, 51, 52, 53, 54, 55, 56, 57, 58, 59, 60, 61, 62, 63, 97, 100, 101, 105, 119, 126, 127, 130, 131, 133, 134, 136, 137, 138, 139, 140, 141, 142, 143, 147, 149, 152, 155, 162, 163

Artificial Intelligence 2, 3, 5, 6, 11, 12, 14, 22, 24, 27, 28, 30, 33, 36, 38, 39, 44, 45, 52, 53, 55, 56, 57, 58, 59, 60, 61, 62, 87, 97, 99, 100, 105, 119, 126, 141, 142, 144, 145, 147, 149, 150, 151, 152, 155, 156, 157, 159, 161, 162, 223, 229, 232

Automation 8, 32, 35, 74, 76, 77, 78, 92, 95, 96, 97, 98, 99, 100, 101, 102, 103, 104, 105, 106, 110, 114, 115, 116, 117, 118, 119, 120, 121, 123, 124, 126, 127, 131, 133, 134, 136, 137, 138, 142, 143, 144, 146, 148, 149, 150, 151, 152, 154, 161, 163, 264

B

Big Data 5, 7, 89, 101, 119, 127, 128, 131, 134, 136, 137, 142, 144, 145, 146, 150, 155, 156, 159, 162

Blockchain 1, 2, 5, 6, 7, 8, 11, 12, 22, 25, 65, 66, 67, 68, 69, 70, 72, 73, 74, 75, 76, 77, 78, 79, 81, 82, 83, 84, 85, 86, 87, 88, 89, 90, 92, 93, 130, 131, 137, 138, 139, 140, 142, 144, 145, 146, 147, 149, 150, 155, 156, 157, 159, 160, 161, 162

Blockchain Technology 2, 7, 12, 65, 66, 67, 68, 69, 70, 72, 73, 74, 75, 76, 77, 79, 81, 82, 83, 84, 85, 86, 88, 89, 90, 92, 93, 130, 131, 137, 146, 149, 150, 155, 157, 160, 161

Board 18, 20, 21, 22, 71, 135, 150, 165, 167, 178, 181, 185, 209, 212, 224, 225, 227, 228, 229, 230, 236, 237, 238, 240, 242, 249, 277, 297, 298, 299, 300, 301, 302, 303, 305, 306, 307, 308, 309, 310, 311, 312, 313, 314, 315, 316, 317, 318, 319, 320, 322, 323, 325, 326, 327, 329

C

Chatbots 27, 28, 35, 36, 37, 38, 44, 55, 59, 62, 63, 161

Chief Accounting Officer 27, 28, 41, 63

Cultural Contexts 9, 300

D

Data Analysis 7, 27, 28, 29, 31, 37, 39, 40, 41, 42, 43, 45, 46, 52, 53, 54, 57,

60, 62, 63, 70, 80, 92, 125, 128, 138, 139, 145, 225
Data Analytics 1, 2, 3, 6, 7, 12, 63, 127, 131, 138, 142, 144, 146, 157
Development 3, 4, 12, 13, 20, 22, 24, 38, 59, 68, 70, 71, 77, 90, 96, 97, 99, 101, 102, 104, 145, 156, 161, 192, 203, 204, 205, 211, 212, 218, 219, 223, 228, 234, 235, 238, 239, 246, 248, 250, 254, 263, 269, 275, 290, 291, 293, 297, 302, 304, 311, 313, 318, 320, 322, 323, 327, 328
Digitalization 6, 8, 68, 123, 124, 125, 126, 127, 128, 129, 130, 131, 132, 133, 134, 135, 136, 137, 138, 139, 140, 141, 144, 145, 148, 150, 151, 152, 154, 157, 160, 161, 162, 163
Disclosure 20, 71, 124, 125, 129, 130, 140, 155, 157, 168, 170, 173, 174, 175, 176, 189, 212, 213, 214, 219, 220, 221, 224, 225, 226, 227, 228, 229, 230, 231, 232, 234, 235, 236, 237, 238, 239, 240, 242, 303

E

Efficiency 2, 7, 21, 33, 39, 41, 43, 54, 59, 60, 73, 74, 80, 92, 99, 100, 104, 105, 113, 114, 115, 116, 118, 123, 125, 126, 127, 128, 129, 131, 132, 133, 134, 135, 137, 139, 143, 149, 161, 162, 163, 168, 191, 205, 223, 229, 251, 253, 260, 269, 273, 275, 277, 278, 283, 285
Emerging Technologies 2, 13, 120, 126, 139, 145, 150, 152, 157, 179
ESG 3, 18, 20, 22, 211, 212, 213, 214, 219, 220, 223, 224, 225, 226, 230, 231, 232, 234, 235, 236, 237, 238, 240, 306, 308, 309, 312, 315, 326, 328, 329

F

Faithful Representation 71, 75, 82, 83, 84, 90, 93, 192, 203
Federal Institute 245, 270
Financial 3, 5, 6, 7, 8, 11, 14, 16, 17, 18, 19, 20, 23, 24, 25, 26, 27, 28, 29, 30, 32, 33, 34, 35, 36, 37, 39, 41, 43, 52, 53, 55, 56, 57, 60, 62, 63, 65, 66, 67, 68, 69, 70, 71, 72, 73, 74, 75, 76, 77, 79, 81, 82, 83, 84, 85, 86, 87, 88, 89, 90, 92, 93, 100, 101, 102, 118, 123, 124, 125, 126, 127, 128, 129, 130, 131, 132, 133, 134, 135, 136, 137, 138, 139, 140, 141, 142, 143, 144, 145, 146, 147, 148, 149, 150, 151, 152, 153, 154, 155, 156, 157, 158, 160, 161, 163, 166, 167, 168, 170, 177, 179, 180, 181, 183, 184, 185, 188, 189, 190, 191, 192, 193, 194, 195, 196, 197, 198, 199, 200, 201, 202, 203, 204, 205, 206, 207, 208, 209, 212, 213, 218, 225, 229, 234, 235, 237, 238, 239, 240, 242, 249, 253, 254, 269, 290, 291, 297, 298, 299, 300, 301, 302, 303, 305, 306, 307, 308, 312, 314, 315, 318, 319, 321, 323, 326, 328, 329
Financial Reporting 3, 6, 17, 18, 20, 24, 25, 65, 66, 67, 70, 71, 72, 73, 74, 75, 76, 77, 79, 81, 82, 83, 84, 85, 86, 89, 90, 92, 123, 125, 126, 127, 128, 129, 130, 131, 132, 133, 134, 135, 136, 137, 138, 139, 140, 141, 143, 144, 146, 149, 150, 151, 152, 153, 154, 155, 157, 160, 161, 163, 166, 167, 168, 177, 180, 181, 183, 184, 185, 189, 190, 191, 192, 194, 195, 197, 198, 199, 200, 201, 202, 203, 204, 205, 206, 207, 208, 209, 212, 213, 234, 239, 240, 242, 297, 298, 299, 300, 301, 302, 303, 305, 308, 314, 315, 318, 319, 323, 328
Financial Welfare 27, 28, 33, 63
French Speaking Sub-Saharan Africa 193

G

Global 5, 7, 9, 16, 17, 18, 20, 24, 25, 26, 37, 38, 39, 43, 57, 60, 61, 69, 76, 100, 126, 132, 143, 145, 148, 155, 158, 159, 167, 185, 187, 190, 206, 213, 217, 220, 225, 226, 227, 228, 229, 231, 232, 234,

297, 300, 319, 320, 322, 323
Goals 63, 156, 178, 218, 235, 239, 247, 251, 252, 261, 272, 273, 285, 304, 323, 327
Governance 5, 6, 19, 20, 25, 151, 153, 155, 157, 192, 203, 207, 212, 213, 223, 229, 230, 231, 234, 235, 239, 240, 242, 245, 246, 247, 249, 250, 251, 252, 253, 257, 260, 261, 269, 270, 272, 273, 274, 276, 281, 285, 286, 287, 288, 289, 290, 291, 292, 293, 298, 299, 300, 302, 304, 305, 306, 307, 313, 314, 316, 318, 319, 320, 321, 323, 324, 325, 327

H

High-Tech Ledger 66, 84, 90

I

IAS 37 165, 167, 168, 171, 172, 173, 174, 175, 176, 177, 178, 182
IFRS Adoption 89, 183, 184, 185, 186, 187, 188, 190, 191, 192, 194, 195, 197, 198, 199, 200, 201, 202, 203, 204, 205, 206, 207, 208
Information Systems 9, 25, 29, 33, 58, 61, 73, 86, 88, 90, 101, 120, 143, 145, 146, 147, 148, 149, 150, 153, 154, 155, 156, 161, 179, 180, 205, 206, 246, 270, 277, 286, 289, 291, 299
Institutional 72, 188, 189, 193, 204, 208, 248, 250, 263, 297, 298, 300, 307, 316, 317, 319, 320, 324, 326, 327
International 5, 16, 17, 20, 23, 24, 61, 71, 76, 77, 85, 86, 88, 90, 118, 119, 120, 132, 135, 141, 143, 144, 145, 146, 147, 148, 149, 150, 151, 152, 153, 154, 155, 156, 157, 158, 159, 160, 161, 165, 167, 168, 178, 179, 180, 181, 182, 183, 184, 185, 187, 188, 190, 202, 203, 204, 205, 206, 207, 208, 209, 212, 213, 218, 235, 236, 237, 238, 239, 240, 242, 243, 244, 246, 250, 254, 256, 257, 269, 276, 288, 289, 290, 291, 292, 293, 304, 307, 319, 321, 323, 324, 327

M

Machine Learning 5, 6, 34, 39, 56, 62, 105, 126, 127, 130, 131, 137, 142, 143, 145, 155, 156, 158, 159, 163, 165, 171, 173, 232
Magnitude 165, 167, 171, 173, 174, 176, 177, 242, 314
Materiality Matrix 212, 213, 232, 235, 236, 240
Message Tone 165, 166, 167, 171, 176
Microsoft Excel 31, 40, 44, 53, 62, 63, 102
Morocco 183, 184, 185, 187, 188, 189, 192, 193, 198, 199, 200, 201, 205, 207, 209

N

Neutrality 65, 71, 81, 84, 86, 88, 90, 278, 279, 281, 283, 285
Non-Financial Information 128, 212

P

Perceived Benefits 98, 106, 183, 194
Productivity 1, 22, 35, 37, 38, 41, 44, 54, 55, 96, 97, 101, 105, 153, 278, 282, 283, 294
Professional Accountant 54, 55, 63, 145

Q

Qualitative Characteristics 70, 71, 72, 74, 75, 76, 81, 85, 88, 90, 183, 184, 185, 191, 192, 194, 198, 200, 201, 202, 208
Quality 22, 32, 67, 70, 72, 74, 78, 79, 81, 82, 85, 86, 88, 89, 90, 92, 98, 99, 100, 102, 118, 128, 143, 146, 152, 157, 168, 170, 172, 181, 182, 190, 191, 192, 195, 202, 203, 204, 206, 207, 208, 217, 223, 229, 235, 237, 248, 250, 252, 254, 258, 278, 282, 283, 288, 294, 297, 298, 299, 300, 301, 302, 303, 308, 315, 318, 319, 323, 324, 325, 326, 328
Quotas 297, 300, 307, 314, 315, 316,

319, 320

R

Regulatory Frameworks 17, 18, 135
Reliability 7, 53, 65, 71, 74, 80, 81, 82, 84, 85, 90, 92, 169, 170, 183, 194, 195, 197, 198, 200, 201, 202, 209, 274, 298, 303, 305, 314
Reporting 3, 5, 6, 17, 18, 19, 20, 24, 25, 27, 28, 63, 65, 66, 67, 70, 71, 72, 73, 74, 75, 76, 77, 78, 79, 81, 82, 83, 84, 85, 86, 88, 89, 90, 92, 103, 123, 125, 126, 127, 128, 129, 130, 131, 132, 133, 134, 135, 136, 137, 138, 139, 140, 141, 143, 144, 146, 148, 149, 150, 151, 152, 153, 154, 155, 157, 160, 161, 162, 163, 166, 167, 168, 177, 180, 181, 183, 184, 185, 186, 189, 190, 191, 192, 194, 195, 197, 198, 199, 200, 201, 202, 203, 204, 205, 206, 207, 208, 209, 212, 213, 214, 217, 218, 220, 225, 232, 233, 234, 235, 236, 237, 238, 239, 240, 242, 243, 273, 297, 298, 299, 300, 301, 302, 303, 304, 305, 306, 308, 314, 315, 318, 319, 323, 328
Risk Management and Compliance 245, 246, 250, 269, 272, 276, 286, 287
Robotic Process Automation 95, 96, 97, 98, 99, 100, 101, 102, 104, 105, 106, 110, 114, 115, 116, 117, 119, 120, 121, 131, 143, 144, 148, 149, 150, 163

S

SDGs 235, 304, 328
Sentiment Analysis 37, 54, 166, 167, 170, 171, 177, 179, 180, 181, 182

Social Responsibility 1, 5, 19, 20, 23, 153, 166, 217, 235, 238, 239, 240, 290, 304, 313, 321, 323, 325
Stakeholders 20, 31, 67, 71, 73, 83, 84, 93, 96, 124, 129, 130, 132, 135, 138, 139, 140, 154, 162, 166, 167, 168, 171, 177, 178, 212, 213, 214, 215, 216, 217, 218, 220, 221, 224, 229, 231, 232, 234, 236, 246, 250, 252, 253, 257, 258, 259, 269, 272, 273, 298, 304
Subjectivity 166, 171, 172, 177, 214, 216, 232
Sustainability 1, 3, 5, 6, 19, 20, 61, 73, 78, 88, 89, 121, 132, 139, 142, 144, 150, 151, 153, 154, 156, 157, 159, 160, 162, 206, 212, 213, 214, 217, 218, 219, 234, 235, 236, 237, 238, 239, 240, 241, 242, 253, 261, 263, 285, 322
Sustainable 20, 25, 63, 133, 144, 156, 160, 217, 218, 219, 223, 227, 234, 235, 236, 237, 238, 239, 248, 258, 297, 304, 311, 313, 318, 320, 327, 328

T

Tactical Decision-Making 27, 28, 31, 53, 63
TAM Model 245, 246, 247, 269, 270, 271, 285, 286
TMT 297, 300, 302, 303, 304, 305, 308, 309, 310, 311, 312, 313, 314, 318, 319, 320, 329
Transparency 5, 6, 7, 16, 17, 18, 20, 65, 66, 73, 77, 83, 89, 96, 123, 125, 126, 129, 130, 131, 132, 134, 135, 136, 137, 139, 140, 144, 148, 149, 153, 155, 157, 158, 160, 161, 162, 163, 167, 179, 190, 213, 217, 242, 246, 251, 252, 253, 260, 261, 272, 298, 317